Penguin Education

# Modern Sociology
## Introductory Readings

Edited by Peter Worsley

D1148608

*Contributing Editors*

Roy Fitzhenry
J. Clyde Mitchell
D. H. J. Morgan
Valdo Pons
Bryan Roberts
W. W. Sharrock
Robin Ward
Peter Worsley

# Modern Sociology
## Introductory Readings

**Selected Readings**
Edited by Peter Worsley

*Contributing Editors:* Roy Fitzhenry, J. Clyde Mitchell,
D. H. J. Morgan, Valdo Pons, Bryan Roberts,
W. W. Sharrock, Robin Ward, Peter Worsley

Penguin Books

Penguin Books Ltd, Harmondsworth,
Middlesex, England
Penguin Books Inc., 7110 Ambassador Road,
Baltimore, Md 21207, U.S.A.
Penguin Books Australia Ltd,
Ringwood, Victoria, Australia

First published 1970
Reprinted 1971
This selection copyright © Peter Worsley and Contributing Editors, 1970
Introduction and notes copyright © Peter Worsley and Contributing Editors, 1970

Made and printed in Great Britain by
Cox & Wyman Ltd, London, Reading and Fakenham
Set in Intertype Times

# Contents

8 Contents

## Part Eight Social Stratification 351

## Part Nine **The Problem of Order** 405

# Introduction

This book of Readings has been designed principally to accompany our textbook, *Introducing Sociology* (Penguin Books, 1970), and the rationale of the general organization of the subject matter is fully explained in the Introduction to that book. But we hope that the Readings will also serve as an introduction to the source material of sociology in their own right.

We have assumed that the reader is approaching the subject for the first time, and have tried to take him through three stages in introducing him to sociology. Firstly in Part One, we discuss the general status of the social sciences and the place of sociology among those sciences, and in Part Two the special characteristics of human society which call for special methods of study also and which, therefore, involve ethical problems of a unique kind.

Having examined the logic of inquiry and the methods and techniques used in sociological research, we move to the second, major stage: the discussion of key institutions and social milieux which all individuals are involved in as they move through the life-cycle: the family, education, work, organizations and 'the community' at various levels (Parts Three to Seven).

In the last stage, with Parts Eight and Nine, we move to the larger issues of societal cohesion and conflict, with an examination of the major lines of division in society, notably social stratification, and an analysis of the forces which make it possible for society to persist at all.

The over-all strategy of the book is to increase the level of theoretical generalization progressively, to move from the concrete to the abstract, from the familiar to the unfamiliar.

Many of the books and articles referred to in the textbook are not easily accessible to interested readers, either because they are only to be found in specialist libraries or because even the best libraries rarely contain more than a few copies, which may be in demand by large numbers of readers.

We have therefore selected key passages from such works, usually from works referred to in the textbook, but by no means always so. We have attempted to provide the reader with materials which bear upon the main themes developed in each chapter of the textbook, though we have divided the subject matter of the original chapter 'Work, industry and organizations' into two separate chapters in this book.

The nature of the selections inevitably varies. They include important statements of general theory, analyses of particular institutions, excerpts from case studies and classical community studies. Some of these you will find written in an easily assimilable manner; others involve more complex arguments and use more technical language. We hope that in this way readers will be introduced to the range of styles that are involved in sociological writing.

We hope, too, that those who are stimulated by any of these excerpts will be encouraged to turn to the original book or article and read more, and we trust that we have presented a sufficient variety of approaches to sociology to cater for people's manifold interests.

Because of the general and introductory nature of these Readings, which makes it desirable that they should be fluent and straightforward to read, we have retained footnotes from the original texts only when they are a necessary amplification of points contained in the text: most references to sources have been deleted. Readers who are sufficiently interested in particular topics to delve further will of course find the references in the original texts.

### Editor's note

I would like to acknowledge the special contribution made by Robin Ward in preparing this book, as well as the assistance of Chris Pickvance in preparing certain of the extracts. The Readings in Part One were selected by myself; those in Part Two by J. Clyde Mitchell; in Part Three by D. H. J. Morgan; in Part Four by Bryan Roberts; in Part Five by D. H. J. Morgan and Robin Ward; in Part Six by Robin Ward; in Part Seven by Valdo Pons; in Part Eight by Roy Fitzhenry; and in Part Nine by Wesley Sharrock.

# Part One Sociology as a Discipline

Sociology has emerged as a specialized social science, with its own particular body of theory and styles of research. But it can never be cut off from the other social sciences nor, indeed, from general thought about society. C. Wright Mills puts this view forcefully in Reading 1. The growth of modern social science, H. Stuart Hughes shows (Reading 2), involved a departure from the methods and assumptions of the natural sciences because consciousness is such a very special feature of human society.

Karl Mannheim (Reading 3) shows how men's thinking about the world is affected by their experience of the past, their hopes or fears for the future, and by their interest in the status quo or their reaction against it.

Thomas S. Kuhn (Reading 4) demonstrates that science always entails systematic thinking and not just mere fact collecting, and shows how we are socialized as scientists into thinking about the world within certain frameworks of thought (which eventually become straightjackets).

Glaser and Strauss (Reading 5) attack the notion that 'theorizing' is a separate kind of activity from empirical research, and insist that our theories must be 'grounded' *in* research.

The inter-relations of the social sciences are such that work by philosophers or social psychologists is often much more relevant for sociology than work by people who are labelled 'sociologists'. Kenneth Burke's discussion (Reading 6) of the complexity of the very notion of the 'act' itself – which he breaks down into a 'pentad' (of five elements) – makes us think much harder about categories such as 'social action', 'behaviour', etc. which we use often too crudely. And George Herbert Mead's classic discussion of the Self as a social product has provided a most fertilizing theory which is developed further in Berger and Luckmann's writing (Reading 8).

Finally the ethical problems which beset anybody engaged in sociological research are clearly and provocatively presented by Norbert Elias (Reading 9).

# 1 C. Wright Mills

## The Sociological Imagination

Excerpt from C. Wright Mills, *The Sociological Imagination,*
Oxford University Press, Inc., 1959, pp. 3–11.

Nowadays men often feel that their private lives are a series of traps.
They sense that within their everyday worlds, they cannot overcome
their troubles, and in this feeling they are often quite correct: what
ordinary men are directly aware of and what they try to do are bounded
by the private orbits in which they live; their visions and their powers are
limited to the close-up scenes of job, family, neighborhood; in other
milieux, they move vicariously and remain spectators. And the more
aware they become, however vaguely, of ambitions and of threats which
transcend their immediate locales, the more trapped they seem to feel.

Underlying this sense of being trapped are seemingly impersonal
changes in the very structure of continent-wide societies. The facts of
contemporary history are also facts about the success and the failure of
individual men and women. When a society is industrialized, a peasant
becomes a worker; a feudal lord is liquidated or becomes a businessman.
When classes rise or fall, a man is employed or unemployed; when the
rate of investment goes up or down, a man takes new heart or goes
broke. When wars happen, an insurance salesman becomes a rocket
launcher; a store clerk, a radar man; a wife lives alone; a child grows up
without a father. Neither the life of an individual nor the history of a
society can be understood without understanding both.

Yet men do not usually define the troubles they endure in terms of
historical change and institutional contradiction. The well-being they
enjoy they do not usually impute to the big ups and downs of the
societies in which they live. Seldom aware of the intricate connexion
between the patterns of their own lives and the course of world history,
ordinary men do not usually know what this connexion means for the
kinds of men they are becoming and for the kinds of history making in
which they might take part. They do not possess the quality of mind
essential to grasp the interplay of man and society, of biography and
history, of self and world. They cannot cope with their personal troubles
in such ways as to control the structural transformations that usually lie
behind them.

Surely it is no wonder. In what period have so many men been so totally exposed at so fast a pace to such earthquakes of change? That Americans have not known such catastrophic changes as have the men and women of other societies is due to historical facts that are now quickly becoming 'merely history'. The history that now affects every man is world history. Within this scene and this period, in the course of a single generation, one-sixth of mankind is transformed from all that is feudal and backward into all that is modern, advanced and fearful. Political colonies are freed; new and less visible forms of imperialism installed. Revolutions occur; men feel the intimate grip of new kinds of authority. Totalitarian societies rise and are smashed to bits – or succeed fabulously. After two centuries of ascendancy, capitalism is shown up as only one way to make society into an industrial apparatus. After two centuries of hope, even formal democracy is restricted to a quite small portion of mankind. Everywhere in the underdeveloped world, ancient ways of life are broken up and vague expectations become urgent demands. Everywhere in the overdeveloped world, the means of authority and of violence becomes total in scope and bureaucratic in form. Humanity itself now lies before us, the super-nation at either pole concentrating its most coordinated and massive efforts upon the preparation of the Third World War.

The very shaping of history now outpaces the ability of men to orient themselves in accordance with cherished values. And which values? Even when they do not panic, men often sense that older ways of feeling and thinking have collapsed and that newer beginnings are ambiguous to the point of moral stasis. Is it any wonder that ordinary men feel they cannot cope with the larger worlds with which they are so suddenly confronted? That they cannot understand the meaning of their epoch for their own lives? That – in defense of selfhood – they become morally insensible, trying to remain altogether private men? Is it any wonder that they come to be possessed by a sense of the trap?

It is not only information that they need – in this Age of Fact, information often dominates their attention and overwhelms their capacities to assimilate it. It is not only the skills of reason that they need – although their struggles to acquire these often exhaust their limited moral energy.

What they need, and what they feel they need, is a quality of mind that will help them to use information and to develop reason in order to achieve lucid summations of what is going on in the world and of what may be happening within themselves. It is this quality, I contend, that journalists and scholars, artists and publics, scientists and editors are coming to expect what may be called the sociological imagination.

The sociological imagination enables its possessor to understand the larger historical scene in terms of its meaning for the inner life and the external career of a variety of individuals. It enables him to take into account how individuals, in the welter of their daily experience, often become falsely conscious of their social positions. Within that welter the framework of modern society is sought, and within that framework the psychologies of a variety of men and women are formulated. By such means the personal uneasiness of individuals is focused upon explicit troubles and the indifference of publics is transformed into involvement with public issues.

The first fruit of this imagination – and the first lesson of the social science that embodies it – is the idea that the individual can understand his own experience and gauge his own fate only by locating himself within his period, that he can know his own chances in life only by becoming aware of those of all individuals in his circumstances. In many ways it is a terrible lesson; in many ways a magnificent one. We do not know the limits of man's capacities for supreme effort or willing degradation, for agony or glee, for pleasurable brutality or the sweetness of reason. But in our time we have come to know that the limits of 'human nature' are frighteningly broad. We have come to know that every individual lives, from one generation to the next, in some society; that he lives out a biography, and that he lives it out within some historical sequence. By the fact of his living he contributes, however minutely, to the shaping of this society and to the course of its history, even as he is made by society and by its historical push and shove.

The sociological imagination enables us to grasp history and biography and the relations between the two within society. That is its task and its promise. To recognize this task and this promise is the mark of the classic social analyst. It is characteristic of Herbert Spencer – turgid, polysyllabic, comprehensive; of E. A. Ross – graceful, muckraking, upright; of Auguste Comte and Emile Durkheim; of the intricate and subtle Karl Mannheim. It is the quality of all that is intellectually excellent in Karl Marx; it is the clue to Thorstein Veblen's brilliant and ironic insight, to Joseph Schumpeter's many-sided constructions of reality; it is the basis of the psychological sweep of W. E. H. Lecky no less than of the profundity and clarity of Max Weber. And it is the signal of what is best in contemporary studies of man and society.

No social study that does not come back to the problems of biography, of history and of their intersections within a society has completed its intellectual journey. Whatever the specific problems of the classic social analysts, however limited or however broad the features of social reality they have examined, those who have been imaginatively aware of the promise of their work have consistently asked three sorts of questions:

1. What is the structure of this particular society as a whole? What are its essential components and how are they related to one another? How does it differ from other varieties of social order? Within it, what is the meaning of any particular feature for its continuance and for its change?

2. Where does this society stand in human history? What are the mechanics by which it is changing? What is its place within and its meaning for the development of humanity as a whole? How does any particular feature we are examining affect, and how is it affected by, the historical period in which it moves? And this period – what are its essential features? How does it differ from other periods? What are its characteristic ways of history making?

3. What varieties of men and women now prevail in this society and in this period? And what varieties are coming to prevail? In what ways are they selected and formed, liberated and repressed, made sensitive and blunted? What kinds of 'human nature' are revealed in the conduct and character we observe in this society in this period? And what is the meaning for 'human nature' of each and every feature of the society we are examining?

Whether the point of interest is a great power state or a minor literary mood, a family, a prison, a creed – these are the kinds of questions the best social analysts have asked. They are the intellectual pivots of classic studies of man in society – and they are the questions inevitably raised by any mind possessing the sociological imagination. For that imagination is the capacity to shift from one perspective to another – from the political to the psychological; from examination of a single family to comparative assessment of the national budgets of the world; from the theological school to the military establishment; from considerations of an oil industry to studies of contemporary poetry. It is the capacity to range from the most impersonal and remote transformations to the most intimate features of the human self – and to see the relations between the two. Back of its use there is always the urge to know the social and historical meaning of the individual in the society and in the period in which he has his quality and his being.

That, in brief, is why it is by means of the sociological imagination that men now hope to grasp what is going on in the world, and to understand what is happening in themselves as minute points of the intersections of biography and history within society. In large part, contemporary man's self-conscious view of himself as at least an outsider, if not a permanent stranger, rests upon an absorbed realization of social relativity and of the transformative power of history. The sociological imagination is the most fruitful of this self-consciousness. By its use men whose mentalities have swept only a series of limited orbits often come to feel as if suddenly awakened in a house with which they had only supposed themselves to be familiar. Correctly or incorrectly, they often come to feel that they can now provide themselves with adequate summations, cohesive assessments, comprehensive orientations. Older decisions that once appeared sound, now seem to them products of a mind unaccountably dense. Their capacity for astonishment is made lively again. They acquire a new way of thinking, they experience a transvaluation of values: in a word, by their reflection and by their sensibility, they realize the cultural meaning of the social sciences.

Perhaps the most fruitful distinction with which the sociological imagination works is between 'the personal troubles of milieu' and 'the public issues of social structure'. This distinction is an essential tool of the sociological imagination and a feature of all classic work in social science.

*Troubles* occur within the character of the individual and within the range of his immediate relations with others; they have to do with his self and with those limited areas of social life of which he is directly and personally aware. Accordingly, the statement and the resolution of troubles properly lie within the individual as a biographical entity and within the scope of his immediate milieu – the social setting that is directly open to his personal experience and to some extent his wilful activity. A trouble is a private matter: values cherished by an individual are felt by him to be threatened.

*Issues* have to do with matters that transcend these local environments of the individual and the range of his inner life. They have to do with the organization of many such milieux into the institutions of an historical society as a whole, with the ways in which various milieux overlap and interpenetrate to form the larger structure of social and historical life. An issue is a public matter: some value cherished by publics is felt to be threatened. Often there is a debate about what the value really is and about what it is that really threatens it. This debate is often without focus if only because it is the very nature of an issue, unlike even widespread trouble, that it cannot very well be defined in terms of the immediate and everyday environments of ordinary men. An issue, in fact, often involves a crisis in institutional arrangements, and often too it involves what Marxists call 'contradictions' or 'antagonisms'.

In these terms, consider employment. When in a city of a hundred million only one man is unemployed, that is his personal trouble, and for its relief we properly look to the character of the man, his skills and his immediate opportunities. But when in a nation of fifty million employees, fifteen million men are unemployed, that is an issue, and we may not hop to find its solution within the range of opportunities open to any one individual. The very structure of opportunities has collapsed. Both the correct statement of the problem and the range of possible solutions require us to consider the economic and political institutions of the society, and not merely the personal situation and character of a scatter of individuals.

Consider war. The personal problem of war, when it occurs, may be how to survive it or how to die in it with honor; how to make money out of it: how to climb into the higher safety of the military apparatus; or how to contribute to the war's termination. In short, according to one's value, to find a set of milieux and within it to survive the war or make one's death in it meaningful. But the structural issues of war have to do with its causes; with what types of men it throws up into command; with its effects upon economic and political, family and religious institutions, with the unorganized irresponsibility of a world of nation-states.

Consider marriage. Inside a marriage a man and a woman may experience personal troubles, but when the divorce rate during the first four years of marriage is 250 out of every 1000 attempts this is an indication of a structural issue having to do with the institutions of marriage and the family and other institutions that bear upon them.

Or consider the metropolis – the horrible, beautiful, ugly, magnificent sprawl of the great city. For many upper-class people, the personal solution to 'the problem of the city' is to have an apartment with private garage under it in the heart of the city and, forty miles out, a house by Henry Hill, garden by Garrett Eckbo, on a hundred acres of private land. In these two controlled environments – with a small staff at each end and a private helicopter connexion – most people could solve many of the problems of personal milieux caused by the facts of the city. But all this, however splendid, does not solve the public issues that the structural fact of the city poses. What should be done with this wonderful monstrosity? Break it all up into scattered units, combining residence and work? Refurbish it as it stands? Or, after evacuation, dynamite it and build new cities according to new plans in new places? What should those plans be? And who is to decide and to accomplish whatever choice is made? These are structural issues; to confront them and to solve them requires us to consider political and economic issues that affect innumerable milieux.

In so far as an economy is so arranged that slumps occur, the problem of unemployment becomes incapable of personal solution. In so far as

war is inherent in the nation-state system and in the uneven industrialization of the world, the ordinary individual in his restricted milieu
will be powerless – with or without psychiatric aid – to solve the troubles
this system or lack of system imposes upon him. In so far as the family as
an institution turns women into darling little slaves and men into their
chief providers and unweaned dependents, the problem of a satisfactory
marriage remains incapable of purely private solution. In so far as the
overdeveloped megalopolis and the overdeveloped automobile are built-
in features of the overdeveloped society, the issues of urban living will
not be solved by personal ingenuity and private wealth.

What we experience in various and specific milieux, I have noted, is
often caused by structural changes. Accordingly, to understand the
changes of many personal milieux we are required to look beyond them.
And the number and variety of such structural changes increase as the
institutions within which we live become more embracing and more
intricately connected with one another. To be aware of the idea of social
structure and to use it with sensibility is to be capable of tracing such
linkages among a great variety of milieux. To be able to do that is to
possess the sociological imagination.

# 2 H. Stuart Hughes

## Consciousness and Society

Excerpts from H. Stuart Hughes, *Consciousness and Society: The Reorientation of European Social Thought 1890–1930*, Knopf, 1958, pp. 35–7, 63–6, 306–8.

Unquestionably the major intellectual innovators of the 1890s were profoundly interested in the problem of irrational motivation in human conduct. They were obsessed, almost intoxicated, with a rediscovery of the nonlogical, the uncivilized, the inexplicable. But to call them 'irrationalists' is to fall into a dangerous ambiguity. It suggests a tolerance or even a preference for the realms of the unconscious. The reverse was actually the case. [. . .]

The main attack against the intellectual heritage of the past was on a narrower front. It was directed primarily against what the writers of the 1890s chose to call 'positivism'. By this they did not mean simply the rather quaint doctrines associated with the name of Auguste Comte, who had originally coined the term. Nor did they mean the social philosophy of Herbert Spencer, which was the guise in which positivist thinking was most apparent in their own time. They used the word in a looser sense to characterize the whole tendency to discuss human behavior in terms of analogies drawn from natural science. In reacting against it, the innovators of the 1890s felt that they were rejecting the most pervasive intellectual tenet of their time. They believed that they were casting off a spiritual yoke that the preceding quarter-century had laid upon them. [. . .]

1. Most basic, perhaps, and the key to all the others was the new interest in the problem of consciousness and the role of the unconscious. [. . .]

2. Closely related to the problem of consciousness was the question of the meaning of time and duration in psychology, philosophy, literature and history. [. . .]

3. Beyond and embracing the questions of consciousness and time there loomed the further problem of the nature of knowledge in what Wilhelm Dilthey had called the 'sciences of the mind'. [. . .] By 1900 it was apparent [. . .] that the nineteenth-century program of building an edifice of historical and sociological knowledge by patient accumulation

and painstaking verification no longer sufficed. By such means it would prove forever impossible to penetrate beneath the surface of human experience. [. . .]

4. If the knowledge of human affairs, then, rested on such tentative foundations, the whole basis of political discussion had been radically altered. No longer could one remain content with the easy assurances of the rationalistic ideologies inherited from the century and a half preceding – liberal, democratic or socialist as the case might be. The task was rather to penetrate behind the fictions of political action, behind what Sorel called the 'myths', Pareto the 'derivations', and Mosca the 'political formulas' of the time. Behind these convenient façades, one could postulate the existence of the actual wielders of power, the creative minorities, the political élites. The discussion of politics, then, had been pushed back from the front of the stage to the wings – from the rhetoric of public discussion to the manipulation of half-conscious sentiments. [. . .]

The essential difference between the natural and the human world, [Weber] contended, lay in the fact that in the latter realm it was impossible to arrive at laws – or causal explanations – that would in any sense give a satisfactory or exhaustive explanation of even the simplest human action. The problem, then, became one of devising a method of arriving at *partial* explanations of a causal character – explanations that for all their patent one-sidedness would be somewhat more rigorous than the conventional procedure in terms of 're-experiencing', 'intuition' or 'feel'.

As his own answer to this problem, Weber devised a most ingenious schema of *hypothetical* analysis. It was based on the conviction that in the study of human affairs the best that a causal explanation could do was to locate the factor which, when removed, would make the decisive difference in a given sequence of events – the factor, that is, which, when thought away, would not permit us to conceive of the event in question as occurring. As applied in a few sample cases, this procedure proved only moderately convincing. But it opened the way to Weber's extremely instructive reflections on 'objectivity' and 'value'.

In proposing his method of hypothetical causal explanation, Weber was careful to specify that the decisive factor in question could be described as decisive only *from the standpoint of the individual investigator*. And this in turn meant that the selection of this factor was based, ultimately, on some explicit or implicit value-system (Weber, 1949, p. 78). The inevitable *choices* among their data that historians and social scientists made faithfully reflected the values they personally cherished: as an individual acting in the world of practical reality, the investigator of society developed an attitude toward life that was subsequently mirrored in his scientific production. [. . .]

A heroic effort was required, then, if the professor was to separate his scientific from his public role. And the struggle was particularly acute in the case of Weber himself, who, as we have seen, was a man of passionate political and social conviction. These convictions Weber had no intention of repressing. He did not argue that it was necessary to combat them in one's own soul. On the contrary, he implied that they were essential to creation in the social-science field: it was only through a kind of sublimation of these very convictions (we are reminded of the later Croce) that significant scientific choice became possible. 'An *attitude of moral indifference*', Weber (1949, p. 60) insisted, 'has no connexion with *scientific* "objectivity".'

Thus in Weber's hands the relationship between scientific objectivity and value-judgement was developed into a peculiarly subtle process of mutual interaction. On the one hand, scientific investigation took its departure from some standpoint in the realm of values. Subsequently this investigation in turn began to illuminate the range of value choices. It could demonstrate what values were consistent or inconsistent with each other; it could determine the consequences or implications of a proposed course of action; it could estimate what 'the attainment of a desired end' would ' "cost" in terms of the predictable loss of other values'. But it could not make the 'act of choice itself': that was the sole responsibility of 'the acting, willing person'; he was obliged to weigh and choose 'from among the values involved according to his own conscience and his personal view of the world'. In short, 'an empirical science' could not 'tell anyone what he *should* do – but rather what he *can* do – and under certain circumstances – what he wishes to do' (see Weber, 1949, pp. 20–21 and 53–4).

Ultimately, however, it was only the values entertained by individual human beings that gave 'meaning' – in the double sense of comprehensibility and purpose – to the existence of man in society. And this meaning was established through what we call culture.

*Reference*

WEBER, M. (1949), *The Methodology of the Social Sciences*, Free Press, translated and edited by E. A. Shils and H. A. Finch.

# 3 Karl Mannheim

Ideology and Utopia

Excerpts from Karl Mannheim, *Ideology and Utopia*, translated by Louis Wirth and Edward Shils, Routledge & Kegan Paul, 1936, pp. 36, 173–4.
First published in German in 1929.

The concept 'ideology' reflects the one discovery which emerged from political conflict, namely, that ruling groups can in their thinking become so intensively interest-bound to a situation that they are simply no longer able to see certain facts which would undermine their sense of domination. There is implicit in the word 'ideology' the insight that in certain situations the collective unconscious of certain groups obscures the real condition of society both to itself and to others and thereby stabilizes it.

The concept of *Utopian* thinking reflects the opposite discovery of the political struggle, namely that certain oppressed groups are intellectually so strongly interested in the destruction and transformation of a given condition of society that they unwittingly see only those elements in the situation which tend to negate it. Their thinking is incapable of correctly diagnosing an existing condition of society. They are not at all concerned with what really exists; rather in their thinking they already seek to change the situation that exists. Their thought is never a diagnosis of the situation; it can be used only as a direction for action. In the Utopian mentality, the collective unconscious, guided by wishful representation and the will to action, hides certain aspects of reality. It turns its back on everything which would shake its belief or paralyse its desire to change things. [. . .]

A state of mind is Utopian when it is incongruous with the state of reality within which it occurs.

This incongruence is always evident in the fact that such a state of mind in experience, in thought and in practice, is oriented towards objects which do not exist in the actual situation. However, we should not regard as Utopian every state of mind which is incongruous with and transcends the immediate situation (and in this sense, 'departs from reality'). Only those orientations transcending reality will be referred to by us as Utopian which, when they pass over into conduct, tend to shatter, either partially or wholly, the order of things prevailing at the time.

In limiting the meaning of the term 'Utopia' to that type of orientation which transcends reality and which at the same time breaks the bonds of the existing order, a distinction is set up between the Utopian and the ideological states of mind. One can orient oneself to objects that are alien to reality and which transcend actual existence – and nevertheless still be effective in the realization and the maintenance of the existing order of things. [. . .] Such an incongruent orientation became Utopian only when in addition it tended to burst the bonds of the existing order. [. . .]

Every period in history has contained ideas transcending the existing order, but these did not function as Utopias; they were rather the appropriate ideologies of this stage of existence as long as they were 'organically' and harmoniously integrated into the world-view characteristic of the period (i.e. did not offer revolutionary possibilities). As long as the clerically and feudally organized medieval order was able to locate its paradise outside of society, in some other-worldly sphere which transcended history and dulled its revolutionary edge, the idea of paradise was still an integral part of medieval society. Not until certain social groups embodied these wish-images into their actual conduct, and tried to realize them, did these ideologies become Utopian.

# 4 Thomas S. Kuhn

## The Structure of Scientific Revolutions

Excerpts from Thomas S. Kuhn, *The Structure of Scientific Revolutions*, University of Chicago Press, 1962, pp. 1–11, 52–3, 77, 82, 89–93, 145–6, 157.

History, if viewed as a repository for more than anecdote or chronology, could produce a decisive transformation in the image of science by which we are now possessed. That image has previously been drawn, even by scientists themselves, mainly from the study of finished scientific achievements as these are recorded in the classics and, more recently, in the textbooks from which each new scientific generation learns to practice its trade. Inevitably, however, the aim of such books is persuasive and pedagogic; a concept of science drawn from them is no more likely to fit the enterprise that produced them than an image of a national culture drawn from a tourist brochure or a language text. This essay attempts to show that we have been misled by them in fundamental ways. Its aim is a sketch of the quite different concept of science that can emerge from the historical record of the research activity itself.

Even from history, however, that new concept will not be forthcoming if historical data continue to be sought and scrutinized mainly to answer questions posed by the unhistorical stereotype drawn from science texts. Those texts have, for example, often seemed to imply that the content of science is uniquely exemplified by the observations, laws and theories described in their pages. Almost as regularly, the same books have been read as saying that scientific methods are simply the ones illustrated by the manipulative techniques used in gathering textbook data, together with the logical operations employed when relating those data to the textbook's theoretical generalizations. The result has been a concept of science with profound implications about its nature and development. [...]

In recent years, however, a few historians of science have been finding it more and more difficult to fulfil the functions that the concept of development-by-accumulation assigns to them. As chroniclers of an incremental process, they discover that additional research makes it harder, not easier, to answer questions like: when was oxygen discovered? Who first conceived of energy conservation? Increasingly, a few of them suspect that these are simply the wrong sorts of questions to ask. Perhaps science does not develop by the accumulation of individual discoveries and inventions. Simultaneously, these same historians confront growing difficulties in distinguishing the 'scientific' component of past observation and belief from what their predecessors had readily labeled 'error' and 'superstition'. The more carefully they study, say, Aristotelean dynamics, phlogistic chemistry or caloric thermodynamics, the more certain they feel that those once current views of nature were, as a whole, neither less scientific nor more the product of human idiosyncrasy than those current today. If these out-of-date beliefs are to be called myths, then myths can be produced by the same sort of methods and held for the same sorts of reasons that now lead to scientific knowledge. If, on the other hand, they are to be called science, then science has included bodies of belief quite incompatible with the ones we hold today. Given these alternatives, the historian must chose the latter. Out-of-date theories are not in principle unscientific because they have been discarded. That choice, however, makes it difficult to see scientific development as a process of accretion. The same historical research that displays the difficulties in isolating individual inventions and discoveries gives ground for profound doubts about the cumulative process through which these individual contributions to science were thought to have been compounded.

The result of all these doubts and difficulties is a historiographic revolution in the study of science, though one that is still in its early stages. Gradually, and often without entirely realizing they are doing so, historians of science have begun to ask new sorts of questions and to trace different, and often less than cumulative, developmental lines for the sciences. Rather than seeking the permanent contributions of an older science to our present vantage, they attempt to display the historical integrity of that science in its own time. They ask, for example, not about the relation of Galileo's views to those of modern science, but rather about the relationship between his views and those of his group, i.e. his teachers, contemporaries and immediate successors in the sciences. Furthermore, they insist upon studying the opinions of that group and other similar ones from the viewpoint – usually very different from that of modern science – that gives those opinions the maximum internal coherence and the closest possible fit to nature. [...] The early developmental stages of most sciences have been characterized by continual competition between a number of distinct views of nature, each partially derived from, and all roughly compatible with, the dictates of scientific observation and method. What differentiated these various schools was not one or another failure method – they were all 'scientific' – but what we shall come to call their incommensurable ways of seeing the world and of practicing science in it. Observation and experience can and must drastically restrict the range of admissible scientific belief, else there would be no science. But they cannot alone determine a particular body of such belief. An apparently arbitrary element, compounded of personal and historical accident, is always a formative ingredient of the beliefs espoused by a given scientific community at a given time.

That element of arbitrariness does not, however, indicate that any scientific group could practice its trade without some set of received beliefs. Nor does it make less consequential the particular constellation to which the group, at a given time, is in fact committed. Effective research scarcely begins before a scientific community thinks it has acquired firm answers to questions like the following: what are the fundamental entities of which the universe is composed? How do these interact with each other and with the senses? What questions may legitimately be asked about such entities and what techniques employed in seeking solutions? At least in the mature sciences, answers (or full substitutes for answers) to questions like these are firmly embedded in the educational initiation that prepares and licenses the student for professional practice. Because education is both rigorous and rigid, these answers come to exert a deep hold on the scientific mind. That they can do so does much to account both for the peculiar efficiency of the normal research activity and for the direction in which it proceeds at any given time. [. . .]

Yet that element of arbitrariness is present, and it too has an important effect on scientific development. [. . .] Normal science, the activity in which most scientists inevitably spend almost all their time, is predicated on the assumption that the scientific community knows what the world is like. Much of the success of the enterprise derives from the community's willingness to defend that assumption, if necessary at considerable cost. Normal science, for example, often suppresses fundamental novelties because they are necessarily subversive of its basic commitments. Nevertheless, so long as those commitments retain an element of the arbitrary, the very nature of normal research ensures that novelty shall not be suppressed for very long. Sometimes a normal problem, one that ought to be solvable by known rules and procedures, resists the reiterated onslaught of the ablest members of the group within whose competence it falls. On other occasions a piece of equipment designed and constructed for the purpose of normal research fails to perform in the anticipated manner, revealing an anomaly that cannot, despite repeated effort, be aligned with professional expectation. In these and other ways besides, normal science repeatedly goes astray. And when it does – when, that is, the profession can no longer evade anomalies that subvert the existing tradition of scientific practice – then begin the extraordinary investigations that lead the profession at last to a new set of commitments, a new basis for the practice of science. The extraordinary episodes in which that shift of professional commitments occurs are the ones known in this essay as scientific revolutions. They are the tradition-shattering complements to the tradition-bound activity of normal science.

The most obvious examples of scientific revolutions are those famous episodes in scientific development that have often been labeled revolutions before. [...] The major turning points in scientific development associated with the names of Copernicus, Newton, Lavoisier and Einstein, more clearly than most other episodes in the history of at least the physical sciences, display what all scientific revolutions are about. Each of them necessitated the community's rejection of one time-honored scientific theory in favor of another incompatible with it. Each produced a consequent shift in the problems available for scientific scrutiny and in the standards by which the profession determined what should count as an admissible problem or as a legitimate problem solution. And each transformed the scientific imagination in ways that we shall ultimately need to describe as a transformation of the world within which scientific work was done. Such changes, together with the controversies that almost always accompany them, are the defining characteristics of scientific revolutions. [...]

Maxwell's equations were as revolutionary as Einstein's and they were resisted accordingly. The invention of other new theories regularly, and appropriately, evokes the same response from some of the specialists on whose area of special competence they impinge. For these men the new theory implies a change in the rules governing the prior practice of normal science. Inevitably, therefore, it reflects upon much scientific work they have already successfully completed. That is why a new theory, however special its range of application, is seldom or never just an increment to what is already known. Its assimilation requires the reconstruction of prior theory and the re-evaluation of prior fact, an intrinsically revolutionary process that is seldom completed by a single man and never overnight. No wonder historians have had difficulty in dating precisely this extended process that their vocabulary impels them to view as an isolated event.

Nor are new inventions of theory the only scientific events that have revolutionary impact upon the specialists in whose domain they occur. The commitments that govern normal science specify not only what sorts of entities the universe does contain but also, by implication, those that it does not. It follows that a discovery like that of oxygen or X-rays does not simply add one more item to the population of the scientist's world. Ultimately it has that effect, but not until the professional community has re-evaluated traditional experimental procedures, altered its conception of entities with which it has long been familiar and, in the process, shifted the network of theory through which it deals with the world. Scientific fact and theory are not categorically separable, except perhaps within a single tradition of normal scientific practice. That is why the unexpected discovery is not simply factual in its import and why the scientist's world is qualitatively transformed as well as quantitatively enriched by fundamental novelties of either fact or theory. [. . .]

A theory of scientific inquiry replaces the confirmation or falsification procedures made familiar by our usual image of science. Competition between segments of the scientific community is the only historical process that ever actually results in the rejection of one previously accepted theory or in the adoption of another. [. . .]

In this essay, 'normal science' means research firmly based upon one or more past scientific achievements, achievements that some particular scientific community acknowledges for a time as supplying the foundation for its further practice. [. . .] Their achievement was sufficiently unprecedented to attract an enduring group of adherents away from competing modes of scientific activity. Simultaneously, it was sufficiently open-ended to leave all sorts of problems for the redefined group of practitioners to resolve.

Achievements that share these two characteristics I shall henceforth refer to as 'paradigms', a term that relates closely to 'normal science'. By choosing it, I mean to suggest that some accepted examples of actual scientific practice – examples which include law, theory, application and instrumentation together – provide models from which spring particular coherent traditions of scientific research. [. . .] The study of paradigms is what mainly prepares the student for membership in the particular scientific community with which he will later practice. Because he there joins men who learned the bases of their field from the same concrete models, his subsequent practice will seldom evoke overt disagreement over fundamentals. Men whose research is based on shared paradigms are committed to the same rules and standards for scientific practice; that commitment and the apparent consensus it produces are prerequisites for normal science, i.e. for the genesis and continuation of a particular research tradition. [. . .]

Discovery commences with the awareness of anomaly, i.e. with the recognition that nature has somehow violated the paradigm-induced expectations that govern normal science. It then continues with a more or less extended exploration of the area of anomaly. And it closes only

Thomas S. Kuhn  31

when the paradigm theory has been adjusted so that the anomalous has become the expected. Assimilating a new sort of fact demands a more than additive adjustment of theory, and until that adjustment is completed – until the scientist has learned to see nature in a different way – the new fact is not quite a scientific fact at all. [. . .]

Once it has achieved the status of paradigm, a scientific theory is declared invalid only if an alternate candidate is available to take its place. No process yet disclosed by the historical study of scientific development at all resembles the methodological stereotype of falsification by direct comparison with nature. That remark does not mean that scientists do not reject scientific theories, nor that experience and experiment are not essential to the process in which they do so. But it does mean – what will ultimately be a central point – that the act of judgement that leads scientists to reject a previously accepted theory is always based upon more than a comparison of that theory with the world. The decision to reject one paradigm is always simultaneously the decision to accept another, and the judgement leading to that decision involves the comparison of both paradigms with nature *and* with each other. [. . .] If an anomaly is to evoke crisis, it must usually be more than just an anomaly. There are always difficulties somewhere in the paradigm-nature fit; most of them are set right sooner or later, often by processes that could not have been foreseen. The scientist who pauses to examine every anomaly he notes will seldom get significant work done. [. . .] Sometimes an anomaly will clearly call into question explicit and fundamental generalizations of the paradigm, as the problem of ether drag did for those who accepted Maxwell's theory. Or, as in the Copernican revolution, an anomaly without apparent fundamental import may evoke crisis if the applications that it inhibits have a particular practical importance, in this case for calendar design and astrology. [. . .]

If any and every failure to fit were grounds for theory rejection, all theories ought to be rejected at all times. On the other hand, if only severe failure to fit justifies theory rejection, then some criterion of 'improbability' or of 'degree of falsification' is required.

Falsification, though it surely occurs, does not happen with, or because of, the emergence of an anomaly or falsifying instance. Instead it is a subsequent and separate process which might equally be called 'verification' since it consists in the triumph of a new paradigm over the old one. To the historian, at least, it makes little sense to suggest that verification is establishing the agreement of fact with theory. All historically significant theories have agreed with the facts, but only more or less. There is no more precise answer to the question whether or how well an individual theory fits the facts. But questions much like that can be asked when theories are taken collectively or even in parts. It makes a great deal of sense to ask which of two actual and competing theories fits the facts *better*.

The man who embraces a new paradigm at an early stage must often do so in defiance of the evidence provided by problem solving. He must, that is, have faith that the new paradigm will succeed with the many large problems that confront it, knowing only that the older paradigm has failed with a few. A decision of that kind can only be made on faith.

Almost always the men who achieve these fundamental inventions of a new paradigm have either been very young or very new to the field whose paradigm they change. And perhaps that point need not have been made explicit, for obviously these are the men who, being little committed by prior practice to the traditional rules of normal science, are particularly likely to see that those rules no longer define a playable game and to conceive another set that can replace them. [. . .]

As in political revolutions, so in paradigm choice – there is no standard higher than the assent of the relevant community. To discover how scientific revolutions are effected, we shall therefore have to examine not only the impact of nature and of logic, but also the techniques of persuasive argumentation effective within the quite special groups that constitute the community of scientists.

# 5 Barney G. Glaser and Anselm L. Strauss

The Discovery of Grounded Theory

Excerpts from Barney G. Glaser and Anselm L. Strauss,
*The Discovery of Grounded Theory: Strategies for Qualitative Research*,
Aldine Press, 1967, pp. 1–35.

The discovery of theory from data – which we call *grounded theory* – is a major task confronting sociology today. [. . .]

The interrelated jobs of theory in sociology are: (a) to enable prediction and explanation of behavior; (b) to be useful in theoretical advance in sociology; (c) to be usable in practical applications – prediction and explanation should be able to give the practitioner understanding and some control of situations; (d) to provide a perspective on behavior – a stance to be taken toward data; and (e) to guide and provide a style for research on particular areas of behavior. [. . .] The theory must also be readily understandable to sociologists of any viewpoint, to students and to significant laymen. Theory that can meet these requirements must fit the situation being researched, and work when put into use. By 'fit' we mean that the categories must be readily (not forcibly) applicable to and indicated by the data under study; by 'work' we mean that they must be meaningfully relevant and to be able to explain the behavior under study. [. . .]

Generating a theory from data means that most hypotheses and concepts not only come from the data, but are systematically worked out in relation to the data during the course of the research. *Generating a theory involves a process of research.* By contrast, the *source* of certain ideas, or even 'models', can come from sources other than the data. The biographies of scientists are replete with stories of occasional flashes of insight, of seminal ideas, garnered from sources outside the data. But the generation of theory from such insights must then be brought into relation to the data, or there is great danger that theory and empirical world will mismatch. [. . .]

While verifying is the researcher's principal and vital task for existing theories, we suggest that his main goal in developing new theories is their purposeful systematic generation from the data of social research. Of course, verifying as much as possible with as accurate evidence as possible is requisite while one discovers and generates his theory – but *not* to the point where verification becomes so paramount as to curb generation. Thus, generation of theory through comparative analysis both subsumes and assumes verifications and accurate descriptions, but *only* to the extent that the latter are in the service of generation. [. . .]

We have chosen the discussional form for several reasons. Our strategy of comparative analysis for generating theory puts a high emphasis on *theory of process*; that is, theory as an ever-developing entity, not as a perfected product. [. . .]

Comparative analysis can be used to generate two basic kinds of theory: substantive and formal. By substantive theory, we mean that developed for a substantive, or empirical, area of sociological inquiry, such as patient care, race relations, professional education, delinquency or research organizations. By formal theory, we mean that developed for a formal, or conceptual, area of sociological inquiry, such as stigma, deviant behavior, formal organization, socialization, status congruency, authority and power reward systems or social mobility. [. . .]

Substantive and formal theories exist on distinguishable levels of generality, which differ only in terms of degree. Therefore, in any one study, each type can shade at points into the other. The analyst, however, should focus clearly on one level or other, or on a specific combination, because the strategies vary for arriving at each one. For example, in our analysis of dying as a nonscheduled status passage, the focus was on the substantive area of dying, not on the formal area of status passage (see Glaser and Strauss, 1965). With the focus on a substantive area such as this, the generation of theory can be achieved by a comparative analysis between or among groups within the same substantive area. In this instance, we compared hospital wards where patients characteristically died at different rates. The substantive theory also could be generated by comparing dying as a status passage with other substantive cases within the formal area of status passage, whether scheduled or not, such as studenthood or engagement for marriage. The comparison would illuminate the substantive theory about dying as a status passage.

However, if the focus were on formal theory, then the comparative analysis would be made among different kinds of substantive cases which fall within the formal area, without relating them to any one substantive area. The focus of comparisons is now on generating a theory of status passage, not on generating theory about a single substantive case of status passage.

Both substantive and formal theories must be grounded in data. Substantive theory faithful to the empirical situation cannot, we believe, be formulated merely by applying a few ideas from an established formal theory to the substantive area. To be sure one goes out and studies an area with a particular sociological perspective, and with a focus, a general question, or a problem in mind. But one can (and we believe should) also study an area without any preconceived theory that dictates, prior to the research, 'relevancies' in concepts and hypotheses. Indeed it is presumptuous to assume that one begins to know the relevant categories and hypotheses until the 'first days in the field', at least, are over. A substantive theory generated from the data must first be formulated, in order to see which of diverse formal theories are, perhaps, applicable for furthering additional substantive formulations.

Ignoring this first task – discovering substantive theory relevant to a given substantive area – is the result, in most instances, of believing that formal theories can be applied directly to a substantive area, and will supply most or all of the necessary concepts and hypotheses. The consequence is often a forcing of data, as well as a neglect of relevant concepts and hypotheses that may emerge. Our approach, allowing substantive concepts and hypotheses to emerge first, on their own, enables the analyst to ascertain which, if any, existing formal theory may help him generate his substantive theories. He can then be more faithful to his data, rather than forcing it to fit a theory. He can be more objective and less theoretically biased. Of course, this also means that he cannot merely apply Parsonian or Mertonian categories at the start, but must wait to see whether they are linked to the emergent substantive theory concerning the issue in focus.

Substantive theory in turn helps to generate new grounded formal theories and to reformulate previously established ones. Thus it becomes a strategic link in the formulation and development of formal theory based on data. For example, in our theory bearing on 'awareness contexts' relevant to dying, two important properties are *cues* leading to awareness and the personal *stakes* involved in the various parties becoming aware. Currently, in generating a formal theory of awareness contexts, we are developing the generalities related to stakes and cues by studying such groups as spies and building subcontractors. A dying patient or a spy has a great stake in any type of awareness context, and a subcontractor has a quantifiable or monetary stake. We use the word *grounded* here to underline the point that the formal theory we are talking about must be contrasted with 'grand' theory that is generated from logical assumptions and speculations about the 'oughts' of social life.

Within these relations existing among social research, substantive theory and formal theory is a design for the cumulative nature of knowledge and theory. The design involves a progressive building up from facts, through substantive to grounded formal theory. To generate substantive theory, we need many facts for the necessary comparative analysis; ethnographic studies, as well as direct gathering of data, are immensely useful for this purpose. Ethnographic studies, substantive theories and direct data collection are all, in turn, necessary for building up by comparative analysis to formal theory. This design, then, locates the place of each level of work within the cumulation of knowledge and theory, and thereby suggests a division of labor in sociological work.

## Reference

GLASER, B. G., and STRAUSS, A. L. (1965), 'Temporal aspects of dying as a nonscheduled status passage', *Amer. J. Sociol.*, vol. 71, pp. 48–59.

# 6 Kenneth Burke

The Five Key Terms of Dramatism

Excerpts from Kenneth Burke, *A Grammar of Motives*, George Braziller, 1955, pp. x–xvi. First published in 1945.

What is involved, when we say what people are doing and why they are doing it? An answer to that question is the subject of this book. The book is concerned with the basic forms of thought which, in accordance with the nature of the world as all men necessarily experience it, are exemplified in the attributing of motives. These forms of thought can be embodied profoundly or trivially, truthfully or falsely. They are equally present in systematically elaborated metaphysical structures, in legal judgements, in poetry and fiction, in political and scientific works, in news and in bits of gossip offered at random.

We shall use five terms as generating principle of our investigation. They are: Act, Scene, Agent, Agency, Purpose. In a rounded statement about motives, you must have some word that names the *act* (names what took place, in thought or deed), and another that names the *scene* (the background of the act, the situation in which it occurred); also, you must indicate what person or kind of person (*agent*) performed the act, what means or instruments he used (*agency*) and the *purpose*. Men may violently disagree about the purposes behind a given act, or about the character of the person who did it, or how he did it or in what kind of situation he acted; or they may even insist upon totally different words to name the act itself. But be that as it may, any complete statement about motives will offer *some kind* of answers to these five questions: what was done (act), when or where it was done (scene), who did it (agent), how he did it (agency) and why (purpose).

If you ask why, with a whole world of terms to choose from, we select these rather than some others as basic, our book itself is offered as the answer. For, to explain our position, we shall show how it can be applied.

Act, Scene, Agent, Agency, Purpose. Although, over the centuries, men have shown great enterprise and inventiveness in pondering matters of human motivation one can simplify the subject by this pentad of key terms, which are understandable almost at a glance. They never need to be abandoned, since all statements that assign motives can be shown to arise out of them and to terminate in them. By examining them quizzically, we can range far; yet the terms are always there for us to reclaim, in their everyday simplicity, their almost miraculous easiness, thus enabling us constantly to begin afresh. When they might become difficult, when we can hardly see them, through having stared at them too intensely, we can of a sudden relax, to look at them as we always have, lightly, glancingly. And having reassured ourselves, we can start out again, once more daring to let them look strange and difficult for a time.

In an exhibit of photographic murals (*Road to Victory*) at the Museum of Modern Art, there was an aerial photograph of two launches, proceeding side by side on a tranquil sea. Their wakes crossed and recrossed each other in almost an infinity of lines. Yet despite the intricateness of this tracery, the picture gave an impression of great simplicity, because one could quickly perceive the generating principle of its design. Such, ideally, is the case with our pentad of terms, used as generating principle. It should provide us with a kind of simplicity that can be developed into considerable complexity, and yet can be discovered beneath its elaborations.

We want to inquire into the purely internal relationships which the five terms bear to one another, considering their possibilities of transformation, their range of permutations and combinations – and then to see how these various resources figure in actual statements about human motives. Strictly speaking, we mean by a grammar of motives a concern with the terms alone, without reference to the ways in which their potentialities have been or can be utilized in actual statements about motives. Speaking broadly we could designate as 'philosophies' any statements in which these grammatical resources are specifically utilized. Random or unsystematic statements about motives could be considered as fragments of a philosophy.

One could think of the grammatical resources as *principles,* and of the various philosophies as *casuistries* which apply these principles to temporal situations. For instance, we may examine the term Scene simply as a blanket term for the concept of background or setting *in general,* a name for *any* situation in which acts or agents are placed. In our usage, this concern would be 'grammatical'. And we move into matters of 'philosophy' when we note that one thinker uses 'God' as his term for the ultimate ground or scene of human action, another uses 'nature', a third uses 'environment', or 'history' or 'means of production', etc. And whereas a statement about the grammatical principles of motivation might lay claim to a universal validity, or complete certainty, the choice of any one philosophic idiom embodying these principles is much more open to question. Even before we know what act is to be discussed, we can say with confidence that rounded discussion of its motives must contain a reference to *some kind* of background. But since each philosophic idiom will characterize this background differently, there will remain the question as to which characterization is 'right' or 'more nearly right'.

It is even likely that, whereas one philosophic idiom offers the best calculus for one case, another case answers best to a totally different calculus. However, we should not think of 'cases' in too restricted a sense. Although, from the standpoint of the grammatical principles inherent in the internal relationships prevailing among our five terms, any given philosophy is to be considered as a casuistry, even a cultural situation extending over centuries is a 'case', and would probably require a much different philosophic idiom as its temporizing calculus of motives than would be required in the case of other cultural situations. [. . .]

A perfectionist might seek to evolve terms free of ambiguity and inconsistency (as with the terministic ideals of symbolic logic and logical positivism). But we have a different purpose in view, one that probably retains traces of its 'cosmic' origin. We take it for granted that, in so far as men cannot themselves create the universe, there must remain something essentially enigmatic about the problem of motives, and that this underlying enigma will manifest itself in inevitable ambiguities and inconsistencies among the terms for motives. Accordingly, what we want is *not terms that avoid ambiguity,* but *terms that clearly reveal the strategic spots at which ambiguities necessarily arise.*

Occasionally, you will encounter a writer who seems to get great exaltation out of proving, with an air of much relentlessness, that some philosophic term or other has been used to cover a variety of meanings, and who would smash and abolish this idol. As a general rule, when a term is singled out for such harsh treatment, if you look closer you will find that it happens to be associated with some cultural or political trend from which the writer would dissociate himself; hence there is a certain notable ambiguity in this very charge of ambiguity, since he presumably feels purged and strengthened by bringing to bear upon this particular term a kind of attack that could, with as much justice, be brought to bear upon any other term (or 'title') in philosophy, including of course the alternative term, or 'title', that the writer would swear by. Since no two things or acts or situations are exactly alike, you cannot apply the same term to both of them without thereby introducing a certain margin of ambiguity, an ambiguity as great as the difference between the two subjects that are given the identical title. And all the more may you expect to find ambiguity in terms so 'titular' as to become the marks of a philosophic school, or even several philosophic schools. Hence, instead of considering it our task to 'dispose of' any ambiguity by merely disclosing the fact that it is an ambiguity, we rather consider it our task to study and clarify the *resources* of ambiguity. [. . .]

Our term, 'Agent', for instance, is a general heading that might, in a given case, require further subdivision, as an agent might have his act modified (hence partly motivated) by friends (co-agents) or enemies (counter-agents). Again, under 'Agent' one could place any personal properties that are assigned a motivational value, such as 'ideas', 'the will', 'fear', 'malice', 'intuition', 'the creative imagination'. A portrait painter may treat the body as a property of the agent (an expression of personality), whereas materialistic medicine would treat it as 'scenic', a purely 'objective material'; and from another point of view it could be classed as an agency, a means by which one gets reports of the world at large. Machines are obviously instruments (that is, Agencies); yet in their vast accumulation they constitute the industrial scene, with its own peculiar set of motivational properties. War may be treated as an Agency, in so far as it is a means to an end; as a collective Act, sub-divisible into many individual acts; as a Purpose, in schemes proclaiming a cult of war. For the man inducted into the army, war is a Scene, a situation that motivates the nature of his training; and in mythologies war is an Agent, or perhaps better a super-agent, in the figure of the war god. We may think of voting as an Act, and of the voter as an Agent; yet votes and voters both are hardly other than a politician's medium or Agency; or from another point of view, they are a part of his Scene. And in so far as a vote is cast without adequate knowledge of its consequences, one might even question whether it should be classed as an activity at all; one might rather call it passive, or perhaps sheer motion (what the behaviorists would call a response to a stimulus).

Or imagine that one were to manipulate the terms, for the imputing of motives, in such a case as this: the hero (Agent) with the help of a friend (co-agent) outwits the villain (counter-agent) by using a file (Agency) that enables him to break his bonds (Act) in order to escape (Purpose) from the room where he has been confined (Scene). In selecting a casuistry here, we might locate the motive in the agent, as were we to credit his escape to some trait integral to his personality, such as 'love of freedom'. Or we might stress the motivational force of the Scene, since nothing is surer to awaken thoughts of escape in a man than a condition of imprisonment. Or we might note the essential part played by the *co-agent*, in assisting our hero to escape – and, with such thoughts as our point of departure, we might conclude that the motivations of this act should be reduced to social origins.

Or if one were given to the brand of speculative enterprise exemplified by certain Christian heretics (for instance, those who worshipped Judas as a saint, on the grounds that his betrayal of Christ, in leading to the Crucifixion, so brought about the opportunity for mankind's redemption), one might locate the necessary motivational origin of the act in the *counter-agent*. For the hero would not have been prodded to escape if there had been no villain to imprison him. [. . .]

As we shall see later, it is by reason of the pliancy among our terms that philosophic systems can pull one way and another. The margins of overlap provide opportunities whereby a thinker can go without a leap from any one of the terms to any of its fellows. (We have also likened the terms to the fingers, which in their extremities are distinct from one another, but merge in the palm of the hand. If you would go from one finger to another without a leap, you need but trace the tendon down into the palm of the hand, and then trace a new course along another tendon.) Hence, no great dialectical enterprise is necessary if you would merge the terms, reducing them even to as few as one; and then, treating this as the 'essential' term, the 'causal ancestor' of the lot, you can proceed in the reverse direction across the margins of overlap, 'deducing' the other terms from it as its logical descendants. [. . .]

The titular word for our own method is 'dramatism', since it invites one to consider the matter of motives in a perspective that, being developed from the analysis of drama, treats language and thought primarily as modes of action. The method is synoptic, though not in the historical sense. A purely historical survey would require no less than a universal history of human culture; for every judgement, exhortation or admonition, every view of natural or supernatural reality, every intention or expectation involves assumptions about motive or cause. Our work must be synoptic in a different sense: in the sense that it offers a system of placement, and should enable us, by the systematic manipulation of the terms, to 'generate' or 'anticipate' the various classes of motivational theory. And a treatment in these terms, we hope to show, reduces the subject synoptically while still permitting us to appreciate its scope and complexity.

# 7 George Herbert Mead

## The Self

Excerpts from Anselm L. Strauss (ed.), *The Social Psychology of George Herbert Mead*, University of Chicago Press, 1956, pp. 217–21, 231–5, 242–3, 252.
First published in George Herbert Mead, *Mind, Self and Society*,
University of Chicago Press, 1934.

The self, as that which can be an object to itself, is essentially a social structure and it arises in social experience. After a self has arisen, it in a certain sense provides for itself its social experiences, and so we can conceive of an absolutely solitary self. But it is impossible to conceive of a self arising outside social experience. When it has arisen we can think of a person in solitary confinement for the rest of his life, but who still has himself as a companion, and is able to think and to converse with himself as he had communicated with others. That process to which I have just referred, of responding to one's self as another responds to it, taking part in one's own conversation with others, being aware of what one is saying and using that awareness of what one is saying to determine what one is going to say thereafter – that is a process with which we are all familiar. We are continually following up our own address to other persons by an understanding of what we are saying, and using that understanding in the direction of our continued speech. We are finding out what we are going to say, what we are going to do, by saying and doing, and in the process we are continually controlling the process itself. In the conversation of gestures what we say calls out a certain response in another and that in turn changes our own action, so that we shift from what we started to do because of the reply the other makes. The conversation of gestures is the beginning of communication. The individual comes to carry on a conversation of gestures with himself. He says something, and that calls out a certain reply in himself which makes him change what he was going to say. He starts to say something, we will presume an unpleasant something, but when he starts to say it he realizes it is cruel. The effect on himself of what he is saying checks him; there is here a conversation of gestures between the individual and himself. We mean by significant speech that the action is one that affects the individual himself, and that the effect upon the individual himself is part of the intelligent carrying-out of the conversation with others. Now we, so to speak, amputate that social phase and dispense with it for the time being, so that one is talking to one's self as one would talk to another person.

This process of abstraction cannot be carried on indefinitely. One inevitably seeks an audience, has to pour one's self out to somebody. In reflective intelligence one thinks to act, and to act solely so that this action remains a part of a social process. Thinking becomes preparatory to social action. The very process of thinking is, of course, simply an inner conversation that goes on, but it is a conversation of gestures which in its completion implies the expression of that which one thinks to an audience. One separates the significance of what one is saying to others from the actual speech and gets it ready before saying it. One thinks it out, and perhaps writes it in the form of a book; but it is still a part of social intercourse in which one is addressing other persons and at the same time addressing one's self, and in which one controls the address to other persons by the response made to one's own gesture. That the person should be responding to himself is necessary to the self, and it is this sort of social conduct which provides behavior within which that self appears. I know of no other form of behavior than the linguistic in which the individual is an object to himself and, so far as I can see, the individual is not a self in the reflexive sense unless he is an object to himself. It is this fact that gives a critical importance to communication, since this is a type of behavior in which the individual does so respond to himself.

We realize in everyday conduct and experience that an individual does not mean a great deal of what he is doing and saying. We frequently say that such an individual is not himself. We come away from an interview with a realization that we have left out important things, that there are parts of the self that did not get into what was said. What determines the amount of the self that gets into communication is the social experience itself. Of course, a good deal of the self does not need to get expression. We carry on a whole series of different relationships to different people. We are one thing to one man and another thing to another. There are parts of the self which exist only for the self in relationship to itself. We divide ourselves up into all sorts of different selves with reference to our acquaintances. We discuss politics with one and religion with another. There are all sorts of different selves answering to all sorts of different social reactions. It is the social process itself that is responsible for the appearance of the self; it is not there as a self apart from this type of experience.

A multiple personality is in a certain sense normal, as I have just pointed out. There is usually an organization of the whole self with reference to the community to which we belong and the situation in which we find ourselves. What the society is, whether we are living with people of the present, people of our own imaginations, people of the past, varies, of course, with different individuals. Normally, within the sort of community as a whole to which we belong, there is a unified self, but that may be broken up. To a person who is somewhat unstable nervously and in whom there is a line of cleavage, certain activities become impossible, and that set of activities may separate and evolve another self. Two separate 'me's and 'I's, two different selves, result, and that is the condition under which there is a tendency to break up the personality. [. . .]

The unity and structure of the complete self reflects the unity and structure of the social process as a whole; and each of the elementary selves of which it is composed reflects the unity and structure of one of the various aspects of that process in which the individual is implicated. In other words, the various elementary selves which constitute, or are organized into, a complete self are the various aspects of the structure of that complete self answering to the various aspects of the structure of the social process as a whole; the structure of the complete self is thus a reflection of the complete social process. The organization and unification of a social group is identical with the organization and unification of any one of the selves arising within the social process in which that group is engaged, or which it is carrying on.

The phenomenon of dissociation of personality is caused by a breaking up of the complete, unitary self into the component selves of which it is composed, and which respectively correspond to different aspects of the social process in which the person is involved, and within which his complete or unitary self has arisen; these aspects being the different social groups to which he belongs within that process. [. . .]

The organized community or social group which gives to the individual his unity of self may be called 'the generalized other'. The attitude of the generalized other is the attitude of the whole community. Thus, for example, in the case of such a social group as a ball team, the team is the generalized other in so far as it enters – as an organized process or social activity – into the experience of any one of the individual members of it.

If the given human individual is to develop a self in the fullest sense, it is not sufficient for him merely to take the attitudes of other human individuals toward himself and toward one another within the human social process, and to bring that social process as a whole into his individual experience merely in these terms. He must also, in the same way that he takes the attitudes of other individuals toward himself and toward one another, take their attitudes toward the various phases or aspects of the common social activity or set of social undertakings in which, as members of an organized society or social group, they are all engaged. And he must then, by generalizing these individual attitudes of that organized society or social group itself, as a whole, act toward different social projects which at any given time it is carrying out, or toward the various larger phases of the general social process which constitutes its life and of which these projects are specific manifestations. This getting of the broad activities of any given social whole or organized society as such within the experiential field of any one of the individuals involved or included in that whole is, in other words, the essential basis and prerequisite of the fullest development of that individual's self: only in so far as he takes the attitudes of the organized social group to which he belongs toward the organized, cooperative social activity or set of such activities in which that group as such is engaged, does he develop a complete self or possess the sort of complete self he has developed. And on the other hand, the complex cooperative processes and activities and institutional functionings of organized human society are also possible only in so far as every individual involved in them or belonging to that society can take the general attitudes of all other such individuals with reference to these processes and activities and institutional functionings, and to the organized social whole of experiential relations and interactions thereby constituted – and can direct his own behavior accordingly.

It in in the form of the generalized other that the social process influences the behavior of the individuals involved in it and carrying it on, i.e. that the community exercises control over the conduct of its individual members; for it is in this form that the social process or community enters as a determining factor into the individual's thinking. In abstract thought the individual takes the attitude of the generalized other toward himself, without reference to its expression in any particular other individuals; and in concrete thought he takes that attitude in so far as it is expressed in the attitudes toward his behavior of those other individuals with whom he is involved in the given social situation or act. But only by taking the attitude of the generalized other toward himself, in one or another of these ways, can he think at all; for only thus can thinking – or the internalized conversation of gestures which constitutes thinking – occur. And only through the taking by individuals of the attitude or attitudes of the generalized other toward themselves is the existence of a universe of discourse, as that system of common or social meanings which thinking presupposes at its context, rendered possible.

The self-conscious human individual, then, takes or assumes the organized social attitudes of the given social group or community (or of some one section thereof) to which he belongs, toward the social problems of various kinds which confront that group or community at any given time, and which arise in connexion with the correspondingly different social projects or organized cooperative enterprises in which that group or community as such is engaged; and as an individual participant in these social projects or cooperative enterprises, he governs his own conduct accordingly. In politics, for example, the individual identifies himself with an entire political party and takes the organized attitudes of that entire party toward the rest of the given social community and toward the problems which confront the party within the given social situation; and he consequently reacts or responds in terms of the organized attitudes of the party as a whole. He thus enters into a special set of social relations with all the other individuals who belong to that political party; and in the same way he enters into various other special sets of social relations, with various other classes of individuals respectively, the individuals of each of these classes being the other-members of some one of the particular organized subgroups (determined in socially functional terms) of which he himself is a member within the entire given society or social community. In the most highly developed, organized and complicated human social communities – those evolved by civilized man – these various socially functional classes or subgroups of individuals to which any given individual belongs (and with the other individual members of which he thus enters into a special set of social relations) are of two kinds. Some of them are concrete social classes or subgroups, such as political parties, clubs, corporations, which are all actually functional social units, in terms of which their individual members are directly related to one another. The others are abstract social classes or subgroups, such as the class of debtors and the class of creditors, in terms of which their individual members are related to one another only more or less indirectly, and which only more or less indirectly function as social units, but which afford or represent unlimited possibilities for the widening and ramifying and enriching of the social relations among all the individual members of the given society as an organized and unified whole. The given individual's membership in several of these abstract social classes or subgroups makes possible his entrance into definite social relations (however indirect) with an almost infinite number of other individuals who also belong to or are included within one or another of these abstract social classes or subgroups cutting across functional lines of demarcation which divide different human social communities from one another, and including individual members from several (in some cases from all) such communities. Of these abstract social classes or subgroups of human individuals the one which is most inclusive and extensive is, of course, the one defined by the logical universe of discourse (or system of universally significant symbols) determined by the participation and communicative interaction of individuals; for of all such classes or subgroups, it is the one which claims the largest number of individual members, and which enables the largest conceivable number of human individuals to enter into some sort of social relation, however indirect or abstract it may be, with one another – a relation arising from the universal functioning of gestures as significant symbols in the general human social process of communication.

I have pointed out, then, that there are two general stages in the full development of the self. At the first of these stages, the individual's self is constituted simply by an organization of the particular attitudes of other individuals toward himself and toward one another in the specific social acts in which he participates with them. But at the second stage in the full development of the individual's self, that self is constituted not only by an organization of these particular individual attitudes, but also by an organization of the social attitudes of the generalized other or the social group as a whole to which he belongs. These social or group attitudes are brought within the individual's field of direct experience, and are included as elements in the structure or constitution of his self in the same way that the attitudes of particular other individuals are; and the individual arrives at them, or succeeds in taking them, by means of further organizing, and then generalizing, the attitudes of particular other individuals in terms of their organized social bearings and implications. So the self reaches its full development by organizing these individual attitudes of others into the organized social or group attitudes, and by thus becoming an individual reflection of the general systematic pattern of social or group behavior in which it and the others are all involved – a pattern which enters as a whole into the individual's experience in terms of these organized group attitudes which, through the mechanism of his central nervous system, he takes toward himself, just as he takes the individual attitudes of others. [. . .]

We may now explicitly raise the question as to the nature of the 'I' which is aware of the social 'me'. I do not mean to raise the metaphysical question of how a person can be both 'I' and 'me', but to ask for the significance of this distinction from the point of view of conduct itself. Where in conduct does the 'I' come in as over against the 'me'? If one determines what one's position is in society and feels one's self as having a certain function and privilege, these are all defined with reference to an 'I', but the 'I' is not a 'me' and cannot become a 'me'. We may have a better self and a worse self, but that again is not the 'I' as over against the 'me', because they are both selves. We approve of one and disapprove of the other, but when we bring up one or the other they are there for such approval as 'me's. The 'I' does not get into the limelight; we talk to ourselves, but do not see ourselves. The 'I' reacts to the self which arises through the taking of the attitudes of others. Through taking those attitudes we have introduced the 'me' and we react to it as an 'I'.

The simplest way of handling the problem would be in terms of memory. I talk to myself, and I remember what I said and perhaps the emotional content that went with it. The 'I' of this moment is present in the 'me' of the next moment. There again I cannot turn around quick enough to catch myself. I become a 'me' in so far as I remember what I said. The 'I' can be given, however, this functional relationship. It is because of the 'I' that we say that we are never fully aware of what we are, that we surprise ourselves by our own action. It is as we act that we are aware of ourselves. It is in memory that the 'I' is constantly present in experience. We can go back directly a few moments in our experience, and then we are dependent upon memory images for the rest. So that the 'I' in memory is there as the spokesman of the self of the second, or minute, or day ago. As given, it is a 'me', but it is a 'me' which was the 'I' at the earlier time. If you ask, then, where directly in your own experience the 'I' comes in, the answer is that it comes in as an historical figure. It is what you were a second ago that is the 'I' of the 'me'. It is another 'me' that has to take the role. You cannot get the immediate response of the 'I' in the process. The 'I' is in a certain sense that with which we do identify ourselves. The getting of it into experience constitutes one of the problems of most of our conscious experience; it is not directly given in experience.

The 'I' is the response of the organism to the attitudes of the others; the 'me' is the organized set of attitudes of others which one himself assumes. The attitudes of the others constitute the organized 'me', and then one reacts toward that as an 'I'. [. . .]

Under what we consider normal conditions, the way in which an individual acts is determined by his taking the attitude of the others in the group, but if the individual is not given the opportunity to come up against people, as a child is not who is held out of intercourse with other people, then there results a situation in which the reaction is uncontrolled.

Social control is the expression of the 'me' over against the expression of the 'I'. It sets the limits, it gives the determination that enables the 'I', so to speak, to use the 'me' as the means of carrying out what is the undertaking that all are interested in.

# 8 Peter L. Berger and Thomas Luckmann

The Social Construction of Reality

Excerpts from Peter L. Berger and Thomas Luckmann, *The Social Construction of Reality*, Allen Lane The Penguin Press, 1967, pp. 26-7, 35-61. First published by Doubleday in 1966.

[In the past] the sociology of knowledge has been concerned with intellectual history, in the sense of the history of ideas. We would stress that this is, indeed, a very important focus of sociological inquiry. We would argue, however, that the problem of 'ideas', including the special problem of ideology, constitutes only part of the larger problem of the sociology of knowledge, and not a central part at that.

*The sociology of knowledge must concern itself with everything that passes for 'knowledge' in society.* As soon as one states this, one realizes that the focus on intellectual history is ill-chosen, or rather, is ill-chosen if it becomes the central focus of the sociology of knowledge. Theoretical thought, 'ideas', *Weltanschauungen* are not *that* important in society. Although every society contains these phenomena, they are part of the sum of what passes for 'knowledge'. Only a very limited group of people in any society engages in theorizing, in the business of 'ideas' and the construction of *Weltanschauungen*. But everyone in society participates in its 'knowledge' in one way or another. Put differently, only a few are concerned with the theoretical interpretation of the world, but everybody lives in a world of some sort. Not only is the focus on theoretical thought unduly restrictive for the sociology of knowledge, it is also unsatisfactory because even this part of socially available 'knowledge' cannot be fully understood if it is not placed in the framework of a more general analysis of 'knowledge'.

To exaggerate the importance of theoretical thought in society and history is a natural failing of theorizers. It is then all the more necessary to correct this intellectualistic misapprehension. The theoretical formulations of reality, whether they be scientific or philosophical or even mythological, do not exhaust what is 'real' for the members of a society. Since this is so, the sociology of knowledge must first of all concern itself with what people 'know' as 'reality' in their everyday, non- or pretheoretical lives. In other words, common-sense 'knowledge' rather than 'ideas' must be the central focus for the sociology of knowledge.

It is precisely this 'knowledge' that constitutes the fabric of meanings without which no society could exist.

The sociology of knowledge, therefore, must concern itself with the social construction of reality. [. . .]

Different objects present themselves to consciousness as constituents of different spheres of reality. I recognize the fellowmen I must deal with in the course of everyday life as pertaining to a reality quite different from the disembodied figures that appear in my dreams. The two sets of objects introduce quite different tensions into my consciousness and I am attentive to them in quite different ways. My consciousness, then, is capable of moving through different spheres of reality. Put differently, I am conscious of the world as consisting of multiple realities. As I move from one reality to another, I experience the transition as a kind of shock. This shock is to be understood as caused by the shift in attentiveness that the transition entails. Waking up from a dream illustrates this shift most simply.

Among the multiple realities there is one that presents itself as the reality *par excellence*. This is the reality of everyday life. Its privileged position entitles it to the designation of paramount reality. The tension of consciousness is highest in everyday life, that is, the latter imposes itself upon consciousness in the most massive, urgent and intense manner. It is impossible to ignore, difficult even to weaken in its imperative presence. Consequently, it forces me to be attentive to it in the fullest way. I experience everyday life in the state of being wide-awake. This wide-awake state of existing in and apprehending the reality of everyday life is taken by me to be normal and self-evident, that is, it constitutes my natural attitude.

I apprehend the reality of everyday life as an ordered reality. Its phenomena are prearranged in patterns that seem to be independent of my apprehension of them and that impose themselves upon the latter. The reality of everyday life appears already objectified, that is, constituted by an order of objects that have been designated *as* objects before my appearance on the scene. The language used in everyday life continuously provides me with the necessary objectifications and posits the order within which these make sense and within which everyday life has meaning for me. I live in a place that is geographically designated; I employ tools, from can-openers to sports cars, which are designated in the technical vocabulary of my society; I live within a web of human relationships, from my chess club to the United States of America, which are also ordered by means of vocabulary. In this manner language marks the coordinates of my life in society and fills that life with meaningful objects.

The reality of everyday life is organized around the 'here' of my body and the 'now' of my present. This 'here and now' is the focus of my attention to the reality of everyday life. What is 'here and now' presented to me in everday life is the *realissimum* of my consciousness. The reality of everyday life is not, however, exhausted by these immediate presences, but embraces phenomena that are not present 'here and now'. This means that I experience everyday life in terms of differing degrees of closeness and remoteness, both spatially and temporally. Closest to me is the zone of everyday life that is directly accessible to my bodily manipulation. This zone contains the world within my reach, the world in which I act so as to modify its reality, or the world in which I work. In this world of working my consciousness is dominated by the pragmatic motive, that is, my attention to this world is mainly determined by what I am doing, have done or plan to do in it. In this way it is *my* world *par excellence*. I know, of course, that the reality of everyday life contains zones that are not accessible to me in this manner. But either I have no pragmatic interest in these zones or my interest in them is indirect in so far as they may be, potentially, manipulative zones for me. Typically, my interest in the far zones is less intense and certainly less urgent. I am intensely interested in the cluster of objects involved in my daily occupation – say, the world of the garage, if I am a mechanic. I am interested, though less directly, in what goes on in the testing laboratories of the automobile industry in Detroit – I am unlikely ever to be in one of these laboratories, but the work done there will eventually affect my everyday life. I may also be interested in what goes on at Cape Kennedy or in outer space, but this interest is a matter of private, 'leisure-time' choice rather than an urgent necessity of my everyday life. [. . .]

The reality of everyday life further presents itself to me as an intersubjective world, a world that I share with others. This intersubjectivity sharply differentiates everyday life from other realities of which I am conscious. I am alone in the world of my dreams, but I know that the world of everyday life is as real to others as it is to myself. Indeed, I cannot exist in everyday life without continually interacting and communicating with others. I know that my natural attitude to this world corresponds to the natural attitude of others, that they also comprehend the objectifications by which this world is ordered, that they also organize this world around the 'here and now' of *their* being in it and have projects for working in it. I also know, of course, that the others have a perspective on this common world that is not identical with mine. My 'here' is their 'there'. My 'now' does not fully overlap with theirs. All the same, I know that I live with them in a common world. Most importantly, I know that there is an ongoing correspondence between *my* meanings and *their* meanings in this world, that we share a common sense about its reality. The natural attitude is the attitude of common-sense consciousness precisely because it refers to a world that is common to many men. Common-sense knowledge is the knowledge I share with others in the normal, self-evident routines of everyday life. [. . .]

Compared to the reality of everyday life, other realities appear as finite provinces of meaning, enclaves within the paramount reality marked by circumscribed meanings and modes of experience. The paramount reality envelops them on all sides, as it were, and consciousness always returns to the paramount reality as from an excursion. This is evident from the illustrations already given, as in the reality of dreams or that of theoretical thought. Similar 'commutations' take place between the world of everyday life and the world of play, both the playing of children and, even more sharply, of adults. The theatre provides an excellent illustration of such playing on the part of adults. The transition between realities is marked by the rising and falling of the curtain. As the curtain rises, the spectator is 'transported to another world', with its own meanings and an order that may or may not have much to do with the order of everyday life. As the curtain falls, the spectator 'returns to reality', that is, to the paramount reality of everyday life by comparison with which the reality presented on the stage now appears tenuous and ephemeral, however vivid the presentation may have been a few moments previously. Aesthetic and religious experience is rich in producing transitions of this kind, inasmuch as art and religion are endemic producers of finite provinces of meaning.

All finite provinces of meaning are characterized by a turning away of attention from the reality of everyday life. While there are, of course, shifts in attention *within* everyday life, the shift to a finite province of meaning is of a much more radical kind. A radical change takes place in the tension of consciousness. In the context of religious experience, this has been aptly called 'leaping'. It is important to stress, however, that the reality of everyday life retains its paramount status even as such 'leaps' take place. If nothing else, language makes sure of this. The common language available to me for the objectification of my experiences is grounded in everyday life and keeps pointing back to it even as I employ it to interpret experiences in finite provinces of meaning. Typically, therefore, I 'distort' the reality of the latter as soon as I begin to use the common language in interpreting them, that is, I 'translate' the non-everyday experiences back into the paramount reality of everyday life. This may be readily seen in terms of dreams, but is also typical of those trying to report about theoretical, aesthetic or religious worlds of meaning. The theoretical physicist tells us that his concept of space cannot be conveyed linguistically, just as the artist does with regard to the meaning of his creations and the mystic with regard to his encounters with the divine. Yet all these – dreamer, physicist, artist and mystic – *also* live in the reality of everyday life. Indeed, one of their important problems is to interpret the co-existence of this reality with the reality enclaves into which they have ventured. [. . .]

The most important experience of others takes place in the face-to-face situation, which is the prototypical case of social interaction. All other cases are derivatives of it.

In the face-to-face situation the other is appresented to me in a vivid present shared by both of us. I know that in the same vivid present I am appresented to him. My and his 'here and now' continuously impinge on each other as long as the face-to-face situation continues. As a result, there is a continuous interchange of my expressivity and his. I see him smile, then react to my frown by stopping the smile, then smiling again as I smile, and so on. Every expression of mine is oriented towards him, and vice versa, and this continuous reciprocity of expressive acts is simultaneously available to both of us. This means that, in the face-to-face situation, the other's subjectivity is available to me through a maximum of symptoms. To be sure, I may misinterpret some of these symptoms. I may think that the other is smiling while in fact he is smirking. Nevertheless, no other form of social relating can reproduce the plenitude of symptoms of subjectivity present in the face-to-face situation. Only here is the other's subjectivity emphatically 'close'. All other forms of relating to the other are, in varying degrees, 'remote'. [. . .]

The reality of everyday life contains typificatory schemes in terms of which others are apprehended and 'dealt with' in face-to-face encounters. Thus I apprehend the other as 'a man', 'a European', 'a buyer', 'a jovial type', and so on. All these typifications ongoingly affect my interaction with him as, say, I decide to show him a good time on the town before trying to sell him my product. Our face-to-face interaction will be patterned by these typifications as long as they do not become problematic through interference on his part. Thus he may come up with evidence that, although 'a man', 'a European' and 'a buyer', he is also a self-righteous moralist, and that what appeared first as joviality is actually an expression of contempt for Americans in general and American salesmen in particular. At this point, of course, my typificatory scheme will have to be modified, and the evening planned differently in accordance with this modification. Unless thus challenged, though, the typifications will hold until further notice and will determine my actions in the situation.

The typificatory schemes entering into face-to-face situations are of course, reciprocal. The other also apprehends me in a typified way – as 'a man', 'an American', 'a salesman', 'an ingratiating fellow', and so on. The other's typifications are as susceptible to my interference as mine are to his. In other words, the two typificatory schemes enter into an ongoing 'negotiation' in the face-to-face situation. In everyday life such 'negotiation' is itself likely to be pre-arranged in a typical manner – as in the typical bargaining process between buyers and salesmen. Thus, most of the time, my encounters with others in everyday life are typical in a double sense – I apprehend the other *as* a type and I interact with him in a situation that is itself typical.

The social reality of everyday life is thus apprehended in a continuum of typifications which are progressively anonymous as they are removed from the 'here and now' of the face-to-face situation. At one pole of the continuum are those others with whom I frequently and intensively interact in face-to-face situations – my 'inner circle', as it were. At the other pole are highly anonymous abstractions which by their very nature can never be available in face-to-face interaction. Social structure is the sum total of these typifications and the recurrent patterns of interaction established by means of them. As such social structure is an essential element of the reality of everyday life. [. . .]

A special but crucially important case of objectivation is signification, that is, the human production of signs. A sign may be distinguished from other objectivations by its explicit intention to serve as an index of subjective meanings. [. . .]

Signs are clustered in a number of systems. Thus there are systems of gesticulatory signs, of patterned bodily movements, of various sets of material artifacts, and so on. Signs and sign systems are objectivations in the sense of being objectively available beyond the expression of subjective intentions 'here and now'. This 'detachability' from the immediate expressions of subjectivity also pertains to signs that require the mediating presence of the body. Thus performing a dance that signifies aggressive intent is an altogether different thing from snarling or clenching fists in an outburst of anger. The latter acts express my subjectivity 'here and now' while the former can be quite detached from this subjectivity – I may not be angry or aggressive at all at this point but merely taking part in the dance because I am paid to do so on behalf of someone else who *is* angry. In other words, the dance can be detached from the subjectivity of the dancer in a way in which the snarling *cannot* from the snarler. Both dancing and snarling are manifestations of bodily expressivity, but only the former has the character of an objectively available sign. Signs and sign systems are all characterized by 'detachability', but they can be differentiated in terms of the degree to which they may be detached from face-to-face situations. Thus a dance is evidently less detached than a material artifact signifying the same subjective meaning.

Language, which may be defined here as a system of vocal signs, is the most important sign system of human society. [. . .] I live in the common-sense world of everyday life equipped with specific bodies of knowledge. What is more, I know that others share at least part of this knowledge, and they know that I know this. My interaction with others in everyday life is, therefore, constantly affected by our common participation in the available social stock of knowledge.

The social stock of knowledge includes knowledge of my situation and its limits. For instance, I know that I am poor and that, therefore, I cannot expect to live in a fashionable suburb. This knowledge is, of course, shared both by those who are poor themselves and those who are in a more privileged situation. Participation in the social stock of knowledge thus permits the 'location' of individuals in society and the 'handling' of them in the appropriate manner. This is not possible for one who does not participate in this knowledge, such as a foreigner, who may not recognize me as poor at all, perhaps because the criteria of poverty are quite different in his society – how can I be poor, when I wear shoes and do not seem to be hungry?

Since everyday life is dominated by the pragmatic motive, recipe knowledge, that is, knowledge limited to pragmatic competence in routine performances, occupies a prominent place in the social stock of knowledge. For example, I use the telephone every day for specific pragmatic purposes of my own. I know how to do this. I also know what to do if my telephone fails to function – which does not mean that I know how to repair it, but that I know whom to call on for assistance. Similarly, I have recipe knowledge of the workings of human relationships. [. . .] *Mutatis mutandis*, a large part of the social stock of knowledge consists of recipes for the mastery of routine problems. Typically, I have little interest in going beyond this pragmatically necessary knowledge as long as the problems can indeed be mastered thereby.

The social stock of knowledge differentiates reality by degrees of familiarity. It provides complex and detailed information concerning those sectors of everyday life with which I must frequently deal. It provides much more general and imprecise information on remoter sectors. Thus my knowledge of my own occupation and its world is very rich and specific, while I have only very sketchy knowledge of the occupational worlds of others. The social stock of knowledge further supplies me with the typificatory schemes required for the major routines of everyday life, not only the typifications of others that have been discussed before, but typifications of all sorts of events and experiences, both social and natural. Thus I live in a world of relatives, fellow-workers and recognizable public functionaries. In this world, consequently, I experience family gatherings, professional meetings and encounters with the traffic police. The natural 'backdrop' of these events is also typified within the stock of knowledge. My world is structured in terms of routines applying in good or bad weather, in the hay-fever season and in situations when a speck of dirt gets caught under my eyelid. 'I know what to do' with regard to all these others and all these events within my everyday life. By presenting itself to me as an integrated whole the social stock of knowledge also provides me with the means to integrate discrete elements of my own knowledge. In other words, 'what everybody knows' has its own logic, and the same logic can be applied to order various things that I know. For example, I know that my friend Henry is an Englishman, and I know that he is always very punctual in keeping appointments. Since 'everybody knows' that punctuality is an English trait, I can now integrate these two elements of my knowledge of Henry into a typification that is meaningful in terms of the social stock of knowledge.

The validity of my knowledge of everyday life is taken for granted by myself and by others until further notice, that is, until a problem arises that cannot be solved in terms of it. As long as my knowlege works satisfactorily, I am generally ready to suspend doubts about it. In certain attitudes detached from every reality – telling a joke, at the theatre or in church, or engaging in philosophical speculation – I may perhaps doubt elements of it. But these doubts are 'not to be taken seriously'. For instance, as a businessman I know that it pays to be inconsiderate of others. I may laugh at a joke in which this maxim leads to failure, I may be moved by an actor or a preacher extolling the virtues of consideration and I may concede in a philosophical mood that all social relations should be governed by the Golden Rule. Having laughed, having been moved and having philosophized, I return to the 'serious' world of business, once more recognize the logic of its maxims, and act accordingly. Only when my maxims fail 'to deliver the goods' in the world to which they are intended to apply are they likely to become problematic to me 'in earnest'. [. . .]

My knowledge of everyday life is structured in terms of relevances. Some of these are determined by immediate pragmatic interests of mine, others by my general situation in society. It is irrelevant to me how my wife goes about cooking my favourite goulash as long as it turns out the way I like it. It is irrelevant to me that the stock of a company is falling, if I do not own such stock; or that Catholics are modernizing their doctrine, if I am an atheist; or that it is now possible to fly non-stop to

Africa, if I do not want to go there. However, my relevance structures intersect with the relevance structures of others at many points, as a result of which we have 'interesting' things to say to each other. An important element of my knowledge of everyday life is the knowledge of the relevance structures of others. Thus I 'know better' than to tell my doctor about my investment problems, my lawyer about my ulcer pains, or my accountant about my quest for religious truth. The basic relevance structures referring to everyday life are presented to me ready-made by the social stock of knowledge itself. I know that 'woman talk' is irrelevant to me as a man, that 'idle speculation' is irrelevant to me as a man of action, and so forth. Finally, the social stock of knowledge as a whole has its own relevance structure. Thus, in terms of the stock of knowledge objectivated in American society, it is irrelevant to study the movements of the stars to predict the stock market, but it is relevant to study an individual's slips of the tongue to find out about his sex life, and so on. Conversely, in other societies, astrology may be highly relevant for economics, speech analysis quite irrelevant for erotic curiosity, and so on.

One final point should be made here about the social distribution of knowledge. I encounter knowledge in everyday life as socially distributed, that is, as possessed differently by different individuals and types of individuals. I do not share my knowledge equally with all my fellowmen, and there may be some knowledge that I share with no one. I share my professional expertise with colleagues, but not with my family, and I may share with nobody my knowledge of how to cheat at cards. The social distribution of knowledge of certain elements of everyday reality can become highly complex and even confusing to the outsider. I not only do not possess the knowledge supposedly required to cure me of a physical ailment, I may even lack the knowledge of which one of a bewildering variety of medical specialists claims jurisdiction over what ails me. In such cases, I require not only the advice of experts, but the prior advice of experts on experts. The social distribution of knowledge thus begins with the simple fact that I do not know everything known to my fellowmen, and vice versa, and culminates in exceedingly complex and esoteric systems of expertise. Knowledge of *how* the socially available stock of knowledge is distributed, at least in outline, is an important element of that same stock of knowledge. In everyday life I know, at least roughly, what I can hide from whom, whom I can turn to for information on what I do not know, and generally which types of individuals may be expected to have which types of knowledge.

# 9 Norbert Elias

Problems of Involvement and Detachment

Excerpts from Norbert Elias, 'Problems of involvement and detachment',
*British Journal of Sociology*, vol. 7, 1956, pp. 226–41.

One cannot say of a man's outlook in any absolute sense that it is detached or involved (or, if one prefers, 'rational' or 'irrational', 'objective' or 'subjective'). Only small babies, and among adults perhaps only insane people, become involved in whatever they experience with complete abandon to their feelings here and now; and again only the insane can remain totally unmoved by what goes on around them. Normally adult behaviour lies on a scale somewhere between these two extremes. In some groups, and in some individuals of these groups, it may come nearer to one of them than in others; it may shift hither and thither as social and mental pressures rise and fall. But social life as we know it would come to an end if standards of adult behaviour went too far in either direction. As far as one can see, the very existence of ordered group life depends on the interplay in men's thoughts and actions of impulses in both directions, those that involve and those that detach keeping each other in check. They may clash and struggle for dominance or compromise and form alloys of many different shades and kinds – however varied, it is the relation between the two which sets people's course. [. . .]

As tools of thinking, therefore, 'involvement' and 'detachment' would remain highly ineffectual if they were understood to adumbrate a sharp division between two independent sets of phenomena. They do not refer to two separate classes of objects; used as universals they are, at best, marginal concepts. In the main, what we observe are people and people's manifestations, such as patterns of speech or of thought, and of other activities, some of which bear the stamp of higher, others of lesser detachment or involvement. [. . .]

Like other people, scientists engaged in the study of nature are, to some extent, prompted in the pursuit of their task by personal wishes and wants; they are often enough influenced by specific needs of the community to which they belong. They may wish to foster their own career. They may hope that the results of their inquiries will be in line with theories they have enunciated before or with the requirements and ideals of groups with which they identify themselves. But these involvements, in the natural sciences, determine as a rule nothing more than the general direction of inquiries; they are, in most cases, counterbalanced and checked by institutionalized procedures which compel scientists, more or less, to detach themselves, for the time being, from the urgent issues at hand. The immediate problems, personal or communal, induce problems of a different kind, scientific problems which are no longer directly related to specific persons or groups. The former, more narrowly time-bound, often serve merely as a motive force; the latter, the scientific problems which they may have induced, owe their form and their meaning to the wider and less time-bound continuum of theories and observations evolved in this or that problem-area by generations of specialists.

Like other human activities scientific inquiries into nature embody sets of values. To say that natural sciences are 'non-evaluating' or 'value-free' is a misuse of terms. But the sets of values, the types of evaluations which play a part in scientific inquiries of this type, differ from those which have as their frame of reference the interests, the well-being or suffering of oneself or of social units to which one belongs. The aim of these inquiries is to find the inherent order of events as it is, independently not of any, but of any particular observer, and the importance, the relevance, the value of what one observes is assessed in accordance with the place and function it appears to have within this order itself.

In the exploration of nature, in short, scientists have learned that any direct encroachment upon their work by short-term interests or needs of specific persons or groups is liable to jeopardize the usefulness which their work may have in the end for themselves or for their own group. The problems which they formulate and, by means of their theories, try to solve, have in relation to personal or social problems of the day a high degree of autonomy; so have the sets of values which they use; their work is not 'value-free', but it is, in contrast to that of many social scientists, protected by firmly established professional standards and other institutional safeguards against the intrusion of heteronomous evaluations. [. . .] Natural scientists seek to find ways of satisfying human needs by means of a detour – the detour via detachment. They set out to find solutions for problems potentially relevant for all human beings and all human groups. The question characteristic of men's involvement: 'What does it mean for me or for us?' has become subordinate to questions like 'What is it?' or 'How are these events connected with others?' In this form, the level of detachment represented by the scientist's work has become more or less institutionalized as part of a scientific tradition reproduced by means of a highly specialized training, maintained by various forms of social control and socially induced emotional restraints; it has become embodied in the conceptual tools, the basic assumptions, the methods of speaking and thinking which scientists use. [. . .]

There are differences between the standards of certainty and achievement of the natural and the social sciences. It is often implied, if it is not stated explicitly, that the 'objects' of the former, by their very nature, lend themselves better than those of the latter to an exploration by means of scientific methods ensuring a high degree of certainty. However, there is no reason to assume that social data, that the relations of persons are less accessible to man's comprehension than the relations of non-human phenomena, or that man's intellectual powers as such are incommensurate to the task of evolving the theories and methods for the study of social data to a level of fitness, comparable to that reached in the study of physical data. What is significantly different in these two fields is the situation of the investigators and, as part of it, their attitudes with regard to their 'objects'; it is, to put it in a nutshell, the *relationship between 'subjects' and 'objects'*. If this relationship, if situation and attitudes are taken into account, the problems and the difficulties of an equal advance in the social sciences stand out more clearly.

The general aim of scientific pursuits is the same in both fields; stripped of a good many philosophical encrustations it is to find out in what way perceived data are connected with each other. But social as distinct from natural sciences are concerned with conjunctions of persons. Here, in one form or the other, men face themselves; the 'objects' are also 'subjects'. The task of social scientists is to explore, and to make men understand, the patterns they form together, the nature and the changing configuration of all that binds them to each other. The investigators themselves form part of these patterns. They cannot help experiencing them, directly or by identification, as immediate participants from within. [. . .]

For the time being, social scientists are liable to be caught in a dilemma. They work and live in a world in which almost everywhere groups, small and great, including their own groups, are engaged in a struggle for position and often enough for survival, some trying to rise and to better themselves in the teeth of strong opposition, some who have risen before trying to hold what they have and some going down.

Under these conditions the members of such groups can hardly help being deeply affected in their thinking about social events by the constant threats arising from these tensions to their way of life or to their standards of life and perhaps to their lives. As members of such groups, scientific specialists engaged in the study of society share these vicissitudes with others. Their experience of themselves as upholders of a particular social and political creed which is threatened, as representatives of a specific way of life in need of defence, like the experience of their fellows, can hardly fail to have a strong emotional undertone. Group images – those, for instance, of classes or of nations, self-justifications – the cases which groups make out for themselves, represent, as a rule, an amalgam of realistic observations and collective fantasies (which like the myths of simpler people are real enough as motive forces of action). To sift out the former from the latter, to hold up before these groups a mirror in which they can see themselves as they might be seen, not by an involved critic from another contemporary group but by an inquirer trying to see in perspective the structure and functioning of their relationship with each other, is not only difficult in itself for anyone whose group is involved in such a struggle; expressed in public, it may also weaken the cohesion and solidarity feeling of his group and, with it, its capacity to survive. There is, in fact, in all these groups a point beyond which none of its members can go in his detachment without appearing and, so far as his group is concerned, without becoming a dangerous heretic, however consistent his ideas or his theories may be in themselves and with observed facts, however much they may approximate to what we call the 'truth'.

And yet, if social scientists although using more specialized procedures and a more technical language are in the last resort not much less affected in their approach to the problems of society by preconceived ideas and ideals, by passions and partisan views than the man in the street, are they really justified in calling themselves 'scientists'?

As things stand, their social task as scientists and the requirements of their position as members of other groups often disagree; and the latter are apt to prevail as long as the pressure of group tensions and passions remains as high as it is.

The problem confronting them is not simply to discard the latter role in favour of the former. They cannot cease to take part in, and to be affected by, the social and political affairs of their groups and their time. Their own participation and involvement, moreover, is itself one of the conditions for comprehending the problems they try to solve as scientists. For while one need not know, in order to understand the structure of molecules, what it feels like to be one of its atoms, in order to understand the functioning of human groups one needs to know, as it were, from inside how human beings experience their own and other groups, and one cannot know without active participation and involvement.

The problem confronting those who study one or the other aspects of human groups is how to keep their two roles as participant and as inquirer clearly and consistently apart and, as a professional group, to establish in their work the undisputed dominance of the latter.

This is so difficult a task that many representatives of social sciences, at present, appear to regard the determination of their inquiries by pre-conceived and religiously held social and political ideals as inevitable. [. . .]

One of the major reasons for the difficulties with which men have to contend in their endeavour to gain more reliable knowledge about themselves is the uncritical and often dogmatic application of categories and concepts highly adequate in relation to problems on the level of matter and energy to other levels of experience, and among them to that of social phenomena. Not only specific expectations as to how perceived data are connected with eath other; specific concepts of causation or of explanation formed in this manner are generalized and used almost as a matter of course in inquiries about relations of men. [. . .]

By and large, theories of science still use as their principal model the physical sciences – often not in their contemporary, but in their classical form. Aspects of their procedures are widely regarded as the most potent and decisive factor responsible for their achievements and as the essential characteristic of sciences generally. By abstracting such aspects from the actual procedures and techniques of the physical sciences, one arrives at a general model of scientific procedure which is known as 'the scientific method'. [. . .]

The assumption is that in this generalized form 'the scientific method' can be transferred from the field where it originated from the physical sciences, to all other fields, to biological as well as to social sciences, regardless of the different nature of their problems; and that wherever it is applied it will work its magic. Among social scientists in particular it is not uncommon to attribute difficulties and inadequacies of their work to the fact that they do not go far enough in copying the method of physical sciences. [. . .]

The abstraction from specific procedures of a general model of the scientific method, and the claim often made for it as the supreme characteristic of research that is scientific, have led to the neglect, or even to the exclusion from the field of systematic research, of wide problem-areas which do not lend themselves easily to an exploration by means of a method for which the physical sciences have provided the prototype. [. . .]

On closer investigation, one will probably find that the tendency to consider a highly formalized picture of this one set of sciences and their method as the norm and ideal of scientific inquiries generally is connected with a specific idea about the aim of sciences. It is, one might think, bound up with the assumption that among propositions of empirical sciences, as among those of pure mathematics and related forms of logic, the only relevant distinction to be made is that between propositions which are true and others which are false; and that the aim of scientific research and of its procedures is simply and solely that of finding the 'truth', of sifting true from false statements. However, the goal towards which positive sciences are striving is not, and by their very nature cannot be, wholly identical with that of fields like logic and mathematics which are concerned with the inherent order of certain tools of thinking alone. It certainly happens in empirical investigations that people make statements which are simply found to be false. But often enough rough dichotomies like 'true' and 'false' are highly inadequate in their case. People engaged in empirical research often put forward propositions or theories whose merit is that they are truer than others or, to use a less hallowed term, that they are *more* adequate, *more* consistent both with observations and in themselves. In general terms, one might say it is characteristic of these scientific as distinct from non-scientific forms of solving problems that, in the acquisition of knowledge, questions emerge and are solved as a result of an uninterrupted two-way traffic between two layers of knowledge: that of general ideas, theories or models and that of observations and perceptions of specific events.

# Part Two
## The Logic and Method of Sociological Inquiry

It is useful to distinguish between the methods and the techniques of sociological research. Methods are those procedures which are shared by other sciences too, for example the formation of concepts and hypotheses, making observations and measurements, performing experiments, building models and theories, providing explanations and making predictions. In contrast, techniques are the specific procedures used in a particular scientific discipline, such as sociology: interviewing techniques, statistical techniques, content analysis, etc. Kaplan (Reading 10) insists on the use of methods and techniques which bring results. We should not be easily impressed by methodologists and other who lay down what *the* scientific method is, and therefore how we should undertake research. Enthusiasm for new techniques is frequently exaggerated and holds back research.

One of the most widely used methods of inquiry is the controlled investigation. In the artificial experiment the variable whose effect is to be determined is manipulated by the researcher. However, the possibilities for artificial experiments on human populations and groups are fairly restricted. Usually sociologists content themselves with the study of natural experiments; for example, the amount and type of education which people receive is beyond the influence of the sociologist, but it can nevertheless be seen as the result of a natural experiment in which the incidence of education on a population has been varied. Although the members of the population have not been manipulated directly, the logic of controlled investigation can be applied to the data describing their different experience. Chapin (Reading 11) describes some of the obstacles encountered in the application of the experimental method.

In a controlled investigation the sociologist's aim is to determine the relationship between some variable whose incidence on a population differs, and some other variable which measures its effect. Often the sociologist has some idea of the relationship he expects, and this is stated in the form of an hypothesis. Direct testing of an hypothesis involves examining the data to see whether the hypothesized relationship occurs or not. Equally important, but less well known, is the method described by Hyman (Reading 12), of indirect testing of relationships between variables which are not expected to be associated. In this case the absence of a relationship may be as significant theoretically as the discovery of a positive or negative relationship.

There are several techniques by which information on the variables of interest can be obtained: observation, conversation and the study of written material. All these techniques are subject to the enthusiasms which Kaplan calls the 'law of the instrument'. The technique of interviewing is a development out of the ordinary conversation. An interview is a conversation with a purpose, and this purpose is decided on by the interviewer. The interview is therefore asymmetric. Observation and interviewing, because they involve interaction with the person or group under study, differ in an important way from the study of written material (records, minutes, statistics, letters, etc.) where the author of the material is not present.

The interview may be more or less structured according to the purposes of the researcher. In the structured interview the interviewer will often make use of an interview schedule containing the precise questions he wishes to put to the respondent. In the unstructured interview, however, the interviewer may only have a list of subjects to cover. Clearly the rationales underlying these two types of interview are very different. In the structured interview, the interviewer is seen as a source of error which must be controlled: standardized questions are used in order to minimize his involvement with the respondent and hence, it is argued, to obtain valid data. In the unstructured interview, the rationale is reversed. The source of error is seen precisely as any formalization or standardization of the situation, and the interviewer is free to adjust his approach according to the respondent's reactions.

Hyman, Cobb, Feldman, Hart and Stember (Reading 13) point out that sociologists are particularly concerned with 'interviewer effect', i.e. the effect of the interviewer contained in the data he obtains, because the participants in an interview are both conscious beings and are aware of the possibility of error. However the techniques of data collection in any science are subject to error; we should not be too pessimistic about those which arise in the interview.

Observation is similar to interviewing in that the sociologist has to maintain his presence in a situation where he would not otherwise be. The interview is transitory and the interviewer's presence is supported and justified by the interviewer role. Observation, however, usually requires the sociologist to maintain a position in a group or community for a longer period of time. This gives rise to the various problems mentioned by Whyte (Reading 14): how should the sociologist identify himself to gain acceptance – since the image he has will influence the range of data available to him, to what extent should he participate, how much should he depend on informants, what effect does his presence have on the activities he is observing, etc.

Documents and written material are the third source of data for the sociologist. The usual problem here is that the purposes of the author of the document differ from those of the sociologist. This limits the use which the sociologist can make of documents to those cases where the documents contain data relating to the variables which are of interest to the sociologist. The technique of content analysis, described in the extract (Reading 15), requires that these variables be translated by operational definition into categories of content, whose occurrence in the document can then be counted. Content analysis thus provides a reliable method of interpreting written material and has frequently been used to analyse newspaper articles.

The case-study, described in our final selection (Reading 16), is not a technique, but a way of organizing data. It has its origin in psychology and medicine where individual cases are studied in detail in order to explain the origins and development of a disease. In sociology, the case-study may refer to an individual, a group, an organization or a community. The common factor is that the case-study aims at a holistic understanding of the phenomena being studied. For this reason it makes use of a variety of techniques and participant observation usually has an important role.

# 10 Abraham Kaplan

The Logic of Inquiry

Excerpts from Abraham Kaplan, *The Conduct of Inquiry*, Chandler Publishing Co., 1964, pp. 13–29.

What in fact goes on in scientific inquiry is usually marked off as belonging to the 'context of discovery', while logic, it is held, deals only with the 'context of justification'. On this view, logic is indifferent to how the scientist arrives at his conclusions, but asks only whether he is justified in reaching them. The distinction between discovery and justification, and between their respective contexts, is valid and important. I suggest, however, that the limitation of logic to the context of justification stems from confusing *this* distinction with the one I have drawn above between logic-in-use and reconstructed logic. Because our reconstructions have occupied themselves with justifications, we have concluded that there is no logic-in-use in making discoveries. If logic is what we methodologists do, not what the scientist does, then it is indeed limited to the context of justification, for this context marks the limit of *our* involvement with the pursuit of truth.

That imagination, inspiration and the like are of enormous importance in science is recognized by everyone. It can be granted that they belong to the context of discovery (including, of course, the discovery of justifications). But does it follow that they are therefore extraneous to logic, that they are a proper subject matter only for the psychology of science? Let me follow the popular though loose usage and refer to all such faculties as 'intuition'. Then the point I am making is that intuition also has its logic-in-use, and so must find a place in any adequate reconstructed logic. There is surely a basic difference between intuition and guesswork – between the intuition of the great creative genius or even of the ordinary experienced scientific worker, and the complete novice's blind, blundering guesswork or mechanical trial and error.

The difference seems to me to lie in this: What we call 'intuition' is any logic-in-use which is (a) preconscious, and (b) outside the inference schema for which we have readily available reconstructions. We speak of intuition, in short, when neither we nor the discoverer himself knows quite how he arrives at his discoveries, while the frequency or pattern of their occurrence makes us reluctant to ascribe them merely to chance.

Countless scientists, like the mathematician Henri Poincaré, have aspired to some self-awareness of their intuitive skills. From a purely psychological standpoint, psychoanalysis has begun to throw some light on the matter. But study of such processes by no means need be limited to a psychological orientation. We can interest ourselves also in the effectiveness of the seeker's operations in achieving their end, and it is this effectiveness that is the concern of logic. From this point of view, for instance, G. Polya has examined the context of mathematical discovery. Similarly, Herbert Simon and Alan Newell have studied the programming of a computer to solve the problems in the propositional calculus, not by a mechanically determinate procedure, but in a way that simulates the efforts of the logician himself to discover a proof. Intuition has 'a logic of its own' only if we let it be 'its own', have no interest in making that logic ours.

The logic of intuition does not in the least minimize the importance to science of serendipity, the chance discovery. But in science – and usually elsewhere, too – luck has to be deserved, as Lagrange once said of Newton. The lucky find must be appreciated to be a 'find' at all: noticed, explored, and interpreted. Six months after Roentgen's chance discovery of X-rays the following interview with him was published: '. . . I had been passing a current through the tube, and I noticed a peculiar black line across the paper.' 'What of that?' 'The effect was one which could only be produced, in ordinary parlance, by the passage of light. No light could come from the tube because the shield which covered it was impervious to any light known, even that of the electric arc.' 'And what did you think?' 'I did not think: I investigated. . . .'

There is a traditional question whether there is a 'logic of discovery' as well as a 'logic of proof'. What is it that is being asked? Clearly, we cannot have reason to predict today what the substance of tomorrow's discoveries will be, for in that case, we would be making the discoveries today. On the other hand, we may well have reason to predict in a general way what discoveries will be made, and even how, in a general way, they will come about. We cannot in 1964 say what our moon rockets will disclose in 1965 or 1970 concerning the volcanic or meteoric origin of the lunar craters, but we might be willing to predict that they will resolve the issue in favour of one alternative or the other. The question then might be: can we formulate logical norms operative beforehand in making such inquiries, or will the norms only tell us afterwards whether a particular inquiry was successful? Can logic tell us how to do science, or only certify that we have in fact done it?

To ask for a systematic procedure which guarantees the making of discoveries as a corresponding procedure guarantees the validity of a proof is surely expecting too much. 'Invention,' says Mill, 'though it can be cultivated, cannot be reduced to rule; there is no science which will enable a man to bethink himself of that which will suit his purpose.' The point is, however, that 'invention' *can* be cultivated. Though the scientific enterprise has a significant element of luck in it, it is not wholly a game of chance, and scientific training surely enhances in some degree the skill of the players. The 'logic of discovery' is, to say, the strategy of playing the game.

Here, I do not mean 'strategy' in the strict sense of the contemporary theory of games: a determination of exactly what move will be made for every possible eventuality that may arise in the play of the game. Such a determination would correspond to a complete set of rules for making discoveries (unless, to be sure, the game is one that we are bound to lose even with optimal play). I mean, rather, strategy in the sense in which it is known to a good chess player. Norms like 'Seize the open file!' and 'Rook behind the pawn!' cannot be demonstrated to produce a win, but the novice is well advised to follow them. [. . .]

That logic can and should concern itself with the process of scientific discovery, with the process of reaching conclusions as well as with the proof of the conclusions reached, is a position taken by many philosophers, from Aristotle to Peirce and Popper. It has been suggested that the 'logic of discovery' can be construed as a study of the reasons for entertaining a hypothesis, in contrast with the logic of proof, which deals with the reasons for accepting a hypothesis. To some extent, unquestionably, these reasons coincide. We entertain hypotheses with high antecedent probability, and this antecedent probability enters into the assessment of its confirmation by the evidence. The maxim 'Look for the woman!' guides the detective, and the hypothesized motive it provides is an important element in the case against the suspect. But not all reasons for entertaining a hypothesis are of a kind which necessarily play a corresponding part in its acceptance.

The drunkard's search is relevant here; the pattern of search, we feel, should be closely related to the probability of the thing sought being in the place where the seeker is looking. But the joke may be on us. It may be sensible to look first in an unlikely place just *because* 'it's light there'. We might reasonably entertain one hypothesis rather than another because it is easier to refute if false, or because it will eliminate a greater number of possibilities, or because it will show us more clearly what steps to take next. We may conduct the search of an area by going up one side and down the other, or by moving outward from the centre in a spiral, or in a variety of other ways, according to circumstances. The optimal pattern of search does not simply mirror the pattern of probability density of what we seek. We accept the hypothesis that a thing sought is in a certain place because we remember having seen it there, or because it is usually in places of that kind, or for like reasons. But we entertain the hypothesis, that is, we look in a certain place, for additional reasons: we happen to be in the place already, others are looking elsewhere, and so on. I do not see that the difference between these kinds of reasons is one only of 'refinement, degree and intensity'.

It might be said that these other sorts of reasons are to be distinguished from purely logical considerations as being of a merely practical kind. I agree to the adjective, but not to the adverb; there is nothing 'mere' about it. If logic relates to scientific practice, it is inescapably concerned with what is 'practical' – that is, with what works in science. I believe that the tendency to exclude such concerns from the domain of our reconstructed logics stems from the demand, of which I spoke earlier, for universality and necessity. What is practical in one set of circumstances may not be so in another, and in any case, we cannot establish that it *must* work. To be sure, logic is interested in the greatest possible range of application of its norms, and in the firmest possible grounding of their claims. But may it not stop short of the ultimate in both respects? Must logicality be, like the Stoic conception of virtue, a perfection which does not admit of degrees? What a scientist does in a particular case may be more or less reasonable, sensible, intelligent. What makes it such is not something in his psychology nor in ours who are appraising what he does, but something in his problem and in the appropriateness to it of the operations of his understanding. This latter something is the subject matter of what I am calling logic.

The word 'methodology', like the words 'physiology', 'history' and 'logic' mentioned earlier, is also one which is used both for a certain discipline and for its subject matter. I mean by *methodology* the study – the description, the explanation and the justification – of methods, and not the methods themselves. Often when we speak of the 'methodology' of, say, economics, we refer to the method or methods used by economists (more likely, some particular school of economists). [. . .]

And methodology is very far from being a sufficient condition for scientific achievement. There was widespread not many years ago – especially among behavioral scientists – what I might call a *myth of methodology*, the notion that the most serious difficulties which confront behavioral science are 'methodological', and that if only we hit upon the right methodology, progress will be rapid and sure. The logicians and the philosophers of science at the time, in the vigor of their attack against 'pseudo science', may unintentionally have given some support to this myth. Or possibly, a more pervasive trait of American culture is manifested in the overemphasis on what methodology can achieve. Riesman has called attention to 'the excessive preoccupation with technique which often sets in when Americans realize that they are not able to do certain things – raise children, make love, make friends – "naturally" '. Whether or not we show this tendency with regard to other activities, we certainly seem to have manifested it in behavioral science. And as Riesman concludes, this methodological preoccupation is 'congenitally self-defeating'. An anxious concern for the condition of the body is not likely to make for a healthy life.

Nothing that I have said about the relation of methodology to science is intended to undermine the normative force and function of methodology. The charge has been made that when methodology takes actual scientific practice as its starting point, and is considered reasonable only when it 'mirrors' such practice, it 'propagates the acceptance of unsatisfactory hypotheses on the ground that this is what everybody is doing. It is conformism covered with high-sounding language. . . . Against such conformism it is of paramount importance to insist upon the normative character of scientific method.' To be sure; but the issue is not whether there *are* norms, but how the norms are grounded. I do not see that the insistence that the norms of scientific practice are validated by that practice implies that they are not norms at all, or that whatever is, is right. For the criterion being put forward is decidedly *not* the question whether everybody's doing it, but the very different question whether anything gets done by it. What I am protesting is the conception of the methodologist as baseball commissioner, writing the rules; or at any rate as umpire, with power to thumb an offending player out of the game. He is at best only a coach, and the merit of his recommendations rests entirely on what the play of the game shows to be effective.

Even sound norms can be unwisely urged. Excessive effort can be diverted from substantive to methodological problems, so that we are forever perfecting how to do something without ever getting around to doing it even imperfectly. Not a little behavioral science has a markedly *programmatic* character, traceable to its methodological sophistication; and while the program, deriving from what must be true 'in principle', may have much philosophical interest, it is likely to be deficient in exploiting the real possibilities of the scientific situation. By pressing methodological norms too far we may inhibit bold and imaginative adventures of ideas. The irony is that methodology itself may make for conformism – conformity to its own favored reconstructions – and a conformity even less productive than one at least imitating scientific colleagues. And the push toward logical completeness may well make for 'premature closure' of scientific conceptions. The situation in science is not unlike that in the arts: the critic with his standards discourages daubers, but he also becomes the mainstay of the Academy and art eventually passes him by.

I believe that actual scientific practice is and must remain at the focus of the methodologist's attention, and that the principle of autonomy of inquiry must not be compromised. A reconstruction of the actuality is always to some extent an idealization, as I have noted earlier. But from this truistic premise the remarkable conclusion has been drawn that, in so far as the methodologist's model and scientific practice differ, so much the worse for science! There are certain philosophers who bravely set out to do battle for Truth, when it is they themselves, like Don Quixote, who stand in need of succour. There have been many, from Kant onwards, who determined to 'save science' from human skepticism; it occurred to few that it was the skeptical philosophy that needed the saving.

Norman Campbell has sharply criticized the assumption that if any branches of learning do really arrive at truth,

it can only be because they conform to logical order and can be expressed by logical formulas. The assumption is quite unjustifiable. Science is true, whatever anyone may say; it has for certain minds, if not for all, the intellectual value which is the ultimate test of truth. If a study can have this value and yet violate the rules of logic, the conclusion to be drawn is that those rules, and not science, are deficient.

This was written, with remarkable prescience, almost a half-century ago. Today behavioral science especially may be as much in need of self-acceptance as of methodological approval.

A corresponding moral is to be drawn by the methodologist. Reconstructed logics have been developed having remarkable subtlety and power, but it is their very virtues that may constitute also their most serious shortcomings. They are too good to be true to their ultimate subject-matter. Methodology must remain alert, Michael Scriven has warned, to 'the logician's perennial temptation – make the portrait neat and perhaps the sitter will become neat. Usually there is more to be learnt from a study of the disarray than is gained by intentionally disregarding it.' It may even be that what we see as a disarray is to more perceptive eyes a style of dress both useful and elegant.

This paper will contain no definition of 'scientific method', whether for the study of man or for any other science. My reason, in part, is that I believe that there are other and often better ways of making meanings clear than by giving definitions. But I also forgo a definition because I believe there is no one thing to be defined. To revert to an earlier metaphor, one could as well speak of 'the method' for baseball. There are ways of pitching, hitting and running bases; ways of fielding; managerial strategies for pinch hitters and relief pitchers; ways of signaling, coaching and maintaining team spirit. All of these, and more besides, enter into playing the game well, and each of them has an indefinite number of variants. We could say, of course, that there is only one way to play: to score runs if you are batting and to prevent them if you are not. And this statement would be about as helpful as any general and abstract definition of 'scientific method'. The questions important to the players arise at a more specific and concrete level. A reconstructed logic is helpful in making clear the unity underlying a multiplicity of particular techniques; it can show, for instance, that a very large class of inferences can be construed as governed by a very few simple rules of deduction. But the simplicity of any one reconstruction of any one method is not meant to deaden awareness of the complexity of the process of inquiry taken as a whole. If we are to do justice to this complexity, I think it is hard to improve on P. W. Bridgman's remark that 'the scientist has no other method than doing his damnedest'.

My uneasiness with the unitary conception of 'scientific method' has, it seems to me, a pragmatic justification quite different from the captious insistence that our logical analyses are never able to take everything fully into account. It is that if a definition of 'scientific method' is specific enough to be of some use in methodology, it is not sufficiently general to embrace all the procedures that scientists may eventually come to find useful. The emphasis by historians and philosophers of science that there is no such thing as *the* scientific method, Conant has said, is a public service. It may well be, at any rate, a service to those scientists who are struggling with ways of working for which their colleagues – to say nothing of methodologists – have little understanding and less sympathy. For the most part, these struggles may come to nothing; but the few which do succeed contribute markedly to the expansion of the frontiers of science. It is less important to draw a fine line between what is 'scientific' and what is not than to cherish every opportunity for scientific growth. There is no need for behavioral science to tighten its immigration laws against subversive aliens. Scientific institutions are not so easily overthrown.

The more realistic danger is that some preferred set of techniques will come to be identified with scientific method as such. The pressures of fad and fashion are as great in science, for all its logic, as in other areas of culture. In his classic work on the design of experiments, R. A. Fisher pointed out that 'any brilliant achievement, on which attention is temporarily focused, may give a prestige to the method employed or to some part of it, even in applications to which it has no special appropriateness'. This observation can be fully documented in the subsequent history of behavioral science.

In addition to the social pressures from the scientific community there is also at work a very human trait of individual scientists. I call it *the law of the instrument*, and it may be formulated as follows: give a small boy a hammer, and he will find that everything he encounters needs pounding. It comes as no particular surprise to discover that a scientist formulates problems in a way which requires for their solution just those techniques in which he himself is especially skilled. To select candidates for training as pilots, one psychologist will conduct depth interviews, another will employ projective tests, a third will apply statistical techniques to questionnaire data, while a fourth will regard the problem as a 'practical' one beyond the capacity of a science which cannot yet fully predict the performance of a rat in a maze. And standing apart from them all may be yet another psychologist laboring in remote majesty – as the rest see him – on a mathematical model of human learning.

The law of the instrument, however, is by no means wholly pernicious in its working. What else is a man to do when he has an idea, Peirce asks, but ride it as hard as he can, and leave it to others to hold it back within proper limits? What is objectionable is not that some techniques are pushed to the utmost, but that others, in consequence, are denied the name of science. The price of training is always a certain 'trained incapacity': the more we know how to do something, the harder it is to learn to do it differently (children learn to speak a foreign language with less of an accent than adults do only because they did not know their own language so well to start with). I believe it is important that training in behavioral science encourage appreciation of the greatest possible range of techniques.

It sometimes even happens that a conspicuously successful technique in some area of behavioral science is not only identified with 'scientific method,' but comes to be so mechanically applied that it undermines the very spirit of scientific inquiry. Electronic computers, game-theoretic models and statistical formulas are but instruments after all; it is not *they* that produce scientific results but the investigator who uses them scientifically. Paul Meehl pointedly asks (in a paper with the question as title): when shall we use our heads instead of the formula? The question is one that behavioral science must continue to face. For having so long been a poor relation of the well-established sciences, it must continuously resist the impulse to see in every new development the promise at last of quick and easy riches.

# 11 F. Stuart Chapin

## Experimental Designs

Excerpts from chapter 7 of F. Stuart Chapin, *Experimental Designs in Social Research*, Harper & Row, 1947, pp. 165–76. First published as 'Some problems in field interviews when using the control group technique in studies in the community', *American Sociological Review*, vol. 8, 1943, pp. 63–8.

Field interviews of individuals in their homes and in the community setting reveal problems not present in experimental designs that are set up in the comparatively simple schoolroom situation, familiar in educational research. The problems of field interview emerging in the community situation in which research uses some experimental design are both methodological and practical. In this section we shall attempt to describe these problems as they arose in three research studies using three different variations of experimental design. Wherever possible, solutions of these problems will be indicated.

To clarify our analyses it should be stated at the outset that by problems of field interview we mean problems of organization and timing of these interviews and not problems of minute personal relationship in interview situations. Since some study has been made of problems that arise in face-to-face contacts of interviewing, and less attention has been given to problems of organization and timing, it is with these latter problems that we shall be concerned, and more specifically with scheduling interviews in home calls chiefly as related to sampling.

The purpose of experimental designs applied to the study of social factors is to measure the effect of one social factor at a time, all other factors in the situation (unknown as well as known) being held constant, that is, controlled. Difficulties arise at once because it is seldom possible to measure one factor alone. Usually the best that we can do is to try to measure a group of factors which operate as social treatment, or as a social program – as, for instance, in an effort to isolate and measure the effect of improved housing upon a group of families formerly slum residents. A second difficulty arises because there are unknown factors at work, that is, unmeasured factors which are not controlled.

Randomization is theoretically the solution to obtaining control of these unknown factors. The procedure is to select a sample at random from the population to be studied. This sample may then be divided at random into the experimental group, which is to receive the social program (e.g. good housing), and the control group, which is excluded from the program (e.g. the slum dwellers). Or two random samples are selected, one to receive the program, the other to act as a control and to be excluded from the program. Since each random sample is by definition selected without bias it will probably contain the unknown or unmeasured factors in equal degree.

The next step is to measure simultaneously each group on some criteria designed to evaluate the effect of the program (e.g. scales that measure morale, adjustment, social status, social participation, etc.). After an interval of a year or more, each group is again measured. Then if the difference in measured changes between the experimental group and the control group shows that the experimental group gains in a degree that occurs very infrequently in chance, the odds are in favor of concluding that we have discovered a difference that is probably a measure of the effect of the social program. So runs the argument.

In community research in practice, however, we encounter an initial difficulty to this apparently smooth logical conclusion. Some cases disappear during the interval of time that the experiment runs. Some are lost by refusals to give information on second interview, some have become deceased and some have moved away and cannot be found. As a consequence the terminal groups are not composed of the same individuals as at the outset. This means that at the terminal date the groups have lost their random character. Certain selective influences have been at work.

A possible solution of this dilemma is to select several random samples for experimental groups and several for control groups, on the assumption that at least one pair of samples will not lose cases and hence will remain random samples throughout the experiment. The practical difficulty to be overcome by this remedy is that of cost. When several samples or pairs of samples are used it is necessary to interview many more cases and this procedure rapidly runs up the expense of research. It increases the cost also because a larger number of interviewers have to be trained and supervised.

More serious than this difficulty is another very practical and fundamental one. It is this. Will the directors of a social program be willing to give their treatment to a randomly selected group and exclude from treatment another identical group to provide a theoretically sound experimental design? When we were asked to study the effects upon the morale of clients resulting from a WPA [Works Projects Administration] program in comparison to that of general relief (local relief), it was not possible to use a procedure of this sort. Who ever heard of a director of WPA or of relief or of public housing willing to court the public criticism that would develop if it became known that selection for treatment or exclusion was made on a random basis? In the WPA study a public controversy was already under way relative to the continuance or limitation of the program. The public atmosphere was therefore not conducive to strengthening support for a research procedure which seemed to favor certain individuals at the expense of others. People resent being chosen to serve as 'guinea pigs'. Would a government administrator permit admission to a public housing project of some families and exclusion of others equally eligible on the basis of random choice? Most administrators are charged with the responsibility to admit to good housing only the most needy families, other factors being equal. This is the way social reform programs are set up to function because those who sponsor them never question their beneficial effects any more than they ever expect to bring such programs to a scientific test of their effects. In the housing experiment cited, there had been much criticism of the project from conservative groups of the community and this created for the administrators many practical difficulties. No public administrator would like to be in the position of seeming to favor one group (in this case the experimental group to be selected at random to have the benefit of treatment) at the expense of another group (in this case the excluded control group, also to be selected at random), without tangible evidence of the greater eligibility on the part of the beneficiaries of the program. Once greater eligibility is accepted as a criterion of admission, the randomness of the group disappears, and with it one of the essential conditions of an ideally theoretical experiment.

Until public administrators of social programs can see their way around this problem, it appears that the use of randomization as a method of control of unknown factors can be ruled out in experimental designs as a method of evaluating social programs in the community situation.

The research student turns, therefore, to the control group technique. This method limits the use of randomization to the selection of the control group. We are obliged to accept as the experimental group any accessible portion of the population eligible to and receiving the program, whether a WPA, relief or housing program. The control group consists of a random sample selected from a similar population not receiving the program. This was the plan followed in the WPA study cited. In the housing study, for reasons of time limitation placed upon the research, it was not possible to select the control group at random. In this case the control group, like the experimental group, consisted of accessible families living in the slum in the same residence for the duration of the experiment.

To reduce variation among other factors the two groups are then matched on as many known factors as possible. These may be age, sex, size of family, income, occupational class, etc. The experiment proceeds from this point as before: measurements are made before and after on selected criteria of effect. [. . .]

We may tentatively summarize the problems of field interview as found in three community studies using the control group technique in a free community situation.

1. The longer the time of each interview (every additional scale or questionnaire to be filled in extends the time of each interview), the fewer the cases that can be canvassed with a given size of field staff in a given time.

2. The longer the period (in days or weeks) over which the interviews run, the greater the likelihood that administrative changes will occur and disrupt the conditions of the experiment.

3. The longer the time interval over which the experiment runs, the greater the loss of cases due to mobility and refusals.

4. Such losses are likely to be more numerous in the control group than in the experimental group.

5. The larger the number of factors used in matching, the greater the number of cases that will be dropped.

6. The cases lost by mobility, refusals, matching, etc., tend on the average to be cases with extreme measurements on criteria of effect. Consequently the trend is toward increasing homogeneity in the experimental and the control groups with resulting diminution in magnitude of differences found on measures of effect. This is to say that losses of cases between 'before' and 'after' measurements tend to leave in the residual groups individuals more alike than was the case at the outset.

In addition to the last point it needs to be recognized that the forms of social treatment which experimental designs attempt to evaluate are usually directed upon populations originally quite homogeneous. To be specific, the kind of people who receive WPA, relief or public housing programs are people at a relatively low and uniform level of income, occupational class and educational attainment when the experiment begins. To this fact of original homogeneity are added the effects of losses of cases, which, as shown above, tend to create still further homogeneity. Consequently if any changes have occurred it becomes evident that these can be described only when the scales that measure effects are sensitive to small differences. Two ways in which such scales may be provided are: (a) to improve existing sociometric scales within their middle ranges by finer calibrations or (b) to utilize the evidence of several minor changes in the same direction by means of computing multiple critical ratios. This latter procedure enables the research student to measure a pattern of change in several factors.

If cost precludes the use of many samples or the use of larger samples to offset the handicaps inherent in samples attenuated from community influences, it would seem that the two procedures just noted may still supply a partial solution of both the methodological and the practical obstacles to using experimental designs which we have enumerated in this book.

Finally, interference with randomization due to practical considerations of an administrative nature does not by any means invalidate the use of experimental designs in the community situation because the results do hold for the groups studied and within the limits of the known controls. The next step is to repeat the experiment on similar groups under like conditions and when possible with additional or more significant controls. The cumulative findings of several similar experiments may prove to be as useful as would fewer experiments based on control of unknowns by randomization within the subgroups of a stratified sample.

# 12 Herbert H. Hyman

Explanation and the Demonstration of Relationships

Excerpts from Herbert H. Hyman, *Survey Design and Analysis*, Free Press, 1955, pp. 226–36.

The analyst is always searching for the explanation of the phenomenon under study. His search is successful when he obtains reliable evidence of the influence of one or more independent variables on the phenomenon. A detailed discussion has been presented already of certain of the empirical procedures that the analyst employs in this search. These procedures *always* involve the examination of the relationship of the phenomenon to *particular* independent variables, and from the findings conclusions are then drawn as to the determinants of the phenomenon. Frequently, the variables that are initially hypothesized as the determinants are the subject of *direct* examination. In such instances, it is most disappointing when *no* relationships can be demonstrated, for it means that the analyst has been unsuccessful in supporting the hypothesis. Consequently, analysts are usually very happy to demonstrate empirical relationships between variables. This pattern of direct demonstrations is so common in the explanatory survey that it has come to be identified with *all* explanatory analyses. The analyst tends to regard success as identical with positive demonstrations of a relationship. He tends to glorify the findings of differences in the phenomenon between individuals or groups contrasted with respect to some independent variable, and to search exclusively for such differences. There is great danger in this pattern of analysis. When the analyst concentrates solely on such differences, he loses a great deal.

This is most obvious in the instance of experimental surveys whose value lies in the *disconfirmation* of previously reported findings. We have already alluded in the previous chapters [not included here] to the possibility that positive findings as to an explanation may be due to some error introduced during the earlier survey process; or that the findings may be real but limited in scope because of the partial and inadequate conceptualization of the phenomenon or because of the particular point in time and human universe that was sampled. Quite often the analyst may or should undertake a new survey, under new conditions of sampling or conceptualization or measurement and the *lack* of a relationship rather than the demonstration of one in the second survey will be of great importance in qualifying the meaning of earlier explanations.

We shall see that there are many other types of explanatory analyses in which success requires that *no* empirical relationship be demonstrated between *particular* variables. All of these analyses are predicated on one central point. The empirical demonstration of the nature of the relationship between particular variables is not the same as the conclusion that is to be drawn about the correlates or cause of the phenomenon. The empirical demonstration often bears on the goal of explaining the phenomenon only in an *indirect* way, for it may well be that the hypothesized explanation is never put to a direct test. The test that is actually made – the demonstration of a relationship between particular variables – may *refer inferentially* to an independent variable which cannot be or deliberately was not examined directly. The analyst for a variety of reasons may be interested in variable or cause 1 but will actually test the influence of cause 2 on the phenomenon. He will by some process of inference then argue as to the significance of cause 1 from the findings observed for cause 2. We shall see that only through such a pattern of analysis which approaches the problem of explanation in a roundabout or indirect manner have we a *unique* key to certain survey problems, and an improved mode of analysis for other survey problems. And the analyst is barred from such *gains* when he neglects the distinction between the conclusion or *inference* which ends the search for an explanation and the *empirical demonstration* of a relationship between particular variables. Not only is he barred from functioning effectively, but he is discouraged when he should not be and he ignores the meaning and value of empirical findings that are negative. We shall first illustrate in detail this indirect approach to explanation from one of the case studies we have used earlier, Durkheim's *Suicide.*

*Durkheim's 'Suicide' – A Case Study of Indirect Explanation Through the Demonstration of No Relationship Between Particular Variables and the Phenomenon:* The reader will recall our discussion [not included here] of Durkheim's analytic approach. Following the model of a descriptive survey analysis. Durkheim initially examines data on suicide rates computed for nations over long periods of time. He observes a regularity in the phenomenon. He notes a distinctive and persistent rate for different nations and is therefore led to or strengthened in the view that the phenomenon is dependent on *causes of 'broad generality'*. He reasons that the explanation of a phenomenon that has a widespread distribution must lie in one or more causes sufficiently widespread to comprehend the phenomenon. Durkheim does not dispute, of course, the possibility of idiosyncratic factors in accounting for the origin of *individual* suicides, but his concern is with suicide rates for larger *aggregates* of people and his train of reasoning is simply that 'individual conditions are *not general enough* to affect the relation between the total number of voluntary deaths and the population. They may perhaps cause this or that separate individual to kill himself, but not give society as a whole a greater or lesser tendency to suicide (Hyman's italics).' The causes must be 'capable of affecting not separate individuals but the group . . . society as a whole'. Durkheim therefore seeks the explanation in variables that are 'expressly social', and tries to test his hypothesis by demonstrating differences in the suicide rate of groups contrasted in certain social respects. In these tests, he hopes to find *positive evidence* of a relationship. Yet prior to all such tests or demonstrations, a whole series of other empirical tests are conducted in which his purpose and hope is to find *no* evidence whatsoever of a relationship, and some *150 pages of text* and analysis are devoted to such procedures. In no instance in these 150 pages are any 'expressly social' factors examined directly. Yet, all of these tests provide evidences *inferentially* in support of the influence of social factors on suicide. They do not constitute a mere digression and are essential to the strengthening of the total work, for Durkheim recognizes the clear distinction between evidence relevant to the search for an explanation and the empirical demonstration that there is a relationship. What is involved?

While Durkheim reasoned from his descriptive data on suicide rates that the regularity and widespread distribution of the phenomenon implied a cause of broad generality, he recognized that there are *two* classes of independent variables that would satisfy this requirement of broad generality, ones that are widespread but *extra-social* and others that are widespread and *social* in character. To Durkheim, the extra-social causes were either 'organic-psychic dispositions' in which are included psychopathology, racial and hereditary factors or factors of the 'physical environment' such as climate or temperature. In so far as nations or groups varied in these extra-social respects, for example, differed in their geographical location and mean temperature, the explanation of the suicide rate might be of an extra-social nature. Consequently, Durkheim could support his theory *indirectly* by a demonstration that the first class of factors shows *no* relationship. By this elimination or exclusion, evidence in support for the *only* other class of factors, the expressly social, would be provided without any recourse to the direct test of the relationship of suicide to social factors. The editor and co-translator of the English edition of the work presents in his preface the design of the procedure:

The early chapters in Durkheim's work are devoted to the *negation* of doc-trines which ascribe suicide to extra-social factors. ... Here in these early chapters Durkheim is involved in a process of *elimination*: all these which require resort to individual or other extra-social causes for suicide are dis-patched, leaving only social causes to be considered. This is used as a found-ation for *reaffirming* his thesis (Hyman's italics).

We shall abstract Durkheim's discussion to emphasize the approach: first, Durkheim examines by a variety of tests the relationship beween psychopathology and the suicide rate. For example, the relation between the rate and proportion of insane and idiots in the population of given countries is examined. The relation between suicide and alcoholic psychoses and total consumption is examined for given large groups. Durkheim remarks, 'no psychopathic state bears a regular and indis-putable relation to suicide'.

Secondly, Durkheim examines by a variety of tests the relationship between 'normal psychological states', i.e. racial and hereditary pre-dispositions, and suicide and concludes that the evidence is negative.

Thirdly, he examines by a variety of tests the relationship between suicide rate and 'cosmic factors'. For example, the climate and suicide rates for given latitudes of Europe are examined. Finally, the influence of individual psychological processes of imitation on the suicide rate is examined, and Durkheim concludes that 'imitation ... does not con-tribute to the unequal tendency in different societies to self-destruction, or to that of smaller social groups within each society. ... Imitation all by itself has no effect on suicide.'

On the basis of this total analysis, which led to the demonstration of *no* relationships, which *denied* all the initial hypotheses advanced, Durk-heim then remarks:

The results of the preceding book are *not wholly negative*. We have in fact shown that for each social group there is a specific tendency to suicide explained *neither* by the organic-psychic constitution of individuals *nor* the nature of the physical environment. Consequently *by elimination* it must *necessarily* depend on social causes and be in itself a collective phenomenon (Hyman's italics).

There are, of course, *methodological* problems associated with such an approach. There are questions of *error* in the analyses, measurements and tests of the influence of the variables. There are questions of the *sampling* basis of the data that are used in the tests. However, all of these problems are *methodological* problems of a general nature which apply equally to demonstrations of relationships of a positive kind and tests of an indirect or negative kind. They have been treated in detail earlier and will be discussed again in later sections.

We shall also see shortly that there are special *analytic* problems in such an approach. For example, the question may well arise as to whether the *choice* of specific variables which are examined and which presumably *exhaust* the class of factors whose influence is to be *rejected* does in fact exhaust the class. Thus, it might be that Durkheim neglected an extra-social factor of significance, even though he considered this question carefully and implies that this is not the case. He remarks on this question: 'There are two sorts of extra-social causes to which one may, *a priori*, attribute an influence on the suicide rate.'

In addition, there is the analytic problem of avoiding *arbitrariness* by the setting of different standards for the rejection of the evidence of a series of such tests and the acceptance of the evidence of other tests. Another one of our cases which also employs negative evidence as inferential support for its central hypothesis provides an illustration of the seriousness of these analytic problems. For the moment we wish merely to emphasize the basic distinction between the empirical demonstration of a relationship and evidence in support of a given explanation. We wish to show the logic of the approach which makes use of indirect evidence and thereby provide the student with additional resources in doing explanatory surveys.

The student may have noted one strange feature in the design followed by Durkheim. After he completed all these *indirect* tests whose sole purpose was the negation of all possible explanations other than social causes, he then proceeded to make direct tests of the influence of social factors. One ponders this fact. If the logical analysis originally made was correct – if suicide can only be due to A or to B – and if Durkheim is able to reject hypotheses other than B – the social, why does he then bother to make direct tests of the social factors? Or one might reverse the question and ask why does Durkheim bother initially with all the indirect tests which are used inferentially to support an hypothesis when he obviously has at his disposal resources for a direct test of his hypotheses and actually conducts such direct tests? While we can, of course, only speculate as to why Durkheim as an analyst followed this design, we can present a rational argument as to the relative advantages of the indirect *v.* the direct test or the advantages of the combined approach of indirect and direct tests.

### Unique use of the indirect test

There are unusual instances in explanatory survey analysis where *in practice* no direct test is possible. Under such conditions, the indirect test provides the only avenue of support for an hypothesis, and the distinction we have been making between explanation and the demonstration of a relationship is crucial for the analyst. It is difficult to find a specific example of such a situation in published survey analyses for one obvious reason. The lack of general awareness of the indirect approach has led analysts to conduct survey research on problems that were manageable or solvable through the use of direct tests. They have rarely exploited indirect tests and the range of findings has unfortunately been restricted. However, Durkheim's own study provides the clue to one type of problem that would be amenable to study mainly via such an approach. We note that Durkheim was interested in independent variables or causes of an *extreme macroscopic* type, the influence of societal factors. As in all survey analysis, *direct* evidence as to the influence of a given variable requires that individuals or groups be *contrasted* with respect to that variable. Durkheim was able to do this directly through the use of *existing records* on suicide rates available for very large aggregates such as nations. Thus he could range over the universe and examine the influence on the suicide rate of the diverse social systems of Denmark and Spain, of the political climate of 1830 and 1849, of military *v.* civilian life. But much survey analysis deals with phenomena which are not represented in existing archives and records, and yet the analyst might well wish to examine the relevance of global social determinants. Generally, he can do little in the way of huge comparative research; his surveys cannot cover the universe or the centuries or even a decade. Yet, following the logic of the indirect test, perhaps these types of explanations can be put to test. For example, to support the notion of a cultural or societal factor in the formation of an opinion, and yet not be able to compare societies directly, one might well examine whether subgroups in a society show different values of the phenomenon. Such groups vary in many respects and are the same only in having some common overarching membership, for example, in the society. If *all* the tests made demonstrate *no* effect of the subgroup factors, one would infer that the determinant lies at the global transcendent level. The analyst under such conditions seeks not to find *differences*, but to find *uniformities* between groups. Our only illustration of such a survey finding constitutes an approximation to this type of indirect test. The British Social Survey conducted an inquiry into the causes of rural depopulation in Scotland. For a period of over fifty years the population had been declining and the Department of Health for Scotland desired guidance. In the course of this survey, residents of a series of regions in Scotland were asked whether they planned to migrate.

Alternative hypotheses as to the explanations of migration might involve either a theory of *specific* factors impinging on particular individuals or a theory of some constellation of factors which characterize rural Scottish life *generally*. Consequently, the relation between the phenomenon of plans to migrate and region *within* rural Scotland was examined. It was found that the proportion 'does not differ significantly between the regions', suggesting that the specific features of the local environment are not the major explanation, but that there is a global social movement related to rural Scottish life as such.

A somewhat parallel analytic approach can be used where one wishes support for a theory of *extreme microscopic* psychological factors, without being able to identify or measure such factors directly and examine their effect on the phenomenon. If one is able to demonstrate that the phenomenon is not frequent, shows marked *variation* within a given society or population and yet is unrelated to any subgroup or social factor, by inference, one draws the conclusion that the determinants must lie at a more idiosyncratic psychological level. Here one seeks to find differences, rather than uniformities, but differences that are inexplicable at a certain gross level.

Many illustrations of such an indirect approach to explanation are available. For example, we can refer to a study we cited earlier of popular surfeit with war news over the radio. Depending on the definition of surfeit and the corresponding index used, a minority of the sample ranging between 15 per cent and 35 per cent were classified as 'surfeited'. The obvious hypothesis about the explanation of why certain individuals are surfeited, while the majority are not, involves some notion of ideological and emotional or psychological factors which determine the tolerance of the individual to stimulation about war. And while some direct tests were actually made of the relationship of surfeit to ideology, no direct tests were made of the influence of factors within the personality. However, inferential support for such an hypothesis is available by use of indirect tests. In three independent studies of the problem it was found that 'being fed up with the amount of war talk on the radio is not closely related to any particular personal characteristics. It does not vary much for different ages or educational levels, by sex or economic level.' Consequently, it strengthens the view that the explanation must lie at a more idiosyncratic psychological level.

A specialized type of such indirect analyses is particularly useful in explanatory surveys of a *programmatic* nature, i.e. those concerned with the amelioration of phenomena involving criticism, dissatisfaction, disruptive or maladaptive behavior. In such surveys, among the group who are found to show the unsatisfactory side of the phenomenon, the explanation may lie either in exposure to stimuli and experiences which would legitimately create dissatisfaction or in more idiosyncratic psychological processes that do not derive directly from the bad features of the environment. The former explanation, if supported by evidence, leads to programs of reform. If the latter explanation is correct, amelioration is of a different order. Now it is often quite difficult to make direct tests of the influence of such psychological processes. However, if the phenomenon is examined for groups varying in their exposure to the unsatisfactory environment, and no relationships are demonstrated, it provides indirect support for the latter theory.

An illustration of this use of the indirect test is available in the study previously cited of Rural Depopulation in Scotland. As the analysts remark: 'it might have been expected that the desire to migrate would have been noticeably more frequent amongst people living in lonely and isolated dwellings, on whom the full force of the disadvantages of rural life is turned'. Yet, there is the alternative hypothesis which involves so-to-speak the notion that loneliness is a state of mind rather than a reaction to specific features of reality. The analysts examine the former hypothesis and find little evidence in support of it. Thus, 84 per cent of those actually living in isolated houses as compared with 84 per cent of those living in social contact in villages wished to remain.

Similarly, for other objective inadequacies in the environment no relationships to desire to migrate can be demonstrated. Partial data bearing on these analyses as summarized from the original report are presented in Table 1. [. . .]

*Table 1* The Relationship of Desire to Migrate among Rural Scottish People and Various Physical Amenities

(An illustration of indirect support for a theory deriving from negative findings)

|  | % who have particular characteristics among those who plan: | |
|  | to remain | to move |
| --- | --- | --- |
| % who have indoor water supply | 66 | 69 |
| % who have plumbing involving main drainage | 61 | 66 |
| % having gas supply | 29 | 36 |
| % having electricity supply | 52 | 59 |
| % having refuse collection service | 54 | 62 |
| % connected to telephone | 15 | 17 |
| % having none of above four services | 27 | 20 |

### Supplementary use of the direct test

Thus far, we have tried to illustrate the way in which the analyst could make use of evidence that there is no relationship of particular variables to the phenomenon to support, by inference, the influence of other determinants. We have suggested that particular types of problems, in practice, may *only* be amenable to this approach. Notable among such problems are ones where the explanation is believed to lie either at a macroscopic social or microscopic psychological level, which cannot be tested directly either because of a lack of resources for comparative study or because the psychological processes are too elusive and subtle. In such instances the indirect approach is crucial.

Now let us consider other uses of the indirect approach. In the Durkheim case after the extra-social factors were rejected, the social factors were put to direct test. [...] In the Scottish study a variety of psychological correlates were explored after the negative findings on amenities. In these instances, the direct test was supplementary. It was *apparently* unnecessary. Yet it was employed. What seems to be involved here? One thing is immediately clear in all of these studies. The logical examination of possible explanatory factors is rather *formal* in character. It merely identifies alternative *classes* of causes. Consequently, when one class of causes is rejected, it permits the inference that the other class is operative but does not identify in any concrete or detailed way what *specific* variables within the remaining class of factors are important. Consequently, the direct tests that are then employed serve the *function of locating,* within the operative class of factors, those that are of importance. Durkheim's study provides an ideal example of this fact, and all that is necessary is to enumerate the great variety of specific social factors whose relationship to suicide is examined in order to demonstrate that the indirect test by itself could not locate the determinants. Among the variables that Durkheim examines are formal religion, educational level, occupational class, marital status, sex, presence of children, size of household, presence of political crisis, membership in the military and presence of economic crisis. Obviously, without recourse to these many direct tests, the prior negative evidence on the influence of extra-social factors could not provide any guidance as to the significance of particular social factors.

Put in another way, Durkheim's well-known finding of three different types of social processes which lead to suicide, then termed *egoistic,* *altruistic* and *anomic* suicide, would otherwise never have been established, for this classification was dependent on the analysis of the specific factors which correlated with suicide.

## Supplementary use of the indirect test

We have suggested that in certain instances negative evidence from a test would be sufficient to confirm indirectly an alternative general hypothesis, but that supplementary analyses would still serve a function of locating the specific explanation. However, the reader might well raise the question as to why it would be necessary or desirable to undertake analyses whose purpose was to reject a given hypothesis. For example, granted that it was wise for Durkheim to make supplementary use of *direct* tests of social factors after the negative findings on extra-social factors, it would seem that the analytic process could still have been simplified. Why not undertake *initially* the direct tests of the social factors. This establishes the merits of the general hypothesis and also locates the specific explanation. Then there would have been no apparent need for conducting the other tests whose purpose was to reject extra-social factors. This might well be true if the logical analysis which is the preliminary basis for setting up the alternative hypotheses in Durkheim's work were sound. In the Durkheim and other examples posed the alternative hypotheses are posed as if they were *exclusive* in character. Suicide must either be due to extra-social *or* social factors. The chronic 'know-nothing' must either be due to external factors *or* to psychological factors. Desire to migrate must either be due to external objective conditions *or* to more subtle psychological processes. But is it not perfectly possible that a phenomenon might be due to *several* sets of factors? If this assumption is correct, then it is clear why positive evidence on behalf of a given hypothesis *initially* would still call for supplementary use of indirect tests whose purpose is to reject another hypothesis. If there are only a limited number of explanations involved, and one is excluded initially, then the second is indirectly supported. But if several explanations may be involved, and one is confirmed, it provides no evidence that the other one is not also operative. One must undertake an empirical demonstration in order to reject the possibility that the other explanations are also involved. Thus, one comes to the simultaneous use of a series of tests, some of which are intended to yield positive, and some of which negative evidence, for it appears to be the analyst's desire usually to show not merely that his explanation is of *some* importance, but is of *primary* importance. Thus, in all these examples the simultaneous use of both kinds of tests has a special – almost polemic – value. It establishes the merits of a theory and it also establishes the *superiority* of that theory to other possible theories. The negative evidence thus serves the function of supporting by inference the superiority or primacy of a given explanation.

# 13 Herbert H. Hyman, William J. Cobb, Jacob J. Feldman, Clyde W. Hart and Charles H. Stember

The Technique of Interviewing

Excerpts from Herbert H. Hyman, William J. Cobb, Jacob J. Feldman, Clyde W. Hart and Charles H. Stember, *Interviewing in Social Research*, University of Chicago Press, 1954, pp. 1–19.

### The setting of the problem

Interviewing as a method of inquiry is universal in the social sciences. The literature of anthropology is a product of the interviewing of informants. Sociologists have made wide use of the method. The writings of psychiatrists, clinicians and psychoanalysts about man and society had their beginnings in an interviewing situation – diagnostic and therapeutic interviews with patients. The periodic censuses of the United States and other countries are monuments to the interview method, and the thousands of students making use of these historical archives, whether conscious of it or not, cannot ignore their ultimate dependence on interview data. New applied fields cutting across the classic disciplines – human relations, industrial relations, communications research, area studies – all make use of interview data. Public-opinion research, as a common resource of the political scientist, public administrator, social psychologist and historian is built upon the foundations of interviewing. [. . .]

Note how contrary to our rules and experience in modern survey research the following prescription for proper social research interviewing is:

The interviewer must have a very good memory. The information has to be obtained in the course of general conversation. . . . Usually the interviewer has to remember all the answers he has obtained and write them out after he has returned to his own place. . . . Usually he has to talk a good deal about general topics, partly to show that he understands the conditions in the region and partly that he is interested in acquiring new knowledge. It will not do for him to make it plain that his interest is to obtain statistical information. . . . It will not do for the interviewer to ask one question after another even when the respondent has shown a willingness to talk. . . . Sometimes several questions worded differently have to be asked in order to obtain one answer, if the first or first few answers are not satisfactory. In such cases these questions . . . must not follow one after another, but other questions or general discussion should intervene in order to take the respondent off guard, or to make him understand exactly what information is wanted. . . . In some cases some sort of pressure has to be exercised on the respondent. The pressure must not be so great as to make the respondent feel he is under compulsion to supply information, nor should it be so slight that he may disregard it entirely.

Yet who is to say that there are not particular conditions under which this prescription is appropriate?

The foregoing quotation is from a description by the Chinese representative on the U N Statistical Commission of the interviewer's task in collecting information, developed out of the difficulties of initiating statistical inquiries among the Chinese people. Lieu even commends to the interviewer such bizarre behavior, arising out of the requirements of his research situation, as the following: 'In the production of polished rice, he must know the quantity that can be obtained from a picul of paddy', and 'the interviewer must choose his respondents, which sometimes makes random sampling very difficult'.

Inevitably, any empirical research on interviewing method can only sample a fragment of so vast an area; yet we seek findings of some generality. Even if we were to limit the area to that of public opinion interviewing within America, we would still encompass such a diversity of procedures, topics, problems, respondents and interviewers that a single methodological inquiry would seem to be gravely inadequate. There is one solution that is available. It is that while we operate within a narrow realm in the *concrete* sense we shall focus on *fundamental* processes within the interview that transcend our specific research setting. That is why a survey specialist seeking specific and elaborate prescriptions and remedies will not find them in this report. They might be inappropriate to his own current interviewing problems; they would certainly be obsolete by 1970; and they would have little relevance to the larger social science audience. As Roethlisberger and Dickson state in their discussion of interviewing method:

It is evident that the interviewing of a child, a psychoneurotic, a native of a primitive community, or the normal adult of a civilized community involves different modifications in the way the interview takes place. ... There is always the danger for the beginner that he attach a significance to the rules of performance that they do not have. He tends to treat them as absolute prescriptions which should never be violated and he tends to multiply them without end ... rules for conducting the interview are substituted for understanding.

In order for us to increase our fundamental understanding, we must inquire, for example, into the social and psychological meaning of an interview for the two parties involved. We shall explore some of the cognitive and motivational processes operating within the interviewer.

We shall ask how his behavior is molded by these processes but in turn modified by the nature of his task. We shall examine some of the reactions of the respondent when he is confronted by an interviewer. Then, we shall elaborate on the relation of errors in the data to ongoing processes within the humans who operate in interviewing situations of various types. By the elaboration of data and theory about such more general and abstract features of *any* interview, we shall hope to achieve some degree of generality. [. . .]

In presenting any detailed research report on one phenomenon, one naturally excludes from discussion many other phenomena which may be relevant to the problem. Thus, in concentrating on understanding interviewer effect, we may run the danger of narrowing our vision too much. In order that the reader should have what we would regard as the appropriate perspective for interpreting our ultimate findings, we shall first discuss some broader matters.

### The evaluation of error – quantitative evidence

The present report is in the nature of a dangerous confession. Research workers using the survey method are willingly exposing themselves to criticism by reporting on a most comprehensive study and demonstration of errors in their findings. This is dangerous, for the natural reaction may be to damn the method summarily because of its fallibility. It is therefore of the utmost importance to evaluate the study and demonstration of error in a proper manner.

Let it be noted that the *demonstration* of error marks an advanced stage of a science. All scientific inquiry is subject to error, and it is far better to be aware of this, to study the sources in an attempt to reduce it, and to estimate the magnitude of such errors in our findings, than to be ignorant of the errors concealed in the data. One must not equate ignorance of error with the lack of error. The lack of demonstration of error in certain fields of inquiry often derives from the nonexistence of methodological research into the problem and merely denotes a less advanced stage of that profession.

We are here studying those errors which occur in survey research as a result of the method of personal interviewing. We shall find many instances of error, which might make the reader regard the interview procedure developed in the survey field as inferior to the interview procedures used in other types of scientific research. Yet in some of these other fields, the errors committed by interviewers may conceivably far exceed those we will demonstrate. [. . .]

The most plausible explanation of the difference in critical attention to interviewer error would seem to lie not in any greater natural sophistication of the survey researcher, but in the differing social organization of research in the respective sciences. Psychiatrists, anthropologists and scholars in many other disciplines traditionally work by themselves, whereas the systematic coverage of large populations and the manipulation of masses of data in survey research require the use of many scientists working cooperatively. It is this difference in the circumstances of work which affects the saliency of the problem of interviewer error and the ease of measuring it. Merton brings this interpretation forcefully to our attention in a discussion of the difference between the European scholar in the Sociology of Knowledge and the American researcher in Mass Communications. Of course, the generality of his remarks goes far beyond these two specific fields.

The lone scholar is not constrained by the very structure of his work situation to deal systematically with reliability as a technical problem. It is a remote and unlikely possibility that some other scholar, off at some other place in the academic community, would independently hit upon precisely the same collection of empirical materials, utilizing the same categories, the same criteria for these categories and conducting the same intellectual operations. . . . There is, consequently, very little in the organization of the European's work situation constraining him to deal *systematically* with the tough problem of reliability of observation or reliability of analysis.

By contrast, in survey research men work in a group situation, and as Merton puts it:

With such research organization, the problem of reliability becomes so compelling that it cannot be neglected or scantily regarded. The need for reliability of observation and analysis, which, of course, exists in the field of research at large, becomes the more visible and the more insistent in the miniature confines of the research team. Different researches at work on the same empirical materials and performing the same operations must presumably reach the same results. . . . Thus, the very structure of the immediate work group with its several and diverse collaborators reinforces the perennial concern of science, including social science, with objectivity; the interpersonal and intergroup reliability of data.
[. . .]

What makes the interview method in all fields singularly exposed to criticism is the fact that the data collected are so *clearly* derived in an interpersonal situation. In other methods where the same sort of indeterminacy may actually operate, the visibility of the problem may not be so marked, and criticisms are unfairly reserved for the interview method. Thus, experimentation with animals is the basis for much of our knowledge in physiology and psychology. But when criticism of such experiments occurs, it is rarely, if ever, on the grounds that the data are in part a product of the peculiar interpersonal relations between animal subject and human experimenter. Such an argument seems too far-fetched. While such sources of indeterminacy are no doubt small in magnitude, it is not beyond the realm of possibility that 'interviewer effects' do occur. Liddell, whose classic research on conditioning in animals extended over many years, remarks:

Another fundamental characteristic of the method is the intimacy which develops during training between animal and experimenter. In the course of months or years this intimate relationship alters infallibly, first in the direction of dependence and solicitation, but later towards avoidance or hostility. We believe that this feature of Pavlov's method differentiates the study of conditioned reflex action from investigations in essential physiology. In chronic physiological experiments of long duration the cooperation of the animal must be secured; but, within the *limits which the physiologist imposes upon his thinking, intimacy between animal subject and investigator is taken for granted and does not enter into the appraisal of the results of the experiment.*

More recently Christie has raised the issue in most general terms of the neglect by animal experimenters of such 'extra-experimental' conditions as the previous experiences of the rats used. (We might well add to this class of conditions the interpersonal relations.) He argues and even demonstrates that these factors affect the results observed but are rarely used as a basis for selection of the animals or the evaluation of the findings. The indeterminancy is present, but neglected here because it is not so patent as in the survey interview.

Granted the possibility of interviewer effects on the data in all social sciences making use of the interview, we might raise the specific issue as to the actual occurrence and relative magnitude of interviewer effects in the survey and other fields.

While it is impossible to estimate the magnitude of error typical of these fields because of the scarcity of empirical data, it can easily be established from the few studies available that interviewer effects do occur. For example, in psychiatry we have a number of large-scale studies revealing considerable variation in the results obtained by different military psychiatrists. [. . .]

It is clear that interviewer effect is a fundamental problem faced by all the social sciences which make use of the interview method in the collection of data. It is in no way exclusive to the survey field. But more than this, interviewer effects in all these fields have their parallel in the errors of observation and measurement or interpretation found in other sciences. When we note that there are observer differences in reading chest X-ray films or in interpreting the results of laboratory tests for syphilis or in appraising the malnutrition of children from medical examinations or of physicians taking a brief medical history or in rating the state of repair of telephone poles or in categorizing short segments of observed behavior or in noting the transit of stars in a telescope, we must acknowledge that fact that interviewing is not uniquely vulnerable.

Bertrand Russell's well-known and penetrating comment on animal psychology illustrates the problem:

The manner in which animals learn has been much studied in recent years, with a great deal of patient observation and experimentation. ... One may say broadly that all the animals that have been carefully observed have behaved so as to confirm the philosophy in which the observer believed before his observation began. Nay more, they have all displayed the national characteristics of the observer. Animals studied by Americans rush about frantically, with an incredible display of hustle and pep, and at last achieve the desired result by chance. Animals observed by Germans sit still and think, and at last evolve the solution out of their inner consciousness.

This brief review suggests that one basic issue is simply the magnitude of errors in the collection of data by different methods of inquiry, efficient ways of estimating their presence in any research, and the safeguards or checks upon such error. Further, it suggests that any fundamental study of interviewer effect in a given field such as survey research may make a larger contribution, since the results have relevance to the improvement of methods in many scientific fields.

### The evaluation of error – larger considerations

The demonstration of error in the the interview must not only be weighed against the prevalence of error in other scientific methods for the collection of data. In addition, whatever crudities and disadvantages characterize the method must be weighed in relation to the gains to be derived through its employment. Some crudity may be the price willingly paid in order to obtain essential information. This practical consideration furnishes one appropriate context for the evaluation of our later findings.

Murray states this calculation eloquently in discussing how the scientist should orient his research into personality. His remarks are eminently pertinent to our problem.

If he continues to hold rigidly to the scientific ideal, to cling to the hope that the results of his researches will approach in accuracy and elegance the formulations of the exact disciplines, he is doomed to failure. He will end his days in the congregation of futile men, of whom the greater number, contractedly withdrawn from critical issues, measure trifles with sanctimonious precision.

H. H. Hyman, W. J. Cobb, J. J. Feldman, C. W. Hart and C. H. Stember  97

And elsewhere in describing his choice of methods, he states:

We tried to design methods appropriate to the variables which we wished to measure; in case of doubt, choosing those that crudely revealed significant things rather than those that precisely revealed insignificant things. Nothing can be more important than an understanding of man's nature, and if the techniques of other sciences do not bring us to it, then so much the worse for them.

The interview, by definition, belongs to a class of methods which yield subjective data – that is, direct descriptions of the world of experience. The interest of many social scientists in the phenomenal world calls for such data, no matter how crude the method of collection may have to be. For example, three of the most prominent emphases in social psychology today – the emphasis on desires, goals, values and the like by students of personality; the current interest in social perception; and emphasis on the concept of attitude – all imply subjective data. While not unique, the interview method has certain advantages for the collection of such data.

Methods exploiting other personal documents such as diaries, life histories or letters do yield an elaborate picture of the individual's world, his desires, and his attitudes. They have many advantages. However, these sources are relatively inflexible or inefficient for certain scientific problems. They may not exist for the particular population of individuals we need to study, or they may be available only for some self-selected and possibly biased subsample of that population. In addition, such documents may not contain information on particular significant variables, since they are generally spontaneous in origin. It is true that even total life histories have been commissioned for a particular scientifically selected sample of individuals who were requested to cover given areas in the document, but this calls for an act of cooperation far greater than is required for many problems and greater than can be required in most instances. In addition, the new applied role of the social scientist as an adjunct to policy making requires continual fact finding or research as events occur or are anticipated, and the interview method in conjunction with sampling is uniquely adapted to such time pressures.

The self-administered questionnaire method provides subjective reports by the respondent and has the advantages of cheapness because of the reduction of interviewer costs and the possibility of group administration, plus applicability on a systematic sampling basis. However, it has limitations which are not characteristic of the personal interview method. Most obvious is the fact that the interview permits the study of illiterates or near-illiterates for whom the written questionnaire is not applicable, and this may be an important limitation for studies involving the national population. So the Research Branch of the Army, which made the most extensive use of self-administered questionnaires, found it necessary to interview all classes of recruits with less than fourth-grade education.

Secondly, since it is always possible for the respondent to read through the entire questionnaire first, or to edit earlier answers in the light of later questions, the advantages of saliency questions becomes dubious, and it is difficult to control the contextual effects of other questions upon a given answer. Such effects have been found to be sizeable. In the interview situation, it is obvious that later questions can be hidden from the knowledge of the respondent and can have no effect on the results of an earlier question.

Thirdly, a variety of gains result from the fact that the interviewer, while he might be a biasing agent, might conceivably be an insightful, helpful person. Thus he may be able to make ratings of given characteristics of the respondent, he might be able to explain or amplify a given question, he might probe for clarification of an ambiguous answer or elaboration of a cryptic report, or he might be able to persuade the respondent to answer a question that he would otherwise skip. All such advantages involving the insightful and resourceful interviewer are lost in the self-administering situation where the mistakes of the respondent have a quality of finality.

A whole class of supposedly objective methods has been applied to these problems. Inferences can be drawn about the inner world of the individual from one or another item of behavior. For example, the individual's behavior may be observed under relatively natural conditions, the observations being made covertly as in studies involving eavesdropping upon conversations, or merely in an informal and unobtrusive manner as in classic participant observation. Or very molecular aspects of behavior may be measured by specialized instruments, these aspects being regarded as indicators of some intervening variable as illustrated in the use of a physiological index. Or indices of attitude may be abstracted from statistical records of past behavior or from the concrete products of past behavior, as illustrated by the analysis of voting records, expenditures or time budgets, or subscription figures, or as illustrated by content analysis of media. Such methods seek to avoid the errors created by the artificiality or nonspontaneous character of a formal interview, and to free us from dealing with purely verbal materials. All have in common an aversion to the subjective, and a reliance on inference.

While the methods have this advantage, they also have certain limitations not characteristic of the interview. Great ingenuity is required if the investigator is to find appropriate indicators of particular intervening variables, and errors may well arise in the process of making circuitous inferences about attitude from very remote behavioral indicators. Vernon states the limitations well when he remarks: 'It is largely owing to the indefiniteness of the behavioral content of traits, attitudes and interests, that verbal methods have been so extensively developed.'

How circuitous the inference from behavior can become is easily illustrated by selecting from the literature such bizarre researches as an analysis of subscription figures to the 'Nation' as an indicator of radical attitudes, or an analysis of the characterization of unmarried women in a sample of novels as an indicator of popular attitudes toward the role of women, or the measurement of sweat secretion as an indicator of the impact of advertisements.

The informal observation of behavior under natural conditions is generally not a flexible method, in that the environment may simply not provide any avenue for the expression of the behavior which is relevant to the particular problem, and then a really tremendous act of inference is necessitated. To find out a person's thoughts one must sometimes ask him a question! This is axiomatic in the case of studies concerned with the past. For example, one of the most lavish governmental social research projects in recent years involved the study of the reactions of the German and Japanese populations to strategic bombing, but these investigations were not undertaken until after the end of hostilities. It is obvious that the natural setting of the post-war world was not appropriate to observing the reaction to the bombing of three years earlier. Here it was necessary to reconstruct the past either through the memories of the respondent reported in the course of interviewing or through historical records.

Just as research may be oriented to a past situation which was not and cannot now be currently observed, so, too, research may be geared to a future and not yet existent situation. People's wishes, plans, desires and anticipations about the future may be central. Here again observation at some point in time permits only bare inference as to the perspective on the future, and it is only through personal documents such as the interview that this dimension of man's thought is revealed.

For other problems, it is theoretically possible to use observational methods. If one could wait around indefinitely, the natural environment would ultimately liberate behavior relevant to a given inference. However, practical limitations preclude such lengthy procedures. As Vernon puts it: 'Words are actions in miniature. Hence by the use of questions and answers we can obtain information about a vast number of actions in a short space of time, the actual observation and measurement of which would be impracticable.'

It should be noted, however, that observational methods were developed in a very efficient and massive form in at least two places and were found adaptable to a host and constant flux of policy problems of an attitudinal sort when handled on a continuing basis. In the United States, for a period of years, the Office of War Information operated what were known as correspondence panels. A nationwide network of correspondent observers reported periodically on the concerns, remarks, attitudes, etc., of people in their communities. To give focus to the reports, these panels received periodic briefings as to what to look for in the way of relevant material. Similarly in England, Mass Observation's national panel of voluntary observers provides a wideflung network of covert observers reporting periodically to headquarters on their observations of behavior, conversation and the like.

An observational approach to attitudes can sometimes achieve adaptability by placing the subject in a specially contrived experimental or laboratory situation in which the behavior relevant to a given inference would appear. Here one can escape the unpleasantness of dealing with mere words, and one can study many problems not amenable to observation under natural conditions. However, it should be noted that the behavior exhibited here is as much bound by the unstated conventions of the contrived situation or laboratory, and by the explicit instructions which are characteristic of all experiments on humans, as is the verbal report by the nature of the formal interview. Moreover, the ability to obtain the participation of ordinary people as experimental subjects is limited. Consequently, generalizations from such procedures may have an inadequate sampling basis.

It should also be noted that the exponents of observation under natural conditions neglect to realize that the behavior observed in real life is conditioned by a host of *unknown momentary* factors operating in the environment just as the verbal report of an individual is bound by the formal interview situation. In brief, one is always playing some role in relation to some situation – whether the situation be that of the laboratory, the arena of everyday life, or the interview – and the real issue is the kind of situation in which the attitudinal findings are liberated and the ability to relate the findings to that situation.

There are many research problems which merely require data that, by definition, are objective. Consequently, there need be no recourse to interviewing. Even here the interview method has had widespread use because of certain practical advantages. The decennial censuses of the United States deal in great measure with data as objective as the presence of 'inside plumbing', and such information could be collected by mere observation of the building. Yet the census enumerates such characteristics by interview. Many other interview surveys for governmental purposes have been conducted on household possessions, the state of repair of given equipment, the job record of the individual, etc. Here again theoretically the information could be collected by observation or by the examination of records. However, the facts may not exist in any set of records, or it may be less expensive and unwieldy to enumerate a whole series of such needed facts in the course of a single interview. In addition, the interview enables one to relate the given datum to other characteristics of that *same individual* which can be measured simultaneously. For example, insurance company records in the aggregate contain objective data on every health insurance policy covering any member of the population, but they do not permit one to analyse such coverage in relation to health needs and experiences, medical expenses, family income and other significant variables. Similarly, voting records reveal the political behavior of individuals, but the ballot does not have any place for the social and psychological characteristics of the voter. Consequently, beyond a certain gross ecological level, it is impossible to analyse the correlates of such behavior merely by the employment of such sources.

All of this suggests that there is an important function which the interview method performs in the collection of subjective and even objective data which should not be forgotten in drawing conclusions from any findings on error. How well the method performs this function is, of course, a legitimate question. One cannot use the argument of essentiality as an excuse for perpetuating errors and crudities that are *remediable*. If anything, the reduction of error becomes all the more crucial in the instance of a method that is widely used and essential in scientific research.

# 14 William F. Whyte

## Participant Observation

Excerpt from William F. Whyte, *Street Corner Society*, University of Chicago Press, rev. edn, 1955, pp. 299–307. First published in 1943.

The spring of 1937 provided me with an intensive course in participant observation. I was learning how to conduct myself, and I learned from various groups but particularly from the Norton Street gang.

As I began hanging about Cornerville, I found that I needed an explanation for myself and for my study. As long as I was with Doc and vouched for by him, no one asked me who I was or what I was doing. When I circulated in other groups or even among the Nortons without him, it was obvious that they were curious about me.

I began with a rather elaborate explanation. I was studying the social history of Cornerville – but I had a new angle. Instead of working from the past up to the present, I was seeking to get a thorough knowledge of present conditions and then work from present to past. I was quite pleased with this explanation at the time, but nobody else seemed to care for it. I gave the explanation on only two occasions, and each time, when I had finished, there was an awkward silence. No one, myself included, knew what to say.

While this explanation had at least the virtue of covering everything that I might eventually want to do in the district, it was apparently too involved to mean anything to Cornerville people.

I soon found that people were developing their own explanation about me: I was writing a book about Cornerville. This might seem entirely too vague an explanation, and yet it sufficed. I found that my acceptance in the district depended on the personal relationships I developed far more than upon any explanations I might give. Whether it was a good thing to write a book about Cornerville depended entirely on people's opinions of me personally. If I was all right, then my project was all right; if I was no good, then no amount of explanation could convince them that the book was a good idea.

Of course people did not satisfy their curiosity about me simply by questions that they addressed to me directly. They turned to Doc, for example, and asked him about me. Doc then answered the questions and provided any reassurance that was needed.

I learned early in my Cornerville period the crucial importance of having the support of the key individuals in any groups or organizations I was studying. Instead of trying to explain myself to everyone, I found I was providing far more information about myself and my study to leaders such as Doc than I volunteered to the average corner boy. I always tried to give the impression that I was willing and eager to tell just as much about my study as anyone wished to know, but it was only with group leaders that I made a particular effort to provide really full information.

My relationship with Doc changed rapidly in this early Cornerville period. At first he was simply a key informant – and also my sponsor. As we spent more time together, I ceased to treat him as a passive informant. I discussed with him quite frankly what I was trying to do, what problems were puzzling me, and so on. Much of our time was spent in this discussion of ideas and observations, so that Doc became, in a very real sense, a collaborator in the research.

This full awareness of the nature of my study stimulated Doc to look for and point out to me the sorts of observations that I was interested in. Often when I picked him up at the flat where he lived with his sister and brother-in-law, he said to me: 'Bill, you should have been around last night. You would have been interested in this.' And then he would go on to tell me what had happened. Such accounts were always interesting and relevant to my study.

Doc found this experience of working with me interesting and enjoyable, and yet the relationship had its drawbacks. He once commented: 'You've slowed me up plenty since you've been down here. Now, when I do something, I have to think what Bill Whyte would want to know about it and how I can explain it. Before, I used to do things by instinct.'

However, Doc did not seem to consider this a serious handicap. Actually, without any training he was such a perceptive observer that it only needed a little stimulus to help him to make explicit much of the dynamics of the social organization of Cornerville. Some of the interpretations I have made are his more than mine, although it is now impossible to disentangle them.

While I worked more closely with Doc than with any other individual, I always sought out the leader in whatever group I was studying. I wanted not only sponsorship from him but also more active collaboration with the study. Since these leaders had the sort of position in the community that enabled them to observe much better than the followers what was going on and since they were in general more skilful observers than the followers, I found that I had much to learn from a more active collaboration with them.

In my interviewing methods I had been instructed not to argue with people or pass moral judgements upon them. This fell in with my own inclinations. I was glad to accept the people and to be accepted by them. However, this attitude did not come out so much in the interviewing, for I did little formal interviewing. I sought to show this interested acceptance of the people and the community in my everyday participation.

I learned to take part in the street corner discussions on baseball and sex. This required no special training, since the topics seemed to be matters of almost universal interest. I was not able to participate so actively in discussions of horse racing. I did begin to follow the races in a rather general and amateur way. I am sure it would have paid me to devote more study to the *Morning Telegraph* and other racing sheets, but my knowledge of baseball at least insured that I would not be left out of the street corner conversations.

While I avoided expressing opinions on sensitive topics, I found that arguing on some matters was simply part of the social pattern and that one could hardly participate without joining in the argument. I often found myself involved in heated but good-natured arguments about the relative merits of certain major-league ball players and managers. Whenever a girl or a group of girls would walk down the street, the fellows on the corner would make mental notes and later would discuss their evaluations of the females. These evaluations would run largely in terms of shape, and here I was glad to argue that Mary had a better 'build' than Anna, or vice versa. Of course, if any of the men on the corner happened to be personally attached to Mary or Anna, no searching comments would be made, and I, too, would avoid this topic.

Sometimes I wondered whether just hanging on the street corner was an active enough process to be dignified by the term 'research'. Perhaps I should be asking these men questions. However, one has to learn when to question and when not to question as well as what questions to ask.

I learned this lesson one night in the early months when I was with Doc in Chichi's gambling joint. A man from another part of the city was regaling us with a tale of the organization of gambling activity. I had been told that he had once been a very big gambling operator, and he talked knowingly about many interesting matters. He did most of the talking, but the others asked questions and threw in comments, so at length I began to feel that I must say something in order to be part of the group. I said: 'I suppose the cops were all paid off?'

The gambler's jaw dropped. He glared at me. Then he denied vehemently that any policemen had been paid off and immediately switched the conversation to another subject. For the rest of that evening I felt very uncomfortable.

The next day Doc explained the lesson of the previous evening. 'Go easy on that "who", "what", "why", "when", "where" stuff, Bill. You ask those questions, and people will clam up on you. If people accept you, you can just hang around, and you'll learn the answers in the long run without even having to ask the questions.'

I found that this was true. As I sat and listened, I learned the answers to questions that I would not even have had the sense to ask if I had been getting my information solely on an interviewing basis. I did not abandon questioning altogether, of course. I simply learned to judge the sensitiveness of the question and my relationship to the people so that I only asked a question in a sensitive area when I was sure that my relationship to the people involved was very solid.

When I had established my position on the street corner, the data simply came to me without very active efforts on my part. It was only now and then, when I was concerned with a particular problem and felt I needed more information from a certain individual, that I would seek an opportunity to get the man alone and carry on a more formal interview.

At first I concentrated upon fitting into Cornerville, but a little later I had to face the question of how far I was to immerse myself in the life of the district. I bumped into that problem one evening as I was walking down the street with the Nortons. Trying to enter into the spirit of the small talk, I cut loose with a string of obscenities and profanity. The walk came to a momentary halt as they all stopped to look at me in surprise. Doc shook his head and said: 'Bill, you're not supposed to talk like that. That doesn't sound like you.'

I tried to explain that I was only using terms that were common on the street corner. Doc insisted, however, that I was different and that they wanted me to be that way.

This lesson went far beyond the use of obscenity and profanity. I learned that people did not expect me to be just like them; in fact, they were interested and pleased to find me different, just so long as I took a friendly interest in them. Therefore, I abandoned my efforts at complete immersion. My behavior was nevertheless affected by street corner life. When John Howard first came down from Harvard to join me in the Cornerville study, he noticed at once that I talked in Cornerville in a manner far different from that which I used at Harvard. This was not a matter of the use of profanity or obscenity, nor did I affect the use of ungrammatical expressions. I talked in the way that seemed natural to me, but what was natural in Cornerville was different from what was natural at Harvard. In Cornerville, I found myself putting much more animation into my speech, dropping terminal 'g's, and using gestures much more actively. (There was also, of course, the difference in the vocabulary that I used. When I was most deeply involved in Cornerville, I found myself rather tongue-tied in my visits to Harvard. I simply could not keep up with the discussions of international relations, of the nature of science, and so on, in which I had once been more or less at home.)

As I became accepted by the Nortons and by several other groups, I tried to make myself pleasant enough so that people would be glad to have me around. And, at the same time, I tried to avoid influencing the group, because I wanted to study the situation as unaffected by my presence as possible. Thus, throughout my Cornerville stay, I avoided accepting office or leadership positions in any of the groups with a single exception. At one time I was nominated as secretary of the Italian Community Club. My first impulse was to decline the nomination, but then I reflected that the secretary's job is normally considered simply a matter of dirty work – writing the minutes and handling the correspondence. I accepted and found that I could write a very full account of the progress of the meeting as it went on under the pretext of keeping notes for the minutes.

While I sought to avoid influencing individuals or groups, I tried to be helpful in the way a friend is expected to help in Cornerville. When one of the boys had to go downtown on an errand and wanted company, I went along with him. When somebody was trying to get a job and had to write a letter about himself, I helped him to compose it, and so on. This sort of behavior presented no problem, but, when it came to the matter of handling money, it was not at all clear just how I should behave. Of course, I sought to spend money on my friends just as they did on me. But what about lending money? It is expected in such a district that a man will help out his friends whenever he can, and often the help needed is financial. I lent money on several occasions, but I always felt uneasy about it. Naturally, a man appreciates it at the time you lend him the money, but how does he feel later when the time has come to pay, and he is not able to do so? Perhaps he is embarrassed and tries to avoid your company. On such occasions I tried to reassure the individual and tell him that I knew he did not have it just then and that I was not worried about it. Or I even told him to forget about the debt altogether. But that did not wipe it off the books; the uneasiness remained. I learned that it is possible to do a favor for a friend and cause a strain in the relationship in the process.

I know no easy solution to this problem. I am sure there will be times when the researcher would be extremely ill-advised to refuse to make a personal loan. On the other hand, I am convinced that, whatever his financial resources, he should not look for opportunities to lend money and should avoid doing so whenever he gracefully can.

If the researcher is trying to fit into more than one group, his field work becomes more complicated. There may be times when the groups come into conflict with each other, and he will be expected to take a stand. There was a time in the spring of 1937 when the boys arranged a bowling match between the Nortons and the Italian Community Club. Doc bowled for the Nortons, of course. Fortunately, my bowling at this time had not advanced to a point where I was in demand for either team, and I was able to sit on the sidelines. From there I tried to applaud impartially the good shots of both teams, although I am afraid it was evident that I was getting more enthusiasm into my cheers for the Nortons.

When I was with members of the Italian Community Club, I did not feel at all called upon to defend the corner boys against disparaging remarks. However, there was one awkward occasion when I was with the corner boys and one of the college boys stopped to talk with me. In the course of the discussion he said: 'Bill, these fellows wouldn't understand what I mean, but I am sure that you understand my point.' There I thought I had to say something. I told him that he greatly underestimated the boys and that college men were not the only smart ones.

While the remark fitted in with my natural inclinations, I am sure it was justified from a strictly practical standpoint. My answer did not shake the feelings of superiority of the college boy, nor did it disrupt our personal relationship. On the other hand, as soon as he left, it became evident how deeply the corner boys felt about his statement. They spent some time giving explosive expressions to their opinion of him, and then they told me that I was different and that they appreciated it and that I knew much more than this fellow and yet I did not show it.

My first spring in Cornerville served to establish for me a firm position in the life of the district. I had only been there several weeks when Doc said to me: 'You're just as much of a fixture around this street corner as that lamp-post.' Perhaps the greatest event signalizing my acceptance on Norton Street was the baseball game that Mike Giovanni organized against the group of Norton Street boys in their late teens. It was the old men who had won glorious victories in the past against the rising youngsters. Mike assigned me to a regular position on the team, not a key position perhaps (I was stationed in right field), but at least I was there. When it was my turn to bat in the last half of the ninth inning, the score was tied, there were two outs, and the bases were loaded. As I reached down to pick up my bat, I heard some of the fellows suggesting to Mike that he ought to put in a pinch-hitter. Mike answered them in a loud voice that must have been meant for me: 'No, I've got confidence in Bill Whyte. He'll come through in the clutch.' So, with Mike's confidence to buck me up, I went up there, missed two swings, and then banged a hard grounder through the hole between second and short. At least that is where they told me it went. I was so busy getting down to first base that I did not know afterward whether I had reached there on an error or a base hit.

That night, when we went down for coffee, Danny presented me with a ring for being a regular fellow and a pretty good ball player. I was particularly impressed by the ring, for it had been made by hand. Danny had started with a clear amber die discarded from his crap game and over long hours had used his lighted cigarette to burn a hole through it and to round the corners so that it came out a heart shape on top. I assured the fellows that I would always treasure the ring.

Perhaps I should add that my game-winning base hit made the score 18-17, so it is evident that I was not the only one who had been hitting the ball. Still, it was a wonderful feeling to come through when they were counting on me, and it made me feel still more that I belonged on Norton Street.

# 15 Philip J. Stone, Dexter C. Dunphy, Marshall S. Smith and Daniel Ogilvie

Content Analysis

Excerpt from Philip J. Stone, Dexter C. Dunphy, Marshall S. Smith and Daniel Ogilvie, *The General Inquirer: A Computer Approach to Content Analysis*, MIT Press, 1966, pp. 14–19.

Our definition presents content analysis as a research tool to be used by the social scientist in making inferences; what is measured in content analysis depends on the theory being investigated. This context is needed not only to gain a proper perspective on content analysis but to differentiate it from other activities that may appear to be similar but are for other purposes. In this section, we shall present a content analysis model, and we shall then use this model to specify what content analysis is not.

Past discussions of content analysis have often given little consideration to its larger context. While Berelson's definition specifies that content analysis is 'a research technique', little further emphasis is made of its research purpose. In fact, Berelson argues that many valid content analysis studies are undertaken solely or primarily to describe characteristics of content:

In a great many studies there is no real problem of inference at all. This is true for all those content analyses in which the description of content itself is the primary objective. Such studies can be said to contain implicit inferences about the causes or the consequences of the content – and some contain them explicitly – but such inferences are in the nature of addenda to or reformulations of the basic data. Thus a trend study of newspaper content can be considered material for inferences about the changing character of press controls and/or about the changing character of public attention. But such 'inferences' are usually nothing but reformulations in other terms of the content analysis itself.

We feel that the researcher has an obligation both to himself and to his public to explicate clearly the inferences he is making. Many content analysts, often preoccupied with measurement, have felt that they should stay at the level of fact and let the reader draw the conclusions. Actually content analysts invariably use at least a rudimentary theoretical framework in the very design of categories and rules for their application. Its rationale, purpose and implications when applied to the data should be made explicit.

Our content analysis model is represented in Figure 1. Primary importance is given to the theory being investigated. The theory determines the texts to be compared (that is, the research design), the categories and rules for application that must be constructed and the kinds of inferences that might be drawn from the results of measurement. The content analysis process is but one part of the model. Upon selection of texts and specification of procedures, the content analysis process makes systematic and objective measurements on the texts by identifying occurrences of specified characteristics. These measurements then serve as a reference for drawing inferences. While the content analysis process is objective and direct, the inferences drawn from the results may be quite subtle and indirect. Whether the measurements and conclusions follow reasonably from the text may be ascertained by checking back to the text.

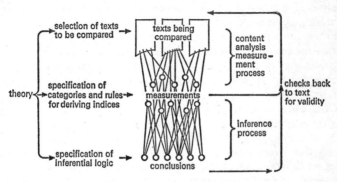

Figure 1 Representation of content analysis model

Often an important part of the inference process (not represented in Figure 1) is information external to the texts themselves, with comparisons made to the text measures. Such external information is used to support inferences made from the content analyses of the texts.

This over-all content analysis model represents the pattern of measurement and inference common to scientific research of all kinds. Measurement is used to define operationally, to single out instances and to describe variations of those aspects of the environment in which the investigator is interested. It is these measurements, made in the context of a research design, that are used to test hypotheses and draw conclusions.

In clinical analysis, as well as in much of literary analysis, emphasis is often placed on understanding as thoroughly as possible a particular instance or event. Inferences are made from the careful inspection of the text itself rather than from the intermediary steps of formal measurement. Each inference is made from the full context of a particular instance or event, rather than from the measures abstracted by the content analysis process.

We have taken the position that these two approaches are complementary, and thus we have designed the procedures described in this book to facilitate the interaction of one with the other. Prior to making a formal content analysis, the investigator can and should carefully inspect a sample of his data, drawing on his intuitive powers to identify the unforeseen circumstances that might be affecting the data. This inspection is used in developing categories and application rules. Formal content analysis is then applied to describe the data as a whole.

Past definitions, such as Berelson's, have emphasized the 'manifest' aspects of content analysis, often putting aside the utility of content analysis in drawing conclusions about 'latent' implications. The content analysis process itself, being systematic and objective, must be based on manifest characteristics of the text. Berelson points out that 'the results of content analysis, however, frequently serve as the basis for these "interpretations" of latent content'. In our model, such interpretations are represented by the stage of inference. The interpretation of 'latent' as well as 'manifest' meanings is a valid exercise within the model.

Often different inferences will be drawn from the same content analysis measure. Thus in one study, a category, 'male-role', consisting of terms he, king, man, prince and so on, might be inferred to indicate simply that overt, manifest attention is being given to persons in male roles, while in another study, the same category may be used to infer an unintentionally expressed concern about masculinity. As a general rule, the more latent the phenomenon inferred, the more internal consistency among categories and external evidence the investigator will want for its support.

By our definition, making inferences from communication content is considered the primary function of content analysis, not addenda nor reformulation. This is not a trivial change from past definitions, for it imposes upon the researcher the burden of integrating theory with method, of being dissatisfied with mere description of phenomena. This does not restrict the researcher to strictly hypothesis-testing studies, but it does require him to construct categories that he believes are relevant, either singly or in combination, to his conceptual framework.

This context, represented by a research model (Figure 1), distinguishes content analysis from several related activities. Considered apart from the emphasis on research design and inference, the content analysis process is basically the task of applying descriptors; that is, of making a particular many-to-few mapping of the text. Viewed this way, it does not differ from any cataloging or concordancing activity, such as produced the index to this book. A book index or catalog may reflect a theoretical orientation. But by our over-all definition, they are not content analyses.

Our definition thus differs from a number of past definitions in distinguishing between the relatively small amount of content analysis research and the large amounts of cataloging done every day. Unfortunately, as broad, operations-centered terms such as 'information processing' or 'information retrieval' come into vogue, investigators sometimes tend to lose sight of their research purposes, and important distinctions can become blurred. The general flexibility of the computer has on occasion led the investigator to forget what he is doing, but this need not be the case.

Our definition also distinguishes content analysis from similar operations in related areas involving the study of language. The term 'semiotic', originally used in medicine to refer to the study of 'signs' or symptoms, was first put forward by John Locke in the latter part of the seventeenth century to refer to the general study of the nature of signs and the use to which the mind puts them in understanding things. The term was subsequently used by philosopher Charles Pierce and gained wide currency from the writings of Charles Morris. Morris divided semiotics into semantics, syntactics and pragmatics:

*Pragmatics* is that portion of semiotics which deals with the origin, uses and effects of signs within the behavior in which they occur; *semantics* deals with the signification of signs in all modes of signifying; *syntactics* deals with combinations of signs without regard for their specific significations or their relation to the behavior in which they occur.

Within semiotics, content analysis becomes one aspect of pragmatics. As a set of operations, however, it closely resembles uses of descriptors in the area of semantics. One cannot read the 'Structure of a semantic theory' in *The Structure of Language* by Katz and Fodor (1964) without sensing a remarkable operational parallel with the content analysis procedures described here. However, content analysis differs in purpose from semantics. For the behavioral scientist, the purpose of content analysis is to infer the 'origin, uses and effects of signs within the behavior in which they occur'.

While it is important to distinguish content analysis from what it is not, we would emphasize that advances in related activities may have important implications for content analysis. Thus, reference to semiotics, information retrieval and information processing may serve a useful purpose in keeping these ties explicit.

Philip J. Stone, Dexter C. Dunphy, Marshall S. Smith and Daniel Ogilvie   113

In summary, content analysis does not study behavior itself; rather it focuses on artifacts produced by behavior; that is, recorded speech and writing. Much as the archaeologist infers the life of a culture from the pattern of remnants, so the content analyst infers the orientation and concerns of a speaker, subculture or culture from the record of what is said.

Studying artifacts rather than studying behavior itself has its drawbacks, but also its advantages. The artifact is static, not a fleeting event as is behavior. Text can be copied and shared with other investigators. It can be analysed and reanalysed until the investigator is satisfied with his work; and it can be reused later to test other hypotheses. Text is usually readily available, often being produced naturally as part of an event; because it extends through history, text is an excellent vehicle for studying long-term changes of attitudes, concerns and styles.

However, like the archaeologist's diggings, the available text fragments may be trivial and insignificant data about the situations they represent. The really significant documents may never become available or, for that matter, may not have been produced. Despite this, the scope of symbolic meaning is wide. The diversity of possible interpretations, the proximity of verbal expression to the pressures of the situation, the multiple levels in which personality is reflected through speech and writing, usually all make the content of what is said an interesting subject of study, suitable for testing a number of hypotheses. Sensitively chosen text, like a well-chosen archaeological site, can yield very worthwhile rewards.

# 16 Howard S. Becker

## The Life History

Excerpts from Howard S. Becker, Introduction to Clifford R. Shaw,
*The Jack-Roller: A Delinquent Boy's Own Story*, University of Chicago Press,
rev. edn, 1966, pp. x–xyiii. First published in 1925.

What are some of the functions that can be usefully performed by a life
history document? In the first place, it can serve as a touchstone with
which to evaluate theories that purport to deal with phenomena like
those of a delinquent career. Whether it is a theory of the psychological
origins of delinquent behavior, a theory of the roots of delinquency in
juvenile gangs or an attempt to explain the distribution of delinquency
throughout a city, any theory of delinquency must, if it is to be considered valid, explain or at least be consistent with the facts of the case.
Thus, even though the life history does not in itself provide definitive
proof of a proposition, it can be a negative case that forces us to decide
a proposed theory is inadequate.

To say this is to take an approach to scientific generalization that
deserves some comment. We may decide to accept a theory if it explains,
let us say, 95 per cent of the cases that fall in its jurisdiction. Many
reputable scientists do. In contrast, one can argue that any theory that
does not explain all cases is inadequate, that other factors than those the
theory specifies must be operating to produce the result we want to
explain. It is primarily a question of strategy. If we assume that exceptions to any rule are a normal occurrence, we will perhaps not search as
hard for further explanatory factors as we otherwise might. But if we
regard exceptions as potential negations of our theory, we will be
spurred to search for them.

More importantly, the negative case will respond to careful analysis
by suggesting the direction the search should take. Inspection of its features will reveal attributes which differ from those of otherwise similar
cases, or processes at work whose steps have not all been fully understood. If we know the case in some detail, as a life history document
allows us to know it, our search is more likely to be successful; it is in
this sense that the life history is a useful theoretical touchstone.

The life history also helps us in areas of research that touch on it only
tangentially. Every piece of research crosses frontiers into new terrain it
does not explore thoroughly, areas important to its main concern in

which it proceeds more by assumption than investigation. A study of a college, for instance, may make assumptions (indeed, must make them) about the character of the city, state and region it is located in, about the social class, background and experience of its students, and about a host of other matters likely to influence the operation of the school and the way it affects students. A study of a mental hospital or prison will make similarly unchecked assumptions about the character of the families whose members end up in the institution. A life history – although it is not the only kind of information that can do this – provides a basis on which those assumptions can be realistically made, a rough approximation of the direction in which the truth lies.

In addition to these matters of neighboring fact, so to speak, the life history can be particularly useful in giving us insight into the subjective side of much-studied institutional processes, about which unverified assumptions are also often made. Sociologists have lately been concerned with processes of adult socialization and with the processes of degradation and 'stripping' associated with socialization into rehabilitative institutions such as prisons and mental hospitals. Although the theories concern themselves with institutional action rather than individual experience, they either assume something about the way people experience such processes or at least raise a question about the nature of that experience. [. . .]

The life history, by virtue again of its wealth of detail, can be important at those times when an area of study has grown stagnant, has pursued the investigation of a few variables with ever-increasing precision but has received dwindling increments of knowledge from the pursuit. When this occurs, investigators might well proceed by gathering personal documents which suggest new variables, new questions and new processes, using the rich though unsystematic data to provide a needed reorientation of the field.

Beneath these specific contributions which the life history is capable of making lies one more fundamental. The life history, more than any other technique except perhaps participant observation, can give meaning to the overworked notion of *process*. Sociologists like to speak of 'ongoing processes' and the like, but their methods usually prevent them from seeing the processes they talk about so glibly.

George Herbert Mead, if we take him seriously, tells us that the reality of social life is a conversation of significant symbols, in the course of which people make tentative moves and then adjust and reorient their activity in the light of the responses (real and imagined) others make to those moves. The formation of the individual act is a process in which conduct is continually reshaped to take account of the expectations of others, as these are expressed in the immediate situation and as the actor supposes they may come to be expressed. Collective activity, of the kind pointed to by concepts like 'organization' or 'social structure', arises out of a continuous process of mutual adjustment of the actions of all the actors involved. Social process, then, is not an imagined interplay of invisible forces or a vector made up of the interacting of multiple social factors, but an observable process of symbolically mediated interaction.

Observable, yes; but not easily observable, at least not for scientific purposes. To observe social process as Mead described it takes a great deal of time. It poses knotty problems of comparability and objectivity in data gathering. It requires an intimate understanding of the lives of others. So social scientists have, most often, settled for less demanding techniques such as the interview and the questionnaire.

These techniques can, I think, tell us much, but only as we are able to relate them to a vision of the underlying Meadian social process we would know had we more adequate data. We can, for instance, give people a questionnaire at two periods in their life and infer an underlying process of change from the differences in their answers. But our interpretation has significance only if our imagery of the underlying process is accurate. And this accuracy of imagery – this congruence of theoretically posited process with what we could observe if we took the necessary time and trouble – can be partially achieved by the use of life history documents. For the life history, if it is done well, will give us the details of that process whose character we would otherwise only be able to speculate about, the process to which our data must ultimately be referred if they are to have theoretical and not just operational and predictive significance. It will describe those crucial interactive episodes in which new lines of individual and collective activity are forged, in which new aspects of the self are brought into being. It is by thus giving a realistic basis to our imagery of the underlying process that the life history serves the purposes of checking assumptions, illuminating organization and reorienting stagnant fields. [. . .]

Given the variety of scientific uses to which the life history may be put, one must wonder at the relative neglect into which it has fallen. Sociologists, it is true, have never given it up altogether. But neither have they made it one of their standard research tools. They read the documents available and assign them for their students to read. But they do not ordinarily think of gathering life history documents themselves or of making the technique part of their research approach.

A number of simultaneous changes probably contributed to the increasing disuse of the life history method. Sociologists became more concerned with the development of abstract theory and correspondingly less interested in full and detailed accounts of specific organizations and communities. They wanted data formulated in the abstract categories of their own theories rather than in the categories that seemed most relevant to the people they studied. The life history was well suited to the latter task, but of little immediately apparent use in the former.

At the same time, sociologists began to separate the field of social psychology from that of sociology proper, creating two specialties in place of two emphases within one field, and focused more on 'structural' variables and synchronic functional analyses than on those factors that manifested themselves in the life and experience of the person. Again, the life history made a clear contribution to the latter task but seemed unrelated to studies that emphasized group attributes and their interconnexions.

But perhaps the major reason for the relatively infrequent use of the technique is that it does not produce the kind of 'findings' that sociologists now expect research to produce. As sociology increasingly rigidifies and 'professionalizes', more and more emphasis has come to be placed on what we may, for simplicity's sake, call the *single study*. I use the term to refer to research projects that are conceived of as self-sufficient and self-contained, which provide all the evidence one needs to accept or reject the conclusions they proffer, whose findings are to be used as another brick in the growing wall of science – a metaphor quite different from that of the mosaic. The single study is integrated with the main body of knowledge in the following way: it derives its hypotheses from an inspection of what is already known; then, after the research is completed, if those hypotheses have been demonstrated, they are added to the wall of what is already scientifically known and used as the basis for further studies. The important point is that the researcher's hypothesis is either proved or disproved on the basis of what he has discovered in doing that one piece of research.

The customs, traditions and organizational practices of contemporary sociology conspire to make us take this view of research. The journal article of standard length, the most common means of scientific communication, is made to order for the presentation of findings that confirm or refute hypotheses. The Ph.D. thesis virtually demands that its author have a set of findings, warranted by his own operations, which yield conclusions he can defend before a faculty committee. The research grant proposal, another ubiquitous sociological literary form, pushes its author to state what his project will have proved when the money has been spent.

If we take the single study as the model of scientific work, we will then use, when we judge research and make decisions about how to organize our research, criteria designed to assure us that the findings of our single study do indeed provide a sound basis on which to accept or reject hypotheses. The canons of inference and proof now in vogue reflect this emphasis. Such methodologists as Stouffer, and others who followed him, developed techniques for assessing hypotheses based on the model of the controlled experiment. Compare two groups, those who have been exposed to the effects of a variable and those who have not, before and after the exposure. The multiple comparisons made possible by this technique allow you to test not only your original hypothesis, but also some of the likely alternative explanations of the same results, should they be what you have predicted. This is the approved model. If we cannot achieve it, our study is deficient unless we can devise workable substitutes. If we do achieve it, we can say with assurance that we have produced scientific findings strong enough to bear the weight of still further studies.

Criteria drawn from the experimental model and used to evaluate single studies in isolation, however useful they may be in a variety of contexts, have had one bad by-product. They have led people to ignore the other functions of research and, particularly, to ignore the contribution made by one study to an over-all research enterprise even when the study, considered in isolation, produced no definitive results of its own. Since, by these criteria, the life history did not produce definitive results, people have been at a loss to make anything of it and by and large have declined to invest the time and effort necessary to acquire life history documents.

We can perhaps hope that a fuller understanding of the complexity of the scientific enterprise will restore sociologists' sense of the versatility and worth of the life history.

# Part Three The Family

Anthropologists have carried out many intensive studies of kinship systems in pre-industrial societies. Comparable studies of family and kinship are rarer in developed societies. We present two excerpts (Readings 17 and 18), however, from studies of Western society, which demonstrate that in modern urban life the elementary 'family of husband, wife and children' is by no means as isolated from wider sets of kin as is commonly assumed. Moreover, the French Canadian extract by Garigue shows that urbanization does not necessarily produce the same kind of kinship system, since cultural values constitute an independent influence on family and kin – in this case the French Canadian culture.

Elizabeth Bott (Reading 19) has provided one of the most stimulating theoretical analyses of the factors which make for variations in the degree to which the spouses in a marriage are independent of each other, by examining the ties each member of the family is involved in outside the home and showing how they react back on the division of labour within the home.

Most such studies have been of working-class or lower-middle-class families. A rare exception is Lupton and Wilson's analysis (Reading 20) of the family links between upper-class people in British society.

Finally, the family is examined in a society which has undergone the experience of revolution: Geiger (Reading 21) discusses both the impact of changes produced as a matter of public policy in the U.S.S.R. and the persistence of the family throughout the period.

# 17 Philippe Garigue

French Canadian Kinship and Urban Life

Philippe Garigue, 'French Canadian kinship and urban life', *American Anthropologist*, vol. 58, 1956, pp. 1090–101.

The present study is aimed at describing the importance and character of kinship among French Canadians of Montreal. It is directed at the problem raised by Wirth and numerous other sociologists, who have assumed that kin ties lose significance in an urban setting. The data were collected between September 1954 and February 1955, from fifty-two persons in forty-three households. As the study was specifically directed at assessing the influence of urbanism on kinship, only informants of urban background were selected, though some households included persons who were born outside Montreal. No significant difference seems to appear between those households whose members were all born in Montreal, and those with members born elsewhere. Thirty genealogical tables were collected from persons whose background was urban from birth. We believe it can safely be assumed that the sample conforms to the dominant urban behavior among French Canadians, even though the extensiveness of interviews and the consequent restriction on the number of people who could be visited in the five months of the field work prevented the taking of a random sample.

All interviews were conducted in French, and took place in the homes of the informants. The informants are mostly of medium income; only three were of high income and five of definitely low income. The study is not intended as an analysis of the total effect of urban life on the kinship system of all Montreal French Canadians – for instance, no attempt was made to study the 'pathology' of urban life – but enough data were collected to answer the more limited question as to the general influence of urbanism upon kinship.

The urban French Canadian kinship system is a variant of that generally reported for Western societies. It is a patronymic bilateral structure, with two major dimensions of lateral range and generation depth. While awareness of descent and pride in the history of a family name is shown by the majority of informants, frequency of contact is highest between members of the same generation, and cuts across consanguineal and affinal ties. These lateral and generation dimensions involve different patterns of behavior: a formal pattern of expected obligations operates between the generations; a more informal choice according to personality preference operates between members of the same generation. The nuclei of the kinship system are the parent-child and sibling relationships of the domestic family, which is held to be an autonomous unit. The expected roles of the members of the broader kin group vary according to their position in the formal and informal patterns, and their closeness to Ego's domestic family. These roles separate the total kin into a number of subgroups having special functions. The total kin group is expected to come into action only for very formal occasions, such as a funeral; in most situations, only the subgroups are involved. Women are more active within the kinship system than men, and this fact, combined with their primary roles as wives and mothers, gives them a great deal of influence and supplies the continuity of the kin group. While all informants showed a high degree of conformity to kinship obligations, they also reported factors which they believed were causing segmentation. The most important of these were said to be social mobility and cultural differentiation, which resulted in a decrease or even loss of contact between members of a kin group.

### The structure of kinship knowledge

Thirty of the fifty-two informants were asked for the range of their genealogical knowledge. The maximum limit of this range was determined by knowledge of the sex of a person, in addition to his family name. For instance, children of lateral kin were included if the informant was aware of their sex in addition to their proper genealogical link. The mean of such knowledge is a range of 215 persons. The smallest range was seventy-five; the ten with least knowledge ranged from this to 120. The next ten ranged from 126 to 243; the highest ten from 252 to a maximum of 484 known kin. These known kin were distributed in a wide lateral range rather than extensive depth of generations. Including Ego's generation, one informant reported three generations, ten informants reported a range of four generations, thirteen informants reported five generations and six informants claimed knowledge of six generations. The three cases with the lowest range of knowledge can be regarded as abnormal. In one instance, the mother's line was not known, and in two more the true bilateralism was distorted by ignorance of the second ascending generation.

The most extensive knowledge of kin was usually concentrated into the generations of Ego and his parents, which together included from one-half to two-thirds of the total persons known. Knowledge of the second ascending generation was often reduced to from one to eight known ancestors. In the third and fourth ascending generations, knowledge was restricted in most instances to a single ancestor. Variations in the lateral range, total size, depth of generations, etc., were linked to the age, sex and marital status of the informants.

The age of the informants varied from nineteen to seventy-two, with an average of thirty and a half years. There was a definite tendency for depth and breadth of range to increase with age. The controlling factor in the ratio of increase seems to be the size of the informant's kin group during adolescence. Among informants up to about forty years of age, their own and their first ascending generation were most important. Among older informants, descending generations became increasingly important. The largest kin knowledge was reported by married persons.

The sex of the informants seemed to be an important factor in kin recognition; only two of the informants who reported the fifteen largest kin groups (186 to 484) were men. All of the ten largest kin groups were reported by women. Sex is also a major factor in determining the stress placed by the informant on the father's or the mother's line. Just over half of the men had a greater knowledge of their father's line; women knew more of their mother's line than their father's by a ratio of three to one. If knowledge of Christian names is taken as a sign of greater kinship awareness, a second and more limited range can be distinguished, which runs from a minimum of fifty-four to a maximum of 288. The proportion of kin whose Christian names are also known, to those known only by family name and sex, varied from one-half to nine-tenths. These ratios do not correlate with the extremes of the first range, and there was only a slight increase in the largest ranges. Ignorance of Christian names was always greatest in the descending generations of the domestic families with which there was little contact.

If kinship ties are graded in order of their importance as foci of activities, the first among them is the sibling tie. This seems to relate to the size of the sibling groups, and to the maintenance of sibling unity after marriage. The average size of the informants' sibling groups was five, with one instance of an informant who was one of sixteen siblings. There is an over-all correlation between total knowledge of kin and the size of the sibling groups closest to the informant: his own, his father's and his mother's. The larger the number of persons in these groups, the greater the total kinship range. Moreover, the scope of lateral kin is increased through marriage of siblings, since these in-law ties tend to be rather firm. Thus, the 'core' of the kinship system is formed by domestic families linked by sibling and parent–child ties, and by lateral ties arising through the marriage of siblings. Recognition outside that core operates according to the lines of descent. In this instance, only some of the members of the sibling groups involved will be known. Some qualification must be introduced between the recognition arising from membership in the core, and through descent. Because of the frequency of cousin marriages among French Canadians, both modes of recognition can operate at the same time. While it is not possible to say whether the importance given to affinal ties through sibling marriages may not be due to the frequency of cousin marriages, there is no doubt that many kinship ties created through the marriage of a sibling are as important as those of cousinship.

Another characteristic of the urban French Canadians is the wide geographical scattering of their kin groups. While all had kin within Montreal, proportions running as high as three-fourths were reported scattered not only within the Province of Quebec, but further afield in Canada and in the United States.

### Important aspects of kinship behavior

Urban French Canadian men and women not only give different stress to kinship, but also have different roles. Men, for instance, reported that they usually thought of their kin groups in terms of their male relatives; their knowledge of their female relatives was more restricted. In all instances, however, their attitudes towards their mothers, wives or sisters, gave these female relatives great influence not only over household matters, but also in many outside affairs. Women seemed to have a greater awareness of the kin group as composed of both sexes. Not only was their knowledge of the total kin group greater, so that in a number of instances wives knew more of their husbands' kin than the husbands themselves did, but they also had a much greater knowledge of the affairs of the kin group. While men reported their kin contacts as being largely for leisure-time activities, the women reported their reasons for contact as most 'family affairs' such as children, births, marriages or illness, etc. A marriage or a funeral was the occasion for intense activity by the women, and it was they who took the initiative in organizing the gathering of relatives, who suggested visits to each other's homes, and who wrote letters or telephoned news to relatives. They also spent more time with their kin than did the majority of men.

While there are individual variations in behavior, this sex differentiation was a formalized expectation. A number of wives reported that while they were intimate with only a limited number of kin in their husband's line, they were expected by most to keep them informed of family affairs by letters or telephone calls. The wife, not the husband, would have been blamed for failure to do this. All informants, male and female, stressed the fact that it was the women who acted as links between the various households of the kin group.

It is beyond the scope of this paper to explore the reasons for this sex differentiation. It may have a close relationship to the fact that, as domestic families are generally large and servants beyond the means of most French Canadians, the women are essentially housewives and only work outside before having children, or because of great economic necessity. It would be wrong, however, to take this predominantly domestic role of women as a sign of their inferior status in the kin group. On the contrary, the continuity of the kinship system over time may be attributed to their dominant position in it. This influence of the women in the kin group is distinct from the authority role of men within each domestic family. The domestic family is headed by the husband, in whom the Civil Code of the Province of Quebec vests a great deal of authority; it is an autonomous unit, with a sole legal representative. Within each household, however, the exercise of this authority is qualified by consultation with one's wife, and outside the domestic family by consultation with one's mother or sisters. But even then, the use of authority is held to be a male prerogative. Within a sibling group it may also happen that the eldest brother, especially at the death of the father, will acquire a position of authority over all the other siblings. Similarly, a grandfather has a great deal of authority. The pattern of authority, even apart from the legal definition given to it by the Civil Code of Quebec, is therefore male, and relates to age and descent.

The equalitarian relationship between father and children or between persons of a different age, reported for the United States, is not present among the French Canadians. While a father allows his children a certain latitude of behavior, it is not marked by any feeling of emotional closeness. Emotional ties are more usually directed toward the mother or the wife, or located within the sibling group. Thus, while a woman's legal status is subordinate, her roles as a mother or wife or sister make her the focus of most of the emotional life of the kin group. While the men determine the status position of their domestic families or of the whole kin group, the women are the 'integraters' of the kin group, and as such its effective leaders. This female leadership role is different from the role of older men, who act as symbols of kinship continuity, but who are not the active agents of the life of the group. The foci of kin links are thus the women, and particular women can actually be regarded as leaders of the kin group. In the case of a grandmother of one of the informants, this leadership role had become a benign dictatorship, and practically all formal kin activities took place at her home.

For both men and women, the frequency of contact with relatives was the result of a number of factors. For instance, while only sixteen of the forty-three households reported relatives in the same parish, all informants reported their highest frequency of contact with their fathers and mothers and with their siblings, even if these lived in distant parishes of Montreal. Only when the degree of kinship was more remote did informants remark that geographical distance influenced contacts. Beside degree of kinship and geographical location, personal preference was an important factor in contact. Personal preference for kin was reported as a factor outside Ego's family of orientation and, if married, his household and his spouse's family of orientation. We may distinguish formal recognition from personal preference in kin relationships. While overlap between these two was reported, the formal dimension operates predominantly between generations, especially upward, while personal preference was especially strong in the selection of contacts with affinals or cousins.

This can best be illustrated by describing the frequency of contact reported by a married man, aged thirty-four, who was a skilled worker in a Montreal factory. He has been chosen as an example because he is about average in the range of kinship recognition, with a total of 233 kin, 203 of whom were alive at the time of the survey. Of these, ninety-three lived in Montreal, scattered in a number of parishes; seventy-two were reported living in various parts of the Province of Quebec, and thirty-eight more were reported in Ontario and in the United States. During each week the informant frequently met members of his two brothers' households, who also lived in Montreal. Contacts with one of these households were more frequent, as they lived in the same parish. There were few week-ends in which the brothers did not meet. He also visited his wife's parents some week-ends, but his wife went more often, taking along their three children. He was very friendly with his wife's brothers, and the husband of one of his wife's sisters; he sometimes went out with either his brothers or his wife's brothers, or with his wife's sister's husband. It was rare, however, that they all came together as a group. Several times a month he met various uncles and cousins who also lived in Montreal, either through a chance meeting or because they were visiting the same household. He saw members of the household of one of his uncles more frequently, as they owned a grocery store where the family sometimes shopped. He reported that he met an average of forty to forty-five relatives each month, including those of generations older and younger than himself. He met far more of them in certain seasons of the year such as Christmas, and during Christmas 1954 he thinks that he must have seen nearly all of the ninety-three relatives who live in Montreal. He also went regularly, about once a month, to see his own parents who lived a few miles outside Montreal. He usually went with one of his brothers who owned a car, and they took their families with them. During the summer his wife and children generally went there for about a fortnight. Each time he visited his parents he usually met one of his married sisters who lived near their parents' home. He would also meet members of another sister's household when they came from the Eastern Townships to Montreal. About every other year, another of his brothers would come up from the United States where he lived with his family, and they would gather for a family reunion, either in Montreal or at their parents' home. The relatives he did not meet he heard about, either through letters or through conversations. Altogether, he had seen 115 of his relatives during 1954, and had heard from another fifty-seven. He admitted that he wasn't always as interested in family affairs as he should be, and that his wife knew more of his own relatives than he did. By way of an excuse, he said that he was a junior executive in his local trade union branch, and had very little time to spare between his work and his union duties.

What seems interesting in this informant's report about his frequency of contact, which was quite different from that of his wife, was that he recognized a strict obligation to see only a certain number of relatives. Outside of this range, frequency of contact and the sense of formal obligation were much less important. However, because all his siblings were married, the range of formal obligation comprised the core of the kinship system and totalled over fifty persons. Yet, since some of these persons were located outside Montreal and were seen less often, the informant reported himself as lax in his kin duties. Informants also made a distinction between obligations to meet relatives who were very close and obligations to meet other kin of ascending generations. They reported that while they were expected by older relatives, other than their father and mother, to fulfil certain kinship obligations, this expectation was satisfied by a low frequency of contact, usually limited to visits at Christmas or the gathering for a family reunion. The frequency of these reunions varied, and most informants reported them as taking place about once a year. They had no fixed dates and usually took place at the home of one of the relatives who acted as a focal point for the activities of the kin group. A very good excuse had to be given for not going, but most informants stated that they went willingly. Sometimes as many as forty or more persons would get together, depending on the size of the home or the economic resources of the persons involved.

The highest frequency of contact took place between relatives of the same generation and, apart from sibling contact, were mostly based on personal preference. This personal preference was recognized as the major factor in the contact, and informants verbalized it in the statement that such meetings were the result of 'just liking to get together'. It can thus be suggested that all the various modes of kinship recognition which have been described operate according to different criteria. Certain kin, such as Ego's parents, siblings, spouse's parents or siblings' spouses, are held to have special claims and are given priority over all others. Recognition of these claims keeps the legally defined autonomy of the domestic family, as well as its life as a unit, at a low threshold, since its members will readily adjust their own lives to the needs of such kin. With other persons, a formal recognition will exist but this recognition can be satisfied by more limited actions, such as attendance at a funeral or a wedding, or by letter writing, so that the autonomy of the domestic family with regard to them is much greater.

The criteria which give rise to these different modes of recognition, and which govern frequency of contact, cannot be presented as clear-cut categories. Involved in the idea of kinship recognition are factors which informants characterize as differences in 'family spirit', or 'family unity', so that there are extensive variations as to who is included in those having 'priority', or just a 'formal' recognition. Many informants, for example, held that cousins were persons who involved some formal recognition, while others would regard close affines as more important to them than cousins. Difficulties in trying to determine the range of each category were often linked to the frequency of cousin marriages. Cousin marriages among the thirty informants who gave their genealogical knowledge varied from one instance of a second-cousin marriage, to two first-cousin and four second-cousin marriages in one kinship group. Altogether, eleven of the thirty informants reported such marriages. In another case, three brothers had married three sisters, and the two kin groups, which had not been previously related, had developed multiple ties which cross-cut the various dimensions of the kin group.

Closely related to the frequency of contact is the frequency of services between relatives. It could be offered as an unverified generalization that those kin who are held by close kinship links, and who see each other most frequently, help each other most frequently. These services included the loan of needed objects, baby sitting, shopping, taking care of the household during the mother's illness, gift giving, the making of extensive loans, or the giving of general economic help. A young mother reported that she was receiving help from her mother, sisters and female cousins. Less frequently, she would also turn to her husband's female relatives.

The pattern of services revealed even more clearly than did the frequency of contact that the kin group of birth is preferred to the kin group of marriage. Not only would there be a preference for one's own line, but also a preference for help from members of one's own sex, within each kin group. However, occasions were reported in which the distinction between the lines was blurred. All the adult females of a kin group, consanguineal and affinal, would help in preparing the family reunion. The buying, preparing and serving of the food, as well as the clearing up, would be the joint task of all the women who came. Another instance of overlap was given by a lawyer, who reported that his relatives, both consanguineal and affinal, came to him for legal advice, for which he charged a fee according to the economic status of the relative. Relatives in the medical profession are also reported as having their services requested by kin. Persons who sell things required by relatives, such as groceries and household utensils, were reported to have their kin as customers. This does not mean that all goods and services were obtained through relatives, but there is a certain degree of economic reciprocity holding the kin group together. Moral problems as well as economic were referred to relatives, especially to those in Holy Orders. Twenty-six of the thirty informants reported relatives in Holy Orders. One informant had eleven such relatives, both priests and nuns. One of these, a priest who was met during one interview, said that he was usually asked to officiate at the baptisms, weddings and funerals of his relatives. Occasionally, they also came to him for advice. The only religious service he did not wish to perform for them was to act as their confessor.

All informants reported that they had received important services from relatives at some time during their lives. One stated that she would not think of going to a place where she had no relatives. Another informant reported that the problem of child rearing in a city was minimized if a mother could have the help of female relatives. One male informant stated that life in Montreal would have been impossible for him and his own domestic family during the depression of the 1930s if his relatives had not helped him. He not only received loans and other economic help, but went to live with his in-laws, and was able to find work through cousins. Of the forty-three households visited, nine either comprised three generations or included other relatives outside the consanguineal unit. Working for a relative is frequently reported, and most informants stated that they knew of kin who were in this position. Certain economic enterprises are operated by persons who are related to each other in various degrees. Instances of this were given for a garage, a hotel, a grocery store and a small industrial plant. Services are sometimes also requested of relatives who are marginal to the frequency of contact. Distant kin who, because of their status and general social position, can give important recommendations or introductions, are sometimes asked to exert their influence. If these relatives are also political figures, their politics will be supported as well as their help sought. The kinship system of urban French Canadians is an important mechanism for manipulating the social environment, and what might be called nepotism, but is referred to by French Canadians as 'family solidarity', is a daily practice.

One of the marked characteristics of French Canadian urban kinship is its high degree of elasticity. Outside the range of 'priority' claims, narrow formal recognition is balanced by selective contact according to personality preference, and the resulting kin group is as much linked to personality preference as to institutionalized formal recognition. This elasticity also permits it to adapt itself to the elements which operate against its continuity in time. Among such elements is the process of social differentiation caused by social mobility. There is, in fact, a close correlation between social status and frequency of contact, and informants who had been upwardly mobile were those who reported the greatest loss of contact with their lateral kin. Social mobility therefore tends to dislocate the lateral range in which personal preference is so important, but it does not seem to separate a person completely from the kin group. Certain formal ties are still recognized, and informants reported instances of a person helping his entire sibling group to move upward. Furthermore, a new kin group forms rapidly at the higher level. Social mobility does not seem to imply a complete loss of the recognition of kin obligations, but merely the movement from a kin group at one level to another kin group at a different level. Cases were quoted in which the acceptance of a spouse into the kin group at the higher social level was conditioned by the possibility of having to accept a number of the spouse's relatives. If the spouse was rejected, there would be a gradual loss of contact with the person who had married 'beneath'. In this instance, there would be a regrouping with the kin group at the lower social level.

Segmentation of the kin group is caused not only by social mobility, but also by the development of cultural differences. Informants quoted instances of relatives who had 'gone English', and with whom little contact was maintained. Cultural differentiation usually arose through marriage with a non-French Canadian. While the majority of marriages reported in the informants' kin groups were with French Canadians, each informant could also list marriages outside, but never more than three for a single kin group. They were to be found at all social levels. Informants stressed that such marriages usually meant a loss of contact unless the spouse was a Catholic, spoke French and accepted the assigned kin role. Again, the lateral kin ties were more vulnerable in such situations; the 'priority' relatives generally kept their association. While parents and siblings usually came to accept these marriages, it was the more distant relatives, with whom personal choice was most important, who showed disapproval and dropped the couple, so that their children grew up with a restricted kin knowledge.

## Conclusions

The collected evidence indicates no trend toward transformation of the present French Canadian urban kinship system into the more restricted system reported for the United States. While difficulties were reported in maintaining a united domestic family or an integrated kin group, there is no reason to suppose that these difficulties were caused primarily by urban living. Moreover, many cases were reported where the kin group re-formed after a period of disunity. There are many reasons for believing that the present system will continue. Far from being incompatible, kinship and urbanism among French Canadians seem to have become functionally related. Each urban domestic family, each household, each person, is normally part of a system of obligations arising from the recognition of kinship ties.

The present system is elastic, and can readily adapt itself to different situations. This is due largely to the limitations placed upon kinship recognition by French Canadians. The 'priority' kin are limited in number compared to the total recognition. The formal extension between generations is satisfied by a low frequency of contact. The wide lateral range offers the greatest freedom of choice through the operation of personal preference. Lastly, because the 'priority' claims are related to a small number of large sibling groups, kinship contact and awareness of kinship obligations must always be multiple. The fact that a French Canadian is normally socialized in a large household conditions him at an early age to multiple kinship obligations. The socialization is carried out in a kinship world in which authority is male and narrowly defined, and emotional needs are satisfied through sibling, cousin, mother–child, and grandmother and aunt relationships. The pattern is continued in adult life, but with a greater freedom since each person can have a wide range of personal preference. The fact that personal preference will bring together persons of roughly the same age, status and background, makes for a great deal of unity in these subgroups. These peer groups not only serve as leisure-activity groups, but after marriage are often the kinship group into which the children of a new couple will become socialized.

It is beyond the scope of this paper to go into the psychological implications of this type of socialization, and the possibility of avoiding the

constraint usually attributed to extensive formal kin obligations by manipulating them to suit personal preference. While the whole kinship
range cannot be thus manipulated, and a 'priority' core remains unchanged to give continuity, enough elasticity is obtained to suit a wide
range of situations. Furthermore, because the women are most active in
kinship affairs, and yet not identified with the legal formal authority
structure, kinship is not conceived of as a pattern of strict 'patriarchal'
obligations but as a reciprocal relationship from which much pride,
pleasure and security can be derived. Lastly, as sibling groups are large,
selection according to personal preference does not unduly decrease the
size of the kin group, but allows emotional ties to unite a large number
of kin according to the emphasis placed on emotional preference. The
resulting personality type seems to be that of an individual who, while he
recognizes many kinds of kinship obligations, actually satisfies these
obligations by selecting kin with whom he has the best relationships.

These characteristics of urban French Canadian kinship are no new
development, but seem to have been in existence since the period of New
France. It can be suggested that one of the reasons for this continuity is
its elasticity, already referred to. All informants agreed that there was a
French Canadian family ideal. While not aware of all its implications,
they would verbalize about it and criticize variations from this ideal on
the basis that to cease to behave like a French Canadian was to become
'English'. These ideals about family and kinship were not isolated but
were part of a cultural complex which included the French language as
spoken in Quebec, a specific system of education, membership in the
Catholic Church and various political theories about the status of French
Canadians in Canada. To be a member of a French Canadian kinship
group implied attitudes and beliefs about some or all of these.

In conclusion, some of the theoretical implications of the research can
be pointed out. One of these is the relationship between the size of
sibling groups and kinship behavior. The hypothesis is offered that
socialization in a family of many siblings results in special perceptions of
kinship obligations. It was found that the size of sibling groups tends to
run in families, and that children raised in large families accepted as
normal the fact of having many children and the implications of multiple kinship recognition. French Canadians, one of the most prolific
groups in the Western world, have made the tradition of a large sibling
group one of the ideals of family life. This raises the problem of assessing
the influence of urbanism on French Canadian kinship. One of the most
widely accepted generalizations about kinship is the proposition that the
greater the urbanization, the smaller the kinship range, and that this
apparent result of city life is everywhere the same. A number of writers

believe that the invariable result of urbanization is to reduce the kinship range to the domestic family. While it is to be accepted that there will be a difference in birth rate between rural and urban areas, this does not necessarily imply that urban kinship is doomed to universal disappearance.

Against this hypothesis of universal similarity, recent studies have shown that kinship recognition is compatible with urban life. While there may be a world trend toward urbanization and industrialization, there is little evidence for the disappearance of kinship awareness. The cluster of social characteristics by which urbanism is usually defined, such as population density, specialized functions and a distinct pattern of social relationship, may exist in a variety of cultures. There is apparently a basic cultural difference in the description of kinship as reported in London and in the United States. Perhaps this difference does not arise from fundamental variations in urbanization, but from variations in concepts about the family and kinship.

One study suggested a great deal of uniformity between the rural and urban kinship systems in the United States. While some societies are undoubtedly more urbanized than others, it seems that the critical factors in diminishing kinship recognition are the cultural values of the society, not its degree of urbanization. For instance, French Canadians share what might be called the techniques of the American way of life. Yet the kinship system of the French Canadians of Montreal seems to be fundamentally different from that reported for the United States. These differences, furthermore, are not due to more extensive rural survivals among the French Canadians, or to longer urban conditioning in the United States, but in each instance seem to be part of the established urban way of life, with its cultural values.

Many writers seem to have identified the effects of urbanization as a worldwide process with the effects of the cultural values to be found in the United States. This is understandable, since most studies of urbanization have been carried out in the United States. However, this study of the French Canadians suggests that the relative influences of urbanization and cultural values of kinship must be seen as distinct.

# 18 Raymond W. Firth and Judith Djamour

Family and Kinship in Western Society

Excerpt from Raymond W. Firth and Judith Djamour, 'Kinship in South
Borough', in Raymond W. Firth (ed.), *Two Studies of Kinship in London*,
Athlone Press, 1956, pp. 12–21.

Most sociological studies stress the importance of the elementary family.
Stress is laid upon the household of husband, wife and children as a self-
sufficient social unit. This view is typified by Margaret Mead when she
speaks of the tiny biological family of the modern American three-room
apartment dwellers who have no kin within a thousand miles. This
emphasis is of course justified. But it is apt to lead to two misconceptions.
The first concerns the structure of the system. The existence of terms for
kin outside the immediate family is recognized. But it is often tacitly
assumed that few relations with such kin occur. The second mis-
conception concerns content. It is often taken for granted that even if
such relations do generally occur, they have no special importance. It is
true that in many cases they may seem insignificant. But the critical
element in the lack of family is probably not the supposed low level of
relations but their variability. Whereas in a primitive society one normally expects to have patterns which can be described as universal for
that society, in modern Western conditions there may be a high degree of
variation. The reason for lack of kinship studies is also, however, as
Talcott Parsons has pointed out, that family studies have been oriented to
an understanding of individual adjustment rather than to a comparative
structural perspective.

To an anthropologist, trained to regard extra-familial kinship as a
major structural and organizational feature of any society, all this comes
as something of a surprise. Is there then any contribution he can make
to this problem? He realizes that he must approach it with caution. In the
first place, his knowledge of the institutional content of a Western social
system is usually very limited. Moreover, as Parsons has shown, anthropological methods have been conventionally used in envisaging such a
major structural aspect as kinship in a society as a whole. Their observations cannot yield this easily in large-scale Western conditions. Some
preliminary comparison of Western kinship with the conventional
anthropological field of inquiry seems therefore advisable.

The anthropologist approaching the problems of kinship in a Western society might pose his preliminary questions in some such form as this: are there significant differences between at least some sectors of Western society and some primitive societies? If, as might seem likely, Western kinship is less formal and less noticeable in the social field, is extra-familial kinship important at all in Western society? If kin relations, and in particular extra-familial kin relations, do have social importance, are there sufficient regularities in the behaviour to allow one to speak of a kinship system? If so, then what is the nature of this system?

Let us take up the first question in some detail. The answer would seem to be that significant differences in the kinship field do exist between primitive societies and some sectors of Western society. These can be set out in the following schematic form:

1. The most obvious is a difference in the situation of the elementary family. Structurally and functionally, it juts out in a prominence which has been recognized by the overwhelming attention paid to it by social scientists. In primitive and peasant societies the elementary family is often so embedded in the larger kin unit and in the household based upon this, that historically its separate existence as a structural unit has sometimes been denied. Even now there is a question as to how far it can be properly recognized in joint family and analogous structures in India. By contrast, the elementary family in a sophisticated Western environment is a highly discrete unit in residence, in property holding, in income control and in social affairs.

2. In a Western social field, there tends to be a functional separation of activities in which, for example, occupational roles are clearly marked off from kinship roles. Or, more precisely, while some occupational roles in the domestic circle of the elementary family – bed making, washing-up, care of infants – tend to have a strong association with kinship status, income-producing activities tend to be separate from kinship ties. Compared with major daily work in a primitive community, that in a sophisticated Western community shows a marked lack of economic co-operation with kin. Father and son, or siblings, or uncle and nephew, may never meet in their daily occupations outside the home. This deprives kinship relations of a very important element of the content which they normally have in a primitive society.

3. By comparison with many, though not all, primitive systems, kinship in a Western society tends to be of relatively narrow range. The number of kin of a person tends to be relatively few (though not so scanty as often seems to be imagined) in recognized as well as in operative terms. Moreover, the lack of a classificatory terminology tends to inhibit the

easy assimilation of genealogically remote to near kin for many social purposes, as is so characteristic of most primitive societies.

4. Kin groups – save in the special circumstances of 'upper class' with substantial status and property to transmit – tend to be shallow in depth and relatively amorphous. Formally defined descent groups of corporate type, if not entirely lacking, tend to be difficult to identify and classify. The kin groups outside the elementary family are not structural groups but organizational groups. They are assemblages *ad hoc* from among the total kin of members of the elementary family that would normally come together in virtue of a special social occasion such as Christmas, or personal occasion such as a wedding or funeral.

5. Relations between kin in a Western society tend to be permissive rather than obligatory. There are certain specific obligations by law, as for instance, those of parent to care for young child, or in some circumstances, for son or daughter to contribute to the maintenance of a dependent parent. There are specific legal prohibitions, as rules against incest. But for the most part, the sanctions for relations between kin are moral rather than legal, and have little weight for extra-familial kin.

6. In line with this, there is great variation in kin behaviour, in respect of the same categories of relatives. This variation tends to be very much greater than with similar categories of relatives in a primitive society. Hence the patterns of extra-familial kin behaviour in a Western society are usually not capable of being stated in terms of ideal rules and degree of departure from them. Where they can be discerned they must be expressed as observed regularities. In the sense of a general contrast, the pattern may be said to be statistical rather than normative in character.

In drawing such contrast, it should be pointed out that such 'polarization' is primarily for heuristic purposes. Kinship systems cannot be completely separated and isolated in terms of geography or of complexity and sophistication of type of society in which they occur. But the contrast, though only in terms of relative magnitudes, does focus on some of the most significant features for inquiry.

The answers to the other questions posed have already been suggested in what has been said, and can be given in detail only by the empirical material in chapters II and III [not included here]. But it will be gathered at this point that to an anthropologist, kinship, including extra-familial ties, is found to be socially significant in those sectors of Western society investigated. There are regularities enough to justify its being considered as having a systematic form.

In attempting to define the character of this system one important general point that has emerged is the need to reconsider some of the basic concepts of kinship, if one is to apply them to the data in a Western society. This does not mean that a new conceptual framework is necessary. But the experience of those investigators who have worked on these problems has shown that the definitions of the anthropologist cannot be simply accepted and applied ready-made to this type of material. Difficulties of field technique could be foreseen: what was not so easily apparent was this need for re-appraisal of some of the theoretical framework.

This arises partly from the permissive nature of the rules of Western kinship, and the high degree of variation of kin behaviour. It also comes partly from the relatively amorphous character of extra-familial kin units.

For instance, in an examination of kin group structure, an anthropologist begins soon to ask about descent principles. In general English speech, descent can refer to transmission of property or title by inheritance as well as to transmission of membership in a kin group. But to anthropologists the term is usually restricted to transmission of kin-group membership alone. (There is a broader sense in which it can apply also to any genealogical tie of direct continuity between generations, as when a grandchild is descended from a grandparent, or two persons are both descended from a common ancestor.) As W. H. R. Rivers pointed out, the precise use of the concept of descent is valid only when the group concerned is unilateral in selection of members. The use of the terms has little sense, he says, and therefore little value, where it is applied to bilateral kin groups. Now it is apt to be assumed that the English kinship system exhibits unilateral descent groups. To quote Rivers: 'Thus, our own family system might be regarded as an example of patrilineal descent, in that we take the name of the father; though it is hardly customary to use the term in this case.' Those groups which control landed property by entail largely follow this system. But there are few circumstances, apart from the surname transmission, which seem to entitle the ordinary English family structure to be regarded as a corporate group type. The unilateral or unilineal principle is therefore difficult to identify. So much is this so that various other emphases have been regarded as characteristic. Talcott Parsons writes of the 'multi-lineal' American family, which in essentials is apparently of the same kind as the English.[1]

The whole problem of what is meant by 'being a Smith', and one's

1. The term 'omnidirectional' has also recently been used by some English anthropologists as a principle of kin affiliation.

precise relation to the Joneses if one's mother was a Jones, is more complex than may at first appear.

For general categorization, terms such as aggregate, set, configuration, constellation, web, network, grouping and group are suggested to describe the entity empirically composed by and represented by the people who communicate or come together on certain social occasions because of their kin relations.

More specifically, one can talk of 'extended family' in some circumstances of collective living arrangements or Christmas festivities; and of 'kindred' in orientation to the circumstances of a particular person. But there is considerable difference of emphasis on the degree of structural cohesion perceived in such entities, and on the principles which are thought to activate the people concerned in constituting an entity. Sometimes there seems to enter into the interpretation an element derived from the previous experience of the investigator. An anthropologist, used to more rigid or more highly formalized systems, is apt to be impressed by the degree of flexibility and personal choice in these Western kinship units. Whereas a sociologist, used to the relative flexibility of the Western social arrangements, is apt to be surprised by the degree of patterning discernible in the kinship field when he turns his attention systematically to it.

The English kinship system has come to be described as a bilateral one in view of the relative lack of differentiation in kinship behaviour between mother's and father's kin, apart from transmission of the father's surname to legitimate children. But the term bilateral when applied to kin groups has come to have two meanings. One is to the set of kin who orient their behaviour to a particular person, Ego, and who trace their relationship to him through his father or his mother as the case may be. This set of persons may constitute a group in virtue of their assembly and common operations in respect of Ego on particular occasions. But they constitute a group of personal orientation. Moreover, they are frequently a group only in a theoretical or ideal sense, since they may never actually assemble as a whole. They are in a sense a group of potential mobilization. They may have no actual corporate existence. Again, their boundaries are relatively undefined. There come points at which it is difficult to say whether there are or are not more persons who should be included in the bilateral kin of Ego. Again, even when it is known that certain persons belong genealogically to this group, there may be uncertainty as to whether they regard themselves as in any active sense members of it. So much is this the case that the term group is often denied to this bilateral set of kin. If used at all it is apt to be restricted to those kin who fairly constantly orient social activity to Ego. Furthermore, the group lacks the principle of continuity. Actual continuity indeed may be preserved to the degree that the relations and responsibilities accepted in regard to Ego are regarded as operative also in the case of Ego's children. In this sense, the sporadic and occasional character often attributed to such kin sets may be empirically false; there may in fact be some continuity of relationship from one generation to another. On the other hand the increasing remoteness of genealogical connexion tends to give good reason for an increasing remoteness of social connexion. Here, proximity of residence and childhood familiarity may play a great part in the maintenance of kin ties. For example, children of Ego's father's father's brother's sons may be reckoned as close patrilineal kin and this relationship may continue without evident diminution to their respective offspring. Such continuity may be stimulated by the absence of siblings for Ego.

It is in this way that the conversion of bilateralism into multilineality occurs. Continuance of the connexion through either mother or father or both into the next generation and the process of cousin assimilation into a sibling position means that the original duplex field of selection has now become multiplied to provide four, eight or more sets of kin who can be referred to.

What is difficult, however, is to ascribe the term descent to this process. In one sense Ego is a member of the set of persons oriented towards him. But this membership is of a different kind than that of the unit ordinarily described as a descent group. By descent is implied the limitation and recognition of the continuity of kin ties for certain social purposes (in particular, membership of continuing named groups) and the accent is on the notion of continuity. In many of the societies studied by anthropologists, these continuing named groups are unilineal in descent principle. Membership of them must be traced genealogically, but the genealogical tie may be through either mother or father, or indeed in some cases through either a male or female more remote ancestor. Such is the type of descent group, corporate in its activities, which has been described as bilateral (or ambilateral).

Different societies vary in the amount of selectivity allowed in claiming and receiving membership. In some, such as the Maori, a person may effectively claim membership of both his father's and his mother's groups, the effective operation of his claim in terms of land and status rights, for example, depending largely upon his residential situation. Ultimately, without any validation by residence, his claim becomes extinguished. (This is what I have termed the ambilateral type.) In others again, choice seems to be more rigid and the person is allowed to belong to one or other of his mother's or father's groups but not both (for this type the term utrolateral has been proposed).

In all these cases, there are, empirically, kin groups of a continuing kind operating multiple social functions (excluding rights over land). But they are not operating unilineally. These form a bilateral kin group in the second sense.

The question is, to what category do the kin groups in the English system belong? As mentioned later, the first term to describe them is patrinominal because of the use of the father's name in transmission of membership.[2] As also described later, the kin relation with the mother is extremely strong. But it does not appear as a formal defining principle and hence does not entitle the system to be termed matrilateral. Whatever term is chosen to designate the system will depend upon the emphasis seen in it by the investigator.

It would seem that the English system has three recognizable types of group. One is the elementary family which for social convenience is referred to patrinominally. The second is an extension of this, usually in three-generation form with incorporation of affines in the form of children's spouses. Again, for social convenience this is commonly referred to, patrinominally, in terms of the original father. In such cases, some grandchildren, offsprings of daughters, are included matrinominally in virtue of the attachment of their mother to her original family, but this represents incorporation only on limited occasions and for limited purposes, as Christmas dinner or a birthday celebration. For other occasions, as for example at school, these daughter's children are known patrinominally. The patrinominally extended family is then only a partially operative, and not a completely regular, social unit. It may well be that for these assemblages and for other contacts between members of this group, it is the original mother who is the focus, the enduring tie. But it should be noted that for naming purposes the group is usually called by her husband's surname.

Finally, there is the type of group which assembles at a wedding or funeral and in which may be represented most of the patrinominal kin groups which have traceable genealogical relation to Ego. This is assembled on a bilateral basis. But in this it is similar to kin groups all over the world.

The upshot then is that in the English kinship system no single emphasis seems to be outstanding enough to give its quality to the system as a whole. There is some patrilineal bias expressed in particular through

2. It has been argued that it might be termed matrinominal since the child always takes the mother's surname. If the mother is married, she bears her husband's surname, if she is unmarried the child takes her surname. But the normal adoption of the husband's surname by the wife renders the term patrinominal for the descent principle appropriate.

the naming system and through some occupational preferences. There is in the ordinary social field a strong matrilineal bias with particular emotional significance. If a single term is felt necessary it is probably best to adopt the suggestion of W. H. R. Rivers and to refer to the English kinship system as a familial system, bearing in mind, *inter alia*, the lack of descent groups of depth.

So far we have discussed mainly kinship structure. What of the content of kin relations? Mention has already been made of the marked lack of economic co-operation with kin in daily life. Compared with the working of a primitive community, the occupational diversity in a Western industrialized society bars easy kinship relations in the field of production. This means that kinship, if it is to operate, must do other things to give body to the relationships.

In many primitive societies, part of this body is given by ritual. In the nineteenth century it might have been said that for certain sections of British society some kinship content was to be found in the ritual field. The custom whereby the younger son might enter the Church and receive a family living is marginal to the problem. But the reciprocal moral and ritual support between family observances and those of the Church was important in many social spheres. This now operates to a much less degree. But kin group relations would still seem to be fairly intimately linked with ritual relations in some circles, say in those of the conventional nonconformist or orthodox Jewish families. Judaism, for instance, has been rightly called a family religion, but it could also be termed a kin-group religion since the emphasis is not simply upon the elementary family but upon the quasi-kinship of the congregation. Moreover, certain kin associations, as in the nomination of Cohen and Levi in the readings of excerpts from the Law, rest putatively upon descent and kinship recognition in traditional terms. However, in British society at large the importance of the ritual factor in kinship is probably slight.

The significance of kin ties outside the elementary family in contemporary British society lies primarily in the positive social contacts in visiting, in recreation, in exchange of news and advice, in attendance on ceremonial occasions and at crises of life, and in the moral obligations that frequently attach to such contacts.

Kinship recognition and relations are important as a part of social living in general rather than as components of specific economic, political or ritual aspects of institutions.

The problems arising may be further expressed in this way. What, under British conditions, is the importance of kin outside the elementary family? What is the character of recognition, the structure and organization of their relationships? Can significant patterns be seen in the apparent maze of interpersonal relations in complex urban conditions where each individual is apparently following his own wishes – significant, that is, for the anthropologist in his frame of reference as a student of comparative social behaviour? In urban conditions, it is generally assumed that there is a marked tendency for individuals and the elementary families in which they are set to live and operate in comparative isolation. This seems to be not merely an inference from empirical observation of the kinds of relationships which people have in an urban environment. It also seems to involve emotional and aesthetic, even moral elements, with the implication that such isolation (if it exists) is repugnant to good living and to be deplored. There is also the set of interpretations which link this notion of isolation with the development of particular kind of facets of personality and character.[3] Precise information is thus desirable about the definition of the kinship universe of an individual and of the elementary family, and of the social use made of it. (Indices of definition of the kinship universe are discussed later.)

The reputed isolation of an individual or elementary family is thought to be due not merely to the general demands, occupational and other, of large-scale social life in modern conditions. It is thought to be specifically related to the severance of ties from kinsfolk by geographical dispersion. The degree of propinquity of members of the elementary family to their kin outside the immediate household may, therefore, be important as a diagnostic feature in the interpretation of kinship recognition and inter-relationship. In every society, an individual needs recognition and support from others in his activities. In modern Western society, he gets it from the members of his elementary family, from his friends, from members of work groups, recreational groups, etc. But it may be argued that not only an individual but also a social unit, such as an elementary family, needs recognition and support. Here, too, it gets this from friends, from associations which it enters into as a group, for example, a church, a sports club, etc. But one important field for recognition and support of the family's activities is that of its kin. In some primitive societies, as in tribal Australia or in Tikopia, every personal contact with a member of the community must be with a kinsman. In others, some choice between kin and non-kin is possible, though there is

3. Three categories of phenomena may be seen under the general head of 'isolation': (a) residential separation; (b) separation from others as regards services and contacts; (c) a psychological, objective feeling of deprivation, better termed loneliness. These three categories are by no means always coincident. Indeed, physical and social isolation may not necessarily imply loneliness at all, but positive preference for separation. We are concerned here primarily with the relation between residential and social separation, i.e. (a) and (b) and not directly with (c) at all.

always some kin base. But the degree of selectivity in contemporary Western society allows not merely of choice between kin, or between kin and non-kin, but also rejection of kin altogether. This is largely true also of the modern African or Asian living in cities, though there may be some difference of degree. But if one assumes that in modern urban life relations with people who live close to one are much more attenuated than they are in rural life – in the urban situation one may not even know one's next-door neighbour at all – then one might put forward a hypothesis. In rural English life, an elementary family is supported by its kin primarily because they are *de facto* in close geographical proximity; and this, even in the rural scene, implies co-operation. In urban English life, on the other hand, an elementary family tends to be supported by its kin because of the lack of full neighbour relations.[4] But experience suggests that such a hypothesis is not likely to be borne out. The general patterns of industrial living have penetrated modern Western rural society far further than is often thought. For instance, in a remote Dorset village, a young man who had grown up there, but been away for a while, said rather ruefully that he did not know the people who were living two doors from him. Even in a country village the neighbour relations have far more of the impersonal quality often attributed solely to urban living than is commonly realized. We have referred to such an hypothesis, even though it may be unacceptable, in order to emphasize the relation between nearness or separation of residence and maintenance or obliteration of kin relations. Any investigation of kinship in an urban environment soon brings out the great degree of variation in relations with kin. The reasons for this are complex, and their force in various types of kin situation is not entirely clear. But among the correlates of the varying recognition and maintenance of kin ties would appear to be the following: residential accessibility; common economic interests, as in occupation, or in property holding; composition of household; composition of elementary family, especially as regards that of the sibling group; the biological range of persons available for kin recognition; the existence of key personalities in the kin field, to take the initiative in kin contacts; and the phase of development in which any given family finds itself. Through these combinations of circumstances runs the element of personal selection, leading again to the question of what regularities can be discerned.

4. One might expect to find then that people living so in rural England would tend to travel much less to visit their kin than people so living in London. This is a question on which we have as yet no adequate information.

Raymond W. Firth and Judith Djamour  145

# 19 Elizabeth Bott

Conjugal Roles and Social Networks

Excerpts from Elizabeth Bott, 'Urban families: conjugal roles and social networks', *Human Relations*, vol. 8, 1955, pp. 345–50.

In this paper I should like to report some of the results of an intensive study of twenty London families. [. . .] Considerable variations were found to occur in the way husbands and wives performed their conjugal roles. At one extreme was a family in which the husband and wife carried out as many tasks as possible separately and independently of each other. There was a strict division of labour within the household, in which she had her tasks and he had his. He gave her a set amount of housekeeping money, and she had little idea of how much he earned or how he spent the money he kept for himself. In their leisure time, he went to football matches with his friends, whereas she visited her relatives or went to a cinema with a neighbour. With the exception of festivities with relatives, this husband and wife spent very little of their leisure time together. They did not consider that they were unusual in this respect. On the contrary, they felt that their behaviour was typical of their social circle. At the other extreme was a family in which husband and wife shared as many activities and spent as much time together as possible. They stressed that husband and wife should be equals; all major decisions should be made together, and even in minor household matters they should help one another as much as possible. This norm was carried out in practice. In their division of labour, many tasks were shared or interchangeable. The husband often did the cooking and sometimes the washing and ironing. The wife did the gardening and often the household repairs as well. Much of their leisure time was spent together, and they shared similar interests in politics, music, literature and in entertaining friends. Like the first couple, this husband and wife felt that their behaviour was typical of their social circle, except that they felt they carried the interchangeability of household tasks a little further than most people.

One may sum up the differences between these two extremes by saying that the first family showed considerable segregation between husband and wife in their role-relationship, whereas in the second family the conjugal role-relationship was as joint as possible. In between these two extremes there were many degrees of variation.

A *joint conjugal role-relationship* is one in which husband and wife carry out many activities together, with a minimum of task differentiation and separation of interests; in such cases husband and wife not only plan the affairs of the family together, but also exchange many household tasks and spend much of their leisure time together. A *segregated conjugal role-relationship* is one in which husband and wife have a clear differentiation of tasks and a considerable number of separate interests and activities; in such cases, husband and wife have a clearly defined division of labour into male tasks and female tasks; they expect to have different leisure pursuits; the husband has his friends outside the home and the wife has hers. It should be stressed, however, that these are only differences of degree. All families must have some division of labour between husband and wife; all families must have some joint activities.

Early in the research, it seemed likely that these differences in degree of segregation of conjugal roles were related somehow to forces in the social environment of the families. In first attempts to explore these forces, an effort was made to explain such segregation in terms of social class. This attempt was not very successful. The husbands who had the most segregated role-relationships with their wives had manual occupations, and the husbands who had the more joint role-relationships with their wives were professionals, but there were several working-class families that had relatively little segregation and there were several professional families in which segregation was considerable. An attempt was also made to relate degree of segregation to the type of local area in which the family lived, since the data suggested that the families with most segregation lived in homogeneous areas of low population turnover, whereas the families with predominantly joint role-relationships lived in heterogeneous areas of high population turnover. Once again, however, there were several exceptions. But there was a more important difficulty in these attempts to correlate segregation of conjugal roles with class position and type of local area. The research was not designed to produce valid statistical correlations, for which a very different method would have been necessary. Our aim was to make a study of the interrelation of various social and psychological factors within each family considered as a social system. Attempts at rudimentary statistical correlation did not make clear how one factor affected another; it seemed impossible to explain exactly how the criteria for class position or the criteria for different types of local area were actually producing an effect on the internal role structure of the family.

It therefore appeared that attempts to correlate segregation of conjugal roles with factors selected from the generalized social environment of the family would not yield a meaningful interpretation. Leaving social class and neighbourhood composition to one side for the time being, I turned to look more closely at the immediate environment of the families, that is, at their actual external relationships with friends, neighbours, relatives, clubs, shops, places of work and so forth. This approach proved to be more fruitful.

First, it appeared that the external social relationships of all families assumed the form of a *network* rather than the form of an organized group.[1] In an organized group, the component individuals make up a larger social whole with common aims, interdependent roles and a distinctive subculture. In network formation, on the other hand, only some but not all of the component individuals have social relationships with one another. For example, supposing that a family, X, maintains relationships with friends, neighbours and relatives who may be designated as A, B, C, D, E, F ... N, one will find that some but not all of these external persons know one another. They do not form an organized group in the sense defined above. B might know A and C but none of the others; D might know F without knowing A, B, C or E. Furthermore, all of these persons will have friends, neighbours and relatives of their own who are not known by family X. In a network, the component external units do not make up a larger social whole; they are not surrounded by a common boundary.

Secondly, although all the research families belonged to networks rather than to groups, there was considerable variation in the *connectedness* of their networks. By connectedness I mean the extent to which the people known by a family know and meet one another independently of the family. I use the term *dispersed network* to describe a network in which there are few relationships amongst the component units, and the term *highly connected network* to describe a network in which there are many such relationships. The difference is represented very schematically in Figure 1. Each family has a network containing five external units, but the network of Family X is more connected than that of Y. There are nine relationships amongst the people of X's network whereas there are only three amongst the people of Y's network. X's network is highly connected, Y's is dispersed.

1. In sociological and anthropological literature, the term 'group' is commonly used in at least two senses. In the first sense it is a very broad term used to describe any collectivity whose members are alike in some way; this definition would include categories, logical classes and aggregates as well as more cohesive social units. The second usage is much more restricted; in this sense, the units must have some distinctive interdependent social relationships with one another; categories, logical classes and aggregates are excluded. To avoid confusion I use the term 'organized group' when it becomes necessary to distinguish the second usage from the first.

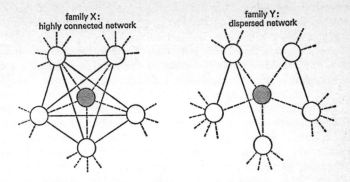

family X:
highly connected network

family Y:
dispersed network

Figure 1 Schematic comparison of the networks of two families. The black circles represent the family; the white circles represent the units of the family's network. The broken lines represent the relationships of the family with external units; the solid lines represent the relationships of the members of the network with one another. The dotted lines leading off from the white circles indicate that each member of a family's network maintains relationships with other people who are not included in the family's network. The representation is, of course, highly schematic; a real family would have many more than five external units in its network.

A detailed examination of the research data reveals that the degree of segregation of conjugal roles is related to the degree of network connectedness. Those families that had a high degree of segregation in the role-relationship of husband and wife had a highly connected network; many of their friends, neighbours and relatives knew one another. Families that had a relatively joint role-relationship between husband and wife had a dispersed network; few of their relatives, neighbours and friends knew one another. There were many degrees of variation in between these two extremes. On the basis of our data, I should therefore like to put forward the following hypothesis: *the degree of segregation in the role-relationship of husband and wife varies directly with the connectedness of the family's social network*. The more connected the network, the more segregation between the roles of husband and wife. The more dispersed the network, the less segregation between the roles of husband and wife. This relationship between network connectedness and segregation of conjugal roles will be more fully illustrated and discussed below.

No claim is made here that network connectedness is the only factor affecting segregation of conjugal roles. Among the other variables affecting the way conjugal roles are performed, the personalities of husband and wife are of crucial importance. We emphasize the effect of network connectedness, however, because the importance of this variable has been insufficiently stressed in previous studies of family role structure.

It thus appears that if one is to understand segregation of conjugal roles, one should examine the effect of the family's immediate social environment of friends, neighbours, relatives and institutions. The question remains, however, as to why some families should have highly connected networks whereas others have dispersed networks. In part, network connectedness depends on the family themselves. One family may choose to introduce their friends, neighbours and relatives to one another, whereas another may not. One family may move around a great deal so that its network becomes dispersed, whereas another family may stay put. But these choices are limited and shaped by a number of forces over which the family does not have direct control. It is at this point that the total social environment becomes relevant. The economic and occupational system, the structure of formal institutions, the ecology of cities and many other factors affect the connectedness of networks, and limit and shape the decisions that families make. Among others, factors associated with social class and neighbourhood composition affect segregation of conjugal roles, not solely and not primarily through direct action on the internal structure of the family, but indirectly through their effect on its network. Conceptually, the network stands between the family and the total social environment. The connectedness of a family's network depends, on the one hand, on certain forces in the total environment and, on the other hand, on the personalities of the members of the family and on the way they react to these forces.

# 20 Tom Lupton and C. Shirley Wilson

The Kinship Connexions of 'Top Decision Makers'

Excerpts from Tom Lupton and C. Shirley Wilson, 'The social backgrounds and connections of "top decision makers"', *Manchester School of Economic and Social Studies*, vol. 27, 1959, pp. 33–51.

The following are the six categories of 'top decision makers' we have chosen to study:

A.  Cabinet Ministers and other Ministers of the Crown.
B.  Senior Civil Servants.
C.  Directors of the Bank of England.
D.  Directors of the 'Big Five' banks.
E.  Directors of 'City' firms.
F.  Directors of insurance companies.

Category A includes all the persons named. Category B includes the twelve senior members of the Treasury Staff and the Permanent Secretaries and their immediate deputies of twenty-one other ministries. Category C includes all directors of the Bank of England (as listed by Mr Cobbold before the Tribunal). Category D comprises all directors of the 'Big Five'. Category E includes the directors of fourteen merchant banks or discount houses, several of which were mentioned before the Tribunal. Some of these are private banks, others public companies, but all have an authorized capital of two million pounds or more. We have taken the directors of only eight insurance companies, all with an authorized capital of over three million pounds to make up category F. The selection of these eight out of all insurance companies with authorized capital of over three million pounds was not entirely random. We made sure that the two large companies mentioned in the evidence were included. The analysis of the education, club membership and connexions of kinship and affinity, is based entirely on published data. [. . .]

The evidence we shall assemble is of a different order to that we have so far studied, and we shall say something to introduce it. It might occur to some readers that the most important feature of the diagrams we present below is the recurrence of certain long established family names, and they might wish to read significance into this in the light of other knowledge and interests, or of preconceived ideas. Others might argue that the diagrams mean nothing because they do not include certain prominent families, or because they are incomplete and biased, and so on. That is why we want to make it clear at the outset that, for this analysis, the diagrams are only intended to show the connexions of kinship and affinity of some persons who are members of our six categories of decision makers. We used the following procedure: we began by taking persons who were prominent in the Tribunal proceedings, for example Lord Kindersley and Mr Cameron Cobbold. We traced the names of parents, siblings, spouses and children, and constructed a small 'family tree'. By following up the names of paternal and maternal kin it often proved possible to join the 'family trees' together into a kinship diagram.[1]

We have not been able to trace the kinship connexions of all persons in the six categories, and it is only possible to present a limited amount of the material so far gathered. To include all connexions of kinship and affinity for even a few dozen people would clearly require a great deal of space and demand greater resources of time and personnel than those available. There may be no kin connexions between a great many of the people we have selected; and there are persons represented on the diagrams who belong to none of the six categories. This has partly arisen because we had already the kin and affinal connexions of some people referred to at the Tribunal before we extended the scope of inquiry.

For ease of exposition the material is presented in a series of small abridged diagrams. The names of some persons who link one diagram with another are enclosed in black rectangles with numbers of linked diagrams in small circles attached. Persons who are members of one or more of the six categories have the appropriate group letter or letters below their names.[2] The names of some persons who are directors of other concerns, industrial or financial and commercial, are indicated, where appropriate, with the letters 'G' and 'H'.

We now trace some of the connexions illustrated, indicating links between diagrams, links which would make one chart in reality. It would take too long to trace every connexion on all the diagrams; the reader is invited to complete this task for himself.

Figure 1 shows some of the connexions of Mr C. F. Cobbold, Governor of the Bank of England and a member of a family of landed gentry. He is related on his father's side to the late Lt.-Col. John Cob-

1. Properly speaking, a diagram of both kinship and affinity. Triangles represent males, and circles females. Unshaded signs represent living people [i.e. in 1959 – Ed.]. The equals sign signifies a marriage connexion and the asterisk a former marriage connexion. ['½' indicates a half-brother or half-sister, and '1' and '2' refer to first and second marriages – Ed.]

2. For reasons of space we have had to shorten some names and titles; we trust no one will take offence at this.

bold, who married a daughter of the 9th Duke of Devonshire. Lt.-Col. Cobbold's sister married Sir Charles Hambro, a Director of the Bank of England. Lt.-Col. H. E. Hambro married the widow of the 5th Earl of Cadogan, whose grandson married a daughter of Lt.-Col. Cobbold (see Figure 9).

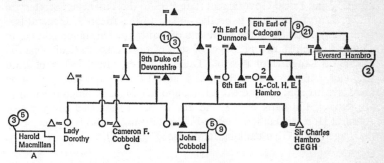

Figure 1

Figure 2 traces links established by the marriage of Sir Everard Hambro with a relative of Lord Norman, who was formerly Governor of the Bank of England. A cousin of Lord Norman married an uncle of the present Home Secretary, the Rt Hon. R. A. Butler. A daughter of this marriage married Sir George Abell, a Director of the Bank of England whose brother-in-law, Mr Nicholas Norman Butler, married into the Hambro family.

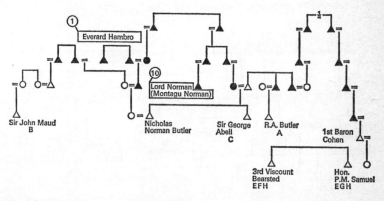

Figure 2

Tom Lupton and C. Shirley Wilson 153

Figure 3 illustrates the marriages of other daughters of the 9th Duke of Devonshire, among them that of Lady Dorothy, wife of the Prime Minister and sister-in-law to Lt.-Col. John Cobbold. One of her cousins (father's brother's daughter) married the 28th Earl of Crawford, whose son, Lord Balniel, is Parliamentary Private Secretary to the Minister of Housing and Local Government (late PPS to the Financial Secretary to the Treasury). The Earl is brother-in-law to the Attorney-General (see Figure 15), and also to the Marquess of Salisbury. This name takes us to Figure 4 which shows marriages of sons of Lord Eustace Cecil. One son married a daughter of the 10th Duke of Leeds, father-in-law of Lord Chandos, Chairman of A.E.I. (see Figure 12). Another son was Baron Rockley; his son, the present Baron, and Mr M. J. Babington Smith (a Director of the Bank of England and of A.E.I.) married daughters of Admiral Hon. Sir Hubert Meade-Fetherstonhaugh, who is connected by marriage to the Glyn banking family (see Figure 21).

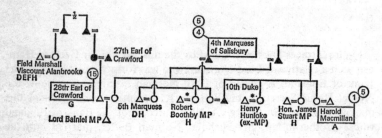

Figure 3

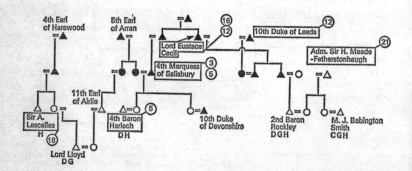

Figure 4

154  The Family

The 4th Marquess of Salisbury connects Figures 4 and 5. His daughter, sister of the present Marquess, married Baron Harlech, the father of the Minister of State for Foreign Affairs, and father-in-law of the Prime Minister's son. Figure 5 also connects with Figure 1, through the late Lt.-Col. John Cobbold; he was related on his mother's side to the 7th Earl of Dunmore, whose granddaughter married Mr D. A. Stirling, a 'Big Five' director. Her brother, the late Viscount Fincastle, brings us to Figure 7. He married a daughter of the 2nd Baron Wyfold; another daughter is married to a son of Sir George Schuster, the brother-in-law of the Chairman of the Tribunal, Lord Chief Justice Parker.

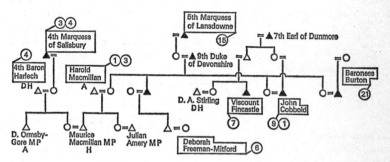

Figure 5

Figure 6 traces some of the connexions of the Prime Minister's nephew by marriage, the 11th Duke of Devonshire, a brother-in-law of the writer Nancy Mitford; she married a son of Lord Rennell. Lord Rennell's wife is a sister of Lord Bicester, a senior director of Morgan Grenfell and Co. and a Director of the Bank of England. Lord Bicester, a witness at the Tribunal, was the 'Rufie' mentioned in the evidence. Lord Rennell links Figures 6 and 22, for one of Nancy Mitford's sisters was married to Lord Moyne, grandson of the 1st Earl of Iveagh. Figure 16 shows that Lord Rennell is also connected to the Keswick family by the marriage of his sister to a brother-in-law of J. H. Keswick. Mr W. J. Keswick, Director of the Bank of England, is related through his wife to Lord Lovat, brother-in-law of two Conservative Members of Parliament.

Figures 8 and 10 are joined by the name of the wife of Mr M. R. Hely-Hutchinson, whose brother is father-in-law to Mr J. M. Stevens, a Director of the Bank of England, who gave evidence at the Tribunal. Her father's family was linked by marriage to Baron Ashcombe, whose brother married a niece of Lord Norman. (Her later marriage is shown in Figure 19.) Baron Norman's brother's wife was a daughter of the 4th Earl

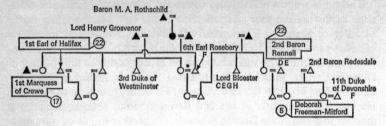

Figure 6

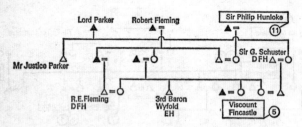

Figure 7

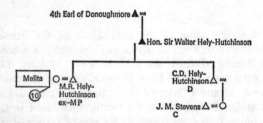

Figure 8

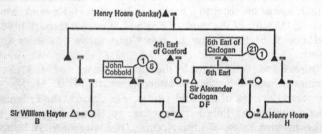

Figure 9

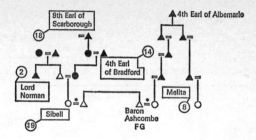

Figure 10

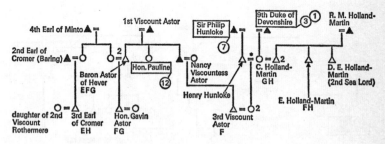

Figure 11

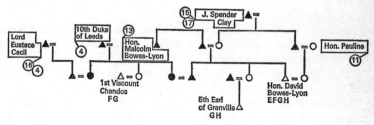

Figure 12

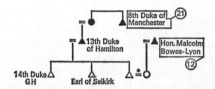

Figure 13

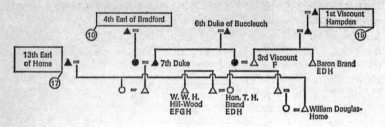

Figure 14

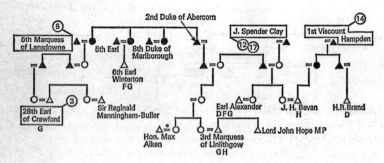

Figure 15

of Bradford, whose grandson, the 6th Earl, is a Crown Estate Commissioner. Another daughter of the Earl of Bradford married the 7th Duke of Buccleuch, brother-in-law to the 3rd Viscount Hampden. Viscount Hampden's son (now the 4th Viscount), managing director of Lazard's, was also a witness at the Tribunal.

The name of Viscount Hampden links Figures 14 and 15, for the 1st Viscount's daughter was mother to Mr J. H. Bevan, brother-in-law of Earl Alexander of Tunis. Earl Alexander married a daughter of the 5th Earl of Lucan, whose wife was a daughter of Mr J. Spender Clay. This brings us back to the diagrams 11 and 12, by-passed in the previous paragraph. A son of Mr J. Spender Clay married a daughter of the 1st Viscount Astor. Figure 11 shows the Astor–Devonshire link; Figure 12 shows that the granddaughter of Mr J. Spender Clay, married the Hon. David Bowes-Lyon, and traces some other marriage connexions of members of his family. A daughter of the Hon. Malcolm Bowes-Lyon married a son of the 13th Duke of Hamilton; another son is First Lord of the Admiralty. The 14th Duke is Lord Steward of the Queen's Household.

Mr H. C. B. Mynors, Deputy Governor of the Bank of England and witness at the Tribunal, is descended on his mother's side from a sister of Mr J. Spender Clay (see Figure 17). His brother, and the Earl of Home, Minister of State for Commonwealth Relations, married sisters, members of the Lyttleton family. The Earl's brother, William Douglas-Home, son-in-law of the 4th Viscount Hampden, links this diagram with Figure 14. Further Lyttleton connexions are shown on Figure 18. The

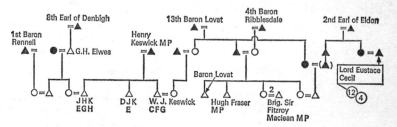

Figure 16

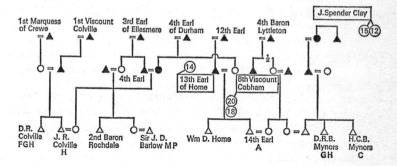

Figure 17

son of Lord Chandos (Oliver Lyttleton) married a daughter of Sir Alan Lascelles (Figure 4), brother-in-law of the 1st Baron Lloyd. The first wife of Lord Chandos's father was a member of the Tennant family, also referred to in the last diagram. This repeats the name of the late Mr R. H. Benson. One of his sons married a daughter of the 2nd Earl of Dudley (Figure 21). The Earl's sister married the 4th Baron Wolverton and a daughter of this marriage became the wife of Mr Nigel Birch, M P. He was Economic Secretary to the Treasury at the time of the decision to raise the Bank Rate and also a member of the Keswick shooting party mentioned in the evidence, a party which also included a member of the

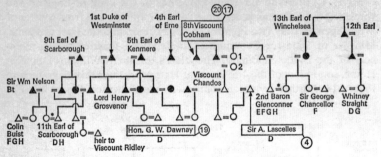

Figure 18

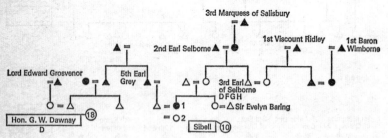

Figure 19

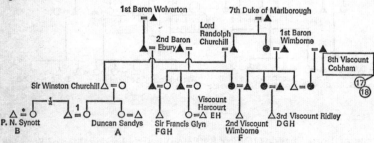

Figure 20

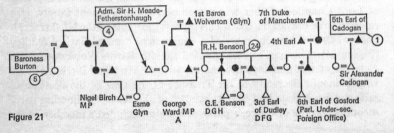

Figure 21

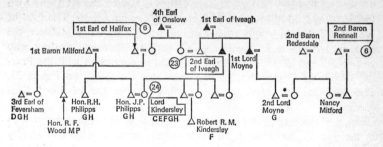

Figure 22

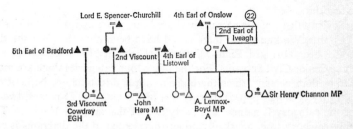

Figure 23

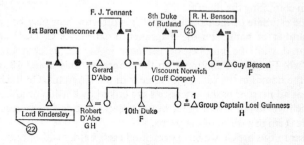

Figure 24

Hambro Bank family. Figure 21 also shows two other members of the Government, the Secretary of State for Air, brother of the 3rd Earl of Dudley, and the Earl of Gosford, Parliamentary Under-Secretary of State to the Foreign Office. Their two families are linked by a marriage in the previous generation.

The next diagram (22) introduces Lord Kindersley, Director of the Bank of England and a prominent Tribunal witness. His brother married a niece of the 2nd Earl of Iveagh, father-in-law of the Rt Hon. Alan Lennox-Boyd, MP, Minister of State for Colonial Affairs. The Earl of Iveagh is father-in-law to a sister of another Conservative Minister, the Rt Hon. John Hare, MP, whose wife is sister to Viscount Cowdray, who was mentioned in evidence at the Tribunal in connexion with the Pearson Group of Companies. These connexions are shown on Figure 23. The final diagram refers to some further connexions of Lord Kindersley.

Some of the diagrams, for example Figure 9, have not been referred to in the text. To have traced all the ramifications of kinship and affinity through all the diagrams would have been confusing, and would have obscured our main aim, that of tracing links between members of the six categories.

Seventy-three of the persons in the six categories appear in the kinship diagrams. We know that there could have been more had not the diagrams been abridged. Eight Ministers are included in the diagrams; and three Senior Civil Servants. For the other four categories there are more names than persons, since there are multiple directorships. Nine of the category C names appear, twenty-five of the category D names, twenty of the category E names, and thirty-two of the category F names. The only category to be markedly under-represented in the diagrams is category B (Senior Civil Servants) with only three included of a total of seventy-three in the category. This may arise partly from the method used in compiling the diagrams.

Some estimate of the extent of multiple directorships may be gained if the number of names on the diagrams in categories C, D, E and F is compared with the number of persons: eighty-six as compared with sixty-two. Finally, in comment on the diagrams, only about 18 per cent of all the names in the categories appear in the diagrams. On the hypothesis that all persons in the categories are linked by kinship or affinity (one to which we do not subscribe) it would take a great deal more research to include them in a series of diagrams.

So far in this article we have presented facts baldly without attempting to assess their meaning and significance. It would have been unwise to have done so in view of the bias of the sample and the incompleteness of the data. Our study must be regarded, then, mainly as a contribution to the 'ethnography' of finance, politics and administration. But we cannot conclude without attempting briefly to relate what we have said to one aspect of social structure which is of particular interest to us.

We have referred to the tradition of intermarriage between banking families. Also by tradition, some merchant bankers become directors of the Bank of England. It is not surprising then that the kinship diagrams show connexions between directors of merchant banks, and between merchant banks and directors of the Bank of England. Nor is it surprising that we find that positions in certain firms are occupied by adjacent generations of the same family. The positions of chairman of Lazard Bros. and director of the Bank of England, for example, are now occupied by Lord Kindersley and were once occupied by his father.

What might seem surprising is that kinship connexions of this kind have persisted through many changes in the scale and functions of banking, in the organization of industry and in the complexity of politics. Bagehot, referring to the family basis of private banking at the end of last century, argued that it was inappropriate for modern large-scale organization. Weber has also argued that bureaucratic, 'civil-service-type' structure, in which recruitment and promotion are based on specific technical qualifications, and in which authority vests in the office and not in the person, is the most appropriate to modern conditions, while traditional structures are unsuitable from the point of view of effectiveness. But Weber also argues that, for effectiveness' sake, decision making and execution ought to be separate. And he notes that: '... administrative structures based on different principles intersect with bureaucratic organization'.

Some of the organizations to which we have referred seem to have the separation of decision making and executive functions to which Weber refers. Possibly they incorporate both traditionalistic and bureaucratic structure. They have both directors and the managers, generally different sets of persons, possibly of different social background and training. While there have been studies of the influence of kinship as a mode of succession amongst managers, we are not aware of any study which has extended to boards of directors.

Weber's point about the intersection of different structural principles has not been followed up by empirical research in the area covered in this article. Gouldner's examination of some hypotheses derived from Weber in the light of facts about factory social structure could be taken as a model for such work.

The intersection of different social principles has another, individual aspect, that of role conflict. Our evidence shows that many people occupy several social roles. For example, a person may have one role in a kinship system, be a member of one or more boards of directors, and a member of various clubs and associations.

The evidence at the Parker Tribunal referred in many places to this problem, but especially as it related to the dual roles of director of a merchant bank and of the Bank of England, which were occupied by Lord Kindersley and Mr W. J. Keswick. Commenting generally on this kind of problem, Mr Cobbold addressed the Parker Tribunal as follows:

It seems to me that a similar position often arises both in business matters and, more generally, in other walks of life, where an honest man must often divorce one set of interests from another. . . . The position arises almost every day in banking, where a banker is not expected to use, for his bank's profit, secret information about a customer's affairs;

and:

. . . the existence of the problem (even if it arises infrequently) must pose the question whether the present arrangement is on balance best suited to the national interest. I am most strongly of the opinion that it is.

Mr Cobbold seemed aware that there were disadvantages in a situation where individuals were faced, as a consequence of discrepancy between structural principles, with conflicts of loyalty or allegiance. But he was personally convinced that these were outweighed by the advantages. This raises a general problem of comparative social structure. The field we have ourselves surveyed provides extensive data relevant to this problem. These data suggest that 'top decision makers' as well as being linked by kinship, business interests and similar background, are also divided by competing, even conflicting interests. Indeed, kinship itself, in certain circumstances, may act as a divisive as well as a uniting force.

To carry out the research into the problems we have briefly outlined would require investigation of a wider field than we have surveyed, and the use of techniques other than those we have used. Interviews, direct observation of behaviour, complete quantitative analysis of such items as leisure time activities, as well as the construction of complete kinship diagrams would be necessary. This latter technique would close many gaps in knowledge of British social structure. Sociologists, including ourselves, have tended to concentrate on the study of working class groups or small local communities where there is much knowledge of the operation of kinship in social life. For our 'top decision makers' we have only biographical material, inspired comment, and little more. It is possible that sociologists have avoided the problem of kinship in 'higher circles' because of the formidable problems presented for empirical field research. We can see that there may be many problems of this kind but there is no reason why the published sources of data should not be fully used.

# 21 H. Kent Geiger

The Family in Soviet Russia

Excerpt from H. Kent Geiger, *The Family in Soviet Russia*, Harvard University Press, 1968, pp. 96–104.

It is clear that responsibility, reproduction and child rearing were in favor at the end of Stalin's régime, and that stable marriages, large families and self-discipline were now more important to the régime than individual freedom, sex equality and ideological consistency.

Equally as fascinating as the story of how Stalin's régime decisively changed its position toward the family is the question of why it did so. A great deal has been written on the subject, and many writers have concluded that the Soviet experience proves that the family cannot be dispensed with. This conclusion is certainly too strong, but it is difficult to establish a definitive interpretation. Perhaps all the evidence on why the new position was adopted will never come to light, for it may be that Stalin simply made a personal decision which he never bothered to explain to his colleagues or to justify in any other form. Interpretations of the new family policy offered by both Soviet and Western analysts are often overly monistic, assigning exclusive weight to only one condition or reasonable cause. It is more likely that the switch in policy was overdetermined, and that at least five sets of conditions were at work: (a) the specific and concrete social problems of the kind described in the preceding chapters [not included here] which called for attention to the family's function of social control; (b) the concessionary mood of Stalin's régime, anxious to gain a measure of popular unity and loyalty among the people, who were by and large in favor of the new, more conservative family policy; (c) a new international situation with a reassuring of the Soviet Union's immediate future on the world political scene and the link between family life and birth rate; (d) the general shift in Soviet policy toward discipline and control over individual freedom, which may simply have swept the family, as it did other institutions of social control and indoctrination, back into a more legitimate status; and (e) a significant and explicit reorientation in Soviet Marxism, stressing the active role of the superstructure in inducing social change.

Several of the social problems faced by the Soviet régime can quite easily be linked with the family. One of the earliest to appear was the gross lack of consistency between the proposals of ideology and the requirements of real life. Since the latter also tended, incidentally, to be more immediately reflected in the norms of the Soviet legal order than in the ideological sphere, these two features of the Soviet system were sometimes out of phase both with one another and with the requirements of successful social organization. For example, though ideological opposition to adoption and to inheritance was quite pronounced, legal support for both concepts was found to be necessary at an early time. Similarly, although the ideological commitment to sex equality was strong, responsibility for care and support of children continued to rest primarily upon the mother both in the normal pattern of everyday family life and in the allocation by court order of the custody of the children of divorced parents. Hence, a certain disharmony or lack of congruence between ideology on the one side and both life and law on the other became a more and more troubling social problem.

Soviet law confronted a series of difficulties as it tried to enforce those ideologically determined principles that did appear within reach. The close interconnexion between the various facets of human affairs is well illustrated by the vexed relationships in family life between two goals of early family policy: individual liberty, such as freedom of divorce, and sex equality. Full freedom of divorce, in the absence of social rearing of children, inevitably led to the unfair burdening of the divorced mother, and a considerable portion of the discussion about family life in the U.S.S.R. has regularly been concerned with technical problems of making certain fine points of ideological principle legally workable even while jeopardizing the attainment of others. Thus legal problems were part of the background of the new family policy, and the advent of the latter afforded the régime a noticeable increment in immediate, if not long-run, administrative convenience. This became most apparent in 1944 when all legal trace of the *de facto* marriage concept ended with the declaration that only registration could make it legal.

Obviously, human suffering itself, the sexual exploitation of women, abuse of the freedom of divorce, and similar matters were part of the explanation. Once again, however, since women had been exploited in this fashion for almost two decades, the relative importance of this factor was clearly low. The questions of homeless children and juvenile delinquency were more important, for both could be laid at the door of irresponsible parents. Studies conducted by Soviet specialists in Leningrad and Moscow strongly suggested that spending leisure in an unorganized way outside the family was characteristic of juvenile delinquents. The leading Soviet expert on family law, Sverdlov, also attributed the rise of the new family policy partly to the problem of juvenile delinquency.

In an even broader sense, the welfare of the children was at stake. As increasing numbers of fathers were absent and mothers employed, upbringing became problematic, and Soviet writing became quite explicit about the task of the family: 'The main importance of the family comes from its work of preparing the new generation for communism.' In an official apologia published in 1936 it was argued that the idea of state rearing of children, now identified as 'Kollontai's theory', was harmful because it 'unwittingly' vindicated parents who did not wish to trouble about their children.

The word 'unwittingly' also seems to be a key to the change in policy. The Soviet man in the street undoubtedly was hard pressed to distinguish between what was appropriate in the 'socialism' of today and what in the 'communism' of the future. In time the confusion was cleared up by a more emphatic distinction between the two eras: the term communism was applied only to the future society, for earlier the people apparently believed, as one writer put it as early as 1926, that ' "the new way of life" is distinguished from "the old" in the fact that there should be no family at all, neither new nor old. This belief was characterized simply as 'wrong thinking', and the new family policy sought to avoid it by specifying what was permitted and what was not in a completely unambiguous fashion. And more sophisticated rascals would now be prevented from the 'attempt to hide their acts of exploitation behind an empty "leftist phrase" '.

The list of social problems could be extended, but the second major circumstance in the great policy change must be considered at this point. Although the extent and fervor of the people's opposition to the radical policies of the early years cannot be definitely established, it seems quite likely that most of the peasantry felt little attracted to free divorce, legal abortion and other practices. Such kinds of freedom – perhaps individual freedom in general – had little to recommend themselves in their social and cultural context. Among Russian peasants the word for freedom, *svoboda*, sometimes seems to call up an image akin to anarchy, as shown by the reply of a peasant refugee to a question about the proper way of requiring discipline from a child: 'Children must obey their parents, but in a free state like the U.S.S.R. this is impossible.' Sexual freedom was a much more serious matter in the peasant villages than in the cities, for behavior of all kinds was more visible to all and the consequences of sexual intercourse much harder to avoid or hide.

Evidence from refugees suggests the general unpopularity of the central plank of the original Bolshevik program for the family, free divorce.

Three out of four among those questioned recorded their approval of the legislation which made the procurement of divorce considerably more difficult. Reactions to some of the more detailed provisions of the law are significant. While it is not possible to vouch for the representativeness of these views, they suggest pre-war attitudes. As to the substantial expense involved: 'It costs a lot of money to get a divorce. That is good. There will be less prostitution.' As to the long and difficult court process: 'People just say, "Right now we are not getting along, so let's get a divorce". It brings depravity to the people. It should go to the court, to make a person think. If not, he just pays a couple of rubles and gets a divorce. That is not good.' To be sure, proof that most features of the new family policy met with approval, even if it could be found, would not indicate that such a fact had been taken into account by Stalin.

Still, and in spite of Stalin's notorious lack of esteem for public opinion, in times of war or other crisis concession to popular demands is a legitimate Bolshevik tactic, and it is probable that in the year 1944 the régime was fully prepared to make any concessions necessary to help unify the population and end the war quickly. Indeed, the tendency to make such tactical concessions appeared as early as 1934 when, in connexion with the trend toward the united front policy, symbols of popular appeal – for example, such words as 'motherland' and 'patriot' – were rehabilitated after many years of official proscription.

A third set of conditions responsible for the new family policy appeared with the new situation in international politics, especially the rise of Hitler's national socialism, which posed a military threat to the U.S.S.R. Hitlerism seems largely responsible for the prohibition of abortion. One of the reasons for repealing the right to legal abortion given at that time, concern for the health of mothers, obviously camouflaged the desire for a rise in the birth rate. 'We have need of people', observed a leading Soviet official. The régime's leaders had long professed to be aware that prohibition of the manufacture and consumption of alcoholic beverages had proved ineffective in the United States. There was every reason to believe that the prohibition of abortion in Russia would produce similarly undesirable reactions, but the policy was nevertheless put through. This fact suggests how anxious Stalin must have been to arrest the sharp decline of the Soviet birth rate. More people meant more soldiers and more workers, and it seemed that the U.S.S.R. would be needing both.

An even broader frame of reference has sometimes been called up to explain the new policy. In this view, after the Five Year Plans and the frenzied drive for collectivization had exhausted and even seriously disorganized the Soviet people, the rapidity and scope of the effort demanded and the social changes induced had brought with them the reactions often found in times of stress — extreme mobility, waves of crime and other types of disorderly personal behavior – to the point where the stability of the Soviet social order itself was endangered. This situation required the imposition of a thoroughgoing new social discipline, and the family can be seen to be only one of several instruments of social control and social coordination that Stalin's régime put to work in the mid-thirties in the interest of personal discipline and social stability. The other main agencies for controlling and disciplining children, school and youth organizations, were also reconstituted, though in a more traditional fashion, with greater stress on regimen and discipline. Similar trends occurred in law, in the armed forces and in industry, for it was necessary to regroup and reorder the chaos in human relations which the frantic pace and desperate struggles of the preceding years had brought about. This was a time for the stabilization of social relations.

Before turning to the ways in which the new policy was framed in the ideology, I should mention one interpretation which has enjoyed some popularity though I myself do not find it compelling. The proponents of this view assert that the family policy of the first fifteen to twenty years was designed largely to divert the control and influence of hostile parents away from youth and that, in the course of time, as political opposition to the régime diminished, the attitude of parents became sufficiently positive so that the régime was, with equal wisdom, able to support the family. In brief, this theory argues that official policy toward the family corresponded to the régime's evaluation of the political attitudes of Soviet parents and its opinion of the ways in which the family rears its children: if parents are seen as against communism, the régime tries to weaken the family; if the parents are in favor of the régime, it tries to strengthen the family.

The most glaring shortcoming of this interpretation is that it disregards the fact that the time of the inception of the new family policy corresponds quite closely with the likely point of maximum political disaffection among the population. Forced collectivization had just been completed, the living standard in the cities had dropped to a point much below that of 1928, and the purges and terror were about to reach a high peak. At such a time Stalin could hardly expect that Soviet parents were making special efforts to rear loyal young communists.

The final consideration at issue in an analysis of the new policy on the family poses the issue somewhat differently. It is curious that although published accounts of the change have made every effort to explain why it occurred, none as yet has considered why it took almost two decades for the régime to decide that the family was of sufficient importance to deserve explicit support. Marxism and its hold over the régime provide an explanation. Three features of Marxist thought are involved: a value premise, a proposition relating two parts of social structure at a concrete level and the Marxist view of how social change occurs – all of which served for many years to obstruct direct participation by the party in the guidance of family behavior.

The value premise, which goes back to Engels, is the insistence on a separation between public and private life, the latter being the realm of individual freedom. In spite of the theory of revolutionary sublimation and sporadic assertions by various influential party leaders to the effect that there must be 'in principle' no such separation, a strong undercurrent of opinion supported it (and still continues to do so). That non-interference in private life, which has usually meant quite specifically family life, is preferred by the Soviet population at large goes without saying. It has also been common in the thinking within the party, which is understandable both because party leaders have always maintained a remarkably rigid wall between these two sides of their lives and because no firm line on such things was taken until 1935. When the policy did change, with official dogma supporting the monogamous husband, the responsible father and the joyous mother, who set aside leisure time to spend with the family, and so on, it was possible for an official apologist to claim that the leftist theories of the early years had gone uncriticized. Though this is not strictly accurate, after Stalin's accession to power, we must remember, 'criticism' had taken on a new meaning; it was now equivalent to condemnation.

Equally influential was the proposition that sex equality could be gained only through the abolition of the women's responsibilities for child rearing and housekeeping. The régime's commitment to sex equality was very strong, and to support the family by praising these two activities was to fly in the face of elementary Marxism.

Finally, the fact that the Marxist theory of social change clearly assigns the more active role to the economic base had made it very difficult for Marxists to forsake the idea that morality is no more than epiphenomenal. The dilemma this heritage has visited upon the Bolsheviks is revealed clearly in an excerpt from a book edited by Yaroslavski in 1924: 'The fundamental question which occupied us earlier, before the October Revolution, was the question of whether communist morality can be worked out in the absence of a communist system, since morality, just as all other ideological norms, is only a superstructure over one or another foundation of the economic set-up of the region.' When morality was regarded as 'only a superstructure', it made little sense to try to set up a moral code for family behavior until a communist base could be brought to life. Thus, in so far as such behavior was not determined by economic factors, it was the realm of private life, and could properly be relegated to the category of 'matters of no concern to the party'.

By the mid-thirties it had become quite clear that the economic base for a radical withering of family life was not forthcoming. At that point a new ethos was pressed into service, and aspects of Lenin's thought were made definitively explicit under Stalin. Most significantly, the superstructure, now a 'socialist' one, was assigned an active role in fomenting social change. Indeed, just as in Soviet economic life, classical Marxism was stood on its head, and the Soviet state under Stalin proclaimed the still continuing campaign to bring the Soviet social order into conformity with its own ideological (that is, 'superstructural') conceptions. The official view of the role of the family in this quest is revealed in the following authoritative formulation, published in 1936:

The increased attention which is lately being paid in the U.S.S.R. to the struggle against all sorts of traditions of exploitation in family life is to be explained, not by any strengthening of these traditions, but by the fact that they are now in striking opposition to the whole socialist system of our state in which socialism has become the social form of existence of the multitudes.

There were other varieties of apologia. Among the writings of those who sought to justify the new family policy in ideological terms, the most dignified tone is found in the works of Krupskaya, Lenin's widow, who confined herself to the unrationalized essence of the new line: 'It is possible to solve this question [the proper conduct of family life] only on the basis of communist morality.' She also referred to the 'great expense' to the Soviet State that was involved in the new decree on the support of motherhood.

No authoritative writers attempted to find justification for the new family policy in Marx, Engels or Lenin, and the efforts that were made by little-known persons seem quite clumsy, internally contradictory and embarrassed. Evading theoretical argumentation of any sophistication, they relied on indoctrination and especially upon that peculiar Soviet form that has been aptly termed the 'imperative-indicative'. Clearly, the truth was too awkward to be faced, and had to be covered up.

The imperative-indicative, which has suffused almost all Soviet writing on the family since the 1930s, is actually a form of socialist realism – that is, a form of mass persuasion. As such it both hides the truth and formulates a course of action: 'in socialist society ... conditions are created which allow woman to combine harmoniously an active participation in productive and social life with the performance of her family function, her duties as a mother'; 'our youth in the choice of a life-friend – wife or husband – know only one motive, one impulse: love. The bourgeois marriage of pecuniary convenience does not exist for our growing generation'; 'motherhood has become a joy ... our women and children are the happiest in the whole world'; and 'in socialist society personal interests and the interests of the family are harmoniously united with the interests of all of society.'

# Part Four The Sociology of Education

The study of education involves methods and theoretical approaches similar to those used in the study of other sectors of society. In this sense, the sociology of education is not a separate intellectual discipline with peculiar methods and theories, and the Readings selected are not only relevant to education but provide material useful in other fields of sociology. For example, the excerpts from Turner (Reading 24) and Bernstein (Reading 26) contribute to the analysis of social stratification and that from Piaget (Reading 29) is important for the analysis of socialization within the family.

Education is, however, an important and readily distinguishable feature of modern society and these Readings are designed to illustrate both the diversity of problems being studied within this field and the various approaches which are being used. The study of education is easily quantified – there are readily available indices of attainment such as examination performance or the stage reached in schooling. Also, the keeping of educational statistics is often better than the keeping of statistics in other areas of social behaviour. This quantification has the advantage that interesting and often unsuspected relationships between education and other features of social life can be demonstrated comparatively and over large populations. Surveys such as those reported in the excerpt from the *Robbins Report* (Reading 22) have shown that educational attainment reflects not only innate intelligence but also factors in a child's social environment. Similar conclusions can, however, be reached by making use of personal experiences and observations, and an important feature of the study of education is that it is a field in which everyone has experience. In the excerpt from Jackson and Marsden (Reading 23) the authors skilfully use observation and personal experiences to explore the multitude of ways in which social environment affects the education a person obtains.

There are, however, disadvantages that result from the ease with which quantification and individual experiences can be used in the study of education. Quantification in educational research can lead to an over-concentration on statistical descriptions and to the assumption that a manipulation of the variables described is sufficient to achieve the desired goal. Much educational planning is of this kind and neglects the importance of describing the processes through which a child learns and of placing these within the context of the total society. Thus, Turner emphasizes that an individual's education is not only affected by factors in his own social background, but also by the way the whole society is organized. Types of schools, the particular sequence of education and different examination systems prepare children according to the values which are dominant within their society and according to the system of social stratification that is present. Consequently, changes in parental income or education may not affect the education of their children unless the relationships between different social groups, and the values they hold, are also changed. Perrucci (Reading 28) summarizes for us the research that relates to this structural context and its importance for the educational aspirations and values which develop within home and school. The excerpt from Lacey (Reading 27) is particularly interesting in this respect since we see that the effect of parental socio-economic status is mediated through the particular types of personal interactions which occur within the school and that this interaction process is itself an important influence on the values and also on the attainment of the children.

Since education is such a normal part of most people's experience, it is difficult for them to regard it as problematic – that is, to regard learning not as an inevitable and natural process but as the product of definite social forces. In the excerpts from Piaget and from Becker and Geer (Reading 25), learning is a consequence of social interaction, depending on the mutual understandings which individuals develop amongst themselves within a given environment. In the Bernstein excerpt this problem is worked out in terms of the languages which develop within different home environments to meet problems of maintaining domestic order. Since formal education is itself partly an instrument of maintaining order in society, the learning process is affected by these languages.

The different methodologies and theoretical concepts in these excerpts relate of three substantive areas of investigation. Most of the excerpts provide material on the role of education in the process of stratification in modern society. Secondly, the excerpts from Piaget, Becker and Geer, Bernstein and Lacey pertain to the study of education as a process of socialization. Lastly, some of the excerpts are concerned with the ways in which the process of learning is affected by being increasingly carried out within formal organizations.

# 22 The Committee on Higher Education (Robbins)

Social Factors in Demand for Higher Education

Excerpt from the Report of the Committee on Higher Education (*Robbins Report*), *Higher Education*, HMSO, Cmnd 2154, 1963, sections 140–43, pp. 51–3.

Clearly the economic circumstances of the home are very influential: even in families of the same occupational level, the proportion of children reaching full-time higher education is four times as high for children from families with one or two children as from those where five or more children have claims on the family's resources. Thus a continuing growth in family incomes is likely to increase still further the demand for higher education. There is also a very important influence from the educational background of the parents (although this is, of course, related to their social class or occupation). As Table 1 shows, the proportion reaching full-time higher education is eight times as high among

*Table 1* Percentage of Children Born in 1940/41 Reaching Full-Time Higher Education: By Father's Age on Completing Full-Time Education Great Britain

| | Full-time higher education | | No full-time higher education | All children | Numbers (=100%) |
|---|---|---|---|---|---|
| | Degree-level | Other | | | |
| Father's age on completing full-time education | | | | | |
| 18 or over | 32 | 11 | 57 | 100 | 22,000 |
| 16 or 17 | 14 | 7 | 79 | 100 | 41,000 |
| under 16 | 2 | 3 | 95 | 100 | 491,000 |

*Source:* Survey of twenty-one year-olds. (See Appendix One, Part II, Section 2 for details.)

*Notes:* 1. The table shows the proportions of children born in 1940/41 who had reached higher education by 1961/2.

2. For definition of degree level courses see note to Table 8 [not included here].

3. The figures for total numbers in each group are population estimates based on the survey. The table excludes those whose fathers' ages for completing full-time education were not known.

*Table 2* Percentage of Leavers from Maintained Grammar Schools Having Two or More Passes at Advanced Level: By Grading in Eleven-Plus and Father's Occupation
England and Wales 1960/61

| Grading in eleven-plus | Father's occupation | Percentage of leavers of all ages who have 2 or more A-levels (1) | Percentage of leavers of all ages who leave aged 18 and over (2) | Percentage of leavers aged 18 and over who have 2 or more A-levels (3) |
|---|---|---|---|---|
| Upper third | Professional and managerial | 57 | 55 | 79 |
| | Clerical | 44 | 39 | 74 |
| | Skilled manual | 38 | 40 | 77 |
| | Semi- and unskilled | 21 | 23 | 81 |
| Middle third | Professional and managerial | 33 | 42 | 63 |
| | Clerical | 18 | 29 | 56 |
| | Skilled manual | 18 | 27 | 59 |
| | Semi- and unskilled | 10 | 15 | 58 |
| Lower third | Professional and managerial | 14 | 32 | 43 |
| | Clerical | 16 | 22 | 58 |
| | Skilled manual | 10 | 18 | 51 |
| | Semi- and unskilled | 4 | 7 | 53 |
| Transfer from secondary-modern school | | 15 | 29 | 49 |
| All groups at eleven-plus | Professional and managerial | 37 | 46 | 67 |
| | Clerical | 26 | 32 | 64 |
| | Skilled manual | 22 | 29 | 65 |
| | Semi- and unskilled | 11 | 17 | 56 |
| All children | | 24 | 31 | 65 |

Source: *Statistics of Education*, 1961, Supplement to Part 2, Table 13. (See also Appendix One, Part II, Section 2.)

children whose fathers continued their own education to the age of eighteen or over as among those whose fathers left school under sixteen. These facts suggest that, just as since the war more children have stayed on at school for a full secondary education, so in turn more of their children will come to demand higher education during the 1970s. The desire for education will tend to spread as more and more parents have themselves received a fuller education.

This in itself is, of course, no guarantee that the quality of students will be maintained if there is an increased entry. There is, however, impressive evidence that large numbers of able young people do not at present enter higher education. Table 2 gives some of the results of a recent Ministry of Education survey of school leavers which, at our request, was extended to provide information on parental occupation and on performance at the age of eleven. Column 1 shows that, of grammar-school leavers with a given measured ability at the age of eleven, the proportion obtaining the qualifications for entry to higher education varies widely according to their social background. Children of manual workers are on average much less successful than children of the same ability in other social groups. This is largely because they leave school earlier. A comparison of columns 1 and 2 of the table shows that the proportion of children of manual workers who stay on to the age when the General Certificate of Education at advanced level is normally attempted is smaller than the proportion of middle-class children who actually achieve two passes at advanced level. But as may be seen from column 3 of the table those children who do stay on are on average as successful as children of the same ability in other social groups.

While the reserves of untapped ability may be greatest in the poorer sections of the community, this is not the whole of the story. It is sometimes imagined that the great increase in recent years in the numbers achieving good school-leaving qualifications has occurred almost entirely among the children of manual workers. This is not so. The increase has been almost as great among the children of professional parents, where the pool of ability might have been thought more nearly exhausted. In these groups the performance of children of a given measured ability has in fact continually improved. The desire for education, leading to better performance at school, appears to be affecting children of all classes and all abilities alike, and it is reasonable to suppose that this trend will continue.

The quality of primary and secondary education and its organization also affects the proportion of children who emerge as capable of entering higher education. Reductions in the size of classes, and the lengthening of the period of higher education for school teachers, should both tend to increase the number of those who achieve good qualifications at school. It is probable that courses leading to the General Certificate of Education will continue to become more widely accessible. The evidence suggests that the degree to which children experience an academic environment has a major influence on whether they make the best of their talents. Table 24 [not included here] for example, shows how in 1960 the proportion of children going into the sixth form varied between areas of differing grammar school provision. Where the provision was liberal, some 12 per cent of children stayed on, compared with only 7 per cent in areas of relatively low provision.

# 23 Brian Jackson and Dennis Marsden

Working-Class Children and Grammar School

Abridged from Brian Jackson and Dennis Marsden, *Education and the Working Class*, Routledge & Kegan Paul, 1962, pp. 86–112.

After the 1944 Education Act the senior parts of the council schools were cut away and formed into secondary-modern schools. The junior sections, covering the years up to eleven, became our primary schools. Both secondary-modern and primary schools tended to gather larger numbers of children within a shorter age span, and the result was that whereas in the old council schools one class for the seven year olds or the thirteen year olds had sufficed, there must now be two or even three classes for each year. Children were divided up into school classes according to ability; the ablest class in each year being the A-stream, and the less fortunate the B or C stream. The division into streams generally took place at seven, and there was not very much movement up or down. This account does not always hold true, but it may be that in the present system where a firmer pre-selection is often accomplished at seven, there is a greater rigidity, a less accommodating way of handling children who develop at different rates and under different pressures. It may be; for there is little certain evidence either way, and one must be wary of overemphasizing the elasticity of the former mode. We had not sufficient informants schooled under the present system of official selection at eleven, and unofficial pre-selection by 'streaming' at seven, to anchor down any firm remarks on the change. But amongst its possible effects could be an increase in the need for very early success by the working-class child, and a heightening of their nascent sense of separateness. For that majority of working-class children who fail the selection examination would find themselves in different classes, not different desks, from the children likely to pass.

The schools' teaching then seemed centred on the grammar-school examination, though not perhaps as attentively and efficiently as it may be today. The atmosphere could be sharply competitive, and at the top of the class one girl said, 'We didn't have friends, we only had rivals.' Given all this, there was still a certain breadth of childish friendship. They found themselves working and playing as members of a wide social group, a more inclusive body than they have belonged to since. Orchards were raided in company with future navvies, plumbers and civil servants; skipping rhymes were picked up from girls who were going to spend their working lives as weavers or bus conductresses, and their first car rides were enjoyed when they were given lifts home by the professional father of a new school friend.

And to some extent they were aware of this at the time. Aware certainly of more tattered and rougher children than themselves, aware too of boys and girls from prosperous homes whose wider experience yielded fuller vocabularies, and an imposing range of reference. Some felt the need to 'cover' themselves against this competition and Malcolm Astin recalled, 'Every year we had to write essays about where we'd been for our holidays, and our family could never go anywhere. But I used to write essays about having gone for a week's holiday to Rhyl. The others were talking about where they'd been, so I'd write my essay too. I knew it was "expected".'

The first weeks at grammar school were strange. For the children who already had contacts, they were exhilarating, the exciting prelude to promised satisfactions. Whole new areas of inviting study presented themselves – algebra, physics, Latin, French. 'I took to Marburton College like a duck to water,' said Ronald Turnbull. For children who had broken most friendships and connexions with the old neighbourhood, here were fresh children, fresh clubs and societies, the school scouts and the school corps to join. The invitation was irresistible, and many were glad to accept it in full and become from the earliest days loyal and eager members of the school. Their wholeheartedness was naturally reflected in their first pieces of work, and finding themselves soon well placed in class, they were conscious of latent power thrusting through, of their ability to command new and more testing situations. We have shown that most of the parents came from the very upper reaches of the working class, and once their child reached grammar school, these parents were wholeheartedly behind the enterprise. In very many small ways they influenced their children to accept, to belong. Both grammar school and home supported the child in orthodox and receptive attitudes. But under particular strains and pressures, this home support could, and did, break down; and this happens more and more often as either the school disturbs the parents (directly in an interview, indirectly through weight of homework and so on), or the parents find no way of obtaining vital knowledge, or coming to terms with the middle-class ethos of the grammar school. The parents may have been 'sunken middle class', but many of these discover how different this can be in knowledge and evaluation from the range of middle-class life endorsed by the grammar school.

For the majority of the children, unlike Ronald Turnbull, the entry to grammar school was uncertain and confused. They had suddenly lost in some measure that mesh of securities, expectations, recognitions, that we have called 'neighbourhood'. 'I had this feeling of not *belonging* anywhere,' said Patricia Joy. They found themselves surrounded by more middle-class children than they had ever met before. These children spoke better, seemed more confident, some already knew bits of French and Latin, their fathers had told them what 'physics' was about, a few even knew the teachers. *They*, evidently, seemed to belong. This insecurity was heightened by confusions over getting the right books, the right sports equipment, the right uniform. 'I didn't like it,' said Rita Watson, 'my uniform seemed too big all round – long sleeves – I suppose my mother had to do it like that so it would last longer, but I felt awful. All the other girls' uniforms seemed all right. *I* was wrong.' On top of this came the new subjects, the new vocabulary (not 'kept in' but 'detention', not 'playtime' but 'break' – and was it 'yard' or 'playground' or 'cloisters'?) the masters' gowns, the prefects, the whole body of customs, small rights and wrongs, that any well-developed grammar school holds. Some of the schools made a practice of teaching the new children aggressively for the first weeks, to 'break them in', and, presumably, to nip behaviour problems in the bud. The effect on children already bewildered was to knock them off balance rather than 'break them in' and to create, rather than cure behaviour problems. This was obvious in our study of the middle-class child where a highly gifted boy could be so robbed of confidence in the first term, as to *seem* dull for several years afterwards. For some of the working-class children, confused by a genuine loss of part of their social life ('neighbourhood'), perplexed by the strangeness and sheer difference of grammar school, conscious of new *social* barriers thickening the normal barriers between pupil and teacher, and unable to turn to parents for explanation and understanding – for these children the beginnings could seem almost hallucinatory. 'I had that feeling like when you were in the forces,' said one boy, 'after you got your jabs and you got inoculation fever, you felt away from it all. You felt in a bit of a haze, everything was a bit bleared. Well, that's how school felt at first. I felt just as I did later when I'd got inoculation fever.'

We recorded a lot of evidence about the school's insensitivity and the child's hypersensitivity; the school's determination to hand on the grammar-school modes, to spread its standards as the best and the only standards, and the child's awkward, clumsy and stubborn desire to preserve the other ways, to remain 'natural'. This gaucherie soon moved into rudeness, tactlessness and the impolite. And the children who clung to 'neighbourhood' seemed to attract to themselves the full weight of the school's punishments. Again it was all part of the 'haze'. 'I got showers of detentions, showers of them, and "Saturday mornings" as well. Canings, tests, detentions, crying at night over my arithmetic homework – that's all I can remember of those years. I don't know why I got so much punishment. I was quite a mild child, and I was interested in my way, too. I just don't know how it was.' At Marburton College one of the punishments was to bring the offending children back on Saturday morning for extra school. 'Yes, you got three detentions and that made it so that you came in on a Saturday morning. But somehow "Saturday mornings" were better than weekday school. The whole school was quieter, more relaxed, less intimidating altogether. Somehow it was better than going to school in mid week.' A similar note could be recorded about the quietness and freedom of the art room, the laboratory after school, or a meeting of the music group. 'I liked relaxing, stretching out on the desks with my feet up on the seat -- all the things that you couldn't do in lessons. And some brainy sixth formers would sit in the master's desk and put these gram records on.'

So it was not then such a simple case of being anti-school. School had its attractions, and for these, its very deep satisfactions, but it was only a part of life and often an alien part of that. 'No,' said Alec Shapely, 'we weren't anti-school. School didn't enter into it. School was like work, you went to school in the daytime and in the evenings you went out to enjoy yourself.' Those who tried to keep all their evenings to themselves seldom lasted into the sixth form, though some did. Others were caught in the tensions between the evening life and the need to do well, to establish themselves securely in terms of marks – as a counter-poise to the ambiguities, the discords, the losses of living. By the third year the lines were clear: on the one hand were the working-class children who had thrown their total self into the school; on the other hand were those children (largely in B-and C-streams now) who clung to neighbourhood, and whose attitude, clumsiness and inarticulate divergencies attracted that rebuke and punishment which merely stiffened the will to resist. Most of these children were moving towards the escape from grammar school at the end of the fifth form. From their ranks only the very small minority survived.

The majority of our sample had preferred school to neighbourhood and become hard-working, accommodating members of the school community. They survived into the sixth form, where they began to assume responsibility to lead and command themselves.

# 24 Ralph H. Turner

## Modes of Social Ascent through Education

Abridged from Ralph H. Turner, 'Modes of social ascent through education: sponsored and contest mobility', in A. H. Halsey, Jean Floud, and C. Arnold Anderson (eds.), *Education, Economy and Society*, Free Press, 1961, pp. 120–33. First published as 'Sponsored and contest ability and the school system', *American Sociological Review*, vol. 25, 1960.

The object of this paper is to suggest a framework for relating certain differences between American and English systems of education to the prevailing norms of upward mobility in each country. Others have noted the tendency for educational systems to support prevailing schemes of stratification, but this statement will dwell specifically on the manner in which the *accepted mode of upward mobility* shapes the school system directly and indirectly through its effects on the values that implement social control. The task will be carried out by describing two ideal-typical normative patterns of upward mobility and suggesting their logical ramifications in the general character of stratification and social control. In addition to showing relationships among a number of differences between American and English schooling, the ideal-types have broader implications than those developed in this paper. First, they suggest a major dimension of stratification, which might profitably be incorporated into a variety of studies on social class. Second, they can be readily applied in further comparisons, between countries other than the United States and England.

Contest mobility is like a sporting event in which many compete for a few recognized prizes. The contest is judged to be fair only if all the players compete on an equal footing. Victory must be won solely by one's own efforts. The most satisfactory outcome is not necessarily a victory of the most able, but of the most deserving. The tortoise who defeats the hare is a folk prototype of the deserving sportsman. Enterprise, initiative, perseverance and craft are admirable qualities if they allow the person initially at a disadvantge to triumph. Even clever manipulation of the rules may be admired if it helps the contestant who is smaller or less muscular or less rapid to win. Applied to mobility, the contest norm means that victory by a person of moderate intelligence accomplished through the use of common sense, craft, enterprise, daring and successful risk taking is more appreciated than victory of the most intelligent or the best educated.

Sponsored mobility, on the other hand, rejects the pattern of the contest and substitutes a controlled selection process. In this process the élite or their agents, who are best qualified to judge merit, *call* those individuals who have the appropriate qualities to élite status. Individuals do not win or seize élite status, but mobility is rather a process of sponsored induction into the élite following selection.

The most obvious application of the distinction between sponsored and contest mobility norms is to afford a partial explanation for the different policies of student selection in the English and American secondary schools. Although American high-school students take different courses of study and sometimes even attend specialized high schools, a major preoccupation has been to avoid any sharp social separation between the superior and inferior students and to keep the channels of movement between courses of study as open as possible. Even recent criticisms of the way in which superior students may be thereby held back in their development usually are qualified by insistence that these students must not, however, be withdrawn from the mainstream of student life. Any such segregation offends the sense of fairness implicit in the contest norm and also arouses the fear that the élite and future élite will lose their sense of fellow-feeling with the masses. Perhaps the most important point, however, is that schooling is presented as an opportunity, and the principal burden of making use of the opportunity depends on the student's own initiative and enterprise.

The English system has undergone a succession of liberalizing changes during this century, but all of them have remained within the pattern of attempting early in the educational program to sort out the promising from the unpromising, so that the former may be segregated and given a special form of training to fit them for higher standing in their adult years. Under the Education Act of 1944, a minority of students have been selected each year by means of a battery of examinations popularly known as 'eleven-plus', supplemented to varying degrees by grade-school record and personal interview impressions, for admission to grammar schools. The remaining students attend secondary-modern or technical schools, in which the opportunities to prepare for college or train for the better occupations are minimal. The grammar schools supply what, by comparative standards, is a high quality of college preparatory education. Such a scheme embodies well the logic of sponsorship, with early selection of those destined for middle-class and better occupations, and specialized training to suit each group for the class in which they are destined to hold membership. The plan facilitates considerable mobility, and recent research reveals surprisingly little bias against the child from a manual-laboring family in the selection for grammar school, when related to measured intelligence. It is altogether possible that adequate comparative research would show a closer correlation of school success with measured intelligence and a closer correlation between school success and family background in England than in the United States. While selection of superior students for mobility opportunity is probably more efficient under such a system, the obstacles to a person not so selected 'making the grade' on the basis of his own initiative or enterprise are probably correspondingly greater.

That the contrasting effects of the two systems accord with the social-control pattern under the two mobility norms is indicated by research into student ambitions in the United States and England. Researches in the United States consistently show that the general level of occupational aspiration reported by high-school students is quite unrealistic in relation to the actual distribution of job opportunities. Comparative study in England shows much less in the way of 'fantasy' aspiration and, specifically, shows a reduction in aspiration among those not selected following the eleven-plus examination. One of the by-products of the sponsorship system is the fact that students from middle-class families whose parents cannot afford to send them to a private school suffer severe personal adjustment problems when they are assigned to secondary-modern schools on the basis of this selection.

While this well-known difference between the early British sorting of students into grammar and modern schools and the American comprehensive high school and junior college is the clearest application of the distinction under discussion, the organizing norms penetrate more deeply into the school systems than is initially apparent. The most telling observation regarding the direct normative operation of these principles would be evidence to support the author's impression that major critics within each country do not usually transcend the logic of their respective mobility norms in their criticisms. Thus, British critics debate the best method for getting people sorted according to ability, without proposing that élite station should be opened to whoever can take it. Although fear of 'Sputnik' in the United States introduced a flurry of sponsored-mobility thinking, the long-standing concern of school critics has been the failure to motivate students adequately. Preoccupation with motivation appears to be an intellectual application of the folk idea that people should *win* their station in society by personal *enterprise*.

The functional operation of a strain toward consistency with the organizing norm of upward mobility may be illustrated by reference to several other features of the school systems in the two countries. First, the value placed upon education itself is different under the two organizing norms. Under sponsored mobility, schooling is valued for its cultivation of élite culture, and those forms of schooling directed toward such cultivation are more highly valued than those which are not. Education of the non-élite is difficult to justify clearly and tends to be half-hearted, while the maximum educational resources are concentrated on 'those who can benefit most from them'. In practice, the latter means those who can learn the élite culture. The secondary-modern schools in England have regularly suffered from less adequate financial provision and a lower teacher–student ratio, from less-well-trained teachers, and from a general lack of prestige, in comparison with the grammar schools.

Under contest mobility in the United States, education is valued as a means of getting ahead, but the contents of education are not highly valued in their own right. There is even a suspicion of the educated man as one who may have gotten ahead without really earning his position. Over a century ago, De Tocqueville had commented on the absence in the United States of a hereditary class 'by which the labors of the intellect are held in honor'. In consequence he remarked that, 'A middling standard is fixed in America for human knowledge.' In spite of recent criticisms of lax standards in American schools, it is in keeping with the general mobility pattern that a Gallup Poll in April 1958 showed that school principals were much more likely to make such criticisms than parents. While 90 per cent of principals thought that '... our schools today demand too little work from the students', only 51 per cent of parents thought so, with 33 per cent saying the work was about right, and 6 per cent that schools demanded too much work.

Second, the logic of preparation for a contest prevails in United States schools, with emphasis on keeping everyone in the running until the final stages. In primary and secondary schools, the assumption tends to be made that those who are learning satisfactorily need little special attention, while the less successful require help to be sure that they remain in the contest and may compete for the final stakes. In December 1958, a nationwide Gallup Poll gave evidence that this attitude had not been radically altered by the international situation. When asked whether teachers should devote extra time to the bright students, 26 per cent said 'yes', and 67 per cent answered 'no'. But the responses changed to 86 per cent 'yes', and only 9 per cent 'no', when the question was asked concerning the 'slow students'.

In western states, the junior college offers many students 'a second chance' to qualify for university, and all state universities have some provision for substandard high-school students to earn admission.

The university itself is run like the true contest, standards being set competitively, students being forced to pass a series of trials each semester, and only a minority of the entrants achieving the prize of graduation. Such a pattern contrasts sharply with the English system in which selection is supposed to have been relatively complete before entry into university, and students may be subject to no testing whatsoever for the first year or more of university study. Although university completion rates have not been estimated in either country, some figures are indicative. The ratio of bachelor's and first-professional degrees in American institutions of higher learning, in 1957–8, to the number of first-time degree-credit enrolments in the fall, four years earlier, was reported to be 0·610 for men and 0·488 for women. The indicated 39 and 51 per cent drop-out rates are probably underestimates, because transfers from two-year junior colleges swell the number of degrees without being included in first-time enrolments. In England, a study following up the careers of individual students, found that in University College London, 81·9 per cent of entering students, between 1948 and 1951, eventually graduated with a degree. A similar study a few years earlier at the University of Liverpool revealed a figure of 86·9 per cent. Under contest mobility, the object is to train as many as possible to the skills necessary for élite status so as to give everyone a chance and to maintain competition at the highest pitch. Under sponsored mobility, the objective is to train in élite culture only those for whom the presumption is that they will enter the élite, lest there be a dangerous number of 'angry young men' who have élite skills without élite station.

Third, systems of mobility precipitate different emphases regarding educational content. Induction into élite culture under sponsored mobility makes for emphasis on school *esprit de corps*, which can be employed to cultivate norms of intraclass loyalty and élite tastes and manners. Likewise, formal schooling built about highly specialized study in fields with entirely intellectual or esthetic concern and no 'practical' value serves the purpose of élite culture. Under contest mobility in the United States, in spite of faculty endorsement of 'liberal education', schooling tends to be measured for its practical benefits and to become, beyond the elementary level, chiefly vocational. Education does not so much provide what is good in itself as provide skills necessary to compete for the real prizes of life, and of these vocational skills are the most important.

An application of these points can be seen in the different national attitude toward students being gainfully employed while in university. More students in the United States than in Britain have part-time employments, and in the United States relatively fewer of the students receive subsidies toward subsistence and living expenses. The most generous programs of state aid in the United States, apart from those applying to veterans and other special groups, do not normally cover expenses other than tuition and institutional fees. British maintenance grants are designed to cover full living expenses, taking into account parents' ability to pay. Under sponsored mobility, gainful employment serves no apprentice or testing function, and is thought merely to prevent the student from gaining the full benefit of his schooling. L. J. Parry speaks of the general opposition to students working and asserts that English university authorities almost unanimously hold that '. . . if a person must work for financial reasons, he should never spend more than four weeks on such work during the whole year.'

Under contest mobility, success in school work is not a sufficient test of practical merit, but must be supplemented by a test in the world of practical affairs. Thus, in didactic folk tales, the professional engineer will also prove himself a superior mechanic, the business tycoon, a superior behind-the-counter salesman. Consequently, by 'working his way through school' the enterprising student 'earns' his education in the fullest sense, keeps in touch with the practical world, and has an apprenticeship into vocational life. Students are often urged to seek part-time employment, even when there is no financial need, and in extreme instances schools have incorporated paid employment as a requirement toward graduation. R. H. Eckleberry states the typical American view: a student willing to work part-time is a 'better bet' than 'the equally bright student who receives all of his financial support from others'.

Finally, social-adjustment training is peculiar to the system of contest mobility. The reason for emphasis on adjustment training is clear when its nature is understood. Adjustment training is preparation to cope with situations in which there are no rules of intercourse or in which the rules are unknown, but in which the good opinions of others cannot be wholly ignored. Under sponsored mobility, the élite recruits are inducted into a homogeneous stratum in which there is consensus regarding the rules, and in which they succeed socially by mastering these rules. Under contest mobility, the élite aspirant must relate himself both to the established élite and to the masses, who follow different rules; and the élite themselves are not sufficiently homogeneous to evolve consensual rules of intercourse. Furthermore, in the contest the rules may vary according to the background of the competitor, so that each aspirant must deal successfully with persons playing the game with slightly different sets of rules. Consequently, adjustment training becomes one of the important skills imparted by the school system. That the emphasis on adjustment training in the schools has had genuine popular support is indicated by a 1945 Fortune Poll, in which a national sample were asked which one of two things would be very important for a son of theirs to get out of college. Over 87 per cent chose 'Ability to get along with and understand people', in answer to the question. This answer was the second most frequently chosen as being the very most important thing to get out of college. In the present connexion, it is possible that British education is better preparation for participation in an orderly and controlled world, while American education prepares better for a less ordered situation. The reputedly superior ability of 'Yanks' to get things done seems to apply to this ability to cope with a chaotic situation.

# 25 Howard S. Becker and Blanche Geer

The Fate of Idealism in Medical School

Excerpt from Howard S. Becker and Blanche Geer, 'The fate of idealism in medical school', in Seymour M. Lipset and Neil J. Smelser (eds.), *Sociology: The Progress of a Decade*, Prentice-Hall, 1961, pp. 293–7. First published in *American Sociological Review*, vol. 23, 1958.

Medical students enter school with what we may think of as the idealistic notion, implicit in lay culture, that the practice of medicine is a wonderful thing and that they are going to devote their lives to service to mankind. They believe that medicine is made up of a great body of well-established facts that they will be taught from the first day on and that these facts will be of immediate practical use to them as physicians. They enter school expecting to work industriously and expecting that if they work hard enough they will be able to master this body of fact and thus become good doctors.

In several ways the first year of medical school does not live up to their expectations. They are disillusioned when they find they will not be near patients at all, that the first year will be just like another year of college. In fact, some feel that it is not even as good as college because their work in certain areas is not as thorough as courses in the same fields in undergraduate school. They come to think that their courses (with the exception of anatomy) are not worth much because, in the first place, the faculty (being PhDs) know nothing about the practice of medicine, and, in the second place, the subject matter itself is irrelevant, or as the students say, 'ancient history'.

The freshmen are further disillusioned when the faculty tells them in a variety of ways that there is more to medicine than they can possibly learn. They realize it may be impossible for them to practice medicine properly. Their disillusionment becomes more profound when they discover that this statement of the faculty is literally true. Experience in trying to master the details of the anatomy of the extremities convinces them that they cannot do so in the time they have. Their expectation of hard work is not disappointed; they put in an eight-hour day of classes and laboratories, and study four or five hours a night and most of the week-end as well.

Some of the students, the brightest, continue to attempt to learn it all, but succeed only in getting more and more worried about their work. The majority decide that, since they can't learn it all, they must select from among all the facts presented to them those they will attempt to learn. There are two ways of making this selection. On the one hand, the student may decide on the basis of his own uninformed notions about the nature of medical practice that many facts are not important, since they relate to things which seldom come up in the actual practice of medicine; therefore, he reasons, it is useless to learn them. On the other hand, the student can decide that the important thing is to pass his examinations and, therefore, that the important facts are those which are likely to be asked on an examination; he uses this as a basis for selecting both facts to memorize and courses for intensive study. For example, the work in physiology is dismissed on both of these grounds, being considered neither relevant to the facts of medical life nor important in terms of the amount of time the faculty devotes to it and the number of examinations in the subject.

A student may use either or both of these bases of selection at the beginning of the year, before many tests have been given. But after a few tests have been taken, the student makes 'what the faculty wants' the chief basis of his selection of what to learn, for he now has a better idea of what this is and also has become aware that it is possible to fail examinations and that he therefore must learn the expectations of the faculty if he wishes to stay in school. The fact that one group of students, that with the highest prestige in the class, took this view early and did well on examinations was decisive in swinging the whole class around to this position. The students were equally influenced to become 'test-wise' by the fact that, although they had all been in the upper range in their colleges, the class average on the first examination was frighteningly low.

In becoming test-wise, the students begin to develop systems for discovering the faculty wishes and learning them. These systems are both methods for studying their texts and short-cuts that can be taken in laboratory work. For instance, they begin to select facts for memorization by looking over the files of old examinations maintained in each of the medical fraternity houses. They share tip-offs from the lectures and offhand remarks of the faculty as to what will be on the examinations. In anatomy, they agree not to bother to dissect out subcutaneous nerves, reasoning that it is both difficult and time-consuming and the information can be secured from books with less effort. The interaction involved in the development of such systems and short-cuts helps to create a social group of a class which had previously been only an aggregation of smaller and less organized groups.

In this medical school, the students learn in this way to distinguish between the activities of the first year and their original view that everything that happens to them in medical school will be important. Thus they become cynical about the value of their activities in the first year. They feel that the real thing – learning which will help them to help mankind – has been postponed, perhaps until the second year, or perhaps even farther, at which time they will be able again to act on idealistic premises. They believe that what they do in their later years in school under supervision will be about the same thing they will do, as physicians, on their own; the first year had disappointed this expectation.

There is one matter, however, about which the students are not disappointed during the first year: the so-called trauma of dealing with the cadaver. But this experience, rather than producing cynicism, reinforces the student's attachment to his idealistic view of medicine by making him feel that he is experiencing at least some of the necessary unpleasantness of the doctor's. Such difficulties, however, do not loom as large for the student as those of solving the problem of just what the faculty wants.

On this and other points, a working consensus develops in the new consolidated group about the interpretation of their experience in medical school and its norms of conduct. This consensus, which we call student culture, focuses their attention *almost completely* on their day-to-day activities in school and obscures or sidetracks their earlier idealistic preoccupations. Cynicism, griping and minor cheating become endemic, but the cynicism is specific to the educational situation, to the first year, and to only parts of it. Thus the students keep their cynicism separate from their idealistic feelings and by postponement protect their belief that medicine is a wonderful thing, that their school is a fine one and that they will become good doctors.

The sophomore year does not differ greatly from the freshman year. Both the work load and anxiety over examinations probably increase. Though they begin some medical activities, as in their attendance at autopsies and particularly in their introductory course in physical diagnosis, most of what they do continues to repeat the pattern of the college science curriculum. Their attention still centers on the problem of getting through school by doing well in examinations.

During the third and fourth, or clinical years, teaching takes a new form. In place of lectures and laboratories, the students' work now consists of the study of actual patients admitted to the hospital or seen in the clinic. Each patient who enters the hospital is assigned to a student who interviews him about his illnesses, past and present, and performs a physical examination. He writes this up for the patient's chart, and appends the diagnosis and the treatment that he would use were he allowed actually to treat the patient. During conferences with faculty physicians, often held at the patient's bedside, the student is quizzed about items of his report and called upon to defend them or to explain their significance. Most of the teaching in the clinical years is of this order.

Contact with patients brings a new set of circumstances with which the student must deal. He no longer feels the great pressure created by tests, for he is told by the faculty, and this is confirmed by his daily experience, that examinations are now less important. His problems now become those of coping with a steady stream of patients in a way that will please the staff man under whom he is working, and of handling what is sometimes a tremendous load of clinical work so as to allow himself time for studying diseases and treatments that interest him and for play and family life.

The students earlier have expected that once they reach the clinical years they will be able to realize their idealistic ambitions to help people and to learn those things immediately useful in aiding people who are ill. But they find themselves working to understand cases as medical problems rather than working to help the sick and memorizing the relevant available facts so that these can be produced immediately for a questioning staff man. When they make ward rounds with a faculty member they are likely to be quizzed about any of the seemingly countless facts possibly related to the condition of the patient for whom they are 'caring'.

Observers speak of the cynicism that overtakes the student and the lack of concern for his patients as human beings. This change does take place, but it is not produced solely by 'the anxiety brought about by the presence of death and suffering'. The student becomes preoccupied with the technical aspects of the cases with which he deals because the faculty requires him to do so. He is questioned about so many technical details that he must spend most of his time learning them.

The frustrations created by his position in the teaching hospital further divert the student from idealistic concerns. He finds himself low man in a hierarchy based on clinical experience, so that he is allowed very little of the medical responsibility he would like to assume. Because of his lack of experience he cannot write orders, and he receives permission to perform medical and surgical procedures (if at all) at a rate he considers far too slow. He usually must content himself with 'mere' vicarious participation in the drama of danger, life and death that he sees as the core of medical practice. The student culture accents these difficulties so that events (and especially those involving patients) are interpreted and reacted to as they push him toward or hold him back from further participation in this drama. He does not think in terms the layman might use.

As a result of the increasingly technical emphasis of his thinking the student appears cynical to the nonmedical outsider, though from his own point of view he is simply seeing what is 'really important'. Instead of reacting with the layman's horror and sympathy for the patient to the sight of a cancerous organ that has been surgically removed, the student is more likely to regret that he was not allowed to close the incision at the completion of the operation, and to rue the hours that he must spend searching in the fatty flesh for the lymph nodes that will reveal how far the disease has spread. As in other lines of work, he drops lay attitudes for those more relevant to the way the event affects someone in his position.

This is not to say that the students lose their original idealism. When issues of idealism are openly raised in a situation they define as appropriate they respond as they might have when they were freshmen. But the influence of the student culture is such that questions which might bring forth this idealism are not brought up. Students are often assigned patients for examination and follow-up whose conditions might be expected to provoke idealistic crises. Students discuss such patients, however, with reference to the problems they create for the *student*. Patients with terminal diseases who are a long time dying, and patients with chronic diseases who show little change from week to week, are more likely to be viewed as creating extra work without extra compensation in knowledge or the opportunity to practice new skills than as examples of illness which raise questions about euthanasia. Such cases require the student to spend time every day checking on progress which he feels will probably not take place and to write long 'progress' notes in the patient's chart although little progress has occurred.

This apparent cynicism is a collective matter. Group activities are built around this kind of workaday perspective, constraining the students in two ways. First, they do not openly express the lay idealistic notions they may hold, for their culture does not sanction such expression; second, they are less likely to have thoughts of this deviant kind when they are engaged in group activity. The collective nature of this 'cynicism' is indicated by the fact that students become more openly idealistic whenever they are removed from the influence of student culture – when they are alone with a sociologist as they near the finish of school and sense the approaching end of student life, for example, or when they are isolated from their classmates and therefore are less influenced by this culture.

# 26 Basil Bernstein

A Socio-Linguistic Approach to Social Learning

Excerpts from Basil Bernstein, 'A socio-linguistic approach to social learning', in J. Gould (ed.), *Penguin Survey of the Social Sciences 1965*, Penguin Books, 1965, pp. 145–66.

In its struggle for recognition, sociology has continuously insisted upon the fact that there exists an order of relations arising out of the inter-actions of members of a society, which constrains and directs behaviour independent of the unique characteristics of its members. Sociologists have been concerned to explain the nature of this order, in particular the processes making for its diversity and change and develop to a formal level a grammar or syntax which controls the conceptualizing of this order. They have studied the major complexes of social forms which shape the social order, their inter-relations and the factors responsible for their change. Language is seen as an integrating or divisive phenomenon; as the major process through which a culture is transmitted; the bearer of the social genes. However, this has rarely given rise to a study of language as a social institution comparable to the analyses made of say the family, religion, etc. As far as speech is concerned this has been viewed as a datum, taken for granted, and not as an object of special inquiry. It is, of course, true that through the writings of George Mead the role of language, really the role of speech, has been explicitly recognized in the formation of a distinctly social self. And yet, in the study of socialization, it is not possible to find an empirical study which systematically examines the role of speech as the process by which a child comes to acquire a specific *social* identity. In fact in the numerous studies of child-rearing, with the exception of very few, there is no account of the patterning of the linguistic environment.[1] Groups are studied, their formal ordering elegantly discussed, but the implications and consequences of *linguistic* aspects of their communications seem to be unworthy of sociological consideration. Graduates are trained to conduct surveys, to construct questionnaires, to interview, without (at least, in England) any explicit and systematic training in what Dell Hymes has called the ethnography of speech – although there is an intuitive or unsystematic recognition of differences in the patterning and consequences of speech events in various subcultures. [. . .]

1. I am ignoring here the many studies limited to the development of speech in children.

## Elaborated and restricted codes

*Definitions and brief description*

Two general types of code can be distinguished: *elaborated* and *restricted*. They can be defined, on a linguistic level, in terms of the probability of predicting for any one speaker which syntactic elements will be used to organize meaning across a representative range of speech. In the case of an elaborated code, the speaker will select from a relatively extensive range of alternatives, and the probability of predicting the organizing elements is considerably reduced. In the case of a restricted code the number of these alternatives is often severely limited and the probability of predicting the elements is greatly increased.

On a psychological level the codes may be distinguished by the extent to which each facilitates (elaborated code) or inhibits (restricted code) an orientation to symbolize intent in a verbally explicit form. Behaviour processed by these codes will, it is proposed, develop different modes of self-regulation and so different forms of orientation. The codes themselves are functions of a particular form of social relationship or, more generally, qualities of social structures.

A distinction will be made between verbal or linguistic, and extra-verbal or para-linguistic components of a communication. The linguistic or verbal component refers to messages where meaning is mediated by words: their selection, combination and organization. The para-linguistic or extra-verbal component refers to meanings mediated through expressive associations of words (rhythm, stress, pitch, etc.) or through gesture, physical set and facial modification.

*Restricted code (lexical prediction).* The pure form of a restricted code would be one where all the words – and hence the organizing structure irrespective of its degree of complexity – are wholly predictable for speakers and listeners. Examples of this pure form would be ritualistic modes of communication: relationships regulated by protocol, types of religious services, cocktail-party routines, some story-telling situations. In these relations individual difference cannot be signalled through the verbal channel except in so far as the *choice* of sequence or routine exists. It is transmitted essentially through variations in extra-verbal signals.

Consider the case of a mother telling her child stories which they both know by heart. 'And Little Red Riding Hood went into the wood' (ritualistic pause). 'And what do you think happened?' (rhetorical question). If the mother wishes to transmit her discrete experience, her uniqueness, she is unable to do this by varying her words. She can only do it by varying the signals transmitted through extra-verbal channels; through changes in intonation, pitch, speech rhythm, facial set, gesture or even through changes in muscular tension, if she is holding the child. The code defines the channels through which new information (i.e. learning) can be made available. The discrete intents of mother and child, interpersonal aspects of the relation, can only be transmitted extra-verbally.

Given the selection of the sequence, new information will be made available through the extra-verbal channels, and these channels are likely to become the object of special perceptual activity. The code defines the form of the social relationship by restricting the *verbal* signalling of individual differences. Individuals relate to each other essentially through *the social position or status they are occupying*. Societies differ in terms of the use made of this code and the conditions which elicit it.

It is suggested that where there is an *exchange* of verbal message of maximal predictability, such as social routines, the context will be one where the participants have *low* predictability about each other's individual attributes. The code offers here the possibility of deferred commitment to the relationship. Decisions about its future form will be based upon the significance given to the exchange of extra-verbal messages.

Consider a cocktail party. Two people are introduced who have never met before. A social routine is likely to develop. This establishes mutual predictability and so the basis of a social relation. What is said is impersonal in that the verbal messages are all previously organized. The individuals will be highly sensitive to extra-verbal signals and so these signals are likely to become the object of special perceptual activity. How the social relation will develop initially depends upon the choice of social routine and the significance accorded to extra-verbal signals. Here, orientation is towards the extra-verbal channels: there is a minimal level of planning involved in the preparation of the speech; the exchange of verbal sequences pre-supposes a shared cultural heritage which controls the verbal communications offered by the occupants of this cocktail-party status.

It is important to note that:

1. The status or positional aspect of the social relationship is important.
2. Orientation is likely to be toward the extra-verbal channels as new information will pass through these channels.
3. Specifically verbal planning is confined to choice of sequence, rather than involving the selection and organization of the sequence.
4. The code restricts the verbal signalling of individual difference.

*Restricted code (syntactic prediction)*. What is more often found is a restricted code, where prediction is only possible at the syntactic level.[2] The lexicon will vary from one case to another, but in all cases it is drawn

2. Prediction here refers to an ability of a special observer *not* of the speakers.

from a narrow range. It is necessary to point out that because a lexicon is drawn from a narrow range this is no criterion for classifying the code as a restricted one. The most general condition for the emergence of this code is a social relationship based upon a common, extensive set of closely shared identifications and expectations self-consciously held by the members.[3] It follows that the social relationship will be one of an inclusive kind. The speech is here refracted through a common cultural identity which reduces the need to verbalize intent so that it becomes explicit, with the consequence that the structure of the speech is simplified, and the lexicon will be drawn from a narrow range. The extra-verbal component of the communication will become a major channel for transmitting individual qualifications and so individual difference. The speech will tend to be impersonal in that it will not be specially prepared to fit a given referent. *How* things are said, *when* they are said, rather than what is said, becomes important. The intent of the listener is likely to be taken for granted. The meanings are likely to be concrete: descriptive or narrative rather than analytical or abstract. In certain areas meanings will be highly condensed. The speech in these social relations is likely to be fast and fluent, articulatory clues are reduced; some meanings are likely to be dislocated, condensed and local; there will be a low level of vocabulary and syntactic selections; *the unique meaning of the individual is likely to be implicit*.

Restricted codes are not necessarily linked to social class. They are used by all members of a society at some time. The major function of this code is to define and reinforce the form of the social relationship by restricting the verbal signalling of individual experience.[4]

*Elaborated code (low syntactic prediction)*. An elaborated code, where prediction is much less possible at the syntactic level, is likely to arise in a social relationship which raises the tension in its members to select from their linguistic resources a *verbal* arrangement which closely fits specific referents. This situation will arise where the intent of the other person cannot be taken for granted, with the consequence that meanings will have to be expanded and raised to the level of *verbal* explicitness. The verbal planning here, unlike the case of a restricted code, promotes a higher level of syntactic organization and lexical selection. The preparation and delivery of relatively explicit meaning is the major function of this code. This does not mean that these meanings are necessarily

3. Restricted codes will arise in prisons, combat units of the armed forces, in the peer group of children and adolescents, etc.

4. A restricted code does not necessarily affect the *amount* of speech, only its form.

abstract, but abstraction inheres in the possibilities. The code will facilitate the *verbal* transmission and elaboration of the individual's unique experience. The condition of the listener, unlike that in the case of a restricted code, will *not* be taken for granted, as the speaker is likely to modify his speech in the light of the special conditions and attributes of the listener. This is not to say that such modifications will always occur, but that this possibility exists. If a restricted code facilitates the construction and exchange of communalized symbols, then an elaborated code facilitates the verbal construction and exchange of individualized or personal symbols. An elaborated code, through its regulation, induces in its speakers a sensitivity to the implications of separateness and difference and points to the possibilities inherent in a complex conceptual hierarchy for the organization of experience.

An example at this point is necessary to show how these various codes control social relations. Imagine a man is at a party where he finds a large number of people whom he has never met before. He goes up to a girl. He will then use, initially, a restricted code (lexicon prediction), which will provide the basis for the social relation. He will attempt to improve upon his understanding of her specific attributes by the meaning he gives to her presence and extra-verbal transmissions. He is then likely to move towards an elaborated code (if he possesses one) so that they may both have a means for elaborating verbally their distinctive experience. The possibility of discovering common ground is in this way increased, and the man may then move into a restricted code (syntactic prediction). The quality of the relationship at this point has shifted, and the girl may then regard this as slightly presumptuous and so force the man back to an elaborated code, or, if he is very unfortunate, to a restricted code (lexicon prediction). On the other hand she may accept the change in the social relation. The important points here are that the codes are induced by the social relation, are expressing it, *and* are regulating it. *The ability to switch codes controls the ability to switch roles.* This is a very simple example but it illustrates all the points made earlier. [. . .]

## Some implications of restricted[5] and elaborated codes

An elaborated code generated originally by the form of the social relation becomes a facility for transmitting individuated verbal responses. As far as any one speaker is concerned, he is not aware of a speech-system or code, but the planning procedures which he is using both in the preparation of his speech and in the receiving of speech creates one. These

5. The reference here and throughout is to a restricted code (high syntactic prediction).

planning procedures promote a relatively higher level of syntactic organization and lexical selection than does a restricted code. What is then made available for learning, by an elaborated code, is of a different order from that made available in the case of a restricted code. The learning generated by these speech systems is quite different. By learning, the reference is to what is significant, what is made relevant: socially, intellectually and emotionally. From a developmental perspective, an elaborated code user comes to perceive language as a set of theoretical possibilities available for the transmission of unique experience. The concept of self, unlike the concept of self of a speaker limited to a restricted code, will be verbally differentiated, so that it becomes in itself the object of special perceptual activity. In the case of a speaker limited to a restricted code, the concept of self will tend to be refracted through the implications of the status arrangements. Here there is no problem of self, *because the problem is not relevant*.

As a child learns an elaborated code he learns to scan a particular syntax, to receive and transmit a particular pattern of meaning, to develop particular verbal planning process, and very early *learns to orient towards the verbal channel*. He learns to manage the role requirements necessary for the effective production of the code. He becomes aware of a certain order of relationships (intellectual, social and emotional) in his environment, and his experience is transformed by these relations. As the code becomes established through its planning procedures, the developing child voluntarily, through his acts of speech, generates these relations. He comes to perceive language as a set of theoretical possibilities for the presentation of his discrete experience to others. An elaborated code, through its regulation, induces developmentally in its speakers an expectation of separateness and difference from others. It points to the possibilities inherent in a complex conceptual hierarchy for the organization of experience.

It is possible to distinguish two modes of an elaborated code. One mode facilitates the verbal elaboration of *interpersonal relations*, and the second facilitates the verbal elaboration of relations between *objects*. These two modes of an elaborated code would differentiate different ranges of experience and would pre-suppose learning to manage different role relations. The two modes possess the general features of an elaborated code. They both carry low syntactic prediction; they both serve as facilities for the verbal elaboration of discrete intent; they orient their users to the expectation of difference; they point to logically similar conceptual orders: *but the referents of the relationships are different*.

An individual going into the arts is likely to possess an elaborated code oriented to the person; whilst an individual going into the sciences, particularly the applied sciences, is likely to possess an elaborated code oriented to object relations. C. P. Snow's two cultures may be related to the experiences differentiated through these two modes of an elaborated code. To be able to switch from one mode to the other may involve a recognition of, and an ability to translate verbally, different orders of experience. It may also involve a *recognition* of and an *ability to manage* the different types of role relations which these modes of speech promote. Over and above genetic dispositions towards person or object relations, it may well be that certain kinds of family settings and schools can orient the child towards, and stabilize, the use of one or both of these two modes of an elaborated code. It is possible for an individual to be limited to an elaborated code and to the role relations of either of its two modes, or to possess both modes, or to possess all forms of elaborated and restricted codes. These alternatives may be subject to considerable environmental influence.

A child *limited* to a restricted code will tend to develop essentially through the regulation inherent in the code. For such a child, speech does not become the object of special perceptual activity, neither does a theoretical attitude develop towards the structural possibilities of sentence organization. The speech is epitomized by a low-level and limiting syntactic organization and there is little motivation or orientation towards increasing vocabulary.

There is a limited and often rigid use of qualifiers (adjectives, adverbs, etc.) and these function as social counters through which individual intent is transmitted. This dramatically reduces the verbal elaboration of intent which, instead, tends to be given meaning through extra-verbal means. Words and speech sequences refer to broad classes of contents rather than to progressive differentiation within a class. The reverse of this is also possible; a range of items within a class may be listed without knowledge of the concept which summarizes the class. The categories referred to tend not to be broken down systematically. This has critical implications if the reference is a subjective state of the speaker. Although the speech possesses a warmth and vitality, it tends to be impersonal in the literal sense of that word. The original social relation between mother and child exerted little pressure on the child to make his experience relatively explicit in a verbally differentiated way. Speech is not perceived as a major means of presenting to the other inner states. The type of learning, the conditions of learning, and the dimensions of relevance initiated and sustained through a restricted code are radically different from learning induced through an elaborated code.

The rigid range of syntactic possibilities leads to difficulty in conveying linguistically logical sequence and stress. The verbal planning function is shortened, and this often creates in substantial speech sequences a large measure of dislocation or disjunction. The thoughts are often strung together like beads on a frame rather than following a planned sequence. A restriction in planning often creates a high degree of redundancy. This means that there may well be a great deal of repetition of information, through sequences which add little to what has already been given. The following passages may illustrate these points:

Its all according like these youths and that if they get into these gangs and that they most have a bit of a lark around and say it goes wrong and that and they probably knock someone off I mean think they just do it to be big getting publicity here and there (boy, age 16. I.Q. verbal 104, non-verbal 100).

Well it should do but it don't seem to nowadays, like there's still murders going on now, any minute now or something like that they get people don't care they might get away with it then they all try it and it might leak out one might tell his mates that he's killed someone it might leak out like it might get around he gets hung for it like that (boy, age 17. I.Q. verbal 99, non-verbal 126).

Role relations may be limited and code switching may be hampered by the regulative consequences of a restricted code. An individual limited to a restricted code will tend to mediate an elaborated code through the regulation of his own.

The structure and function of the speech of children and adults limited to a restricted code is of the *same general order* as the speech induced by social relations generating a restricted code outlined earlier. Some children have access to no other code; their only code is a restricted one. Clearly one code is not better than another; each possesses its own aesthetic, its own possibilities. Society, however, may place different values on the orders of experience elicited, maintained and progressively strengthened through the different coding systems.

The orientation towards the codes, elaborated and restricted, may be independent of the psychology of the child, independent of his native ability, although the *level* at which a code is used will undoubtedly reflect purely psychological attributes. The orientation towards these codes may be governed entirely by the form of the social relation, or more generally by the quality of the social structure. The intellectual and social procedures by which individuals relate themselves to their environment may be very much a question of their speech models within the family and the codes these speech models use.

I should like to draw attention to the relations between social class and the two coding systems. The subcultural implications of social class give rise to different socialization procedures. The different normative systems create different family-role systems operating with different modes of social control. It is considered that the normative systems associated with the middle class and associated strata are likely to give rise to the modes of an elaborated code whilst those associated with some sections of the working class are likely to create individuals limited to a restricted code. Clearly social class is an extremely crude index for the codes and more specific conditions for their emergence have been given in this paper. Variations in behaviour found within groups who fall within a particular class (defined in terms of occupation and education) within a mobile society are often very great. It is possible to locate the two codes and their modes more precisely by considering the orientation of the family-role system, the mode of social control and the resultant linguistic relations. Variations in the orientation of the family-role system can be linked to the external social network of the family and to occupational roles. It is not possible to do more than mention the possibilities of these more sensitive indices.

Children socialized within the middle class and associated strata can be expected to possess both an elaborated *and* a restricted code, whilst children socialized within some sections of the working-class strata, particularly the lower working class, can be expected to be *limited* to a restricted code. If a child is to succeed as he progresses through school it becomes critical for him to possess, or at least to be oriented towards, an elaborated code.

The relative backwardness of lower-working-class children may well be a form of culturally induced backwardness transmitted to the child through the implications of the linguistic process. The code the child brings to the school symbolizes his social identity. It relates him to his kin and to his local social relations. The code orients the child progressively towards a pattern of relationships which constitute for the child his psychological reality and this reality is reinforced every time he speaks.

## Conclusion

Two general linguistic codes or speech-systems have been discussed, their social origins explored and their regulative consequences briefly discussed. It is thought that the theory might throw some light on the social determinants of educability. Where a child is sensitive to an elaborated code the school experience for such a child is one of symbolic and social development; for the child limited to a restricted code the school experience is one of symbolic and social change. It is important to realize that a restricted code carries its own aesthetic. It will tend to develop a metaphoric range of considerable power, a simplicity and directness, a vitality and rhythm; it should not be disvalued. Psychologically, it unites the speaker to his kin and to his local community. A change of code involves changes in the *means* whereby social identity and reality are created. This argument means that educational institutions in a fluid society carry within themselves alienating tendencies. To say this is *not* to argue for the preservation of a pseudo-folk culture but rather to argue for certain changes in the social structure of educational institutions; it is also to argue for increased sensitivity on the part of teachers towards both the cultural and cognitive requirements of the formal educational relationship. The problem goes deeper than this. It raises the question of a society which measures human worth, accords respect, grants significance by means of a scale of purely occupational achievement.

From a more academic point of view it is tentatively thought that the thesis might well have a more general application. Elaborated and restricted codes and their variants should be found in any society where their originating conditions exist. The definitions should, in principle, be capable of application to a wide range of languages (and to other symbolic forms, e.g. music), although in any one case elaboration and restriction will be relative. The theory might be seen as a part, but clearly not the whole, of the answer to the problem of how the psychic is transformed into the social. The theory is sociological and is limited by the nature of these assumptions. Individual differences in the use of a particular code cannot be dealt with except on an insensitive more-or-less basis. It is also clear that there is more to culture and communication than what might be revealed by a consideration of limited aspects of speech. Finally, it is thought imperative that sociologists recognize in their analyses the fact that man speaks.

# 27 Colin Lacey

The Formation of Student Subcultures in a
Northern Grammar School

Abridged from Colin Lacey, *Hightown Grammar*, Manchester University Press,
1970, pp. 53–64.

## The model

As soon as the highly selected first-year population meets at the grammar
school and is allocated to the four first-year classes, a complex process of
interaction begins. It takes place through a variety of encounters. Boys
talk and listen to each other; talk and listen to teachers; listen to conversations; notice details of accent, gesture, clothing; watch others at
work and at play in various situations and in innumerable different permutations.

During the first few days much of this interaction appears to take
place in a fairly random way, influenced mainly by the physical and
organizational arrangements. Soon, patterns of selection begin to
emerge. Various initial interactions yield information and experience,
which are retained by the individual and provide some basis for the
interpretation and partial control of other interactions. This partial control is extremely important because it soon gives rise to a recognizable,
although unstable and changing, structure.

I now suggest a model which describes the passage of pupils through
the grammar school. Two terms should first be explained: *differentiation*
and *polarization*. By differentiation I mean the separation and ranking of
students according to a multiple set of criteria which makes up the normative, academically orientated, value system of the grammar school.
Differentiation is defined here as being largely carried out by teachers in
the course of their normal duties.

Polarization, on the other hand, takes place within the student body,
partly as a result of differentiation, but influenced by external factors
and with an autonomy of its own. It is a process of subculture formation
in which the school-dominated, normative culture is opposed by an
alternative culture which I refer to as the 'anti-group' culture. The content of the anti-group culture will, of course, be very much influenced
by the school and its social setting. For example, it may range from a
folk music CND group in a minor public school to a delinquent

subculture at a secondary-modern school in an old urban area. In Hightown Grammar School it fell between these extremes and was influenced by the large working-class and Jewish communities of Hightown.

## Differentiation

There are a number of scales on which a master habitually rates a boy. For the purpose of the analysis, two will be considered:

1. *Academic scale.*

2. *Behaviour scale.* This would include considerations as varied as general classroom behaviour and attitudes; politeness; attention; helpfulness; time spent in school societies and sports. The two are not independent. Behaviour affects academic standards not only because good behaviour involves listening and attending, but because a master becomes favourably disposed towards a boy who is well behaved and trying hard. The teacher therefore tends to help him and even to mark him up. I have found in my own marking of books that when I know the form (i.e. the good and bad pupils), I mark much more quickly. For example, I might partly read an essay and recognize the writing: 'Oh, Brown. Let's see, he tries hard. Good, neat work, missed one or two ideas – seven out of ten.' Or, 'This is a bit scruffy – no margin, not underlined; seems to have got the hang of it though. Who is it? Oh, Jones, that nuisance – five out of ten!'

## Polarization

There is another reason why good behaviour is correlated with academic achievement. A boy who does well and wishes to do well academically is predisposed to accept the grammar school's system of values, that is, he behaves well. The system gives him high prestige, and it is therefore in his interest to support it; the correlation between membership of the choir and performance in class illustrates this point. He is supporting his position of prestige. On the other hand, a boy who does badly academically is predisposed to criticize, reject or even sabotage the system where he can, since it places him in an inferior position.

A boy showing the extreme development of this phenomenon may subscribe to values which are actually the inverted values of the school. He obtains prestige for cheeking a teacher, playing truant, not doing homework, for smoking, drinking and even stealing. As it develops, the anti-group produces its own impetus. The boy who takes refuge in such a group because his work is poor finds that the group commits him to a behaviour pattern which means that his work will stay poor – and in fact often gets progressively worse.

The following extracts from an essay entitled 'Abuse', written by a first-form boy for his housemaster, illustrate a development of anti-group values which is extreme for a first-year pupil:

I am writing this essay about abuse in the toilets. . . . What they (the prefects) call abuse and what I call abuse are two different things altogether.

All the people where I live say I am growing up to be a 'Ted' so I try to please them by acting as much like one as I possibly can. I go around kicking a ball against the wall that is nearest to their house and making as much noise as I can and I intend to carry on doing this until they can leave me alone. . . . It seems to me the Grammar School knows nothing about abuse for *I would much rather be a hooligan and get some fun out of life than be a snob always being the dear little nice boy doing what he is told* (Lacey's italics).

In section 1 above [not included here], we saw that at the beginning of the first year the pupils constitute a relatively homogeneous, undifferentiated group. They were uniformly enthusiastic and eager to please, both through their work and in their behaviour. The pupils who are noticed first are the good ones and the bad ones. Even by the spring term, some masters are still unsure of the names of quiet pupils in the undifferentiated middle of the classes they teach.

It is somewhat rare for an anti-group to develop in the first year. Although one or two individuals may develop marked anti-group values, they are likely to remain isolates. In the 1962 first year, I was able to recognize only one, Badman, the author of the essay. He wished to be transferred to a secondary-modern school.

In the second year the process of differentiation continues. If streaming takes place between the first and second years, as it did in the year group I studied, it helps speed the process and a new crop of cases of emotional disturbance occurs. In the 1963 second year most of them were associated with boys who were failing to make the grade in the top stream and boys who were in the lower half of the bottom stream. Early on, the symptoms are mainly individual; later, after a prolonged period of interaction and the impact of streaming, they are expressed mainly in group attitudes. After six months in the second year this bottom stream was already regarded as a difficult form to teach because, to quote two teachers, 'They're unacademic, they can't cope with the work'; 'Give them half a chance and they'll give you the run-around.'

The true anti-group starts to emerge in the second year, and it develops markedly in the third and fourth years. It is then that strenuous efforts are made to get rid of anti-group pupils. Considerable pressure is put on the headmaster by the teachers who take the boys. He in turn transmits it to the board of governors. In most cases, application to leave will also be made by the boys and their parents. In Hightown, the board of governors was often loath to give permission for a boy to leave or transfer, for two reasons: (a) the governors were also the governors for the secondary modern schools in the area and could not readily agree to passing on disciplinary problems from the grammar school to the secondary modern; (b) they were generally suspicious of grammar-school teachers and felt reluctant to risk an injustice to a pupil who was often a working-class boy.

## Quantitative indices

The indices developed below are prepared from two questionnaires completed by all members of the 1962 intake. One questionnaire was given at the end of the first year and one at the end of the second. The indices are designed to illustrate the processes of differentiation and polarization. On both occasions the boys were asked who had been their close friends over the last year. They were asked to restrict themselves to boys in the school and to six choices, unless they felt they definitely could not do so.

There was virtually no difference in the average number of choices *received* per boy in the four *unstreamed* first-year classes (Table 1).

*Table 1*  Average Number of Friendship Choices Received Per Boy in Each First-Year Class*

| Form | Choices per boy |
| --- | --- |
| 1A | 4·1 |
| 1B | 4·1 |
| 1C | 4·2 |
| 1D | 4·5 |

\* The choices are 'received' from boys in their own form and from the other first-year forms.

When the boys were streamed on academic criteria at the end of the first year, these *same* friendship choices were related to the new forms 2E, 2A, 2B, 2C (Table 2).

Not only do the figures reveal striking differences, but these differences are related to academic achievement. At the end of the first year, the higher up the academic scale a boy was placed, the more likely he was to attract a large number of friendship choices.

At the end of the second year, the boys were asked the same question. The response was equally striking. Column (b) of Table 2 shows that the year spent among a new class of boys has hardly changed the over-all

*Table 2*  Average Number of Friendship Choices Received Per Boy
at the End of First Year and Second Year, for Each of
the Second-Year Classes

| *Average number of choices per boy in in each class* | | |
| Form | (a) First year* | (b) Second year |
| --- | --- | --- |
| 2E | 4·8 | 4·8 |
| 2A | 4·5 | 4·6 |
| 2B | 3·9 | 4·0 |
| 2C | 3·3 | 4·3 |

* The choices in column (a) were made at the end of the first year and are the same as those averaged in Table 1, but they have been averaged for the classes the pupils were about to enter.

The choices in column (b) were made at the end of the second year and are averaged for the classes in which the pupils have spent the year.

positions of 2E, 2A and 2B, although the actual friendship choices for any one boy will have undergone considerable change. However, 2C has undergone a substantial change. The increase from 3·3 to 4·8 for 2C represents an increase of something like thirty choices, in a class of thirty boys. That the new popularity of boys in 2C is brought about by the growth of a new set of norms and values or the beginnings of the anti-group subculture is demonstrated by Table 3. The boys of 2C have become popular for the very reasons they were unpopular in the first year.

The boys of 2E and 2A who, according to our hypothesis, *should* be positively influenced by the academic grading, since they are successful in relation to it, show that it does have a marked positive influence on their choice of friends (for example, 2E make twenty-six choices into 2A, fourteen choices into 2B and only seven into 2C). There is no element in the organization of the school that could bring this about. Similarly, 2A makes twenty-eight choices into 2E, sixteen into 2B and only six into 2C.

In 2B a change takes place. Their choices into 2E and 2A have the expected form but there is an unexpectedly large number of choices into 2C – twenty-three, more than into 2E or 2A. Similarly, the boys of 2C show a marked tendency to choose their friends outside 2C and 2B, rather than from 2E and 2A. There must be a basis, other than the school-imposed academic values, on which these friends are chosen. This alternative set of norms and values I have already referred to as the anti-group subculture.

*Table 3* Distribution of Friendship Choices According to Class: Second Year, 1963 (1962 Intake at End of Second Year)

Read *across* for choices made, *down* for choices received by each class

| Form (number in each class in brackets) | 2E | 2A | 2B | 2C | Others | Total of choices made | Percentage of choices in own class |
|---|---|---|---|---|---|---|---|
| 2E (31) | 91 | 26 | 14 | 7 | 12 | 150 | 60·7 |
| 2A (31) | 28 | 94 | 16 | 6 | 14 | 158 | 59·5 |
| 2B (28) | 20 | 17 | 63 | 23 | 20 | 143 | 44·0 |
| 2C (30) | 9 | 4 | 18 | 92 | 13 | 136 | 67·7 |
| Total (of choices received) | 148 | 141 | 111 | 128 | 58 | 588 | |

# 28 Robert Perrucci

## The Structural Context of Mobility

Abridged from Robert Perrucci, 'Education stratification and mobility', in
Donald A. Hansen and Joel E. Gerstl (eds.), *On Education: Sociological Perspectives*,
Wiley, 1967, pp. 132–9.

The role of values, aspirations and motivation as positive or negative
factors in the mobility process is clearly of considerable importance. But
it is only a part of the story. Values and aspirations have their origin
within specific group contexts, and they are encouraged, nourished or
extinguished in these same contexts. Networks of social relationships, or
social structures, are the paths through which ideas concerning mobility
are transmitted. Yet social structures do more than simply channel and
transmit values to those persons implicated within them. They also generate their own peculiar set of inducements and constraints upon the
mobility process. Families of varying size and composition can create
bonds of kinship so strong as to inhibit any motivation to 'leave' one's
family of origin. Community size and structure can affect the existing
opportunity structure and, as a result, the individual's perception of and
aspiration for occupational mobility. School climates, in terms of pupils,
faculty and curriculum, are also a significant set of constraints upon the
mobility process. In this section we shall examine some of the structural
contexts in which the desire, expectation and opportunity for mobility
are found.

Let us begin with a view of social structure as a set of channels for the
transmission of mobility-relevant values and aspirations. Since social
structures represent patterns of social relationships that persist over time,
the information transmitted through the relationship networks will have
a tendency to maintain and reinforce established patterns of living. In
the case of the social structure of stationary lower-class families, for
example, we may offer the following structural explanation for intergenerational immobility: given unfavorable conditions for real improvement, individuals will adapt in such fashion as to reduce occupational
and educational aspirations. These initial adaptations develop supportive
values and norms which take on their own reasons for existence and are
transmitted through established networks of social relationships. With
this separate existence as cultural patterns, values and norms which
emerged as adaptive responses now function to perpetuate immobility.

Stated in this form, such a description of intergenerational immobility does not provide a good fit to reality. There is enough upward and downward mobility in all classes to indicate that social structures must also transmit values and aspirations that are not in keeping with the dominant values of a particular class. How is it that some lower-class youth endorse values and aspirations that are the modal patterns of another social stratum? What are the mechanisms by which values which move through one social structure are transmitted through another social structure? Are there particular persons in a social structure who are the 'carriers' of foreign values and who provide the necessary support for the maintenance of these values?

The structural patterns suggest a very interesting tendency among mobile lower-class youth, as compared to middle-class youth, to look outside the family for information, advice and support for upward mobility. This tendency seems to be related to the functional role played by loose family ties in the process of mobility. Strodtbeck, for example, has pointed to the manner in which 'familism' values interfere with mobility values and result in lower achievement among Italians as compared to Jews. Involvement in extended family relationships and concern with leaving the family as a result of job mobility has also been found to limit mobility and migration among persons in rural depressed areas. Thus it appears that structural supports for mobility outside the family may also reinforce the need of the mobile person to leave behind the old-established ties and take on new ties.

To this point in this section we have stressed the significance of social structure for mobility in terms of the capacity of various social structures to provide channels for transmitting mobility-oriented values and aspirations. However, structural contexts are important for understanding mobility not only from the point of view of value transmission, but for their capacity for providing personal qualities, skills, self-confidence, personal control and independence as a function of the type of relationships that children are exposed to. A family structure, for example, can become the 'small society' in which the child learns the rules for coping with, adapting to, or mastering relationships in the larger society. As Strodtbeck has put it in his study of mobility among Italians and Jews:

The general question is: what is the arrangement of power and support among the three roles of father, mother and son which is maximally related to attitudes for achievement and to subsequent adjustment to success outside the family? . . .

Two possible ways in which power relationships may affect a boy's subsequent achievement immediately suggest themselves. The first involves the ease with which the son identifies with his father. Proper father-identification, which is probably related to adequate performance in the male role, could very well be facilitated or inhibited by different power relationships among father, mother and son. The second concerns the fact that the power distribution in the family will condition the way a boy expects power to be distributed in the outside world, and that his adjustment to family power will, therefore, generalize to external systems.

Strodtbeck's findings on the role of family relationships in mobility are most revealing. Italian and Jewish boys who were more likely to believe the world was subject to rational mastery and independent achievement were those who reported democratic relationships with their father and equalitarian relationships between parents. Perhaps even more interesting is the finding that the son's achievement and mastery values are correlated with the nature of the power relationships but not with whether the father held the values of mastery and achievement. In effect, the father's pattern of relationships with other family members – in this case, father domination – serves to negate the very values he might seek to transmit in his relationships with his son. As Strodtbeck most pointedly puts it: 'The son is more likely, at least in this stage of life, to resign himself to the notion that there are forces beyond his control – in this instance, father.'

The final structural context related to the encouragement and transmission of mobility-related values and aspirations is that of school climate. In speaking of school climate we are interested in two things. The first is the normative climate of the school, which in large part is related to the characteristics of the student body. Does the particular social composition of the student body provide a normative environment that becomes a constraining force on the values, aspirations and performance of individual students? Our second interest turns attention away from the student, to the teachers and type and quality of curriculum and instruction.

One of the most extensive and systematic investigations of school climate and its effects upon education is Coleman's study of the social structure and value climate of ten high schools in northern Illinois. Among the more important findings was that school climates, as exemplified by those students who were the social élites and members of leading crowds, contained a strong emphasis upon social activities, sports and popularity as contrasted with intellectual activity. Such value emphases were found to exist in the working-class school and the upper-middle-class school as well. To quote Coleman:

As has been evident throughout this research, the variation among schools in the status of scholastic achievement is not nearly so striking as the fact that in all of them, academic achievement did not 'count' for as much as did other activities in the school. Many other attributes were most important. In every school the boys named as best athletes and those named as most popular with girls were far more often mentioned as members of the leading crowd, and as someone to 'be like' than were the boys named as best students. And the girls who were named as best dressed, and those named as most popular with boys, were in every school far more often mentioned as being in the leading crowd and as someone to be like, than were the girls named as best students.

The relative unimportance of academic achievement . . . suggests that the adolescent subcultures in these schools exert a rather strong deterrent to academic achievement.

The existence of such adolescent subcultures in high schools is important for understanding mobility. For the lower-class youth, such an environment simply becomes an added barrier to his own mobility. For if he relies more heavily upon sources outside the family for support of mobility aspirations as suggested earlier, the nonintellectual high-school climate operates as a mobility inhibiting factor. Or to put it another way, if he is to get support for intellectual values through involvement with others of similar inclination, he does so at the expense of lowered status within the school status system. As a double burden, he would probably also lose status among his lower-class peers outside the school for his interest in things intellectual.

The middle-class youth, on the other hand, may not 'suffer' as much from such a school climate. It is possible that the adolescent subculture is a luxury he can afford, at least from the point of view of the likelihood that it will lead away from a college career. Since he is more likely to have mobility-inducing support from the family, not to mention the economic resources which make higher education an established expectation, there will be a discrepancy between the adolescent and adult world in which mobility-inhibiting values are not reinforced. And perhaps most important is that Coleman's findings refer to the pursuit of high standards of academic achievement which, while important for the encouragement and fostering of exceptional talent, is not necessarily related to expectations regarding college attendance and occupational aspirations. Thus, the middle-class boy can devalue intellectual pursuits without impairing his desire to go to college (for he may find the college and high school environments to be quite similar), but the lower-class youth who devalues intellectual pursuits is too apt to find ready sources of support and reinforcement for devaluing education.

# 29 Jean Piaget

On Intellectual Growth

Excerpt from Jean Piaget, *The Language and Thought of the Child*, Routledge
& Kegan Paul, 1967 reprint of 3rd edn, pp. 38-41. This translation first published
in 1926. First published in French in 1923.

Egocentrism must not be confused with secrecy. Reflexion in the child
does not admit of privacy. Apart from thinking by images or autistic
symbols which cannot be directly communicated, the child up to an age,
as yet undetermined but probably somewhere about seven, is incapable
of keeping to himself the thoughts which enter his mind. He says everything. He has no verbal continence. Does this mean that he socializes his
thought more than we do? That is the whole question, and it is for us to
see to whom the child really speaks. It may be to others. We think on the
contrary that it is first and foremost to himself, and that speech, before it
can be used to socialize thought, serves to accompany and reinforce
individual activity. Let us try to examine more closely the difference
between thought which is socialized but capable of secrecy, and infantile
thought which is egocentric but incapable of secrecy.

The adult, even in his most personal and private occupations, even
when he is engaged on an inquiry which is incomprehensible to his fel-
low-beings, thinks socially, has continually in his mind's eye his collaborators or opponents, actual or eventual, at any rate members of his
own profession to whom sooner or later he will announce the result of his
labours. This mental picture pursues him throughout his task. The task
itself is henceforth socialized at almost every stage of its development.
Invention eludes this process, but the need for checking and demonstrating calls into being an inner speech addressed throughout to a hypothetical opponent, whom the imagination often pictures as one of flesh and
blood. When, therefore, the adult is brought face to face with his fellow-
beings, what he announces to them is something already socially elaborated, and therefore roughly adapted to his audience, that is, it is
comprehensible. Indeed, the further a man has advanced in his own
line of thought, the better able is he to see things from the point of
view of others and to make himself understood by them.

The child, on the other hand, placed in the conditions which we have
described, seems to talk far more than the adult. Almost everything he
does is to the tune of remarks such as 'I'm drawing a hat', 'I'm doing it

better than you', etc. Child thought, therefore, seems more social, less capable of sustained and solitary research. This is so only in appearance. The child has less verbal continence simply because he does not know what it is to keep a thing to himself. Although he talks almost incessantly to his neighbours, he rarely places himself at their point of view. He speaks to them for the most part as if he were alone, and as if he were thinking aloud. He speaks, therefore, in a language which disregards the precise shade of meaning in things and ignores the particular angle from which they are viewed, and which above all is always making assertions, even in argument, instead of justifying them. Nothing could be harder to understand than the note-books which we have filled with the conversation of Pie and Lev. Without full commentaries, taken down at the same time as the children's remarks, they would be incomprehensible. Everything is indicated by allusion, by pronouns and demonstrative articles – 'he, she, the, mine, him, etc.' – which can mean anything in turn, regardless of the demands of clarity or even of intelligibility. ... In a word, the child hardly ever even asks himself whether he has been understood. For him, that goes without saying, for he does not think about others when he talks. He utters a 'collective monologue'. His language only begins to resemble that of adults when he is directly interested in making himself understood; when he gives orders or asks questions. To put it quite simply, we may say that the adult thinks socially, even when he is alone, and that the child under seven thinks egocentrically, even in the society of others.

What is the reason for this? It is, in our opinion, twofold. It is due, in the first place, to the absence of any sustained social intercourse between the children of less than seven or eight, and in the second place to the fact that the language used in the fundamental activity of the child – play – is one of gestures, movement and mimicry as much as of words. There is, as we have said, no real social life between children of less than seven or eight years. The type of children's society represented in a classroom of the *Maison des Petits* is obviously of a fragmentary character, in which consequently there is neither division of work, centralization of effort, nor unity of conversation. We may go further, and say that it is a society in which, strictly speaking, individual and social life are not differentiated. An adult is at once far more highly individualized and far more highly socialized than a child forming part of such a society. He is more individualized, since he can work in private without perpetually announcing what he is doing, and without imitating his neighbours. He is more socialized for the reasons which have just been given. The child is neither individualized, since he cannot keep a single thought secret, and since everything done by one member of the group is repeated through a sort of imitative repercussion by almost every other member. Nor is he socialized, since this imitation is not accompanied by what may properly be called an interchange of thought, about half the remarks made by children being egocentric in character. If, as Baldwin and Janet maintain, imitation is accompanied by a sort of confusion between one's own action and that of others, then we may find in this fragmentary type of society based on imitation some sort of explanation of the paradoxical character of the conversation of children who, while they are continually announcing their doings, yet talk only for themselves, without listening to anyone else.

# Part Five  Work and Industry

Work has always been a basic feature of human society. With the Industrial Revolution, however, significant changes have occurred in the way work is organized. Most clearly, work is now on the whole performed in factories rather than at home. Thompson (Reading 30) refers to a change which is less obvious, the transition from work based on natural periods of time to work based on the clock. In Reading 31 Bakke examines the fundamental meaning of work by referring to the minority who are distinguished by *not* being employed. Those who are at work, he shows (Reading 32), base their assessment of their situation on a comparison with others who may be better or worse off than themselves.

Sociologists have described in a number of different ways the structure of relations at the workplace. The approach of Mayo (see Reading 33) stressed the importance of motivating employees in an appropriate manner, thus laying the foundation for the 'human relations' school of management. In contrast, when Goldthorpe and his colleagues (see Reading 34) look at car-assembly workers they stress the extent to which their orientation to their work is a product not of the policies of management, nor of their satisfaction with the work they are doing, but of their role within the community. This leads them to put a higher value on consistent and high wages than upon any of the other types of satisfaction which people gain from their work. Tunstall (Reading 35), however, in his study of fishermen, shows that this is by no means the only approach to work. And in contrast to the car-assembly workers, who live relatively 'privatized' lives in modern housing estates, work and social life in the trawler industry still spill over into each other to a considerable extent.

Finally, we include an article by Merton (Reading 36) which, while not referring specifically to behaviour within work organizations, provides a theoretical approach which allows us to understand the conflicts which occur when managers and employees alike are faced with conflicting expectations as to how to perform their work roles.

# 30 E. P. Thompson

Time and Work Discipline

Excerpt from E. P. Thompson, 'Time, work discipline and industrial capitalism', *Past and Present*, vol. 38, 1967, pp. 60–61.

Labour from dawn to dusk can appear to be 'natural' in a farming community, especially in the harvest months: nature demands that the grain be harvested before the thunderstorms set in. And we may note similar 'natural' work-rhythms which attend other rural or industrial occupations: sheep must be attended at lambing time and guarded from predators; cows must be milked; the charcoal fire must be attended and not burn away through the turfs (and the charcoal burners must sleep beside it); once iron is in the making, the furnaces must not be allowed to fail.

The notation of time which arises in such contexts has been described as task-orientation. It is perhaps the most effective orientation in peasant societies, and it remains important in village and domestic industries. It has by no means lost all relevance in rural parts of Britain today. Three points may be proposed about task-orientation. First, there is a sense in which it is more humanly comprehensible than timed labour. The peasant or labourer appears to attend upon what is an observed necessity. Second, a community in which task-orientation is common appears to show least demarcation between 'work' and 'life'. Social intercourse and labour are intermingled – the working-day lengthens or contracts according to the task – and there is no great sense of conflict between labour and 'passing the time of day'. Third, to men accustomed to labour timed by the clock, this attitude to labour appears to be wasteful and lacking in urgency.

Such a clear distinction supposes, of course, the independent peasant or craftsman as referent. But the question of task-orientation becomes greatly more complex at the point where labour is employed. The entire family economy of the small farmer may be task-orientated; but within it there may be a division of labour, and allocation of roles, and the discipline of an employer–employed relationship between the farmer and his children. Even here time is beginning to become money, the employer's money. As soon as actual hands are employed the shift from task-orientation to timed labour is marked. It is true that the timing of work can be done independently of any time-piece – and indeed precedes the diffusion of the clock. Still, in the mid-seventeenth century substantial farmers calculated their expectations of employed labour (as did Henry Best) in 'dayworkes' – 'the Cunnigarth, with its bottomes, is four large dayworkes for a good mower', 'the Spellowe is four indifferent dayworkes', etc.; and what Best did for his own farm, Markham attempted to present in general form:

A man ... may mow of Corn, as Barley and Oats, if it be thick, loggy and beaten down to the earth, making fair work, and not cutting off the heads of the ears, and leaving the straw still growing one acre and a half in a day: but if it be good thick and fast standing corn, then he may mow two acres, or two acres and a half in a day; but if the corn be short and thin, then he may mow three, and sometimes four acres in a day, and not be overlaboured.

The computation is difficult, and dependent upon many variables. Clearly, a straightforward time-measurement was more convenient.

This measurement embodies a simple relationship. Those who are employed experience a distinction between their employer's time and their 'own' time. And the employer must *use* the time of his labour, and see it is not wasted: not the task but the value of time when reduced to money is dominant. Time is now currency: it is not passed but spent.

# 31 E. Wight Bakke

The Environment of Unemployment

Excerpts from E. Wight Bakke, *The Unemployed Man: A Social Study*, Nisbet, 1933, pp. 62–72.

The first important characteristic which ran through the attitudes of every skilled worker and all but a very few of the labourers with whom I talked was the sense of being lost without the work to which they were accustomed:

It takes it out of you when you've been working all yer life, and it puts years on to you. It's put years on my head, this past eleven months has. Us men that's learned to work are lost without it. – a riveter.

It ain't the money any more than it is the fact that you don't have nothin' to do. Your money at the Labour helps out a bit, but it don't give you no work to do, and that's what I miss. – a brewery hand.

You've heard tell that the worker today don't get no satisfaction out of his work. Well let me tell you something. He gets a lot more satisfaction out of it than he does living without it on unemployment benefit. – a sheet-metal worker.

One ship repairer became so desperate without work after a period of six months that he offered to raffle himself. It wasn't need for food or clothing that forced him to such a proposal. He declared that he could bear the idleness no longer. So he proposed to offer himself at a raffle, give half the receipts to a hospital and work for the winner for such time as the other half might be considered cover.

This sense of being 'out of stride', of being forced into a state of idleness, is a factor the exact opposite of the element of laziness which is declared by some to cause men to follow the path of least resistance. The number of semiskilled men with large families who said they would 'jump at the chance' to go back to work, even if they received no more than their insurance benefit, is an indication that even in a machine age there are other rewards for work than the money reward. Said one former employee of the London County Council:

Everybody does some work in this world. You can go as far back as Adam, and you'll find that they all work someway, with their brains if not with their hands. That's one thing that makes us human; we don't wait for things to happen to us, we work for them. And if you can't find any work to do, you have the feeling that you're not human. You're out of place. You're so different from all the rest of the people around that you think something is wrong with you. I don't care what your job is, you feel a lot more important when you come home at night than if you had been tramping around the streets all day. The next time you see a lot of fellows standing and watching a gang laying a pavement or putting up a house, *just ask yourself how much fun it is to stand and watch other men work.*

The lack of such work discipline is one of the factors in making the problem of the unemployed young men so difficult of solution. They have not the same habitual experience of working day after day, week after week, and year after year, which the older men have. Work does not have the same pull on them as it does on the men to whom the job has become the cornerstone of their whole life.

It may also be noted in this connexion that the few cases in which this attractiveness of the job as a giver of status was absent were cases of unskilled labourers whose work was casual, unsteady and offered little satisfaction aside from the wage.

Five of the men whom I met early in the period devoted to this study remained in my acquaintance for more than four months. I kept records of my periodic meetings and conversations with them. Those progressive records give evidence of the increasing severity with which unemployment makes itself felt as the days change to weeks and the weeks to months. Two of them, typical of the others, are given here. The first case is that of a young man of twenty-eight. He was experienced as a mechanic and as a motor-lorry driver. After leaving the Central School he had gone to technical school and had had ten years of experience driving lorries on long-distance jobs. I shall call him A.

I met A one evening after we had been listening to a political speech on the street corner. He had just come out of work three days before. He was confident of getting another job soon. There weren't any vacancies at the Labour Exchange, but 'You don't need to expect much there, anyway. There's plenty of jobs for a man with my experience. I've never been out more than a week or so before. I'll soon be back. The governor never had no complaint to make about my work though we had a little fracas when I left.' He was a good man and he knew it. The fact that he had no job didn't discourage him, he had weathered the same kind of experience before.

*Three weeks later.* 'I'm beginning to wonder how plentiful jobs are. It's a funny thing. It's never been like this before. It's most discouragin', Mr Bakke, most discouragin'. You feel like you're no good, if you get what I mean.' During these three weeks he had written in response to every 'ad' for drivers, in the London district, which appeared in *The Times* and the *Telegraph*. He was living with his parents so that he didn't worry about his board and room, except that he didn't like to 'sponge off them' any longer than he had to. He was still hopeful that he had just missed the jobs and that something would come his way, soon.

*Eight weeks.* I went down to A's house to request that he keep a record of his week's activities for me. I went at nine o'clock in the evening. His mother informed me that he had not yet returned from looking for work. He had gone to Highgate (about ten miles) in answer to a sign up in the Employment Exchange. They were running low on cash so he had decided to walk rather than to pay bus fare. 'He says as long as he isn't doing anything to earn money, he isn't going to spend it.' I returned the next night at nine o'clock. He had just come in from a long tramp in search of work. 'I'm beginning to wonder what is wrong with me. I've tried every way. I've had to walk in the back way in order to get at the governor. Then he says, "How'd you get in here?" And then he tells me he don't need me. Then I have to dodge the company police to get into another place. It makes you cunnin', you know. Then they say, "How long you been out?" And you don't like to, but you lie. I never thought I'd lie even to get a job. But I know if I tell them two months they'll say, "What's wrong?" And even if I prove my character is right, I'm started on the wrong foot with him. I don't like it. "We'll take your name and address", they says. How many times I have heard that! But those words don't give you work to do.'

*Eleven weeks.* During the intervening period, I had kept in touch with A. The diligence with which he explored every possibility of work aroused my admiration. He worked far harder and far longer hours at this task than at his regular job. The confidence which I had noticed in my first conversation with him was completely gone. In its place there had come a dogged determination to find some kind of work. He had lost the hope that careful following of leads would secure him a job. He had turned to an unplanned, gate-to-gate search for work. Here was his comment at the end of eleven weeks. 'There's one of two things, either I'm no good, or there is something wrong with business around here. Of course, I know that things are slack. But I've always said that a good man could get a job even in slack times. That's not so. And the man who says so is a liar. I wouldn't say this very loud, but I'm telling you that I'm beginning to hate England. Do you suppose if I went to the States I could get started? I feel when I walk down the streets here that all my old mates are looking at me and saying, "Wonder what's wrong with A. He never used to keep away from work so long." Even my family is beginning to think I'm not trying. So I can't talk much with them any more. I get in some nights as late as ten, eat a bite and then go to bed. Some nights we never say a word. Then I lay and try to plan like I used to when one job came to an end. But somehow the plans don't come like they used to. I reckon I've tried them all. And it's up at five-thirty or six in the morning to start out again. But you don't wake up feeling like going again. For you don't know which way to go. But you do.'

*Seventeenth week.* A didn't say much the last time I saw him. He was sullen and despondent. He wasn't completely discouraged yet. The search for a job had lost all of its zest for him, and had settled down to a drab search for what experience told him he could not find. It was during this last interview that he expressed what lies at the root of the demoralization of such fine workers as he, after a long period of unemployment:

*It isn't the hard work of tramping about so much, although that is bad enough. It's the hopelessness of every step you take when you go in search of a job you know isn't there. [. . .]*

Practically every man who had a family showed evidences of the blow his self-confidence had suffered from the fact that the traditional head of the family was not able to perform his normal function. He had married in the confidence that he was able to support a family. He was failing in that. The blow was all the harder because he felt that the failure was not all his own fault. He would be able to support his family if he had a chance to work. The state of mind of this group of men with families is focused sharply in the statement of a boilermaker:

It's nasty out tonight, isn't it? But you can't stay indoors, can you? It gets on your mind, to see the kids around and you know you're not bringing anything to them. I used to like to have them run to meet me when I came home from work. But now. . . . Well – I almost wish they wouldn't come. It's hell when a man can't even support his own family.

The effect of this loss of satisfaction in the doing of the day's task should not be forgotten when the diligence of the search for work is being assessed. As a carpenter said, 'It's a lot harder looking for work than doing it, mate.' I do not intend to discuss the effect of mental attitudes on increasing or decreasing the amount of fatigue which accompanies the doing of any work. Whatever the degree of that effect may be, certainly the looking for a job, particularly after several months of no success, is surrounded by the minimum of those factors which decrease the actual physical fatigue attendant upon such effort. Such tiredness is likely to be mistaken by the casual observer for laziness. It would be closer to the truth to describe it as physical and mental exhaustion from the doing of work (search for a job) which is unaccompanied by any reward or hope of reward.

One further fact with respect to the mental effects of unemployment struck me as more significant than the rest. Robbed of a job, the difference in ability as between individuals has only one chance for expression – *more or less initiative in finding work*. Until work is found, the greater ability, the greater efficiency, the better attitude towards work – these are of no value. The job is the medium in which these qualities acquire significance. Without this job, they are useless.

But this added aggressiveness in looking for work is just the factor which throws a man, if unsuccessful, against rebuff after rebuff; and the sensitiveness to the importance of one's place as a worker will cause him to get disheartened more quickly than the man who has less sensitiveness on this point. I was not surprised, therefore, to find among the men with whom I associated for several months that the most ambitious lost heart most quickly. The quality that *on the job* leads to rapid achievement of greater and greater satisfactions, *off the job* leads to rapid retreat into hopelessness and discontent, despair and even sullenness. The incentive to work hard, the desire to push ahead, the ambition to perfect one's technique, these are basic qualities for satisfaction at work. They are just the qualities that make it hardest for a man to be out of work.

Unemployment Insurance eases the physical hardship of all and the mental distress of the unambitious, but it does not prove true medicine for the mental attitudes of the highly skilled or even the unskilled workman who is ambitious.

With a job, there is a future; without a job, there is slow death of all that makes a man ambitious, industrious and glad to be alive.

E. Wight Bakke   227

# 32 E. Wight Bakke

Workers and Wages

E. Wight Bakke, 'Workers and Wages', in E. Wight Bakke, Clark Kerr and
C. W. Anrod (eds.), *Unions, Management and the Public*, Harcourt, Brace & World,
3rd edn, 1967, pp. 557–9. First published in a slightly different form in
E. Wight Bakke, *The Unemployed Worker*, Yale University Press, 1940.

High on the list of circumstances which set boundaries to the worker's
field of activity and achievement is income. There are few subjects about
which there is more talk, less understanding and more feeling than this.
Few workers in America *make* a living. Each *buys* a living with money
received primarily from wages. That fact is an important clue to what
they do and think and hope for. The pay envelope or the salary check
gives to each an individual claim upon what all in cooperation have
produced. But wages are more than that – they set standards of prestige,
they give a measure of a man's worth, they make spending habits a
measure of character and they furnish a whole set of practices which
make our culture distinctive. In an earlier day when money was not the
key to most of life, money did not drive men on to exceptional effort, nor
the lack of it to drink.

In America in the twentieth century, if one were to take away the
making and the spending of money, most societal arrangements would
collapse. We should be confused about who was successful and why.
Society bluebooks would have to be revised. The development of enterprises involving billions of dollars would no longer startle the imagination and we should have to get our vicarious thrills from thinking about
those who went looking for a sacred cup. We should be forced to find
another set of qualifications for some (not all) of our directors of non-
profit agencies. The 'upper' classes would have to find some way other
than spending money to make them different from the 'lower' classes.
We should not be considering wages as one of the major facts in the lives
of American workers.

For it is the fact that we have arranged in our society to give a man a
pay envelope for doing his work and then leave him free to live or not, to
save or not, to spend or not, to marry or not, to have children or not, to
work or not – it is just that fact that makes the amount and the steadiness
of the wage, and the arrangements we make to fill in the gap when there
is no envelope, so important.

Now the fact that wages and the buying of a living with wages and the determining of a social status by wages are all part of the folkways is in itself no more a distinctive problem for workers than is the fact that it is customary for men to wear low-heeled shoes. It is the fact that those wages do not buy the kind of living men would like to have ... that makes wages a workers' problem. Mr Dooley once put a part of the issue this way: 'Wan iv the strangest things about life is that th' poor, who need the money th' most, ar-re the viry wans that niver have it.' ... They need no union organizer to tell them that. The feeling is a product of the inadequacy of the wages they receive to meet their problems of living comfortably. It is not a product of comparison of their wage with the value they give to their employer nor of a comparison with what *he* has. Ideas of the relationship of wages to work may be seen from a very typical response. 'What is a fair wage? Now you've got me: but it would be enough to live on without worry and it would come regular. I guess really what I mean when I say *fair* wages is *more* wages.'

What the worker considers to be a 'fair' wage is probably a point somewhere between the amount necessary to support his family on their present plane of living and the amount necessary to achieve an eventual standard of living desired. Although the horizon of this standard is limited, it is not fixed. Actually we know little that is definite about either the lower or upper limits below or above which the effort is not worth the compensation. The absolute minimum is probably very close to the amount a family could get on relief. Interviews with thousands of workers in the course of our research at the Institute of Human Relations would suggest a conservative definition of the upper limits. Certainly the immediate standard of economic security is determined for most of these workers by the standard of living customary for the most favored of his immediate associates.

Alger books to the contrary, the horizon of working-class people extends very little beyond the standards attained by other members of their own class with whose situation they were acquainted, so far as their personal ambitions were concerned. For their children they desire an education higher than that which they had attained. For them they hold out the hope that something better than factory work awaits them as a career. Many a working-class family is integrated around the effort to provide children with educational and training equipment which would make possible for them a nonworking-class life. ...

The wish for security is amplified by a longing for the regularity of income. Workers have had to adapt themselves to great fluctuations in income and work. But no degree of acceptance destroys the difficulty, if not the absolute impossibility, of planning under such circumstances.

That obstacle to comfortable living for ordinary people who try to eliminate the unexpected as much as possible from their lives is an unsolvable problem. The conditions upon which the evenness of work and income depend are out of their control.

The desire for economic security is further amplified by the wish to win a comfortable margin beyond mere maintenance requirements. I was reminded in talking with American workers of Whiting Williams's reference to Wanamaker's advertisement for woolen blankets, 'It is the part of the blanket that hangs over which keeps you warm.' Not much of the blanket hung over for most of those with whom in one relation or another we associated.

Economic security means, then, increasing within the possibilities of working-class income and in view of the standards set by working-class associates, the regularity of income and a comfortable margin beyond the minimum of livelihood demanded by the standard of living set by the group.

The realization of such security does not require approximation to the economic status of wealthy persons; it requires merely evidence of some progress from the point at which one started. That is an achievement which is possible in a relatively short period of life for workers, say between the ages of twenty-one and forty. At the latter age children who have been contributing begin to leave home, and unless one can hold on to the job he has had, satisfactory and remunerative employment opportunities rapidly decrease. But during these years 'with fair luck' one has the sense of making at least small progress from the economic starting point.

These are the considerations which define what workers are struggling for when they use the term 'security'. It is obviously not a guaranteed maintenance, nor is it a guarantee of standards and safeguards which would be satisfactory to most middle-class individuals. It is the obtaining of some hope that they may secure some margin of safety above the standard which *their* associates require of the self-respecting man. ...

Within these boundaries of the minimum required for maintenance at a relief level and the social standards of economic success certain recurring definitions of a fair wage were evident. ... We list a few of the 'fair wage' standards most frequently cited:

1. As much as others are getting for the same work in the same plant.

2. As much as is paid for the same work in other plants in the same city.

3. As much as other employees of the same company are getting for the same work in other cities.

4. Enough to provide a proper differential above those who do work in the same plant which is less skilled, valuable or responsible.

5. Enough so that the wife and children do not have to work.

6. Enough so the children can finish high school.

7. Enough to permit laying something aside for a rainy day and for old age.

8. The union rate (for union men).

It is evident that as far as workers are concerned, a fair-wage concept is geared more to their standing among their fellows, to a comparison with their rates, and to the amount needed for living than to remuneration consistent with the profitability of their services to the employer.

## 33 Reinhard Bendix

The Contribution of Elton Mayo to Managerial Ideology

Abridged from Reinhard Bendix, *Work and Authority in Industry*, Harper & Row, 1963, pp. 311–18. First published in 1956.

Major contributions in the history of ideas often consist in an author's striking summary of old ideas. I believe this is true of Mayo's work. There are traces of the 'New Thought' movement in his emphasis upon the strategic importance of mental and emotional factors in the make-up of managers and workers. The promise of success is rather lacking in Mayo in keeping with the changing images of man in industry, which I have traced. Cooperation in industry is identified by Mayo with society's capacity to survive; and this belief is akin to, if not identical with, the ideal of cooperation which inspired the employee-representation plans and the open-shop campaign of the 1920s. Mayo's neglect of trade unions and of their role in industry is well in line with the open-shop campaign also, for in this campaign employers were not only fighting unions, but also introducing many measures designed to forestall them by satisfying the demands of workers in line with managerial objectives.

Some managers had also anticipated Mayo with regard to a reassessment of the motivation of workers. During the 1920s, several writers had pointed out that it was wrong to think workers were interested only in money. Instead workers wanted to feel they were doing something worth while and that they had the respect of others. They wanted 'to be somebody other than an unidentified human unit in an industrial organization'. Failure to take this into account would wreck even the best intentioned welfare plans.

Mayo used scientific investigations to prove workers were not self-interested individuals but persons with attitudes and feelings which had to be considered in terms other than a test of their aptitudes for better job placement.

A comparison and contrast between Mayo and Taylor is most illuminating in this connexion. Mayo certainly shared Taylor's belief in science as the foundation upon which an enlightened management should base its approach. Taylor had advanced the idea of a managerial élite, which by means of a 'mental revolution' could increase wages as well as profits.

To do so it had only to base its shop management and the selection and training of workers upon the results of scientific studies. Though Mayo did not accept Taylor's techniques, his conception of a managerial or administrative élite which would bring about industrial harmony and increased production had much in common with Taylor's idea of a managerial élite. Both men were concerned with discovering the causes of low productivity or of output restriction; both insisted that industrial conflicts were harmful and that the cooperation of employers and workers should be increased; and both attributed the output restrictions of workers to the mistaken views of labor *and* management.

Nevertheless, Taylor differed from Mayo on certain major points. He thought workers were justified to restrict their output as long as their increased productivity was *not* reflected in higher earnings. In this respect Taylor was certainly not typical of the managers, whose ideas and practices he sought to influence. Yet he and they were at one in their endeavor to test each worker *as an individual*, since in their judgement it was his aptitude for work which counted, not his relations to his fellow-workers. As a group, workers were regarded as intrinsically hostile to management, since they tended to promote both the organization of trade unions and the output restriction which trade unions encouraged. In these respects Taylor and his followers continued the tradition of regarding each worker as a wage-maximizing individual in isolation.

Elton Mayo broke with that tradition. His research confirmed his belief that workers acted in natural solidarity with their fellows, not as isolated individuals. As a result of Mayo's work, there was a marked increase in the existing tendency of managers and their spokesmen to concern themselves with the attitudes and feelings of workers. Moreover, Mayo extended his analysis to the qualities and practices of management and he reinterpreted the meaning of managerial authority in industry.

Critics of Mayo and his school have pointed out that both the willing teamwork of the six relay assemblers and the output restriction of fourteen workers in the Bank Wiring Room were instances of cooperation. But in a managerial context this objection is beside the point.

The change from output restriction to willing cooperation depends in both instances upon an indirect inducement. Hence, Mayo's view of the managerial task may be defined as the endeavor to provide an organizational environment in which employees can fulfil their 'eager human desire for cooperative activity'. The major objective of management is to foster cooperative teamwork among its employees.

To deny that in modern enterprises authority can be exercised against the will of subordinates is tantamount to the assertion that authority is ineffective without 'spontaneous cooperation'. In this view the demand for willing cooperation with management stands at least on a par with the efforts to enlist this cooperation through financial incentives. Such incentives are not excluded, of course, but under progressive management, work should be done out of an inner persuasion, according to Mayo and his many followers. They seem to say that, by working, an employee manifests his allegiance as much as he earns a living. And they seem to be in no doubt that the satisfaction derived from such allegiance outweighs the satisfaction derived from material benefits.

# 34 J. H. Goldthorpe, David Lockwood, Frank Bechhofer and Jennifer Platt

## Industrial Attitudes of Affluent Workers

Excerpt from J. H. Goldthorpe, David Lockwood, Frank Bechhofer and Jennifer Platt, *The Affluent Worker: Industrial Attitudes and Behaviour*, Cambridge University Press, 1968, pp. 174–8.

Our sample is not one on the basis of which any far-ranging generalizations of a direct kind can safely be made: on the contrary, it was expressly devised so as to represent a special, critical case. And, as we have repeatedly tried to show in course of the monograph, the attitudes and behaviour of our respondents appear often divergent from those of most other industrial workers who have been studied in different, more 'traditional' contexts. Nevertheless, while these contrasts are, of course, central to the argument of the monograph, we have at certain points found reason to speculate that our affluent workers may perhaps be revealing a pattern of industrial life which will in the fairly near future become far more widespread. The main respects in which we believe this may prove to be the case, and our grounds for thinking so, are as follows.

1. It is in our view probable that, in the conditions of modern British society, the tendency will increase for industrial workers, *particularly unskilled or semi-skilled men*, to define their work in a largely instrumental manner; that is, as essentially a means to ends which are extrinsic to their work situation. The more traditional modes of working-class life are now steadily being eroded both by such factors as urban redevelopment and greater geographical mobility and also, one may suppose, by the 'demonstration effect' of those workers and their families who have already become 'affluent'. One may then expect that as this process continues, the pressure on the mass of manual workers to increase their consumer power will intensify. Models of new standards and styles of living will become both more evident and more compelling. In the case of those men at least who do not possess skills which are in high demand, there will be mounting inducements to relegate work to the level of merely instrumental activity and to seek employment which offers a high economic return if only as compensation for its inherent 'disutility'. Moreover, such a tendency is likely to be encouraged by the re-orientation of working-class family and community life which would now seem to be taking place on a fairly large scale. One major outcome

of this is to bring the conjugal family into a more central position than previously in the life of the manual worker, and thus to widen and strengthen the expectations which are held of him as husband, father and family provider. And to the extent, then, that his out-of-work life becomes dominated by home and family concerns, the link between this and the worker's occupational life is likely to be narrowed down to one of a largely economic kind. In other words, a privatized social life and an instrumental orientation to work may in this way be seen as mutually supportive aspects of a particular life-style.

2. Following on from the above, we would also expect our affluent workers to be to some extent 'prototypical' in the limited, affectively neutral, nature of their involvement in their work organizations. We are not inclined, on existing evidence, to share in the view of Blauner and others who see the more advanced forms of production technology as being generally conducive to more normatively integrated industrial enterprises. We would not give the same weight as these writers to the effects of technology in determining attitudes to work and the structure of work relationships. As a factor of greater potential importance, we would again refer to ongoing changes in working-class life outside work, and most notably in this respect to changes *within* the family. In consequence of the conjugal family assuming a more 'companionate' or partnership-like form, relations both between husband and wife and between parents and children would seem likely to become closer and more inherently rewarding; certainly more so than could generally have been the case under the economic and social conditions of the traditional working-class community. If workers are better able to satisfy their expressive and affective needs through family relationships, it may be anticipated that those men at least who enjoy no special occupational skills or responsibilities will less commonly regard their workplace as a *milieu* in which they are in search of satisfactions of this kind. Rather, time spent in work-based association will more probably be seen as detracting from time available for family life and thus as representing a social cost. Correspondingly, work-linked obligations or social attachments, beyond those essential to retaining employment, will tend to be avoided. Furthermore, as we have already suggested, workers of the kind in question are likely to be subject to increasing pressure to give priority in their employment to maximizing economic returns; that is, to define their work as a means of gaining resources for the pursuit of extrinsic – largely familial – ends. Finally, so far as the enterprise itself is concerned, it must be remembered that, independently to some extent of the pattern of technological change, the *scale* of plants and establishments is likely to

increase further, and also the degree of bureaucratic control and administration to which employees are exposed. Thus, the continuing rationalization of work in these ways is yet another factor which may be expected to inhibit workers' identification with, and commitment to, the enterprise in any moral sense.

3. As regards trade unionism, it is clear that in one respect at least our affluent workers[1] merely reveal – though in extreme form – a pattern of behaviour which is very general and in no way recent; that is, in their low participation in branch affairs. However, of greater interest is the question of whether they may be regarded as indicative of newer trends in their *concurrent* relatively high involvement in unionism at workplace level; that is, in union activity focused on the particular, largely economic, issues of their own shop and factory. In our view, the almost complete divorce between the unionism of the branch and of the workplace which is manifest here *is* likely to develop on a much wider scale, as also may associated views of the functions of trade unions of a distinctively limited and instrumental kind. Such a trend in unionism we would see as the most probable concomitant of the trends in orientations to work and to family and community life to which we have already referred. To the extent that wants and expectations from work are confined to high-level economic returns, so the meaning of trade unionism will tend to be interpreted in a similarly instrumental way. And to the extent that individuals' central life interests are to be found in the cultivation and enjoyment of their private, domestic lives, commitment to trade unionism, understood as a social movement or as an expression of class or occupational solidarity, is unlikely to be widespread. On the other hand, where there is a strong drive to increase the material rewards of work, and thus consumer power, then involvement in union activity concerned with matters of wages and conditions of service of immediate interest to workers may of course, be expected – and involvement, perhaps, of some intensity. While militancy directed towards such ends as greater worker control may well become more difficult to sustain among home-centred employees, we would regard greater aggressiveness in the field of 'cash-based' bargaining as a very probable development.

4. Finally, on the question of aspirations for the future, we would think that there is at least one general characteristic of our affluent workers which will become increasingly common; namely, their awareness of themselves as carrying through some individual, or more probably family, project – their awareness of being engaged in a course of action aimed at effecting some basic change in their life situation and, perhaps,

1. The craftsmen excepted.

in their social identity. As we noted earlier, such an outlook is in marked contrast to the fatalistic social philosophy which was frequently encountered among the inhabitants of the traditional working-class community. However, as the proportion of manual workers with personal experience of long-term economic insecurity diminishes, more optimistic attitudes towards the future may be expected to develop more widely. And as the normative force of traditional ways of life is weakened, through both their physical disruption and the presentation of attractive alternatives, it may be anticipated that to an increasing extent manual workers and their families will pursue new goals and standards in a relatively purposive and planful fashion. In this respect, we would suggest, the workers we studied can be regarded as being in some sense both pioneers and exemplars. The life-styles which they are now creating for themselves may well set the patterns and the norms for subsequent recruits to the 'new' working class and at the same time stand as inducements to others still to seek in their turn a road which leads to affluence.

In these several ways it is our view that the subjects of our Luton inquiry will prove to be more typical of the future than they are of the present time. But it need scarcely be added that the foregoing paragraphs should in no way be understood as implying unconditional predictions about the future course of events. They are intended rather as an attempt at outlining, in the light of our research, some probable consequences for working-class economic life of already observable trends of change within British society at large. Such trends may, of course, be checked or reversed in ways which cannot be foreseen; and it is only on the condition that they continue that our analysis can stand.

# 35 Jeremy Tunstall

## Work and the Social Life of Fishermen

Excerpts from Jeremy Tunstall, *The Fishermen*, MacGibbon & Kee, 1962, pp. 89–94, 135–8.

Let us now take a quick look at one terrace in Hessle Road to see something of what living in the fish-dock area means.

Andrew's Terrace is on one of the streets which leads off Hessle Road on the south side, down to the fish-dock. At the time when I was there the street was not under immediate threat of demolition, but it was on the 'worse' side of Hessle Road and everybody knew it would be coming down in the next few years.

The street has about 300 houses of which over half are in terraces leading off at right angles. It had a higher proportion of fishermen than most other streets in Hessle Road, but even so there were only fifty-eight fishermen in the street. In the fourteen households there are four fishermen. In addition there are two ex-fishermen, one a retired skipper and another a trawler engineer who now works on a pilot ship. Several other people in the terrace work in the fishing industry and only one adult does not have a close relative in some part of it.

During the day lorries rumble down the street to a fish-house and to the fish-dock itself just beyond. In the evening men pass along the street on their way to and from a working-men's club which caters almost entirely for fishermen and fish-workers. Just before 2 a.m. the sound of bobbers' wooden clogs can be heard clumping down the street to the dock, breaking the stillness of the night. By seven in the morning the first workers are going down to the fish-house to get things started for the day.

In Andrew's Terrace there are fourteen houses, and they face each other, seven a side, across a narrow piece of asphalt. Each house has two bedrooms and from the front one you can just about spit onto the doorstep of the house opposite. On the ground floor there are two rooms with a tiny cubby-hole at the back which is the kitchen. The lavatory is outside in a small yard, with a narrow backalley behind. The front door leads straight from the terrace into the front room, but in crowded families this room is often partitioned off, with more or less carpentry and deftness, into a third bedroom. Where this has happened the family lives all its communal life in the back room. Here is a table and chairs, a radio and usually a television, a budgerigar in a cage, and except in midsummer a coal fire burning in the grate. The walls of the house are very thin, and somebody going upstairs seems to shake the whole structure. Intimate sounds come through the walls. There can be little privacy between those who live in one of these two-up and two-down houses. Sounds also come through from house to house and neighbours can listen to any family rows which may occur.

These are the terrace's fourteen households with each person's age in brackets:

No. 1.  Railway man (34), wife (30), son (12).
No. 2.  Pensioner widower – retired trawler skipper (73).
No. 3.  Unemployed pilot-ship engineer (58), wife (49), daughter (25) and her husband (30) and son (4); other daughters (12, 6), son (10).
No. 4.  Pensioner widow (73).
No. 5.  Shop manager (41), wife (38), daughters (14, 11), sons (12, 7, 4).
No. 6.  Building plasterer (39), wife (35), daughters (12, 10, 8, 2, 1), sons (9, 5).
No. 7.  Fish filleter (26), wife (23), son (2), daughter (1).
No. 8.  Unemployed ship boiler-scaler (50), wife (38), daughter (17), son (6).
No. 9.  Trawler deckhand (43), wife (39), sons (17, 13), daughter (15).
No. 10. Bobber (58), wife (59), son (28), daughter (18).
No. 11. Bricklayer's labourer (60), wife (58), grandson (18).
No. 12. Pensioner widow (67).
No. 13. Warehouse worker (45), wife (43), sons (24, 21), daughter, married and separated (22) and her sons (4, 2).
No. 14. Bobber (53), wife (48), sons (28, 24, 21, 16, 13), daughters (26, 20, 10, 8, 4).

It can easily be seen that there is a very wide range of experience and fortune in Andrew's Terrace. One of the old-age pensioners spent several years as a young woman in Holland and speaks Flemish, while others in the terrace have never been out of the East Riding. One pensioner lives on £2 10s. a week, while the total weekly income of the people in some of the big families is £40 and more. Three of the houses are occupied by pensioners living alone, but well over half the terrace's people live in households of seven or more.

The pensioners tend to keep to themselves, despite the fact that they all know each other from some time back. The old skipper in no. 2 was a friend of the husband of the widow in no. 12 and has been a neighbour of the widow in no. 4 for forty years. The latter sees her son in no. 1 but no one else in the terrace.

The families in the end houses do not seem to take much part in the terrace's social life. This seems to be because both the wives are busy and because these people do not have to pass the other doors in the terrace to reach their own.

Although these five of the fourteen households play little part in the terrace's social life, there is a good deal of mixing among the others. Most of them have the common interest of young children. The children play on the narrow asphalt strip between the two rows of houses, while babies in prams are also put out here – inevitably establishing contact between the mothers. Three of the most active of the terrace's socialites appear to be the very young wives in nos. 3, 7 and 13. They are all relatively free to move about, having their mothers in the terrace, two of them living in the same house. The young wife in no. 7 has her sister and mother across the way at no. 13. The ties between these young women also bring two of the terrace's older women into the social group and a bridge is thus made between the women of different ages.

Going into each house in turn I was continually meeting familiar faces. In some houses women neighbours entered without knocking and doors were left ajar for this purpose. It was as if the women in this group regarded themselves as being communally engaged in the tasks of housekeeping and childrearing. In the day-time the terrace seemed to be like a factory and each house was only private to the extent that a work-bench is private. Of course, when the husbands came home the position would be different, but even so, on fine evenings women take chairs outside and continue their sociability. One women braided trawl nets at home, and doing this outside in the terrace during fine weather she was a focus of interest. [. . .]

The concentration of fishermen is greatest on the south side of the Road, and thins out quickly to the north.[1] In many cases, as in Andrew's Terrace, they come from the less respectable larger families. (Fishermen have an average of five living brothers and sisters.) In turn the overcrowding in such families probably tends to motivate boys towards fishing, which gets them away from the crowded bedrooms and the back room packed with chattering women.

From this point of view a number of fishermen in a street is partly due to a lack of 'respectability' as locally understood. It also comes to be used

1. Within half a mile of the dock in 1955 lived 27·9 per cent of all fishermen and 5·5 per cent of Hull's population. Within a mile of the dock lived 17·3 per cent of Hull's population – over three times as much – and 56·4 per cent of the fishermen, or just over twice as many.

as one rough indicator of status.[2] People who are insisting on the respect-ability of their street say things like: 'No, there aren't any fishermen in this street. Except one, and you wouldn't know he was a fisherman.'

This attitude of many Hessle Road people to fishermen is ambivalent. They don't want their sons to go into it and they regard it as second-best to almost any job on shore. On the other hand they know that people in other parts of Hull think of fishing and Hessle Road as being one and the same thing. Because of this, almost all Hessle Road people, when con-fronted by a middle-class interviewer who hints that fishermen are not very respectable, will vigorously defend the fishermen, realizing that in this context they are defending themselves. [. . .]

Most fishing-recruits probably do their first serious drinking actually on trawlers. A lad of fifteen will take a dram of whisky or rum and knock it back in one gulp, making a fierce grimace to hide the tears.

Some people ashore are under the impression that a great deal of drinking is done at sea. One of the schoolboys already quoted seemed to think fishermen consumed large quantities of rum while chopping away ice in winter. In fact only a very small portion of duty-free drink is taken to sea, and then only during winter. The men are allowed half a bottle of spirits each and some beer. Any heavy drinking at sea must rely on the men taking with them bottles bought at the normal price ashore. Many men take a dozen bottles of beer and a bottle or two of spirits. This, however, is usually consumed well before fishing starts and sometimes even before the trawler is out of the Humber; it can have disastrous consequences. Recently in Hull the papers described an inquest on a fisherman who had been lost overboard. No mention was made in the paper of the following circumstances related to me by one of the crew:

It was all hushed up, like. Everybody on board was drunk except the skipper and the watch on the bridge. I was leaning out of a porthole back aft. Some-thing flew by into the sea, I thought it was the cook throwing garbage away. Then I saw it was a body. I ran up to the bridge. Another bastard was so drunk he shouted out. 'Tell me what the water's like, maybe I'll take a swim too.' When I got to the bridge and told the skipper he turned the ship round, but we didn't find the body. It was washed up at Flamborough Head a week later. Some of the lads were so pissed up when we got back to Hull a few hours later, they didn't even know this man had been lost over.

But for the most part, however, one can assume that after the first day or two very little drinking is done at sea. Indeed, their having to go three weeks at a time parched of liquor is one reason why fishermen drink so heavily when ashore. A popular stereotype in Hull is that all fishermen

2. This is similar to coal-mining areas, where the number of miners in a street is inversely proportional to the status-level of the street.

drink very heavily. This is not true – I have spoken to several fishermen who are non-drinkers. However, non-drinkers tend to live on housing estates and they are not popular sociable men. Others are not heavy drinkers, but these are often older men who when younger indulged more heavily. In a conversation about drink one chief engineer said: 'Not all fishermen drink heavy. Look at me. I used to drink a lot, spirits and all. Now I'm not drunk from one year to the next. I haven't drunk more than five pints at a time for several years.' The assumption behind such statements, however, is that most fishermen do drink fairly heavily. Most young fishermen can tell you of a recent occasion after a good trip when they spent £40 or more in a few drunken days.

When a young recruit strains to adjust himself to the manly behaviour of the adult fishermen he is acutely aware that a sign of successful integration with them is an ability to drink. Hessle Road, as we have seen, has no social amenities to offer adolescent boys of the kind who go fishing, but when they are able to go into pubs and clubs, a rich web of social life opens up.

Why is it that fishermen drink so much? In many cases it is not even true to say that they do drink more than the average man – they are merely concentrating their drinking. But those who take a bottle or two of spirits to sea do drink more than most people. Another obvious explanation is that they are trying to forget the cold, black void of the Arctic which awaits them once again. Fishermen say: 'Of course fishermen get drunk. Anybody who does what we do has to get drunk to stay sane.'

Fishermen go to sea partly to avoid the fate of the non-skilled shore worker – low pay and low status. They make more money than unskilled workers ashore yet they do not move out of their class. Many fishermen like to smarten up their homes. New carpets, expensive television sets and washing machines are usual. But even if a fisherman is buying his home, his attitudes are never grander than those of the 'respectable' working-class. He does not indulge in middle-class kinds of spending. Few fishermen buy cars, foreign holidays are rare, and none send their children to fee-paying schools. With the kind of social life that a fisherman is used to and wants, he has cash to spare. He did not go to sea on trawlers because he wanted to become posh, be middle class, but because he wanted a little status, some spare money to spend in the kind of social sphere he already moved in.

At sea a fisherman suffers, but when ashore he has money to spare. He is unlikely to have any self-improving hobbies. His favourite relaxation is drinking, mainly with other fishermen, because only they are free all day when ashore, have the same attitude to life and the same spare cash.

Jeremy Tunstall   243

When fishermen drink they buy rounds compulsively. Giving away drinks buys a man status – even if only temporary. Some young lads when they get drunk start buying drinks for total strangers. In their sober moments, they will refer to such people as bums and scroungers, but for the moment the fisherman buys their deference and gains for himself the centre of the stage. When he throws his money away on drink, he is trying not only to shut out the thought of another trip to the Arctic, but also he is trying to forget his lowly position in society – an awareness of which originally contributed to his desire to go trawling.[3]

One of the special features of fishermen's drinking is that much of it is done in clubs. Working-men's clubs are a marked feature of social life in Yorkshire, and this is especially so in Hull. In Hessle Road there are two very popular clubs one of which has the same name as the fish-dock – Saint Andrew's – and these are regarded by fishermen as their exclusive preserve. There are also about another half dozen clubs in the Hessle Road area to which fishermen belong in large numbers. Many fishermen belong to several clubs, but are usually rather vague as to when they last paid the subscription.

A normal first day ashore might go like this: at 10 a.m. the man goes down to the fish-dock to 'settle', to collect the poundage money which is due to him. At 11 a.m. he goes into a Hessle Road pub. Later with some pals he goes by taxi to another pub in the centre of Hull. At 3 o'clock a move is made again by taxi back to Hessle Road, and drinking continues in a club. This closes at 5 p.m. and the man goes home. He's out again for the evening session in one of the clubs, and after closing-time may well go to a party where there is more drinking. Fishermen don't drink draught bitter much, but draught mild, bottled beer, whisky, rum and gin are all popular.

3. *The Gift*, by Marcel Mauss (Cohen & West), 1954, p. 72 (first published as *Essai sur le Don*, in 1925): 'To give is to show one's superiority, to show that one is something more and higher, that one is *magister*. To accept without returning or repaying more is to face subordination, to become a client and subservient, to become *minister*.'

# 36 Robert K. Merton

## The Role-Set

Excerpt from Robert K. Merton, 'The role-set: problems in sociological theory', *British Journal of Sociology*, vol. 8, 1957, pp. 110–20.

However much they may differ in other respects, contemporary sociological theorists are largely at one in adopting the premise that social statuses and social roles comprise major building blocks of social structure. This has been the case, since the influential writings of Ralph Linton on the subject, a generation ago. By status, and T. H. Marshall has indicated the great diversity of meanings attached to this term since the time of Maine, Linton meant a position in a social system involving designated rights and obligations; by role, the behaviour oriented to these patterned expectations of others. In these terms, status and roles become concepts serving to connect culturally defined expectations with the patterned conduct and relationships which make up a social structure. Linton went on to state the long-recognized and basic fact that each person in society inevitably occupies multiple statuses and that each of these statuses has an associated role.

It is at this point that I find it useful to depart from Linton's conception. The difference is initially a small one, some might say so small as not to deserve notice, but it involves a shift in the angle of vision which leads, I believe, to successively greater differences of a fundamental kind. Unlike Linton, I begin with the premise that each social status involves not a single associated role, but an array of roles. This basic feature of social structure can be registered by the distinctive but not formidable term, role-set. To repeat, then, by role-set I mean that complement of role-relationships in which persons are involved by virtue of occupying a particular social status. Thus, in our current studies of medical schools, we have begun with the view that the status of a medical student entails not only the role of a student *vis-à-vis* his teachers, but also an array of other roles relating him diversely to other students, physicians, nurses, social workers, medical technicians, and the like. Again, the status of school teacher in the United States has its distinctive role-set, in which are found pupils, colleagues, the school principal and superintendent, the Board of Education, professional associations and, on occasion, local patriotic organizations.

It should be made plain that the role-set differs from what sociologists have long described as 'multiple roles'. By established usage, the term multiple role refers not to the complex of roles associated with a single social status, but with the various social statuses (often, in differing institutional spheres) in which people find themselves – for illustration, the statuses of physician, husband, father, professor, church elder, Conservative Party member and army captain. (This complement of distinct statuses of a person each of these in turn having its own role-set, I would designate as a status-set. This concept gives rise to its own range of analytical problems which cannot be considered here.)

The notion of the role-set reminds us, in the unlikely event that we need to be reminded of this obstinate fact, that even the seemingly simple social structure is fairly complex. All societies face the functional problem of articulating the components of numerous role-sets, the functional problem of managing somehow to organize these so that an appreciable degree of social regularity obtains, sufficient to enable most people most of the time to go about their business of social life, without encountering extreme conflict in their role-sets as the normal, rather than the exceptional, state of affairs.

If this relatively simple idea of role-set has any theoretical worth, it should at the least generate distinctive problems for sociological theory, which come to our attention only from the perspective afforded by this idea, or by one like it. This the notion of role-set does. It raises the general problem of identifying the social mechanisms which serve to articulate the expectations of those in the role-set so that the occupant of a status is confronted with less conflict than would obtain if these mechanisms were not at work. It is to these social mechanisms that I would devote the rest of this discussion.

Before doing so, I should like to recapitulate the argument thus far. We depart from the simple idea, unlike that which has been rather widely assumed, that a single status in society involves, not a single role, but an array of associated roles, relating the status-occupant to diverse others. Secondly, we note that this structural fact, expressed in the term role-set, gives rise to distinctive analytical problems and to corresponding questions for empirical inquiry. The basic problem, which I deal with here, is that of identifying social mechanisms, that is, processes having designated effects for designated parts of the social structure, which serve to articulate the role-set more nearly than would be the case, if these mechanisms did not operate. Third, unlike the problems centred upon the notion of 'multiple roles', this one is concerned with social arrangements integrating the expectations of those in the role-set; it is not primarily concerned with the familiar problem of how the occupant of a status manages to cope with the many, and sometimes conflicting, demands made of him. It is thus a problem of social structure, not an exercise in the no doubt important but different problem of how individuals happen to deal with the complex structures of relations in which they find themselves. Finally, by way of setting the analytical problem, the logic of analysis exhibited in this case is developed wholly in terms of the elements of social structure, rather than in terms of providing concrete historical description of a social system.

All this presupposes, of course, that there is always a *potential* for differing and sometimes conflicting expectations of the conduct appropriate to a status-occupant among those in the role-set. The basic source of this potential for conflict, I suggest – and here we are at one with theorists as disparate as Spencer and Marx, Simmel and Parsons – is that the members of a role-set are, to some degree, apt to hold social positions differing from that of the occupant of the status in question. To the extent that they are diversely located in the social structure, they are apt to have interests and sentiments, values and moral expectations differing from those of the status-occupant himself. This, after all, is one of the principal assumptions of Marxist theory, as it is of all sociological theory: social differentiation generates distinct interests among those variously located in the structure of the society. To continue with one of our examples: the members of a school board are often in social and economic strata which differ greatly from that of the school teacher; and their interests, values and expectations are consequently apt to differ, to some extent, from those of the teacher. The teacher may thus become subject to conflicting role-expectations among such members of his role-set as professional colleagues, influential members of the school board and, say, the Americanism Committee of the American Legion. What is an educational essential for the one may be judged as an education frill, or as downright subversion, by the other. These disparate and contradictory evaluations by members of the role-set greatly complicate the task of coping with them all. The familiar case of the teacher may be taken as paradigmatic. What holds conspicuously for this one status holds, in varying degree, for the occupants of all other statuses who are structurally related, through their role-set, to others who themselves occupy diverse positions in society.

This, then, is the basic structural basis for potential disturbance of a role-set. And it gives rise, in turn, to a double question: which social mechanisms, if any, operate to counteract such instability of role-sets and, correlatively, under which circumstances do these social mechanisms fail to operate, with resulting confusion and conflict. This is not to say, of course, that role-sets do invariably operate with substantial efficiency. We are concerned here, not with a broad historical generalization to the effect that social order prevails, but with an analytical problem of identifying social mechanisms which produce a greater degree of order than would obtain, if these mechanisms were not called into play. Otherwise put, it is theoretical sociology, not history, which is of interest here.

## Social mechanisms articulating role-sets

### Relative importance of various statuses

The first of these mechanisms derives from the oft-noticed sociological circumstance that social structures designate certain statuses as having greater importance than others. Family and job obligations, for example, are defined in American society as having priority over membership in voluntary associations. As a result, a particular role-relationship may be of peripheral concern for some; for others it may be central. Our hypothetical teacher, for whom this status holds primary significance, may by this circumstance be better able to withstand the demands for conformity with the differing expectations of those comprising this role-set. For at least some of these others, the relationship has only peripheral significance. This does not mean, of course, that teachers are not vulnerable to demands which are at odds with their own professional commitments. It means only that when powerful members of their role-set are only little concerned with this particular relationship, teachers are less vulnerable than they would otherwise be (or sometimes are). Were all those involved in the role-set *equally* concerned with this relationship, the plight of the teacher would be considerably more sorrowful than it often is. What holds for the particular case of the teacher presumably holds for the occupants of other statuses: the impact upon them of diverse expectations among those in their role-set is mitigated by the basic structural fact of differentials of involvement in the relationship among those comprising their role-set.

### Differences of power of those in the role-set

A second potential mechanism for stabilizing the role-set is found in the distribution of power and authority. By power, in this connexion, is meant the observed and predictable capacity to impose one's will in a social action, even against the opposition of others taking part in that action; by authority, the culturally legitimized organization of power.

As a consequence of social stratification, the members of a role-set are not apt to be equally powerful in shaping the behaviour of status-occupants. However, it does not follow that the individuals, group or stratum in the role-set which are *separately* most powerful uniformly succeed in imposing their demands upon the status-occupant, say, the teacher. This would be so only in the circumstance that the one member of the role-set has either a monopoly of power in the situation or outweighs the combined power of the others. Failing this special but, of course, not infrequent, situation, there may develop *coalitions of power* among some members of the role-set which enable the status-occupants to go their own way. The familiar pattern of a balance of power is of course not confined to the conventionally defined political realm. In less easily visible form, it can be found in the workings of role-sets generally, as the boy who succeeds in having his father's decision offset his mother's opposed decision has ample occasion to know. To the extent that conflicting powers in his role-set neutralize one another, the status-occupant has relative freedom to proceed as he intended in the first place.

Thus, even in those potentially unstable structures in which the members of a role-set hold contrasting expectations of what the status-occupant should do, the latter is not wholly at the mercy of the most powerful among them. Moreover, the structural variations of engagement in the role-structure, which I have mentioned, can serve to reinforce the relative power of the status-occupant. For to the extent that powerful members of his role-set are not centrally concerned with this particular relationship, they will be the less motivated to exercise their potential power to the full. Within varying margins of his activity, the status-occupant will then be free to act as he would.

Once again, to reiterate that which lends itself to misunderstanding, I do not say that the status-occupant subject to conflicting expectations among members of his role-set is in fact immune to control by them. I suggest only that the power and authority-structure of role-sets is often such that he has a larger measure of autonomy than he would have had if this structure of competing power did not obtain.

*Insulation of role-activities from observability by members of the role-set*

People do not engage in continuous interaction with all those in their role-sets. This is not an incidental fact, to be ignored because familiar, but one integral to the operation of social structure. Interaction with each member of a role-set tends to be variously intermittent. This fundamental fact allows for role-behaviour which is at odds with the expectations of some in the role-set to proceed without undue stress. For effective social control presupposes social arrangements making for the observability of behaviour. (By observability, a conception which I have borrowed from Simmel and tried to develop, I mean the extent to which social norms and role-performances can readily become known to others in the social system. This is, I believe, a variable crucial to structural analysis, a belief which I cannot, unhappily, undertake to defend here.)

To the extent that the social structure insulates the individual from having his activities known to members of his role-set, he is the less subject to competing pressures. It should be emphasized that we are dealing here with structural arrangements for such insulation, not with the fact that this or that person *happens* to conceal part of his role-behaviour from others. The structural fact is that social statuses differ in the extent to which the conduct of those in them are regularly insulated from observability by members of the role-set. Some have a functionally significant insulation of this kind, as for example, the status of the university teacher, in so far as norms hold that what is said in the classroom is privileged. In this familiar type of case, the norm clearly has the function of maintaining some degree of autonomy for the teacher. For if they were forever subject to observation by all those in the role-set, with their often differing expectations, teachers might be driven to teach not what they know or what the evidence leads them to believe, but to teach what will placate the numerous and diverse people who are ostensibly concerned with 'the education of youth'. That this sometimes occurs is evident. But it would presumably be more frequent, were it not for the relative exemption from observability by all and sundry who may wish to impose their will upon the instructor.

More broadly, the concept of privileged information and confidential communication in the professions has this same function of insulating clients from observability of their behaviour and beliefs by others in their role-set. Were physicians or priests free to tell all they have learned about the private lives of their clients, the needed information would not be forthcoming and they could not adequately discharge their functions. More generally, if all the facts of one's conducts and beliefs were freely available to anyone, social structures could not operate. What is often described as 'the need for privacy' – that is, insulation of actions and beliefs from surveillance by others – is the individual counterpart to the functional requirement of social structure that some measure of exemption from full observability be provided. 'Privacy' is not only a personal predilection, though it may be that, too. It is also a requirement of social systems which must provide for a measure, as they say in France, of *quant-à-soi,* a portion of the self which is kept apart, immune from observation by others.

Like other social mechanisms, this one of insulation from full observability can, of course, miscarry. Were the activities of the politician or, if one prefers, the statesman, fully removed from the public spotlight, social control of his behaviour would be correspondingly reduced. And as we all know, anonymous power anonymously exercised does not make for a stable social structure meeting the values of a society. So, too, the teacher or physician who is largely insulated from observability may fail to live up to the minimum requirements of his status. All this means only that some measure of observability of role-performance by members of the role-set is required, if the indispensable social requirement of accountability is to be met. This statement does not contradict an earlier statement to the effect that some measure of insulation from observability is also required for the effective operation of social structures. Instead, the two statements, taken in conjunction, imply that there is an optimum zone of observability, difficult to identify in precise terms and doubtless varying for different social statuses, which will simultaneously make both for accountability and for substantial autonomy, rather than for a frightened acquiescence with the distribution of power which happens, at a particular moment, to obtain in the role-set.

### Observability of conflicting demands by members of a role-set

This mechanism is implied by what has been said and therefore needs only passing comment here. As long as members of the role-set are happily ignorant that their demands upon the occupants of a status are incompatible, each member may press his own case. The pattern is then many against one. But when it becomes plain that the demands of some are in full contradiction with the demands of others, it becomes, in part, the task of members of the role-set, rather than that of the status-occupant, to resolve these contradictions, either by a struggle for over-riding power or by some degree of compromise.

In such circumstances, the status-occupant subjected to conflicting demands often becomes cast in the role of the *tertius gaudens,* the third (or more often, the *n*th) party who draws advantage from the conflict of the others. Originally at the focus of the conflict, he can virtually become a bystander whose function it is to highlight the conflicting demands being made by members of his role-set. It becomes a problem for them, rather than for him, to resolve their contradictory demands. At the least, this serves to make evident that it is not wilful misfeasance on his part which keeps him from conforming to all the contradictory expectations imposed upon him.[1] When most effective, this serves to articu-

1. See the observations by William G. Carr, the executive secretary of the National Education Association, who has summarized some of the conflicting pressures exerted upon school curricula by voluntary organizations, such as the American Legion, the Association for the United Nations, the National Safety Council, the Better Business Bureau, the American Federation of Labor and the Daughters of the American Revolution. His summary may serve through concrete example to indicate the extent of

late the expectations of those in the role-set beyond a degree which would occur, if this mechanism of making contradictory expectations manifest were not at work.

## Mutual social support among status-occupants

Whatever he may believe to the contrary, the occupant of a social status is not alone. The very fact that he is placed in a social position means that there are others more or less like-circumstanced. To this extent, the actual or potential experience of facing a conflict of expectations among members of the role-set is variously common to all occupants of the status. The particular persons subject to these conflicts need not, therefore, meet them as wholly private problems which must be coped with in wholly private fashion.

It is this familiar and fundamental fact of social structure, of course, which is the basis for those in the same social status forming the associations intermediate to the individual and the larger society in a pluralistic system. These organizations constitute a structural response to the problems of coping with the (potentially or actually) conflicting demands by those in the role-sets of the status. Whatever the intent, these constitute

---

competing expectations among those in the complex role-set of school superintendents and local school boards in as differentiated a society as our own. Sometimes, Mr Carr reports, these voluntary organizations 'speak their collective opinions temperately, sometimes scurrilously, but always insistently. They organize contests, drives, collections, exhibits, special days, special weeks and anniversaries that run all year long.

They demand that the public schools give more attention to Little League baseball, first aid, mental hygiene, speech correction, Spanish in the first grade, military preparedness, international understanding, modern music, world history, American history, and local history, geography and home-making, Canada and South America, the Arabs and the Israelis, the Turks and the Greeks, Christopher Columbus and Leif Ericsson, Robert E. Lee and Woodrow Wilson, nutrition, care of the teeth, free enterprise, labor relations, cancer prevention, human relationships, atomic energy, the use of firearms, the Constitution, tobacco, temperance, kindness to animals, Esperanto, the 3 Rs, the 3 Cs and the 4 Fs, use of the typewriter and legible penmanship, moral values, physical fitness, ethical concepts, civil defence, religious literacy, thrift, law observance, consumer education, narcotics, mathematics, dramatics, physics, ceramics, and (that latest of all educational discoveries) phonics.

Each of these groups is anxious to avoid overloading the curriculum. All any of them ask is that the non-essentials be dropped in order to get their material in. Most of them insist that they do not want a special course – they just want their ideas to permeate the entire daily programme. Every one of them proclaims a firm belief in local control of education and an apprehensive hatred of national control.

Nevertheless, if their national organization programme in education is not adopted forthwith, many of them use the pressure of the press, the radiance of the radio, and all the props of propaganda to bypass their elected school board.'

An address at the inauguration of Hollis Leland Caswell Teachers College, Columbia University, November 1955.

social formations serving to counter the power of the role-set; of being, not merely amenable to its demands, but of helping to shape them. Such organizations – so familiar a part of the social landscape of differentiated societies – also develop normative systems which are designed to anticipate and thereby to mitigate such conflicting expectations. They provide social support to the individuals in the status under attack. They minimize the need for their improvising personal adjustments to patterned types of conflicting expectations. Emerging codes which state in advance what the socially-supported conduct of the status-occupant should be, also serve this social function. This function becomes all the more significant in the structural circumstances when status-occupants are highly vulnerable to pressures from their role-set because they are relatively isolated from one another. Thus, thousands of librarians sparsely distributed among the towns and villages of America and not infrequently subject to censorial pressures, received strong support from the code on censorship developed by the American Library Association. This only illustrates the general mechanisms whereby status-peers curb the pressures exerted upon them individually by drawing upon the organizational and normative support of their peers.

*Abridging the role-set*

There is, of course, a limiting case in the modes of coping with incompatible demands by the role-set. Role-relations are broken off, leaving a greater consensus of role-expectations among those who remain. But this mode of adaptation by amputating the role-set is possible only under special and limited conditions. It can be effectively utilized only in those circumstances where it is still possible for status-occupants to perform their other roles, without the support of those with whom they have discontinued relations. It presupposes that the social structure provides this option. By and large, however, this option is infrequent and limited, since the composition of the role-set is ordinarily not a matter of personal choice but a matter of the social organization in which the status is embedded. More typically, the individual goes, and the social structure remains.

**Residual conflict in the role-set**

Doubtless, these are only some of the mechanisms which serve to articulate the expectations of those in the role-set. Further inquiry will uncover others, just as it will probably modify the preceding account of those we have provisionally identified. But, however much the substance may change, I believe that the logic of the analysis will remain largely intact. This can be briefly recapitulated.

First, it is assumed that each social status has its organized complement of role-relationships which can be thought of as comprising a role-set. Second, relationships hold not only between the occupant of the particular status and each member of the role-set, but always potentially and often actually, between members of the role-set itself. Third, to the extent that members of the role-set themselves hold substantially differing statuses, they will tend to have some differing expectations (moral and actuarial) of the conduct appropriate for the status-occupant. Fourth, this gives rise to the sociological problem of how their diverse expectations become sufficiently articulated for the status-structure and the role-structure to operate with a modicum of effectiveness. Fifth, inadequate articulation of these role-expectations tends to call one or more social mechanisms into play, which serve to reduce the extent of patterned conflict below the level which would be involved if these mechanisms were not at work.

And now, sixth, finally and importantly, even when these (and probably other) mechanisms are operating, they may not, in particular cases, prove sufficient to reduce the conflict of expectations below the level required for the social structure to operate with substantial effectiveness. This residual conflict within the role-set may be enough to interfere materially with the effective performance of roles by the occupant of the status in question. Indeed, it may well turn out that this condition is the most frequent one – role-systems operating at considerably less than full efficiency. Without trying to draw tempting analogies with other types of systems, I suggest only that this is not unlike the case of engines which cannot fully utilize heat energy. If the analogy lacks force, it may nevertheless have the merit of excluding the Utopian figment of a perfectly effective social system.

We do not yet know some of the requirements for fuller articulation of the relations between the occupant of a status and members of his role-set, on the one hand, and for fuller articulation of the values and expectations among those comprising the role set, on the other. As we have seen, even those requirements which can now be identified are not readily satisfied, without fault, in social systems. To the extent that they are not, social systems are forced to limp along with that measure of ineffectiveness and inefficiency which is often accepted because the realistic prospect of decided improvement seems so remote as sometimes not to be visible at all.

# Part Six Organizations

Why are organizations important? A superficial answer would be that in modern industrial society most people are affected by organizations in one way or another for most of the time. March and Simon in Reading 37 refer to this, but go on to stress some of the characteristics which make organizations sociologically important: in contrast to wider social life, members of organizations tend to play stable roles, which are clearly defined and easily recognized; formal channels are used by members to communicate with each other and with the world outside and their communications reflect a special knowledge which springs directly from their involvement in common tasks.

Most organizations have this in common. They differ, however, in many significant ways. In Reading 38 Stinchcombe sets out four important types of organization which have been discussed by sociologists, and especially by Max Weber. For Weber (see Reading 39), the basic question which distinguished the different types was the means used to decide whose authority was legitimate. One of these types, the modern bureaucracy, was of crucial importance in understanding industrial society. Our next selection comes from Weber's discussion of the characteristics of bureaucracy.

In bureaucratic organizations, control is based on the common recognition by officials of a special knowledge, either technical expertise or the detailed knowledge which is accumulated by officials in their specific positions – knowledge which is filed. Technically, the bureaucratic form of organization is the most efficient means of carrying out administrative tasks, and can be found in churches and clubs, prisons and political parties, as well as in business organizations – wherever, in fact, routine work has to be done. It is both a cause and a consequence of capitalism; on the other hand, socialism requires an even higher degree of bureaucratization.

But while almost all modern organizations will contain an element of bureaucracy, they still differ substantially in many ways. Etzioni (Reading 40) stresses that the fundamental difference is the means used by the leaders of a body to control the lower participants. Organizations cannot operate satisfactorily without a system of rewards and sanctions which are distributed over the various offices. But there are three kinds of power which give these controls their character. Institutions such as prisons are characterized by the use of coercive power; in factories, relations between management and workers are based on utility; and in bodies such as churches, symbolic means are used by the leaders to exercise their authority – they appeal to the set of norms which are held in common by clergy and parishioners. Etzioni argues that if we analyse the kind of power used by the leaders – and to varying degrees these three kinds are combined in practice – we can predict many other features of organizations, and in particular the kind of response which members make to the exercise of control by their superiors.

Goffman (Reading 41) stresses the peculiar character of a different category of organizations, which he calls 'total institutions'. There are organizations in which we work (such as factories), others in which we spend our leisure time (such as bingo clubs) and others in which we sleep (such as hotels). What is distinctive about total institutions is that the barriers which normally keep these three areas of life separate are broken down: in total institutions, such as prisons, hospitals and monasteries, we sleep *and* play *and* work. In contrast to bureaucracies, there is a basic split between the staff and the inmates; new incentives must be found for members to perform their work, and the work itself often takes on an unusual character; for total institutions are not administrative bodies but, in Goffman's words, 'forcing houses for changing persons'.

Our last two selections refer to the effect of the social context on performance inside the organization. Blau and Scott (Reading 42) discuss ways in which the environment moulds the orientation of members to their role within the organization. Thus employees have distinctive expectations about their work: they may value a good, steady wage far more than a satisfying job, though this is not always the case; norms exist in the community which to some extent are carried over into the work context; and the networks which members form both inside and outside the factory are relevant to understanding the way in which they attempt to safeguard their interests when these are jeopardized. Blau and Scott show that bureaucracies cannot exist unaffected by the culture of the community in which they are located. For example, the traditional values of Japanese society have led to the development of bodies substantially different from Weber's ideal type. In some societies, indeed, it may not be viable for bureaucracies to exist at all.

Kapferer's case study (Reading 43) concerns a dispute which broke out within a group of African mine employees in the Cell Room of an electro-zinc plant of the mine. It illustrates the interplay between factors internal to the organization and those social characteristics which are brought in from the outside, such as age, religion and tribal background. All of these factors helped to determine the pattern of relations within the Cell Room, and together they gave rise to a set of norms which workers selected and appealed to in justifying courses of action inside the work place.

# 37 James G. March and Herbert A. Simon

The Significance of Organizations as Social Institutions

Excerpt from James G. March and Herbert A. Simon, *Organizations*, Wiley, 1958, pp. 2–4.

Why are organizations important? A superficial answer is that organizations are important because people spend so much of their time in them. The working force – that is to say, the bulk of the adult population – spends more than a third of its waking hours in the organizations by which it is employed. The life of the child takes place to almost an equal extent in the environment of the school organization; and an uncountable host of other organizations, mostly voluntary, account for a large chunk of leisure time of child and adult alike. In our society, preschool children and nonworking housewives are the only large groups of persons whose behavior is not substantially 'organizational'.

The ubiquitousness of organizations is not their sole or principal claim for attention. As social scientists we are interested in explaining human behavior. Taking the viewpoint of the social psychologist, we are interested in what influences impinge upon the individual human being from his environment and how he responds to these influences. For most people formal organizations represent a major part of the environment. Moreover, we would expect organizations to have an even more significant effect upon behavior than is suggested merely by looking at the time budget as we have done above. If we wished to sum up in a single quality the distinctive characteristics of influence processes in organizations, as contrasted with many other influence processes of our society, we would point to the *specificity* of the former as contrasted with the *diffuseness* of the latter.

A concrete example will help to point up the contrast we have in mind. Compare rumor transmission with the transmission of a customer order through a manufacturing company. Rumor transmission is truly a process of diffusion. Seldom does a rumor move outward along a single channel; indeed, in most cases it would soon die if it did not spread out broadly from its original source. The customer order, on the other hand, is transmitted along definite channels, and usually relatively few of them, to specific destinations. We do not wish to imply that there is *no* selectivity in the transmission of rumors, or *no* uncertainty in the destination of formal organizational communications. There certainly is a great deal of both. But the difference in degree in the specificity of channels betwen the two cases is striking.

Not only are organizational communications characteristically specific with respect to the channels they follow, but they also exhibit a high degree of specificity with respect to content. Here there is a strong contrast between organizational communications and communications through mass media. The audiences to whom newspapers and radio address themselves possess no common technical vocabulary; there is no subject about which they have any shared special knowledge; there is no good way of predicting what they will be thinking about when the mass communication reaches them. In principle at least, the recipient of an organizational communication is at the opposite pole. A great deal is known about his special abilities and characteristics. This knowledge is gained from considerable past experience with him and from a detailed knowledge of the work environment in which he operates.

When a mass medium exerts influence or attempts to give instruction, its messages are usually of the simplest variety – 'go to your corner druggist now, and ...' – and its appeals are to widely shared motivations. Organizational instructions, on the contrary, frequently contain great detail; often motivation can be assumed. Not only can organization communication be detailed, but it can be cryptic, relying on a highly developed and precise common technical language understood by both sender and recipient. Again we do not wish to imply any contrast of black and white, which would clearly be contrary to fact, but only to point to characteristic differences of degree that are large in magnitude and highly significant.

The great specificity that characterizes communications in organizations can be described in a slightly different way, using the sociological concept of *role*. Roles in organizations, as contrasted with many of the other roles that individuals fill, tend to be highly elaborated, relatively stable and defined to a considerable extent in explicit and even written terms. Not only is the role defined for the individual who occupies it, but it is known in considerable detail to others in the organization who have occasion to deal with him. Hence, the environment of other persons that surrounds each member of an organization tends to become a highly stable and predictable one. It is this predictability, together with certain related structural features of organizations to be discussed presently, that accounts for the ability of organizations to deal in a coordinated way with their environments.

The high degree of coordination of organization behavior can be illustrated by comparing coordination in organizations with the coordination that takes place in economic markets. To be sure, markets often exhibit considerable stability and predictability. A seller can bring his goods into the market with a fair notion of the total quantity that will be supplied and the prices at which goods will be exchanged. But he does not know in advance who specifically will be the buyer of his wares or at what precise price. Transactions that take place within organizations, far more than in markets, are preplanned and precoordinated. The automobile engine division knows exactly how many engine blocks to put into production – not because it has made a forecast of the market, but because its production plan has been coordinated with the plans for producing completed automobiles in other departments of the company.

A biological analogy is apt here, if we do not take it literally or too seriously. Organizations are assemblages of interacting hnuman beings and they are the largest assemblages in our society that have anything resembling a central coordinative system. Let us grant that these coordinative systems are not developed nearly to the extent of the central nervous system in higher biological organisms – that organizations are more earthworm than ape. Nevertheless, the high specificity of structure and coordination within organizations – as contrasted with the diffuse and variable relations *among* organizations and among unorganized individuals – marks off the individual organization as a sociological unit comparable in significance to the individual organism in biology.

# 38 Arthur L. Stinchcombe

## Some Main Types of Organizations

Excerpt from Arthur L. Stinchcombe, 'Formal organizations', in Neil J. Smelser (ed.), *Sociology: An Introduction*, Wiley, 1967, pp. 169–72.

It is useful to outline four types of organizations that have played an important role in sociological thinking about organizations since the categories were developed by Max Weber in the first part of this century. These four types are (a) the *charismatic retinue* of followers or disciples of a leader, (b) *feudal administration* of fief-holders, (c) *modern bureaucracies,* such as steel plants or government departments and (d) *modern professional organizations*, such as universities or hospitals.

The key difference that Weber noted among these organizations is the basis on which the organization decides the truth of the theory on which planning is based. Since this theory is what justifies the exercise of authority and is what makes authority legitimate, Weber called these criteria of truth 'principles of legitimacy'.

First, he noted that organizations in which the truth of the theory is decided on the basis of *what an inspired leader says* tend to have a distinct form of organization. He called the principle of legitimacy in this case *charisma*, which is a religious word meaning the 'gift of grace'. If people delegate authority to a man because they think he has an extraordinary gift, genius or inspiration, we call this 'charismatic authority'.

We find the charismatic retinue among the followers of inspired religious leaders, among the research assistants at the disposal of a scientist who is thought to be a genius, or among the aides of a president who is thought to represent in his person the wishes of the people. That is, charismatic administration occurs whenever people believe that, in the particular area of organizational activity, 'history is the lengthened shadow of a man'. In these cases the genius, inspiration or election make the sayings of the leader the principal criterion of truth and worth. The organizations, therefore, tend to be created so that the other people serve to *increase the powers* of the genius or inspired leader.

A good example of a charismatic retinue is the group of research assistants of any famous scientist. These assistants do not have defined jobs and responsibilities but, instead, are supposed to do what the famous scientist thinks is worth doing. The financing of the group is usually by irregular and unpredictable contributions from foundations. The foundations donate the money only as long as they believe in the genius of the scientist, which is only as long as he obtains results. This combination is typical of charismatic retinues: subordinates are at the disposal of the chief rather than possessing defined responsibilities or authority of their own, and irregular financing is by contributions from those who believe in the extraordinary qualities of the chief. These same essentials are found in the group of disciples of Jesus Christ, the 'Kitchen Cabinets' of the Presidents of the United States or the street-corner gang following an exceptional gang leader.

In feudal administration (broadly conceived), the basis of truth of the theory on which social activity is planned is tradition. There are several types of traditional administrations, but the most common one is that in which each official in the organization maintains a traditional territory in which he has certain hallowed rights – rights that he administers in his own interest. Combined with his traditional rights, he has traditional duties to the source from which the rights originated. In classical feudalism the source was usually the king or the church. Very similar forms of administration, in the modern world, are dealerships for new cars.

For example, the franchise holder for an automobile company performs a number of functions for the company. He advertises to the community, gives the service provided for in the warranty, stops the development of wildcat discount operators who would cut profit margins, often arranges financing of car sales and does other things. The automobile manufacturer supposes that the dealer will do these things because of self-interest if he is given more or less complete control of the area. But the dealer has some obligations to the company. For instance, he usually cannot sell his competitors' makes of new cars. This kind of informal administrative system rests on traditional loyalties and obligations, which in modern times are written into a contract. But unlike a charismatic or bureaucratic administration, there is no constant flow of orders from the superior to the subordinate. The subordinate serves the superior because of his own interests and his own sense of honor.

When the organizational theory is based on a mixture of legal principles and rational decisions of a top leadership, a *bureaucracy* tends to develop. Officials hold office for which they draw a salary; the organization as a legal personality holds the resources; and the official, typically, has a career within the organization.

Modern utility companies are perhaps the extreme examples of bureaucratic administration, whether they are governmental (as the Post Office in the United States) or private (as the American Telephone and

Telegraph Company). The key cause of extreme bureaucratization in utilities is that they must provide the same service to millions of people – and the same service day after day to those millions. One does not need genius or inspiration today to supply the same electricity to the same people as yesterday. But the electrical system is too interdependent to be parceled out among franchise holders. On the other hand, a good plan decided upon this month for serving a new public or for cheaper electrical production will keep earning the company money day after day for years. In short, routine administration of highly interdependent systems with a steady income produces bureaucracy. Responsibility is finely divided, but each man reports to a superior with wider responsibilities. Men move systematically from positions near the bottom to positions near the top. Unlike the early church, not even being the Son of God would help a person become the head of an electrical utility company at thirty years of age.

When the truth of the theory of organizational activity is certified by specialized knowledge of the trained members of the organization – rather than by a leader-genius, by tradition, or by top management – we tend to get a *professional* type of organization. In this type, people are delegated wide responsibility for planning activities in their sphere of competence, after their competence has been certified by a group of peers. Universities and hospitals are typical examples of this type of organization.

In a university, people are recruited to teach and perform research according to the judgement of the group of professionals in each discipline. The president of the university cannot hope to judge for himself the competence of biophysicists, political scientists and linguists. Moreover, he cannot direct their work, once they are hired. Consequently, the professionals in each discipline hire people, and usually the person hired decides himself what needs to be done. If he is competent, he alone knows best what to teach and how to perform research in his special field. Extreme decentralization of responsibility to men chosen as competent by their professional peers is distinctive of professional organizations.

# 39 Max Weber

The Essentials of Bureaucratic Organization

Excerpts from Max Weber, *The Theory of Social and Economic Organization*, translated by A. M. Henderson and Talcott Parsons, revised and edited by Talcott Parsons, Oxford University Press, Inc., 1947, pp. 333–40. First published in German in 1922.

The purest type of exercise of legal authority is that which employs a bureaucratic administrative staff. Only the supreme chief of the organization occupies his position of authority by virtue of appropriation, of election or of having been designated for the succcession. But even *his* authority consists in a sphere of legal 'competence'. The whole administrative staff under the supreme authority then consists, in the purest type, of individual officials who are appointed and function according to the following criteria:

1. They are personally free and subject to authority only with respect to their impersonal official obligations.

2. They are organized in a clearly defined hierarchy of offices.

3. Each office has a clearly defined sphere of competence in the legal sense.

4. The office is filled by a free contractual relationship. Thus, in principle, there is free selection.

5. Candidates are selected on the basis of technical qualifications. In the most rational case, this is tested by examination or guaranteed by diplomas certifying technical training, or both. They are *appointed*, not elected.

6. They are remunerated by fixed salaries in money, for the most part with a right to pensions. Only under certain circumstances does the employing authority, especially in private organizations, have a right to terminate the appointment, but the official is always free to resign. The salary scale is primarily graded according to rank in the hierarchy; but in addition to this criterion, the responsibility of the position and the requirements of the incumbent's social status may be taken into account.

7. The office is treated as the sole, or at least the primary, occupation of the incumbent.

8. It constitutes a career. There is a system of 'promotion' according to

seniority or to achievement, or both. Promotion is dependent on the judgement of superiors.

9. The official works entirely separated from ownership of the means of administration and without appropriation of his position.

10. He is subject to strict and systematic discipline and control in the conduct of the office.

This type of organization is in principle applicable with equal facility to a wide variety of different fields. It may be applied in profit-making business or in charitable organizations, or in any number of other types of private enterprises serving ideal or material ends. It is equally applicable to political and to religious organizations. With varying degrees of approximation to a pure type, its historical existence can be demonstrated in all these fields.

1. For example, this type of bureaucracy is found in private clinics, as well as in endowed hospitals or the hospitals maintained by religious orders. Bureaucratic organization has played a major role in the Catholic Church. [. . .] The same phenomena are found in the large-scale capitalistic enterprise; and the larger it is, the greater their role. And this is not less true of political parties, which will be discussed separately. Finally, the modern army is essentially a bureaucratic organization administered by that peculiar type of military functionary, the 'officer'.

2. Bureaucratic authority is carried out in its purest form where it is most clearly dominated by the principle of appointment. [. . .]

3. Appointment by free contract, which makes free selection possible, is essential to modern bureaucracy. [. . .]

4. The role of technical qualifications in bureaucratic organizations is continually increasing. Even an official in a party or a trade-union organization is in need of specialized knowledge, though it is usually of an empirical character, developed by experience, rather than by formal training. In the modern state, the only 'offices' for which no technical qualifications are required are those of ministers and presidents. This only goes to prove that they are 'officials' only in a formal sense, and not substantively, as is true of the managing director or president of a large business corporation. [. . .]

5. The bureaucratic official normally receives a fixed salary. [. . .]

6. 'Offices' which do not constitute the incumbent's principal occupation, in particular 'honorary' offices, belong in other categories. . . . The typical 'bureaucratic' official occupies the office as his principal occupation.

7. With respect to the separation of the official from ownership of the means of administration, the situation is essentially the same in the field of public administration and in private bureaucratic organizations, such as the large-scale capitalistic enterprise.

8. At the present time collegial bodies are rapidly decreasing in importance in favor of types of organization which are in fact, and for the most part formally as well, subject to the authority of a single head. For instance, the collegial 'governments' in Prussia have long since given way to the monocratic 'district president'. The decisive factor in this development has been the need for rapid, clear decisions, free of the necessity of compromise between different opinions and also free of shifting majorities.

9. The modern army officer is a type of appointed official who is clearly marked off by certain class distinctions. [. . .]

## The monocratic type of bureaucratic administration

Experience tends universally to show that the purely bureaucratic type of administrative organization – that is, the monocratic variety of bureaucracy – is, from a purely technical point of view, capable of attaining the highest degree of efficiency and is in this sense formally the most rational known means of carrying out imperative control over human beings. It is superior to any other form in precision, in stability, in the stringency of its discipline and in its reliability. It thus makes possible a particularly high degree of calculability of results for the heads of the organization and for those acting in relation to it. It is finally superior both in intensive efficiency and in the scope of its operations, and is formally capable of application to all kinds of administrative tasks.

The development of the modern form of the organization of corporate groups in all fields is nothing less than identical with the development and continual spread of bureaucratic administration. This is true of church and state, of armies, political parties, economic enterprises, organizations to promote all kinds of causes, private associations, clubs and many others. Its development is, to take the most striking case, the most crucial phenomenon of the modern Western State. However many forms there may be which do not appear to fit this pattern, such as collegial representative bodies, parliamentary committees, soviets, honorary officers, lay judges and what not, and however much people may complain about the 'evils of bureaucracy', it would be sheer illusion to think for a moment that continuous administrative work can be carried out in any field except by means of officials working in offices. The whole pattern of everyday life is cut to fit this framework. For bureaucratic administration is, other things being equal, always, from a formal, technical point of view, the most rational type. For the needs of mass administration today, it is completely indispensable. The choice is only that between bureaucracy and dilettantism in the field of administration.

The primary source of the superiority of bureaucratic administration lies in the role of technical knowledge which, through the development of modern technology and business methods in the production of goods, has become completely indispensable. In this respect, it makes no difference whether the economic system is organized on a capitalistic or a socialistic basis. Indeed, if in the latter case a comparable level of technical efficiency were to be achieved, it would mean a tremendous increase in the importance of specialized bureaucracy. [. . .]

The question is always who controls the existing bureaucratic machinery? And such control is possible only in a very limited degree to persons who are not technical specialists. Generally speaking, the trained permanent official is more likely to get his way in the long run than his nominal superior, the Cabinet Minister, who is not a specialist.

Though by no means alone, the capitalistic system has undeniably played a major role in the development of bureaucracy. Indeed, without it capitalistic production could not continue and any rational type of socialism would have simply to take it over and increase its importance. Its development, largely under capitalistic auspices, has created an urgent need for stable, strict, intensive and calculable administration. It is this need which gives bureaucracy a crucial role in our society as the central element in any kind of large-scale administration. Only by reversion in every field – political, religious, economic, etc. – to small-scale organization would it be possible to any considerable extent to escape its influence. On the one hand, capitalism in its modern stages of development strongly tends to foster the development of bureaucracy, though both capitalism and bureaucracy have arisen from many different historical sources. Conversely, capitalism is the most rational economic basis for bureaucratic administration and enables it to develop in the most rational form, especially because, from a fiscal point of view, it supplies the necessary money resources. [. . .]

Bureaucratic administration means fundamentally the exercise of control on the basis of knowledge. This is the feature of it which makes it specifically rational. This consists on the one hand in technical knowledge which, by itself, is sufficient to ensure it a position of extraordinary power. But in addition to this, bureaucratic organizations, or the holders of power who make use of them, have the tendency to increase their power still further by the knowledge growing out of experience in the service. For they acquire through the conduct of office a special knowledge of facts and have available a store of documentary material peculiar to themselves. [. . .]

The following are the principal more general social consequences of bureaucratic control:

1. The tendency to 'levelling' in the interest of the broadest possible basis of recruitment in terms of technical competence.

2. The tendency to plutocracy growing out of the interest in the greatest possible length of technical training. Today this often lasts up to the age of thirty.

3. The dominance of a spirit of formalistic impersonality, *'sine ira et studio'*, without hatred or passion, and hence without affection or enthusiasm. The dominant norms are concepts of straightforward duty without regard to personal considerations. Everyone is subject to formal equality of treatment; that is, everyone in the same empirical situation. This is the spirit in which the ideal official conducts his office.

# 40 Amitai Etzioni

## Organizational Control

Excerpts from Amitai Etzioni, *Modern Organizations*, Prentice-Hall, 1964, pp. 58–61

Nowhere is the strain between the organization's needs and the participant's needs – between effectiveness, efficiency and satisfaction – more evident than in the area of organizational control. In part, the two sets of needs support each other. An increase in the income of a corporation might allow it to increase the wages and salaries it pays; an increase in the prestige of a school might increase the prestige of the teachers who work there. To the degree that two sets of needs are compatible, little control is necessary. The participants will tend to do what is best for the organization in order to gratify their own needs, and the organization in seeking to serve its needs will serve theirs. But such meshing of needs is never complete, and is usually quite incomplete. The corporation's profit might grow, but the wages not be increased. Hence deliberate efforts have to be made by the organization to reward those who conform to its regulations and orders and to penalize those who do not. Thus the success of an organization is largely dependent on its ability to maintain control of its participants.

All social units control their members, but the problem of control in organizations is especially acute. Organizations as social units that serve specific purposes are artificial social units. They are planned, deliberately structured; they constantly and self-consciously review their performances and restructure themselves accordingly. In this sense they are unlike natural social units, such as the family, ethnic group or community. The artificial quality of organizations, their high concern with performance, their tendency to be far more complex than natural units, all make informal control inadequate and reliance on identification with the job impossible. Most organizations most of the time cannot rely on most of their participants to internalize their obligations, to carry out their assignments voluntarily, without additional incentives. Hence, organizations require formally structured distribution of rewards and sanctions to support compliance with their norms, regulations and orders.

To fulfil its control function the organization must distribute its rewards and sanctions according to performance so that those whose performance is in line with the organizational norms will be rewarded and those whose performance deviates from it will be penalized. [. . .]

## Classification of means of control

The means of control applied by an organization can be classified into three analytical categories: physical, material or symbolic. The use of a gun, a whip or a lock is physical since it affects the body; the threat to use physical sanctions is viewed as physical because the effect on the subject is similar in kind, though not in intensity, to the actual use. Control based on application of physical means is ascribed as *coercive power*.

Material rewards consist of goods and services. The granting of symbols (e.g. money) which allow one to acquire goods and services is classified as material because the effect on the recipient is similar to that of material means. The use of material means for control purposes constitutes *utilitarian power*.

Pure symbols are those whose use does not constitute a physical threat or a claim on material rewards. These include normative symbols, those of prestige and esteem; and social symbols, those of love and acceptance. When physical contact is used to symbolize love, or material objects to symbolize prestige, such contacts or objects are viewed as symbols because their effect on the recipient is similar to that of 'pure' symbols. The use of symbols for control purposes is referred to as *normative, normative-social* or *social power*. Normative power is exercised by those in higher ranks to control the lower ranks directly as when an officer gives a pep talk to his men. Normative-social power is used indirectly, as when the higher in rank appeals to the peer group of a subordinate to control him (e.g. as a teacher will call on a class to ignore the distractions of an exhibitionist child). Social power is the power which peers exercise over one another.

The use of various classes of means for control purposes – for power, in short – has different consequences in terms of the nature of the discipline elicited. All other things being equal, at least in most cultures, the use of coercive power is more alienating to those subject to it than is the use of utilitarian power, and the use of utilitarian power is more alienating than is the use of normative power.[1] Or, to put it the other way around, normative power tends to generate more commitment than

1. Unless specified otherwise, 'normative power' is used to refer to both normative and normative-social power. Social power is not discussed because as such it is not an organizational power.

utilitarian, and utilitarian more than coercive. In other words, the application of symbolic means of control tends to convince people, that of material means tends to build up their self-oriented interests in conforming, and the use of physical means tends to force them to comply.

The powers organizations use differ largely according to the ranks of the participants that are controlled. Most organizations use less alienating means to control their higher rather than their lower ranks. For instance, coercive power – if used at all – is applied to lower participants; e.g. prisoners are put in solitary confinement if they try to escape. Higher participants, e.g. guards, are more often rewarded or sanctioned materially to insure their performances (e.g. tardiness is fined). In making comparative observations, it is hence essential to compare participants of the same rank in different kinds of organizations or different ranks within the same organization. If such precaution is not observed, it is difficult to tell if the findings differ because of differences in rank or in the nature of the organizations, or both.

Comparing the controls applied to the lower ranks of different organizations is a fruitful way of classifying organizations, since differences in the nature of controls is indicative of and in this sense predicts many other differences among organizations. Most organizations most of the time use more than one kind of power. Control might be predominantly coercive, utilitarian or normative. Among organizations in which the same mode of control predominates, there are still differences in the degree to which the predominant control is stressed. Ordering organizations from high to low according to the degree to which coercion is stressed, we find concentration camps, prisons, traditional correctional institutions, custodial mental hospitals and prisoner-of-war camps. Ordering organizations from high to low according to the degree to which utilitarian power is predominant, we find blue-collar organizations such as factories, white-collar organizations such as insurance companies, banks and the civil service, and peacetime military organizations. Normative power is predominant in religious organizations, ideological-political organizations, colleges and universities, voluntary associations, schools and therapeutic mental hospitals.

Not every organizational type has one predominant pattern of control. Labor unions, for instance, fall into each of the three analytical categories. There are labor unions which rely heavily on coercive power to check deviant members, as in those unions that border on 'underworld' organizations; there are 'business-unions' in which control is largely built on the ability of the union representatives to 'deliver the goods', i.e. to secure wage increases and other material improvements. Finally, there are unions in which control is based on manipulation of ideological symbols, such as commitment to a Socialist ideology ('those who do not pay their dues retard the service of the union to the cause of the laboring classes'), or in which the community of workers is recruited to exert informal pressures on members to follow the norms and orders of the organization ('strike-breakers are poor friends'). [. . .]

The response of the participants to a particular use of power or combination of powers is determined not only by that use of power but also by the participants' social and cultural personalities. For instance, the same exercise of coercive power – a foreman slapping a worker – would elicit a more alienated response in working-class persons than it would in persons on 'skid row'; in contemporary Britain than the Britain of three generations ago; in France than on the Ivory Coast; in an aggressive than in a subservient person. When, however, the effect of all these factors is 'checked', when the effect of various means of control on the same group of workers is compared, the more normative the means of control used, the less alienating the exercise of power, and the more coercive the means, the more alienating the use of power. Utilitarian power rarely elicits as alienating a response as coercive power, nor does it as a rule generate as much commitment as normative power. To state it more concretely, most factory workers rarely feel as alienated as prisoners or as committed as church members.

# 41 Erving Goffman

On the Characteristics of Total Institutions

Excerpts from Erving Goffman, *Asylums: Essays on the Social Situation of Mental Patients and Other Inmates*, Doubleday, 1961, pp. 3–12.

Social establishments – institutions in the everyday sense of that term – are places such as rooms, suites of rooms, buildings or plants in which activity of a particular kind regularly goes on. In sociology we do not have a very apt way of classifying them. Some establishments, like Grand Central Station, are open to anyone who is decently behaved; others, like the Union League Club of New York or the laboratories at Los Alamos, are felt to be somewhat snippy about who is let in. Some, like shops and post offices, have a few fixed members who provide a service and a continuous flow of members who receive it. Others, like homes and factories, involve a less changing set of participants. Some institutions provide the place for activities from which the individual is felt to draw his social status, however enjoyable or lax these pursuits may be; other institutions, in contrast, provide a place for associations felt to be elective and unserious, calling for a contribution of time left over from more serious demands. In this book another category of institutions is singled out and claimed as a natural and fruitful one because its members appear to have so much in common – so much, in fact, that to learn about one of these institutions we would be well advised to look at the others.

Every institution captures something of the time and interest of its members and provides something of a world for them; in brief, every institution has encompassing tendencies. When we review the different institutions in our Western society, we find some that are encompassing to a degree discontinuously greater than the ones next in line. Their encompassing or total character is symbolized by the barrier to social intercourse with the outside and to departure that is often built right into the physical plant, such as locked doors, high walls, barbed wire, cliffs, water, forests or moors. These establishments I am calling *total institutions*, and it is their general characteristics I want to explore.

The total institutions of our society can be listed in five rough groupings. First, there are institutions established to care for persons felt to be both incapable and harmless; these are the homes for the blind, the aged, the orphaned and the indigent. Second, there are places established to care for persons felt to be both incapable of looking after themselves and a threat to the community, albeit an unintended one: TB sanataria, mental hospitals and leprosaria. A third type of total institution is organized to protect the community against what are felt to be intentional dangers to it, with the welfare of the persons thus sequestered not the immediate issue: jails, penitentiaries, POW camps and concentration camps. Fourth, there are institutions purportedly established the better to pursue some worklike task and justifying themselves only on these instrumental grounds: army barracks, ships, boarding schools, work camps, colonial compounds and large mansions from the point of view of those who live in the servants' quarters. Finally, there are those establishments designed as retreats from the world even while often serving also as training stations for the religious; examples are abbeys, monasteries, convents and other cloisters. This classification of total institutions is not neat, exhaustive nor of immediately analytical use, but it does provide a purely denotative definition of the category as a concrete starting point. [. . .]

None of the elements I will describe seems peculiar to total institutions, and none seems to be shared by every one of them; what is distinctive about total institutions is that each exhibits to an intense degree many items in this family of attributes. [. . .]

A basic social arrangement in modern society is that the individual tends to sleep, play and work in different places, with different co-participants, under different authorities, and without an over-all rational plan. The central feature of total institutions can be described as a breakdown of the barriers ordinarily separating these three spheres of life. First, all aspects of life are conducted in the same place and under the same single authority. Second, each phase of the member's daily activity is carried on in the immediate company of a large batch of others, all of whom are treated alike and required to do the same thing together. Third, all phases of the day's activities are tightly scheduled, with one activity leading at a prearranged time into the next, the whole sequence of activities being imposed from above by a system of explicit formal rulings and a body of officials. Finally, the various enforced activities are brought together into a single rational plan purportedly designed to fulfil the official aims of the institution.

Individually, these features are found in places other than total institutions. For example, our large commercial, industrial and educational establishments are increasingly providing cafeterias and free-time recreation for their members; use of these extended facilities remains voluntary in many particulars, however, and special care is taken to see that the ordinary line of authority does not extend to them. Similarly, house-wives or farm families may have all their major spheres of life within the same fenced-in area, but these persons are not collectively regimented and do not march through the day's activities in the immediate company of a batch of similar others.

The handling of many human needs by the bureaucratic organization of whole blocks of people – whether or not this is a necessary or effective means of social organization in the circumstances – is the key fact of total institutions. From this follow certain important implications.

When persons are moved in blocks, they can be supervised by personnel whose chief activity is not guidance or periodic inspection (as in many employer–employee relations) but rather surveillance – a seeing to it that everyone does what he has been clearly told is required of him, under conditions where one person's infraction is likely to stand out in relief against the visible, constantly examined compliance of the others. Which comes first, the large blocks of managed people, or the small supervisory staff, is not here at issue; the point is that each is made for the other.

In total institutions there is a basic split between a large managed group, conveniently called inmates, and a small supervisory staff. Inmates typically live in the institution and have restricted contact with the world outside the walls; staff often operate on an eight-hour day and are socially integrated into the outside world. Each grouping tends to conceive of the other in terms of narrow hostile stereotypes, staff often seeing inmates as bitter, secretive and untrustworthy, while inmates often see staff as condescending, highhanded and mean. Staff tend to feel superior and righteous; inmates tend, in some ways at least, to feel inferior, weak, blameworthy and guilty.

Social mobility between the two strata is grossly restricted; social distance is typically great and often formally prescribed. Even talk across the boundaries may be conducted in a special tone of voice. [. . .]

Just as talk across the boundary is restricted, so, too, is the passage of information, especially information about the staff's plans for inmates. Characteristically, the inmate is excluded from knowledge of the decisions taken regarding his fate. Whether the official grounds are military, as in concealing travel destination from enlisted men, or medical, as in concealing diagnosis, plan of treatment and approximate length of stay from tuberculosis patients, such exclusion gives staff a special basis of distance from and control over inmates.

All these restrictions of contact presumably help to maintain the antagonistic stereotypes. Two different social and cultural worlds develop, jogging alongside each other with points of official contact but little mutual penetration. Significantly, the institutional plant and name come to be identified by both staff and inmates as somehow belonging to staff, so that when either grouping refers to the views or interests of 'the institution', by implication they are referring (as I shall also) to the views and concerns of the staff.

The staff–inmate split is one major implication of the bureaucratic management of large blocks of persons; a second pertains to work.

In the ordinary arrangements of living in our society, the authority of the work place stops with the worker's receipt of a money payment; the spending of this in a domestic and recreational setting is the worker's private affair and constitutes a mechanism through which the authority of the work place is kept within strict bounds. But to say that inmates of total institutions have their full day scheduled for them is to say that all their essential needs will have to be planned for. Whatever the incentive given for work, then, this incentive will not have the structural significance it has on the outside. There will have to be different motives for work and different attitudes toward it. This is a basic adjustment required of the inmates and of those who must induce them to work.

Sometimes so little work is required that inmates, often untrained in leisurely pursuits, suffer extremes of boredom. Work that is required may be carried on at a very slow pace and may be geared into a system of minor, often ceremonial, payments, such as the weekly tobacco ration and the Christmas presents that lead some mental patients to stay on their jobs. In other cases, of course, more than a full day's hard labor is required, induced not by reward but by threat of physical punishment. In some total institutions, such as logging camps and merchant ships, the practice of forced saving postpones the usual relation to the world that money can buy; all needs are organized by the institution, and payment is given only when a work season is over and the men leave the premises. In some institutions there is a kind of slavery, with the inmate's full time placed at the convenience of staff; here the inmate's sense of self and sense of possession can become alienated from his work capacity. T. E. Lawrence (*The Mint*) gives an illustration in his record of service in an RAF training depot:

The six-weeks men we meet on fatigues shock our moral sense by their easy-going. 'You're silly —, you rookies, to sweat yourselves' they say. Is it our new keenness, or a relic of civility in us? For by the RAF we shall be paid all the twenty-four hours a day, at three halfpence an hour; paid to work, paid to eat, paid to sleep: always those halfpence are adding up. Impossible, therefore, to dignify a job by doing it well. It must take as much time as it can for afterwards there is not a fireside waiting, but another job.

Whether there is too much work or too little, the individual who was work-oriented on the outside tends to become demoralized by the work system of the total institution. An example of such demoralization is the practice in state mental hospitals of 'bumming' or 'working someone for' a nickel or dime to spend in the canteen. Persons do this – often with some defiance – who on the outside would consider such actions beneath their self-respect. (Staff members, interpreting this begging pattern in terms of their own civilian orientation to earning, tend to see it as a symptom of mental illness and one further bit of evidence that inmates really are unwell.)

There is an incompatibility, then, between total institutions and the basic work-payment structure of our society. Total institutions are also incompatible with another crucial element of our society, the family. Family life is sometimes contrasted with solitary living, but in fact the more pertinent contrast is with batch living, for those who eat and sleep at work, with a group of fellow workers, can hardly sustain a meaningful domestic existence. Conversely, maintaining families off the grounds often permits staff members to remain integrated with the outside community and to escape the encompassing tendency of the total institution.

Whether a particular total institution acts as a good or bad force in civil society, force it will have, and this will in part depend on the suppression of a whole circle of actual or potential households. Conversely, the formation of households provides a structural guarantee that total institutions will not be without resistance. The incompatibility of these two forms of social organization should tell us something about the wider social functions of them both.

The total institution is a social hybrid, part residential community, part formal organization; therein lies its special sociological interest. There are other reasons for being interested in these establishments, too. In our society, they are the forcing houses for changing persons; each is a natural experiment on what can be done to the self.

# 42 Peter M. Blau and W. R. Scott

The Social Environment of Organizations

Excerpts from Peter M. Blau and W. R. Scott, *Formal Organizations: A Comparative Approach*, Routledge & Kegan Paul, 1963, pp. 199–205. First published in 1961.

Community norms are often the basis on which management hires and promotes employees, as illustrated by the treatment of racial and ethnic groups in organizations (see Collins, 1946) and, specifically, by differences in personnel practices in the South and the North, even when branches of the same firm are compared. Another example of community influence is provided by a study comparing the performance of social workers of a state welfare department in offices of varying sizes (see Thomas, 1959). It was found that workers in small offices were more likely to have a service orientation and to perform better as caseworkers than those in large offices. However, further analysis indicated that the crucial factor was probably not size of office but size of community. The small offices were all located in small communities, where workers were more likely than those in anonymous cities to be concerned with the welfare of their clients, who were not complete strangers but neighbours; their greater interest in helping clients improved case-work service.

A study by Kerr and Siegel (1954) suggests a relation between community structure and strike propensity among industrial workers. Propensity to strike was measured by man-days lost due to strikes and lockouts, comparable data being available on about fifteen industries in eleven different countries. The highest propensity to strike in most countries was in the mining, maritime and longshore industries; the lowest, in agriculture, trade and the railroad industry. The explanatory hypothesis offered for the strike patterns discovered is that men whose work isolates them from the regular social life of the rest of the community tend to form an isolated mass with strong union solidarity, whereas workers who are integrated into the larger community do not. Workers in the isolated mass were also more likely to be active participants in their unions, and factionalism was high in their unions. Other studies on union participation and solidarity tend to confirm their conclusion. [. . .]

A case study of a strike in a New England community provides additional confirmation of the Kerr and Siegel hypothesis (Warner and

Low, 1947). Warner and Low attribute a strike in a large shoe manufacturing company to the breakdown in the skill hierarchy resulting from mass-production methods, which alienated workers from their jobs and undermined their status and their integration with the rest of the community. As a result, shoe operatives were more apt than other workers to confine their social contacts to members of the working class. The removal of managerial control from a local Yankee City owner to outsiders led to further deterioration in management–worker relations. A loss of craft skills and alienation from a powerful distant management caused workers to feel like an isolated mass and to associate primarily with others of their own social class, thus encouraging their participation in the union and in the strike. [. . .]

A study of factories in Japan conducted by Abegglen (1958, esp. pp. 11–54) provides information on non-Western organizations. Abegglen's data were obtained from qualitative interviews and observations in fifty-three factories of varying size. All of these organizations were found to be governed by traditional values, in sharp contrast to the pervasive impersonality in Western organizations. Employment in a company was looked upon as a personal commitment both by workers and management; hence, workers rarely were laid off or left their jobs. One result of such an employment policy was that most firms usually had a surplus of labour. This situation impeded adjustment to economic change and discouraged the introduction of technological innovations, since the cost of new machines could not be compensated for by reducing the cost of labour. Recruitment to various levels in these firms was largely based on formal education, and education depended to a considerable extent on family background and income, so that a person's status in the factory tended to be governed by his family's status in the community. Compensation was based on such features as age, education and number in the family rather than being closely geared to performance, the worker being rewarded for his status and his loyalty to the firm and not his specific contributions to the production process. There was little demarcation between the worker's private life and his business life: 'Management is involved in such diverse matters as the personal finances of the worker, the education of his children, religious activities, and the training of the worker's wife' (Abegglen, 1958, p. 129). In general it appears that industrialization in Japan was accompanied by much less change in its traditional social organization and social relations than was the case in Western countries. [. . .]

A study by Fallers (n.d., see esp. pp. 126–35, 151–2, 241–3) of the governmental and administrative organization of the Soga, a Bantu-speaking people of East Africa, allows us to examine bureaucracy in a non-literate society. Unlike most tribes, the Bantu had a central government before the Europeans came. Fallers suggests that the ambiguity of the Soga descent system created a structural need for an administrative corps recruited on a non-kinship and non-hereditary basis. Hence, in addition to the hereditary ruler and the princes who were the ruler's classificatory siblings, there was an administrative staff composed of commoners raised to their position by the chief on the basis of their abilities and services to him and directly dependent upon him for their position. Although this staff was bound to the ruler by traditional authority, it was a hierarchical and non-kinship structure based on achieved status and as such was more receptive to bureaucratization when a Western nation took over the country than were the less centralized, more traditional political systems of other tribes. Moreover, the conflict between lineage and state inherent in the dual political structure facilitated bureaucratization by the British, since the ruler, insecure in his position and facing the threat of revolt by the princes, welcomed the British as allies. Among the Southern Bantu, where the lineage-state problem was of less importance, Westernization did not proceed as readily. Once the Soga rulers were committed to the new order – being dependent on the British as allies and sending their sons typically to schools in England – the British could introduce further bureaucratization, replacing the tribute system by salaries and the personal-appointment system by civil-service procedures. Attempts to introduce bureaucratic practices at the lower levels (for example, among the village headmen) were less successful, since these chiefs depended less for their authority on an administrative hierarchy and more on local personal ties with their villagers.

## References

ABEGGLEN, J. G. (1958), *The Japanese Factory*, Free Press.

COLLINS, O. (1946), 'Ethnic behavior in industry', *Amer. J. Sociol.*, vol. 51, pp. 293–8.

FALLERS, L. A. (n.d.), *Bantu Bureaucracy*, East African Institute of Social Research, Cambridge, England.

KERR, C., and SIEGEL, A. (1954), 'The interindustry propensity to strike – an international comparison', in A. Kornhauser *et al.* (eds.), *Industrial Conflict*, McGraw-Hill, pp. 189–212.

THOMAS, E. J. (1959), 'Role conceptions and organizational size', *Amer. soc. Rev.*, vol. 24, pp. 30–37.

WARNER, W. L., and LOW, J. O. (1947), *The Social System of the Modern Factory*, Yale University Press.

# 43 B. Kapferer

Norms and the Manipulation of Relationships in a Work Context

Excerpts from B. Kapferer, 'Norms and the manipulation of relationships in a work context', in J. C. Mitchell (ed.), *Social Networks in Urban Situations*, Manchester University Press, 1969, pp. 189–209.

While admitting the influence of a person's job and his position in the production process on the type and number of individuals he has direct relationships with, these are not the only factors affecting interaction in the Cell Room. Workers have relationships with other employees which are not demanded as part of the production process. Some individuals whose work imposes restrictions on their movement have a wide variety of direct contacts in the situation, whereas other workers whose job is associated with freedom of movement throughout the work place include only a small number of persons within their direct set of relationships. These considerations suggest the influence of other factors which may inhibit or facilitate interaction between workers in the Cell Room. Thus various social characteristics such as those of tribal background, age and religion or the possession of power and/or authority in the work context affect the degree to which individuals come into contact with one another. [. . .]

The following is a brief account of a dispute which broke out between two co-workers of the same occupational status in unit 3. It tells of Abraham's objection to the fast working pace of a fellow stripper, Donald, who works at stand IV with Abel (see Figure 1); Donald's brief period of angry opposition to Abraham's suggestion that he should slow down his work rate; and, finally, his eventual acquiescence to Abraham's demands.

The normal clamour and hum of the Cell Room is suddenly broken by Abraham who shouts across to Donald at stand IV, '*Buyantanshe* (Progress), slow down and wait for us.' A hush now settles on the Unit. For a while Donald takes no notice and Abraham calls '*Buyantanshe*' once more. This evokes a reaction and Donald retorts that he is not to be called by his nickname as he already has a proper name. Abraham replies that he only knows Donald by his nickname, '*Buyantanshe*'. His blood up, Donald shouts, 'We young men must be very careful about being bewitched.' Abraham assents, 'You are quite right, you will be bewitched if you don't respect your elders.' Donald is now almost beside himself with rage, and goes straight to lodge a formal protest with the Shop Steward, Lotson, against what he considers to be

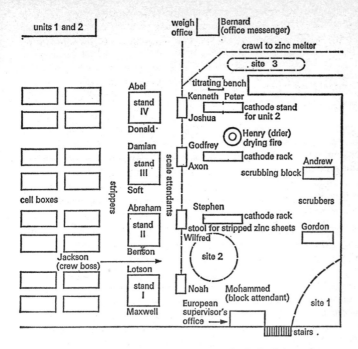

Figure 1 A schematic drawing of the Cell Room showing in detail the work area of unit 3 and approximate working positions of those Cell Room employees who are engaged for most or part of their time in unit 3

Abraham's threat of witchcraft. This done he then goes down the stripping stands reporting the matter to the strippers and those scale attendants working nearby. He is just passing stand III when he hears, as do others close at hand, Soft's very audible comment to Joshua that Donald must be drunk or else they (the unit 3 workers) should not be seeing such behaviour. Donald storms across to Soft, and the latter, in an attempt to pacify him and to persuade him to return to his stand, says, 'I didn't mean *you* when I said that.' Jackson, the Crew Boss, who has hitherto been amusedly observing the dispute from the sidelines, now steps in and orders Donald to return to work, which the latter does, muttering angrily all the way back to his stand, 'I don't wish anyone to call me "*Buyantanshe*", I have my own name, Donald.'

Work now returns more or less to normal. Occasionally small clusters of workers collect to discuss or inquire about the dispute; but the event is once more brought fully to the attention of the unit workers when Soft comes to seat himself near Lotson at break time. Lotson asks him why he has quarrelled with Donald at work. 'It's my own business; Donald didn't hear me properly,' mutters Soft. Others who are seated near Soft and Lotson now stop whatever they have been talking about and crane forward to listen. Damian and Jackson come from where they have been standing near stand 1 and hover at the outskirts of the group surrounding Lotson and Soft. Soft now elaborates, 'Donald has taken too much beer and this is what has caused him to behave like this. Surely we all call him by his nickname!' Donald, who has been listening nearby, and prior to this had been discussing his version of the dispute with two of his friends, Godfrey and Stephen, impatiently breaks in, 'In my case, please, I don't want anyone calling me *Buyantanshe* as I have my proper name, Donald. Drinking doesn't enter the case – the quarrel was caused by Abraham who insisted on calling me by my nickname and instead of answering properly to my protests, threatened to bewitch me.' At this Lotson bursts out with a disbelieving laugh and asks Donald for the real reasons behind his outburst: 'Was it because Soft called you a drunk? If so, this is not a real case.' Soft now intervenes and states that Donald has reacted in such a way because the comment came from a young man. 'Really,' he declares, 'there is no excuse for Donald's behaviour.'

Abraham, who is seated near stand 1, calls across to Donald to join him where he is sitting. (He addresses the latter as 'Donald'.) Everybody seated with Donald urges him to go, and after much prompting he does so. Lotson, Abel and Soft joke together that now Donald need not fear being bewitched any longer. Immediately on Donald's arrival at Abraham's seating place, Abraham asks him to go and sharpen his stripping hook. After having completed this service Donald returns the hook to its owner and then joins a group of scale attendants and titrators who are seated near the Weigh Office.

For most workers in the unit, including Abraham, the dispute seemed to be at an end. But that this was not so for Donald, was demonstrated a few days later. Donald again accused Abraham of witchcraft and used his suspicions of Abraham's malevolence as a pretext for applying for a transfer from the Cell Room to another section of the mine. His application was successful and he was transferred to underground work.

It is immediately apparent that the various individuals involved in the dispute invoked a number of norms in the situation to support their own particular stand. These expressed norms also relate to the varied social factors, interests and beliefs which lie at the root of all Cell Room relationships. Thus in an attempt to obtain a clearer understanding of the processes involved in the dispute and the issues at stake, these expressed norms must be placed in the context of the social mosaic formed out of the inter-meshing of Cell Room relationships.

The dispute between Abraham and Donald was precipitated by Abraham, who in shouting across to Donald to slow down his working rate called him *Buyantanshe*. Donald took no notice of Abraham's words and did not slacken his pace, but instead made an issue out of being addressed by his nickname. Thus the major issue which had been introduced at the very start of the dispute was Abraham's implied accusation that Donald was a 'ratebuster'. [. . .]

Abraham's reference to Donald's 'ratebusting' has an edge to it other than the implication that Donald by working fast was generally threatening the Cell Room workers' position in relation to management. The accusation had another purpose, that of protecting the interests of the older workers against the younger workers in the Room. This is revealed in the altercation between the two men which ensued after Donald's first reaction to being called *Buyantanshe* and which involved Donald's shouting across to Abraham, 'We young men must be careful of being bewitched.' The norm which serves to regulate the work speed of the strippers operates more in the interests of the older than the younger strippers. Many of the older strippers in unit 3 are nearing retirement age and it is a very real fear among them that if their work noticeably flags behind the rate of the younger strippers they would run the risk of being sacked or retired.[1] In addition Figure 1 illustrates that with the exception of stand IV where two relatively young workers, Donald and Abel, are employed, all the young workers are paired with older workers. Some of these older workers, as for example, Damian, Maxwell and Abraham, because of their age, find the work very taxing physically, and are dependent on the younger men on their stands, in those instances where they are paired with them, to take some of their load as well. Thus in a sense the younger men may have an interest in breaking the norm in an attempt to get rid of the older workers some of whose work they must on occasions assist with. However, because of the nature of the work it is not easy for a young stripper paired with an older stripper to ratebust. The exception is stand IV where two relatively young strippers are paired and it is therefore significant that they should be involved in the norm breaking. Also, because the stand at which Abraham works is the one in the unit where two older workers are employed may explain why the accusation should come from this stand. These facts are given greater force when it is realized that for a number of days prior to the dispute, although they had not been working fast before break, Donald and Abel had been finishing their work well ahead of the others. In addition, from information collected over a period of twenty-six days before the dispute the two older strippers, Abraham and Benson on stand II, with only three exceptions were the last to finish. Not only had Donald and Abel been working fast but they had also been demonstrating very convincingly the greater speed in which a task can be

1. During the study Abraham and Maxwell *were* approached by the European General Foreman who informed them that they were under consideration by the Company for retirement.

completed when both the strippers are young, than when the stripping pair consists of at least one older worker, or in stand II's case, two older workers. Therefore a number of further considerations in relation to the case must be stressed. The norm which regulates work speed can be interpreted in one sense as protecting the interests of all workers concerned in the Cell Room, but in another way it could be seen as really having its main efficacy in protecting the interests of the older workers in the Room. In certain cases some of the young strippers have to carry the weight of a very much older worker's work and may, in fact, have as much reason to break the norm as to maintain it. By breaking the norm they may be able to rid themselves of the older workers, thereby lightening their work load. Thus Donald by working fast could have been seen as doing the other young workers in the Room who are saddled with much older work partners, a service; and by showing up the latter's lack of suitability for the work he may well have merited the receipt of support in the dispute.

Another point is also worthy of attention. In certain circumstances, as fast work can be regarded by Cell Room workers and particularly the older workers as being ratebusting threatening the maintenance of their present working conditions, so slow work could also be viewed as a similar threat. By 'dragging the chain' as Abraham and Benson might be regarded as doing, a stripper will hold up the time of task completion of others in the work situation. The speed of work of scrubbers and scale attendants is largely dependent on the rate set by strippers. If a stripper's work speed is slow this extends the time taken to complete the tasks of scrubbers and scale attendants well beyond the accepted four hours work time in the Cell Room. This could cause considerable inconvenience. Not only does it shorten the leisure time of the persons concerned but if they are involved in other economic ventures outside Mine employment the necessity to stay at work could seriously upset their satisfactory operation. It was largely because of Abraham's and Benson's slow work that at least one scrubber and some of the scale attendants had to work overtime for which they received no extra payment.

In the analysis of the various norms and attitudes so far relevant to the dispute it is clear that a variety of interpretations can be placed on them. The dispute cannot be explained simply in terms of Abraham's view that Donald was a ratebuster; for upon closer examination Donald's offence does not seem as serious as it might have first appeared and it is even possible that some case could be made out in support of his action. However, the analysis of the factors involved in the dispute to date does provide a partial explanation of at least some of the characteristics of the case. In the first place it can be understood why the accusation of ratebusting should come from a person working in stand II and why it should be directed at a man on stand IV. Secondly because it has been shown that some sympathy could be generated for Donald's action it is conceivable that no other worker involved in the dispute should raise the issue of ratebusting. But other problems remain or are raised. Why, for instance, was Abraham the accuser and not Benson? Why was Donald accused and not Abel, as the latter on this occasion was just as guilty as the former? Why, if some case can be made out to support Donald, was he deserted by the workers in the unit who apparently threw in their support for Abraham? Perhaps by examining the other issues which entered as the dispute progressed some solution to these problems may be found.

Donald expressed a fear to Abraham that the latter might sanction his disapproval of Donald's behaviour by the use of witchcraft. Abraham jokingly replied that this was a possibility as Donald had shown disrespect to an elder. Here two additional norms which govern workers' behaviour in the Cell Room must be discussed: as Abraham pointed out and Donald realized, Donald had disregarded another norm in the situation which is that respect must be shown by younger to older men in the work context. Age is a factor together with other social characteristics, such as seniority of service in the Cell Room and occupational status, which demands deference from younger and more junior employees. Although these factors are subject to varied interpretation according to the particular persons involved, Donald's subordination to Abraham was institutionalized in a fictitious 'father–son' relation recognized by themselves and by others in the situation.

Donald rarely comes into contact with Abraham except to exchange greetings on arrival at work, but when they do greet each other Donald often addresses Abraham as '*tata*' (father) and Abraham reciprocates by calling Donald '*mwana*' (son). In the Cell Room a large number of kinship terms and occasionally other forms of address terms are applied by the employees to one another. Also, as in Abraham and Donald's occasional adoption of kinship terminology in their address to each other, the use of kin terms between workers does not in general imply an actual kinship connexion. But as is usual when specific kinds of kin terms are used between pairs of persons in any context, irrespective of whether an actual kin link exists or not, a certain mode of behaviour is expected between them. In town and in the Cell Room, as in the rural areas, the terms for 'father' and 'son' denote both respect and social distance and indicate the one's dominant position over the other. Ideally a son should be subordinate to the wishes and demands of his father and should not show the latter disrespect. A further point must also be noted. The usage of certain types of address terms (kin or otherwise) between workers not only expresses the nature of their relationship to the particular persons involved but also communicates its character to others in the work situation. Therefore, by their use of particular kin terms in the address of one another the position in which Donald stood in relation to Abraham and the ideal mode of behaviour which could be expected between them was communicated to the other workers in the situation. Thus their expected behaviour towards each other was public knowledge in the unit. Donald, by reacting strongly to Abraham's use of his nickname and by not slowing down his work speed, had breached another norm which frames behaviour in the Cell Room, viz. that a younger man should show respect to an older man; a norm reinforced by the fact that a recognized 'father–son' relationship existed between them. Donald's breach of this norm might have tipped the balance of the scales more in Abraham's favour, and more clearly defined the terms on which support for Abraham could have been based. It might also appear to answer one of the previously stated problems, as to why, when no other person took up Abraham's accusation of ratebusting – there even seeming to be a case for some support for Donald, at least from the younger workers – all the support flowed towards Abraham. For example, it was when Abraham drew his attention to Donald's disrespect of an older man that Soft seemingly gave his allegiance to Abraham, suggesting that Donald must be drunk to behave in such a way.

But in his realization of his disrespect for Abraham, Donald made reference to a much more serious issue, the threatened use of witchcraft. What made matters worse was that Abraham endorsed Donald's claim by stating that his future use of witchcraft was a possibility if Donald did not come to heel. Most workers believe that witchcraft can cause grave personal misfortune such as illness, death, work accidents or premature retirement or delay promotion to the benefit of other seemingly less qualified members of the Room. Not all illness, accidents, retirements and delays in promotion etc. are regarded as the result of witchcraft. Witchcraft is only sought as an explanation for such misfortune when no other immediately evident explanation is available.

It is widely accepted in the Cell Room that witchcraft which is harmful to others should not be used, not only because it is dangerous to the persons against whom it is directed but also because its use drives a wedge, as the workers perceive it, between people who must co-operate both at work and in their dealings with management. However, the very nature of the work situation strengthens the belief in the existence of witchcraft in the Cell Room and fosters witchcraft accusations between the workers. The skill to perform various tasks within the Cell Room is acquired easily and quickly, employees being transferred from one job to another without any special induction training, except in the cast of titrating. In fact when workers, due to illness or some other personal crisis are absent from work, men normally occupied in different tasks within the Cell Room will be momentarily transferred to fill vacancies occasioned by such absenteeism. This is particularly so when a person involved in a critical task on which the production process depends, such as stripping, is absent from work. In this instance, an employee who is a scale attendant or dryer, both tasks that are less critical in that slightly fewer men doing these jobs does not greatly impede the work flow, will be transferred to perform the task in the stripper's absense. Because of the ease by which employees can be transferred from one job to another, no man can regard himself, or be considered by the company, as indispensable or providing difficulties for replacement. A considerable feeling of insecurity is thereby generated, and it is felt, not without cause, that an illness or accident which prevents attendance at work for any period of time could cost a man his job. Furthermore there are wage differences operating between the various Cell Room tasks, workers in high-grade tasks such as stripping, receiving higher wages than employees in lower-grade work. Short of combined union action for general wage increases covering all Cell Room jobs, and perhaps the Mine Plant generally, the only way by which workers can increase their pay is to seek promotion. But the only time when a worker can hope for a promotion is when a vacancy arises in a higher-grade job.[2] These are few and far between as no new jobs are being created by the company in the Cell Room at higher levels, and the rate of labour turnover is low, the latter undoubtedly being conditioned by the attractiveness of the Cell Room work conditions. Therefore employees who can be promoted in terms of the Cell Room work structure will compete with each other for promotion when a vacancy occurs: this competition is all the more fierce because the Cell Room workers are competing for scarce resources. Men with apparently similar qualifications for promotion to a specific task will compete, with only one man being successful. It is not surprising that the use of witchcraft in such a case is suspected as an aid to a successful promotion, and accusations of witchcraft in these instances are not uncommon. In addition to witchcraft accusations flowing between people

2. Except for the positions of titrator and crew boss, where some education including knowledge of written and spoken English is required, no special educational achievement is needed for promotion. Other factors such as length of service, behaviour at work and the physical strength to carry out the heavier work often demanded in the higher job grades, are influential in the company's choice as to who is promoted. However, it is important that it is not always clear what factors influence promotion when it occurs.

of the same wage grade, particularly when they are thrown into competition with each other for promotion, accusations also flow between workers of different wage grades. Because of the limited number of jobs which fall vacant, people in higher paid jobs suspect the operation of witchcraft against them by lower paid workers to induce illness, accidents and even death in an attempt to create vacancies. This results in another pattern of witchcraft accusations when certain illnesses or accidents occur for instance, flowing from employees in highly paid jobs to workers in low-paid tasks.

Witchcraft is also believed to be used by specific individuals at work as a sanction to reinforce their power and authority in the Room and to warn other workers in the work place against forms of behaviour which might threaten these former individuals' security. Although all men are thought capable of exercising witchcraft in the Cell Room it is generally believed that some of the older men, largely because of their age and supposed familiarity with 'traditional' witchcraft practices, are the most dangerous and skilful exponents of the art. When accused of witchcraft they will deny the accusation vehemently, passing it off as ridiculous, 'for who would wish to bewitch a workmate?' But it must be stressed that the old men are not loath to foster the belief in their witchcraft powers amongst the younger men. The belief in their extraordinary powers is an important weapon in their hands, for the constant threat of its possible use is a valuable sanction with which the older men can control certain forms of work behaviour such as Donald's, which could threaten their continued employment in the Cell Room. In unit 3 Abraham, Maxwell and Damian are the most feared for their witchcraft powers. On one occasion considerable consternation spread throughout the room when Damian appeared at work with his green boiler suit covered in yellow clay. The clay happened to be of the same colour as that in the Broken Hill cemetery and it was thought that Damian had visited the place the previous evening for the purpose of robbing corpses of their vital organs for the practice of his witchcraft. In fact Damian had only been cultivating his gardens on the outskirts of the Mine township. [. . .]

One way in which I have attempted to assess the many norms, values, etc., expressed or implied in the conflict as it progressed was in terms of their utility for the rallying of support to the cause of one or the other parties involved. I was thus concerned with the mobilization of support. But at the risk of overstressing my position, I now want to suggest that the general norms, values, attitudes and beliefs which are overt in a situation of conflict are more the banners under which people act: they do not necessarily betray the underlying reasons for their action. Other norms and expectations which are more restricted to the governing of behaviour in the relationships between specific *pairs* of individuals will also influence the particular nature of the mobilization in a conflict situation. Norms which are general and accepted by most people in a situation facilitate better the communication to others of the reasons for an individual's action or alignment, than those norms and expectations which are restricted to the relationships operating between certain pairs of actors.

# Part Seven
# The Community and Community Studies

In an essay written in 1933 and reproduced in part in Reading 44(c), Louis Wirth complains that 'the term "community" ... has been used with an abandon reminiscent of poetic licence'. This is certainly true, and even strictly sociological definitions of community are numerous and varied. Any attempt to reproduce a representative cross section would thus require a far larger selection of Readings than it is possible to include here. Nor, in our view, would this be particularly useful. We are more concerned to convey how sociologists delineate communities and study aspects of them than how they define the term.

We do, however, begin with a few excerpts which convey five strikingly different conceptions of community. These are given in Reading 44. They range from Tönnies's classical conception of *Gemeinschaft* as a set of intimate and closely interwoven relationships, to Long's totally different view of a local community as a set of structured activities which co-exist and intermesh without any over-all 'organization', and to Webber's conception of 'interest community' in which spatial proximity is not a *necessary* condition.

We then give a selection of extracts from several field studies of widely differing communities. Reading 45 is a brief statement on the nature of the Lynds's pioneer community study, *Middletown*. Few sociologists conducting a community study would now try to emulate the Lynds's attempt to produce 'a total-situation study'. Yet many still derive insights and stimulation from *Middletown*. The Readings by Arensberg and Kimball and by Seeley, Sim and Loosley are given as good illustrations of the fruitful use of conceptions of community in two very different field situations.

In his study of a Chicago slum, Suttles (Reading 48) does not use any particular conception of community. Indeed, he lays stress not on 'community organization' as such but on the way in which 'a segmentary system of spatial and ethnic units' contributes to order in a community which most middle-class laymen would tend to regard as essentially 'disorganized'. In the extracts from Margaret Stacey's study of Banbury and

Pons's of Stanleyville, there is again no particular concern with problems of community delineation and the main interest is in aspects of differentiation and division *within* two very different communities. Both studies provide good examples of the kind of exploratory endeavour which community studies usually are. In Margaret Stacey's study we are told how the distinction between Banburians and recent immigrants to Banbury led the author to see the opposition between traditionalism and non-traditionalism as a key to the social structure of the community. In Pons's study we are shown how the small-scale study of a single neighbourhood was used, in conjunction with census-type data on the population of Stanleyville as a whole, to develop a working conception of how and why there was so much internal variation in the processes of urban integration operating in the town.

Finally, in Reading 51 we give two extracts from writings on the integration operating in the town.

# 44 Conceptions of Community

## (a) Ferdinand Tönnies

### The Contrast between *Gemeinschaft* and *Gesellschaft*

Excerpts from Ferdinand Tönnies, *Community and Association*, Routledge & Kegan Paul, 1955, pp. 37–9. First published in German in 1887.

All intimate, private and exclusive living together is understood as life in *Gemeinschaft* (community). *Gesellschaft* (society) is public life – it is the world itself. In *Gemeinschaft* (community) with one's family, one lives from birth on bound to it in weal and woe. One goes into *Gesellschaft* (society) as one goes into a strange country. A young man is warned against bad *Gesellschaft* (society), but the expression bad *Gemeinschaft* (community) violates the meaning of the word. Lawyers may speak of domestic *Gesellschaft* (society) thinking only of the legalistic concept of a social association, but the domestic *Gemeinschaft* (community) or home life with its immeasurable influence upon the human soul has been felt by everyone who ever shared it. Likewise, each member of a bridal couple knows that he or she goes into marriage as a complete *Gemeinschaft* (community) of life. A *Gesellschaft* (society) of life would be a contradiction in and of itself. One keeps or enjoys another's *Gesellschaft* (society or company) but not his *Gemeinschaft* (community) in this sense. One becomes a part of a religious *Gemeinschaft* (community); religious *Gesellschaften* (associations, or societies) like any other groups formed for given purposes, exist only in so far as they, viewed from without, take their places among the institutions of a political body or as they represent conceptual elements of a theory; they do not touch upon the religious *Gemeinschaft* as such. There exists a *Gemeinschaft* (community) of language, of folkways or mores, or of beliefs; but, by way of contrast, *Gesellschaft* (society or company) exists in the realm of business, travel or sciences. So of special importance are the commercial *Gesellschaften* (societies or companies), whereas, even though a certain familiarity and *Gemeinschaft* (community) may exist among business partners, one could indeed hardly speak of commercial *Gemeinschaft* (community). To make the word combination 'joint-stock *Gemeinschaft*' would be abominable. On the other hand, there exists a *Gemeinschaft* (community) of ownership in fields, forest and pasture. The *Gemeinschaft* (community) of property between man and wife cannot be called *Gesellschaft* (society) of property. Thus many differences become apparent. [. . .]

*Gemeinschaft* (community) is old; *Gesellschaft* (society) is new as a name as well as a phenomenon. [. . .] All praise of rural life has pointed out that the *Gemeinschaft* (community) among people is stronger there and more alive; it is the lasting and genuine form of living together. In contrast to *Gemeinschaft, Gesellschaft* (society) is transitory and superficial. Accordingly, *Gemeinschaft* (community) should be understood as a living organism, *Gesellschaft* (society) as a mechanical aggregate and artifact.

## (b) R. M. MacIver and Charles H. Page

## The Mark of a Community is That One's Life May Be Lived Wholly Within It'

Excerpts from R. M. MacIver and Charles H. Page, *Society: An Introductory Analysis*, Macmillan Co., 1961, pp. 8–10. First published in 1949. Revised version of R. M. MacIver, *Society: A Textbook of Society*, Macmillan Co., 1937.

Community is the term we apply to a pioneer settlement, a village, a city, a tribe or a nation. Wherever the members of any group, small or large, live together in such a way that they share, not this or that particular interest, but the basic conditions of a common life, we call that group a community. The mark of a community is that one's life *may* be lived wholly within it. One cannot live wholly within a business organization or a church; one can live wholly within a tribe or a city. The basic criterion of community, then, is that all of one's social relationships may be found within it.

Some communities are all-inclusive and independent of others. Among primitive peoples we sometimes find communities of no more than a hundred persons, as, for example, among the Yurok tribes of California, which are almost or altogether isolated. But modern communities, even very large ones, are much less self-contained. Economic and, increasingly so, political interdependence is a major characteristic of our great modern communities.

We may live in a metropolis and yet be members of a very small community because our interests are circumscribed within a narrow area. Or we may live in a village and yet belong to a community as wide as the whole area of our civilization or even wider. No civilized community has walls around it to cut it completely off from a larger one, whatever 'iron curtains' may be drawn by the rulers of this nation or that. Communities exist within greater communities: the town within a region, the region within a nation, and the nation within the world community which, perhaps, is in the process of development.

A community then is an area of social living marked by some degree of *social coherence*. The bases of community are *locality* and *community sentiment*.

A community always occupies a territorial area. Even a nomad community, a band of gypsies, for example, has a local, though changing, habitation. At every moment its members occupy together a definite place on the earth's surface. Most communities are settled and derive from the conditions of their locality a strong bond of solidarity. To some extent this local bond has been weakened in the modern world by the extending facilities of communication; this is especially apparent in the penetration into rural areas of dominant urban patterns. But the extension of communication is itself the condition of a larger but still territorial community.

The importance of the conception of community is in large measure that it underscores the relation between social coherence and the geographical area. [. . .]

But today we find, what never existed in primitive societies – people occupying specific local areas which lack the social coherence necessary to give them a community character. For example, the residents of a ward or district of a large city may lack sufficient contacts or common interests to instill conscious identification with the area. Such a 'neighborhood' is not a community because it does not possess a feeling of belonging together – it lacks community sentiment. [. . .] A community, to repeat, is an area of common living. There must be the common living with its *awareness* of sharing a way of life as well as the common earth.


## (c) Louis Wirth

### Towards a Definition of the Local Community

Excerpts from Louis Wirth, 'The scope and problems of the community', in A. J. Reiss, Jr (ed.), *Louis Wirth on Cities and Social Life*, University of Chicago Press, 1964, pp. 165–75. First published in *Publications of the Sociological Society of America*, vol. 27, 1933, pp. 61–73.

The term 'community', like other concepts taken over from common-sense usage, has been used with an abandon reminiscent of poetic license.

In the case of some writers community has stood for those organic relationships that obtain in the plant and animal world and that may be found in human relations as well as between organisms of the same or of different species living together on a symbiotic basis. Others have referred to the community as a psychical rather than an organic relationship and have consequently emphasized consensus over symbiosis and collective action over the division of labor.

This seems to be the fundamental difference between the point of view of Herbert Spencer and that of Auguste Comte. While the former emphasized one aspect of the social complex, namely, the division of labor, competition and interdependence, the latter regarded consensus, i.e. common culture, common experiences, aims and understanding as the more fundamental fact in social cohesion. The emphasis upon one or the other of these dual aspects of human group life reappears persistently in the history of our discipline. It is implicit in Sir Henry Maine's distinction between 'status' and 'contract', in Durkheim's discrimination between the two kinds of mutual dependence or *solidarité*, the one organic and the other mechanical, and it has crystallized in the difference of meaning between 'community' and 'society', expressed in the works of Tönnies, Max Weber, Park and Burgess, and MacIver. [. . .]

Historically the community has been an expression that emphasized the unity of the common life of a people or of mankind. Even a superficial retrospect, however, reveals that this common life itself has undergone profound changes which have been reflected in changing scientific interests in the community. One of the chief tasks in every human group is that of generating a sense of all belonging together. In the face of the increasing mechanization of living, of national and cultural provincialism, of the more thoroughgoing segmentation of life and the more minute division of labor, this task has become, as MacIver says, 'not less necessary but more difficult'. In the transition from a type of social organization based on kinship, status and a crude division of labor, to a type of social organization characterized by rapid technological developments, mobility, the rise of special interest groups and formal social control, the community has acquired new meaning and has revealed new problems.

At one time territorial, kinship and interest relations were, apparently, more coterminous than they are now. The folk community was apparently more of a primary group, as Cooley used the term, than the prevailing form of group life is today in Western civilization. As folk life gives way to technological civilization, new bases for social integration must appear if men are to retain the capacity to act collectively in the face of divergent interests and increasing interdependence. The change from status to contract, of which the trend from the family to the state as the predominant form of social organization is representative, and the change from a relatively high degree of local self-sufficiency to a delicately and unstably equilibrated international interdependence, best represented by the change from barter and local markets to international trade, finance and politics, suggest a wider territorial basis for community life and the tenuous character of modern opinion and action. The territorial limits of modern communities cannot be drawn on the basis of a single criterion. Every important interest in community life may have a varying range of influence, and may in turn be subject to repercussions from without of an indirect and remote sort. The multiplication of corporate groups in modern times, the wide dispersion of the membership and the increasing number of ties of identification and affiliation of the individual with diverse societies often obscure the fact that every society is also in some degree a community. [. . .]

As research interests have turned from the more abstract consideration of community life to the study of specific areas, villages, towns, cities and regions, the importance of relatively stable and comparable unit areas and of continuous moving indexes of changes in community life has become apparent. But here, as elsewhere, facts do not lie around at random merely waiting to be picked up by inquiring sociologists. Data have relevance only to specific problems, and each problem may call for a different set of facts to be discovered, organized and interpreted in order to be concluded. We must be clear, therefore, on the questions to which we seek answers before we can say what data will be relevant.

In so far as we are interested in the community of scientists, rather than as technicians and politicians, we raise a series of questions about it which are more general, more abstract and probably more universal than those which arise in the practical affairs of everyday life. In so far as this is true, it should be possible also to formulate data that would be considered the minimum requisite for the sociological study of any community. These data, if our theory is correct, should also prove basic in dealing with practical and technical problems of communal existence. Indeed, any acceptable definition of the community would be fruitful only to the extent that it not merely delimited a field of study but also suggested a set of questions or hypotheses which could provide the basis for specific sets of collected data.

One aspect of every community is its territorial base. To discover the center and the boundaries of a community is therefore a preliminary task in any study. In the past, before the interests of the sociologists were as clearly defined as they are now, the area of a community was either staked out arbitrarily or was defined by political or administrative boundaries. The tendency at present, even in such an official procedure as the definition of metropolitan areas by the census, seems to be to stake out the territory on the basis of definite tests of internal cohesiveness of the community and the determination of the margins of influence of different communities with reference to one another. The Census Bureau, in determining the periphery of metropolitan districts, has employed such criteria as the administrative boundaries, the retail trade areas, the commutation area, the local postal or freight-rate zones. The more we interest ourselves in regions as communities, the more we are inclined to take account of other factors, such as newspaper circulation, wholesale trade areas, banking areas and wider cultural areas over which a given settlement exercises its dominance. [. . .]

Another approach to the community is suggested if one thinks of it as a constellation of institutions. These include not merely such formal and established social structures as schools, churches, courts, business houses and settlements but also such phenomena as families, neighborhood organizations, political parties, rooming houses, gangs, clubs, newspapers and recreation centers. Institutions have a history and a natural history which is linked to, and a segment of, the communities in which they arise. They might be studied from the standpoint of their location, from the point of view of the spatial distribution of the people in whose life they function, the changing roles they play in community life, and as competing and conflicting with one another in their effort to enlist the interest and loyalty of the population. [. . .]

A more distinctly social-psychological approach to the community is represented by the view of a community as a constellation of types of personalities. The more objective and external data about communities mentioned above need obviously to be supplemented by the more subjective material to be obtained only through personal contact with, and the personal documents of, human beings. The statistical data contained in the census figures can be made meaningful only through the understanding of the culture of which personalities are the active, dynamic constituent parts. Every community may be set certain limits to the possibilities for personal development; there is usually a wide range of personality types to be analysed and classified in every community; and there are, as Adam Smith observed, some types of personality that can only be found in great cities. The distribution of competence, talent and genius may be very uneven in the various areas of a city, and in country and town. In some communities distinctive types of personality may be found which are unique to the area and are a faithful mirror of its life.

The concentration of specific types of personalities in specific areas where they find or create for themselves a hospitable culture is one of the factors which has given distinctive color to the city.

## (d) Melvin M. Webber

### Towards a Definition of the Interest Community

Excerpt from Melvin M. Webber, 'The urban place and the nonplace urban realm', in Melvin M. Webber, J. W. Dyckman, D. L. Foley, A. Z. Guttenberg, W. L. C. Wheaton and C. B. Wurster, *Explorations into Urban Structure*, University of Pennsylvania Press, 1964, pp. 108–11.

Both the idea of city and the idea of region have been traditionally tied to the idea of place. Whether conceived as physical objects, as inter-related systems of activities, as interacting populations or as govern-mental dominions, a city or a region has been distinguishable from any other city or region by the fact of territorial separation.

The idea of community has similarly been tied to the idea of place. Although other conditions are associated with the community – including 'sense of belonging', a body of shared values, a system of social organization and interdependency – spatial proximity continues to be considered a *necessary* condition.

But it is now becoming apparent that it is the accessibility rather than the propinquity of 'place' that is the necessary condition. As accessibility becomes further freed from propinquity, cohabitation of a territorial place – whether it be a neighborhood, a suburb, a metropolis, a region or a nation – is becoming less important to the maintenance of social communities.

The free-standing town of colonial America may have fixed the im-ages that are still with us. At that time, when the difficulties and the costs of communicating and traveling were high, most of the townsman's associations were with other residents of the town he lived in. In turn, intratown intercourse tended to strengthen and stabilize the shared values and the systems of social organization; they must surely have reinforced the individual's 'sense of belonging to his town'. But even in colonial days when most men dealt solely with their neighbors, there were some who were simultaneously in close touch with others in distant towns, who were members of social communities that were not delimited to their home-town territories. As recently as two hundred years ago these long-distance communicators were uncommon, for the range of specialization and the range of interests among colonial populations were quite narrow. But today, the man who does not participate in such spatially extensive communities is the uncommon one.

Specialized professionals, particularly, now maintain webs of intimate contact with other professionals, wherever they may be. They share a particular body of values; their roles are defined by the organized structures of their groups; they undoubtedly have a sense of belonging to the groups; and, by the nature of the alliances, all share in a community of interests. Thus, these groups exhibit all the characteristics that we attribute to communities – except physical propinquity.

Spatial distribution is not the crucial determinant of membership in these professional societies, but interaction is. It is clearly no linguistic accident that 'community' and 'communication' share the Latin root *communis*, 'in common'. Communities comprise people with common interests who communicate with each other.

Though it is undoubtedly true that the most frequent interactions are among those members of professional communities who live and work within close distances of each other, the most productive contacts – those in which the content of the communication is the richest – are not necessarily the most frequent ones nor those that are made with associates who happen to be close by. Although specialized professionals are a rather extreme example, we can observe the same kinds of associational patterns among participants in the various types of nonprofessional communities as well.

All this is generally recognized. There is no novelty in noting that members of occupational groups are members thereby of limited-interest fraternities. Similarly, it is commonly recognized that members of churches, clubs, political parties, unions and business organizations, and that hobbyists, sportsmen and consumers of literature and of the performing arts are thereby also members of limited-interest groups whose spatial domains extend beyond any given urban settlement. A 'true' community, on the other hand, is usually seen as a multi-interest group, somewhat heterogeneous, whose unity comes from interdependencies that arise among groups when they pursue their various special interests *at a common place*.

I do not challenge the utility of this idea for certain purposes. A metropolis is indeed a complex system in which interrelated and interdependent groups support each other by producing and distributing a wide assortment of services, goods, information, friendships and funds. Groups located in a given metropolis, where they carry out activities of all sorts, certainly do thereby create a systematic structure through which they work; they do indeed form a community whose common interests lie in continuing the operations of the place-based metropolitan system.

Nevertheless, the place-community represents only a limited and special case of the larger genus of communities, deriving its basis from the common interests that attach to propinquity alone. Those who live near each other share an interest in lowering the social costs of doing so, and they share an interest in the quality of certain services and goods that can be supplied only locally. It is this thread of common interests in traffic flow on streets, garbage collection, facilities for child rearing, protection from miscreant neighbors and from the inhospitable elements, and the like, that furnishes the reason-for-being of municipal government. This thread is also the basis for certain business firms and voluntary institutions that supply other goods and services which inhabitants and firms in the place-community demand with frequent recurrence. But, over time, these place-related interests represent a decreasing proportion of the total bundle of interests that each of the participants holds.

## (e) Norton E. Long

## The Local Community as an Ecology of Games

Excerpts from Norton E. Long, 'The local community as an ecology of games', *American Journal of Sociology*, vol. 64, 1958, pp. 251–5.

The local community whether viewed as a polity, an economy or a society, represents itself as an order in which expectations are met and functions performed. In some cases, as in a new, company-planned mining town, the order is the willed product of centralized control, but for the most part the order is the product of a history rather than the imposed effect of any central nervous system of the community. For historic reasons we readily conceive the massive task of feeding New York to be achieved through the unplanned, historically developed cooperation of thousands of actors largely unconscious of their collaboration to this individually unsought end. The efficiency of this system is attested to by the extraordinary difficulties of the War Production Board and Service of Supply in accomplishing similar logistical objectives through an explicit system of orders and directives. In so far as conscious rationality plays a role, it is a function of the parts rather than the whole.

Particular structures working for their own end within the whole may provide their members with goals, strategies and roles that support rational action. The results of the interaction of the rational strivings after particular ends are in part collectively functional if unplanned. All this is the well-worn doctrine of Adam Smith, though one need accept no more of the doctrine of beneficence than that an unplanned economy can function.

While such a view is accepted for the economy, it is generally rejected for the polity. Without a sovereign, Leviathan is generally supposed to disintegrate and fall apart. Even if Locke's more hopeful view of the naturalness of the social order is taken, the polity seems more of a contrived artifact than the economy. Furthermore, there is both the hangover of Austinian sovereignty and the Greek view of ethical primacy to make political institutions seem different in kind and ultimately inclusive in purpose and for this reason to give them an over-all social directive end. To see political institutions as the same kind of thing as other institutions in society rather than as different, superior and inclusive (both in the sense of being sovereign and ethically more significant) is a form of relativistic pluralism that is difficult to entertain. At the local level, however, it is easier to look at the municipal government, its departments and the agencies of state and national government as so many institutions, resembling banks, newspapers, trade unions, chambers of commerce, churches, etc., occupying a territorial field and interacting with one another. This interaction can be conceptualized as a system without reducing the interacting institutions and individuals to membership in any single comprehensive group. [. . .]

Observation of certain local communities makes it appear that inclusive over-all organization for many general purposes is weak or non-existent. Much of what occurs seems to just happen with accidental trends becoming cumulative over time and producing results intended by nobody. A great deal of the communities' activities consist of undirected cooperation of particular social structures, each seeking particular goals and, in doing so, meshing with others. [. . .]

It is the contention of this paper that the structured group activities that coexist in a particular territorial system can be looked at as games. These games provide the players with a set of goals that give them a sense of success or failure. They provide them determinate roles and calculable strategies and tactics. In addition, they provide the players with an élite and general public that is in varying degrees able to tell the score. There is a good deal of evidence to be found in common parlance that many participants in contemporary group structures regard their occupations as at least analogous to games. And, at least in the American culture, and not only since Eisenhower, the conception of being on a 'team' has been fairly widespread. [. . .]

Looked at this way, in the territorial system there is a political game, a banking game, a contracting game, a newspaper game, a civic organization game, an ecclesiastical game and many others. Within each game there is a well-established set of goals whose achievement indicates success or failure for the participants, a set of socialized roles making participant behavior highly predictable, a set of strategies and tactics handed down through experience and occasionally subject to improvement and change, an élite public whose approbation is appreciated and, finally, a general public which has some appreciation for the standing of the players. Within the game the players can be rational in the varying degrees that the structure permits. At the very least, they know how to behave, and they know the score.

Individuals may play in a number of games but, for the most part, their major preoccupation is with one, and their sense of major achievement is through success in one. Transfer from one game to another is, of course, possible, and the simultaneous playing of roles in two or more games is an important manner of linking separate games.

Sharing a common territorial field and collaborating for different and particular ends in the achievement of over-all social functions, the players in one game make use of the players in another and are, in turn, made use of by them. Thus the banker makes use of the newspaperman, the politician, the contractor, the ecclesiastic, the labor leader, the civic leader – all to further his success in the banking game – but, reciprocally, he is used to further the others' success in the newspaper, political, contracting, ecclesiastical, labor and civic games. Each is a piece in the chess game of the other, sometimes a willing piece, but, to the extent that the games are different, with a different end in view. [. . .]

It is perhaps the existence of some kind of a general public, however rudimentary, that most clearly differentiates the local territorial system from a natural ecology. The five-acre woodlot in which the owls and the field mice, the oaks and the acorns, and other flora and fauna have evolved a balanced system has no public opinion, however rudimentary. The cooperation is an unconscious affair. For much of what goes on in the local territorial system cooperation is equally unconscious and perhaps, but for the occasional social scientist, unnoticed. This unconscious cooperation, however, like that of the five-acre woodlot, produces results. The ecology of games in the local territorial system accomplishes unplanned but largely functional results. The games and their players mesh in their particular pursuits to bring about over-all results; the territorial system is fed and ordered. Its inhabitants are rational within limited aeas and, pursuing the ends of these areas, accomplish socially functional ends. [. . .]

In many cases the territorial system is impressive in the degree of intensity of its particular games, its banks, its newspapers, its downtown stores, its manufacturing companies, its contractors, its churches, its politicians, and its other differentiated structured, goal-oriented activities. Games go on within the territory, occasionally extending beyond it, though centred in it. But, while the particular games show clarity of goals and intensity, few, if any, treat the territory as their proper object. [. . .]

The lack of over-all institutions in the territorial system and the weakness of those that exist insure that coordination is largely ecological rather than a matter of conscious rational contriving. In the metropolitan area in most cases there are no over-all economic or social institutions. People are playing particular games, and their playgrounds are less or more than the metropolitan area. But even in a city where the municipal corporation provides an apparent over-all government, the appearance is deceptive. The politicians who hold the offices do not regard themselves as governors of the municipal territory but largely as mediators or players in a particular game that makes use of the other inhabitants. Their roles, as they conceive them, do not approach those of the directors of a TVA developing a territory. The ideology of local government is a highly limited affair in which the office-holders respond to demands and mediate conflicts. They play politics, and politics is vastly different from government if the latter is conceived as the rational, responsible ordering of the community.

# 45 R. S. Lynd and H. M. Lynd

A Pioneer Community Study

Excerpts from R. S. Lynd and H. M. Lynd, *Middletown: A Study in American Culture*, Harcourt, Brace & World, 1929, pp. 3–6.

The aim of the field investigation recorded in Middletown was to study synchronously the interwoven trends that are the life of a small American city. A typical city, strictly speaking, does not exist, but the city studied was selected as having many features common to a wide group of communities. Neither field work nor report has attempted to prove any thesis; the aim has been, rather, to record observed phenomena, thereby raising questions and suggesting possible fresh points of departure in the study of group behavior. [. . .]

Two major difficulties present themselves at the outset of such a total-situation study of a contemporary civilization: *first,* the danger, never wholly avoidable, of not being completely objective in viewing a culture in which one's life is imbedded, of falling into the old error of starting out, despite oneself, with emotionally weighted presuppositions and consequently failing ever to get outside the field one set out so bravely to objectify and study; and, *second*, granted that no one phase of living can be adequately understood without a study of all the rest, how is one to set about the investigation of anything as multifarious as the gross-total thing that is Schenectady, Akron, Dallas or Keokuk?

A clew to the securing both of the maximum objectivity and of some kind of orderly procedure in such a maze may be found in the approach of the cultural anthropologist. There are, after all, despite infinite variations in detail, not so many major kinds of things that people do. Whether in an Arunta village in Central Australia or in our own seemingly intricate institutional life of corporations, dividends, coming-out parties, prayer meetings, freshmen and Congress, human behavior appears to consist in variations upon a few major lines of activity: getting the material necessities for food, clothing, shelter; mating; initiating the young into the group habits of thought and behavior; and so on. This study, accordingly, proceeds on the assumption that all the things people do in this American city may be viewed as falling under one or another of the following six main-trunk activities:

Getting a living.
Making a home.
Training the young.
Using leisure in various forms of play, art and so on.
Engaging in religious practices.
Engaging in community activities.

This particular grouping of activities is used with no idea of its exclusive merit but simply as a methodological expedient. By viewing the institutional life of this city as simply the form which human behavior under this particular set of conditions has come to assume, it is hoped that the study has been lifted on to an impersonal plane that will save it from the otherwise inevitable charge at certain points of seeming to deal in personalities or to criticize the local life. For, after all, having one's accustomed ways scrutinized by an outsider may be disconcerting at best. Like Aunt Polly in Donald Ogden Stewart's *Aunt Polly's Story of Mankind*, many of us are prone to view the process of evolution as the ascent from the nasty amoeba to Uncle Frederick triumphantly standing at the top of the long and tortuous course in a Prince Albert with one gloved hand resting upon the First National Bank and the other upon the Presbyterian church. To many of us who might be quite willing to discuss dispassionately the quaintly patterned ways of behaving that make up the customs of uncivilized peoples, it is distinctly distasteful to turn with equal candor to the life of which we are a local ornament. Yet nothing can be more enlightening than to gain precisely that degree of objectivity and perspective with which we view 'savage' peoples. Even though such a venture in contemporary anthropology may be somewhat hazy and distorted, the very trial may yield a degree of detachment indispensable for clearer vision.

It is a commonplace to say that an outstanding characteristic of the ways of living of any people at any given time is that they are in process of change, the rate and direction of change depending upon proximity to strong centers of cultural diffusion, the appearance of new inventions, migration and other factors which alter the process. We are coming to realize, moreover, that we today are probably living in one of the eras of greatest rapidity of change in the history of human institutions. New tools and techniques are being developed with stupendous celerity, while in the wake of these technical developments increasingly frequent and strong culture waves sweep over us from without, drenching us with the material and non-material habits of other centers. In the face of such a situation it would be a serious defect to omit this developmental aspect from a study of contemporary life.

The further device of using as a groundwork for the observed behavior of today the reconstructed and in so far as possible equally objectively observed behavior of 1890 has, therefore, been adopted in this investigation, wherever the data available permitted. The year 1890 was selected as the base-line against which to project the culture of today because of greater availability of data from that year onward and because not until the end of 1886 was natural gas struck in the city under study and the boom begun which was to transform the placid county-seat during the nineties into a manufacturing city. This narrow strip of thirty-five years comprehends for hundreds of American communities the industrial revolution that has descended upon villages and towns, metamorphosing them into a thing of Rotary Clubs, central trade councils and Chamber of Commerce contests for 'bigger and better' cities.

Had time and available funds permitted, it would obviously have been desirable to plot more points in observed trends between 1890 and the present. But the procedure followed enables us to view the city of today against the background of the city of a generation ago out of which it has grown and by which it is conditioned, to see the present situation as the most recent point in a moving trend.

To sum up, then: the following pages aim to present a dynamic, functional study of the contemporary life of this specific American community in the light of the trends of changing behavior observable in it during the last thirty-five years.

So comprehensive an approach necessarily involves the use of data of widely varying degrees of overtness and statistical adequacy. Some types of behavior in the city studied lie open to observation over the whole period since 1890; in other cases only slight wisps of evidence are obtainable. Much folk talk, for instance – the rattle of conversation that goes on around a luncheon table, on street corners, or while waiting for a basketball game to commence – is here presented, not because it offers scientifically valid evidence, but because it affords indispensable insights into the moods and habits of thought of the city. In the attempt to combine these various types of data into a total-situation picture, omissions and faults in proportion will appear. But two saving facts must be borne in mind: no effort is being made to prove any thesis with the data presented, and every effort is made throughout to warn where the ice is thin.

# 46 Conrad M. Arensberg and Solon T. Kimball

## A Rural Community in Ireland

Excerpts from Conrad M. Arensberg and Solon T. Kimball, *Family and Community in Ireland*, Harvard University Press, 2nd edn 1968, pp. 273-9. First published in 1948.

In rural Ireland what we have called the 'rural community' is no simply defined geographical area. Any one of the recognized divisions of the countryside in Ireland, a townland, a group of townlands, a parish, an old barony, a mountain upland, a portion of a valley floor or plain, except perhaps the newer administrative divisions, is in a sense a community. The lines of relationship among the small farmers are continuous from one of these to another across the land. Geographic barriers serve only to deflect the lines of this continuum, not to divide it.

We observe of a farmer of Luogh, for example, that he 'coors' largely in Luogh townland. But he has kinsmen scattered around about as far as Mount Elva, four miles to the north, and Liscannor, three miles to the south. He attends the parish church of Killilagh, a two-mile walk from his house, but sends his children to school at Ballycotton, only a mile off. He does most of his shopping in Roadford, a crossroad settlement two miles away. Yet he takes his larger produce for sale and his larger needs of purchase to the market town of Ennistymon some eight miles off, or the smaller one of Lisdoonvarna some five miles off. He votes and pays his taxes as a member of a certain electoral district which overlaps exactly none of these regions. He associates himself in tradition with Clare and Munster as a North Clare man, rather than with Galway and Connaught, though he may have seen very little of either beyond his market towns. The small farmer of Luogh has allegiances to all these communities. He is quite ready to find his emotion stirred in any one of them. He is ready to back the men of Luogh against the men of the neighboring townland; to back those of the mountain region against those of the valley lands; those of his parish against the rest; those of the countryside against the towns of Lisdoonvarna and Ennistymon; those of North Clare against other sections of the county; those of Clare against all other counties; those of his class against all others; of his religion against all others; of his nation against all others. Each one of these allegiances has a geographical base, though in the last analysis each one of these is built up out of his personal experience of human relations.

A study of the local community among the small farmers must thus be a study of the geographic basis of their relationships. In the course of such study an inquiry into the spatial relationships involved in the distribution of produce and shop goods between the farms and the market towns is a first step.

The chief agencies of distribution in the countryside draw upon well-marked areas. Each crossroad shop, each hamlet, each market town, each fair, has its own hinterland. In recent years creameries have grown up at strategic places. Likewise, in the same years, larger towns have pushed their hinterlands farther back into the country districts, and motor lorries go even into the back roads.

The definition of such market areas and the demarcation of those into which such a rural county as Clare can be divided is a relatively simple task. It can be reached by plotting out on the map lists of customers' names and addresses obtained from each of the myriad crossroad centers and clusters of shops sprinkled over the county, combining them with others obtained from records of tolls paid by farmers in larger centers. This information can be checked with the testimony of farmers themselves as to where they do their buying and selling. It can be checked again with testimony upon the part of shopkeepers in the market towns as to the area from which they draw their clientele.

Plotting out these lists gives a picture of many superimposed areas. The smallest of all of them groups only a few townlands together about a crossroad or a hamlet. These areas about hamlets cluster together in turn, along the roads, to form larger areas about a village. The area about a village groups together with that round other villages, again depending upon the terrain and the roads, to form a larger district around one of the larger towns. These town-encircling areas themselves fall together to form still larger districts embracing all the farms trading in the largest centers such as Ennis, the county seat of 6000 population, Kilrush, the metropolis of the West Clare peninsula of 4000 population, and the city of Limerick. For Limerick draws farmers along the main roads as far as Newmarket-on-Fergus, fifteen miles into Clare. The whole county, of course, centers ultimately in Limerick, since rail, road and river all lead there rather than over the upland divides to Galway city to the north.

Local fairs figure in this plotting. Traditional long-established fairs are sometimes not held within the confines of a town of the present day, though all but a few of them now take place in the streets of some town or on a modern fair-green set aside at one edge of a town. Nevertheless, the areas from which farmers come to fairs yield the same picture of overlapping distributions. The smaller fairs of little attendance draw from the smaller areas, which group together in turn. Widest of all are the areas of the largest fairs, held at Ennis and Kilrush. And there is not a village to be found on the map that does not have its fairs, carefully scheduled so that within the immediate area there will be no conflict of schedules. The farmer may go this week to a small village fair two miles or so away in one direction, next week three miles or so in another, and the third week to a larger town. [. . .]

In these ever-larger overlapping market areas the natural physical divisions of the countryside are well represented. The great central mass of Mount Callan divides West Clare from the rest of the county. It divides as well the market districts of Ennis and Kilrush. In the valley of the Fergus River, which drains the highlands of Mid-Clare to the north and East Clare beyond the corcasses (rough marshlands) to the east, the human flow of trade and produce exchange tends downwards to the towns of Ennis and Clarecastle, at the head of tidewater. The high country marking the divides over into the Inagh and Cullinagh rivers and into the lake country of North Clare, just south of the gaunt hills of Burren, divides the market district of Ennis from the smaller districts upon which the villages of Ennistymon, Corrofin and Lisdoonvarna draw. Yet these villages in their turn are within the region of Clare from which the farmers converge upon Ennis. In each case a center, whether a larger market town or one of the smaller villages, serves a natural area demarcated by the configuration of the land and the course of the roads.

In such natural regions, particularly in more remote and mountainous country, the roads determine the intercourse of the communities with one another. Today each focal point is joined with another by a motor road. As the roads wind out from the larger centers, shops come to be placed at the strategic crossroad; a public house springs up; perhaps a schoolhouse, a parochial house, a chapel of the parish, rise beside them. Nowadays creameries are put up at these or still other points along the roads, where they are most conveniently accessible to small and medium farms producing milk. Even more recently lorries have begun to come direct to the crossroad to pick up produce that once, before motor traffic, had to be carried by the farmers themselves all the way to town.

Plotting out the market areas of the towns and villages of the countryside reveals a characteristic of social and economic space even here where the deepest hinterlands are never more than a half-day's leisurely trip by horse and cart. Any list of customers plotted by residence around a minor center gives an area which extends considerably farther in the direction away from the nearest larger center than it does in the direction leading to it. The minor centers draw principally from the hinterlands behind them and their areas extend only a little way along the roads in the direction of the next larger center. Ennistymon in North Clare draws custom twelve miles to the north, but to the south its influence reaches only three miles up the valley of the Inagh River, where the region of the larger center, Ennis, begins. Ennis itself serves all Clare, and its own immediate area extends, to judge from the residences of the farmers who come to buy and sell in her markets, beyond Ennistymon to the north and as far as Killadysert to the south. In the direction of Limerick, the metropolis of south-west Ireland, however, the influence of Ennis ends at Newmarket-on-Fergus, a scant five miles off.

# 47 J. R. Seeley, R. A. Sim and E. W. Loosley

A Middle-Class Community in a Modern Metropolis

Excerpts from J. R. Seeley, R. A. Sim and E. W. Loosley, *Crestwood Heights*,
Basic Books, 1963, pp. 3–11.

This book [*Crestwood Heights*] attempts to depict, in part, the life of a
community. North Americans may know its external features well, for
some community like it is to be seen in and around almost any great city
on this continent, from New York to San Francisco, from Halifax to
Vancouver. In infinite variety, yet with an eternal sameness, it flashes on
the movie screen, in one of those neat comedies about the upper-middle-
class family which Hollywood delights to repeat again and again as nur-
ture for the American Dream. It fills the pages of glossy magazines
devoted to the current best in architecture, house decoration, food, dress
and social behavior. The innumerable service occupations bred of an
urban culture will think anxiously about people in such a community in
terms of what 'they' will buy or use this year. Any authority in the field of
art, literature or science probably at some time has had, or will have, its
name on a lecture itinerary. A teacher will consider it a privilege to serve
in its schools. For those thousands of North Americans who struggle to
translate the promise of America into a concrete reality for themselves
and, even more important, for their children, it is in some sense a
Mecca.

The book attempts to pin down in time and space this thing of dreams
for the many, and actual experience for the very few. One such community from among the many of its kind has been chosen. It will be
called 'Crestwood Heights'. It is 'somewhere in central Canada'; the time
falls in the years immediately following the Second World War.

Since the word 'community' will be used throughout this study in
reference to Crestwood Heights, it is important that the sense in which
the term is apt be established in the very beginning. Although Crestwood Heights is officially a separate municipality within a greater metropolitan area, it is also something else. It exists *as a community* because of
the relationships that exist between people – relationships revealed in the
functioning of the institutions which they have created: family, school,
church, community center, club, association, summer camp and other
more peripheral institutions and services. (Some of the many groups to

which Crestwooders belong are to be found within the geographic boundaries of Crestwood Heights, though some are outside the area altogether.) These relationships develop within a material setting of brick, stone, wood, concrete and steel – and of flowering gardens, shaded in several sections by trees which once arched over an earlier and very different enterprise, the clearing of the forest by a more simple type of pioneer. Yet the Crestwood resident of the present day is also, in his way, a pioneer.

This complex network of human relationships which *is* the community exists from the viewpoint of the participants for a definite purpose. In Crestwood Heights the major institutional focus is upon child rearing. How is a Crestwood Heights adult to be made? How will he grow and mature into manhood? What ideals are to be placed before him? What are the pressures to be laid upon him for conformity? What are the obstacles to orderly, predictable growth? What are to be the stages of maturation? What is to be understood by 'maturity' itself, and how is it finally to be achieved? Here are eminent local preoccupations.

These questions, which once primarily concerned poet, novelist, dramatist and philosopher, now also supply data for scientific scrutiny. In this study, we as social scientists have attempted to look at some facts about child growth as it takes place in a comparatively homogeneous, prosperous, modern, urban and suburban environment. [. . .]

Crestwood Heights is built on a choice brow of land, overlooking a wide sweep of the metropolitan area. Yet, although it is literally a city built upon a hill, the closest investigation of the terrain from the air would fail to reveal definite boundaries. Should an intruder from outside wander through its streets, he would find little, except a slight difference in sign-posts, to distinguish Crestwood Heights from Big City – or from other suburbs near it.

There is, however, a subtle but decided line drawn between Crestwood Heights and Big City. The very name 'Crestwood Heights' expresses to perfection the 'total personality' of the community, particularly in its relation to the metropolis of which it is a part. That name suggests, as it is clearly meant to do, the sylvan, the natural and the romantic, the lofty and serene, the distant but not withdrawn; the suburb that looks out upon, and over the city, not in it or of it, but at its border and on its crest. The name is a source of pride, a guide for differential conduct (to some degree at least), but first and foremost a symbol evoking deference. Crestwood Heights is bound inescapably to Big City by many ties, but the proximity of the heterogeneous metropolitan area provides chiefly a foil against which Crestwood Heights can measure its own superiority and exclusiveness, core of its communal identity. The psychological climate of Crestwood Heights is, otherwise, no easier to assess than are its physical contours. [. . .]

Crestwood Heights, at the local level, maintains a symbiotic relationship with the sprawling, variegated metropolitan area. As a separate municipality with a population of roughly 17,000 it does maintain some services: a council, municipal police and fire departments, schools. It has a voluntary community council, a community center, a very active Home and School Association, as well as some minor organizations. But, on the other hand, Crestwood Heights has no industry, no hospital, no large stores, no sewage disposal plant, no Community Chest or other social agencies; and virtually no slums, no service clubs and only one church. Thus Crestwood Heights, together with other comparable upper middle class neighborhoods, is highly interdependent with the metropolitan area, however much it tries to hold itself aloof, for each offers services which make it attractive and necessary to the other. The institutional meshing between Crestwood Heights and Big City is well illustrated in the occupational pattern. Few of those employed in the institutions of Crestwood Heights live in the community. They commute there to work, leaving their families behind in some other, less expensive, section of the metropolis. Conversely, the institutions of Big City provide the incomes which maintain the homes of Crestwood Heights.

In the highly organized industrial and commercial civilization into which this urban complex fits, there is a growing need for highly trained, highly specialized persons in management and professional positions. Their importance to that civilization is reflected in the favorable incomes which they receive, and by the relatively high standard of consumption enjoyed by them because of their status. These are the people who can afford the exclusive environment of Crestwood Heights, who, in very truth, *must* be able to afford it as part of their careers. The Crestwood resident proudly feels that he is outside the city – but by no means beyond the reach of urban amenities and conveniences. Although to the casual observer this distinction might seem tenuous, the Crestwooder jealously guards his privileged suburban status. Harder work, struggle, anxiety and sacrifice are not considered too high a price to pay for a Crestwood Heights address, an address which symbolizes the screening out of the unpleasant features of urban existence, leaving only the rewards and joys.

It is not that Crestwood is merely a dormitory within the metropolis, though sleep is one common bond which brings family members with otherwise diverse interests together. The sharing of food and of many other forms of familial and communal activity and association, also play their part in making Crestwood the locus of a common life. While the

Crestwood Heights father, and any other wage-earning members of the family, do carry on their occupations beyond the physical limits of Crestwood Heights, their removal is much less complete than it would be from a more distant commuting center. Frequent interchanges by telephone between downtown and Crestwood Heights, a member of the family picking up the car at the office, a luncheon rendezvous with friends or family at a Big City restaurant – all are easily arranged. Conversely, a series of services enters the back door as the wage-earning member takes his leave through the front. Cleaning women, deliveries of all kinds, repair services, stream into the community from the city. These are the men and women who help in multitudinous ways to sustain the prosperous but servantless modern household of Crestwood Heights.

The fact that employment, golf clubs, symphonies and like activities are almost all extra-communal tends to specialize, if not to deepen, those relations which are left exclusively local. These ties are institutionalized primarily in the family, secondarily in the school and its affiliated activities, and less powerfully, in the municipal services. The institutions of Crestwood Heights tend therefore to converge upon the family, existing as they do to regulate the life of a purely residential community devoted to child rearing.

# 48 G. D. Suttles

A Slum Community in Chicago

Excerpts from G. D. Suttles, *The Social Order of the Slum*,
University of Chicago Press, 1968, pp. 13–35.

In its heyday the Near West Side of Chicago was the stronghold of such
men as Al 'Scarface' Capone and Frank 'The Enforcer' Nitti and was the
kindergarten for several figures still active in the underworld. For convenience, I will call this part of Chicago the Addams area after Jane
Addams, who founded Hull House there. [. . .]

To the north the area is bounded by a huge expressway that is the
main east–west artery of the city. On the east is a large block of industry
and 'The Loop' or the downtown part of the city. To the west is one
of the world's largest complexes of hospitals and associated institutions.
The southern boundary is a little less distinct, starting with a shipping
district along Roosevelt Road that fades into the open air markets of
Maxwell Street and then stops abruptly with a series of railroad tracks
that cover two full city blocks.

None of these are natural boundaries in the sense that they can or do
effectively block the establishment of human relations and social contacts. Yet according to local views, they are important landmarks used in
making judgements about how one will behave as well as in assessing and
describing the behaviour of others. Across the expressway is one of
Chicago's 'skid rows', an area set aside for drunkenness, ill-dress, de-
bauchery, minor prostitution, begging and other vices. Below Roosevelt
Road is Maxwell Street or 'Jew Town', where gypsy fortune tellers and
Jewish merchants share the daytime hours with the Negro residents. At
night, however, this area is off limits to any whites. In the medical center
there is a large number of doctors, medical students and student nurses,
most of whom commute to the area. For the most part, these people and
the residents of the Addams area find each other's behavior incomprehensible and have neither grounds for conflict nor peaceful exchange.
In any case their lives are carried out in such different fashions that they
seldom come in contact and can easily 'keep their distance'.

For persons in the Addams area only the adjacent neighborhoods are
well defined (see Figure 1). Beyond this, their notion of established
boundaries become vague and uncertain. Even when they are in un-

familiar territory, however, there is the general assumption that boundaries exist and that the area included must 'belong' to someone. Thus, the city is seen as something like an irregular lattice work from which a person's behavior and appearance can be gauged, interpreted and reacted to depending upon the section to which he belongs. This does not mean, however, that Addams area residents believe that persons from other areas are secretly at war with them or have a way of life that is totally alien to their own. On the contrary, the general assumption seems

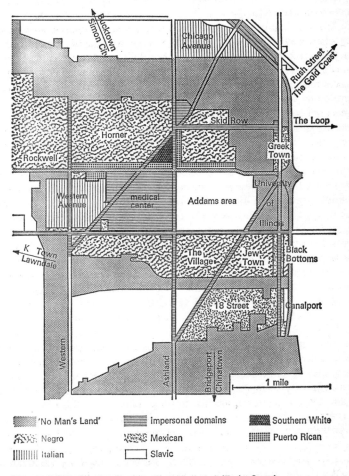

Figure 1 Neighborhoods adjacent to the Addams area (Taylor Street)

to be that others are driven by much the same urges and needs as themselves. Each little section is taken to be a self-sufficient world where residents carry out almost all of their legitimate pursuits. A person who leaves his own area, then, is suspect so long as he has no visible and justifiable reason for straying from his home grounds. The first and most immediate evidence for making inferences about where a person 'belongs' are his clothing, apparent ethnicity, demeanor, sex, age, companions, location and plausible destination. In combination, these become the signs on which residents rely to define a person and to determine their own course of action. [. . .]

Life in the Addams area is extremely provincial and what goes on a few blocks away may hardly affect the daily routine of commercial transactions, social engagements and family life. After the eastern portion of the area had been demolished, those who remained carried on their lives much as they always had. The lack of marked disruption of the entire neighborhood is due largely to its general structure. The Addams area consists of several ethnic segments which are relatively independent, although they sometimes combine in an orderly way. With the clearance of the eastern portion, one Italian and one Mexican section were excised. While these ethnic sections could no longer combine with those remaining in the area, the remaining sections were left almost wholly intact. In turn, these sections continued to observe the same principles both in their opposition and in their alliances.

Probably the hardest hit were several home owners and businessmen at the western periphery of the university site. Typically, Addams area residents do not buy or improve a building for speculative purposes, but as a home which they can outfit to please themselves and a few long-term friends, relatives and neighbors. It is useless to assure them that they will be adequately compensated for the loss of their home or that the remaining buildings and rentals will rise in value. If their friends, relatives and neighbors are removed, they are like an actor with a huge but empty auditorium.

In the Addams area, most business establishments are not just a way of making a living but also of enjoying an enduring set of social relations where money is only one of the tokens that change hands. Besides, businesses in the Addams area cater to the very restricted needs, preferences and background of a specific group of persons. In this case, customers are simply not interchangeable. Reimbursement for a lost business thus can never quite be translated into its equivalent elsewhere.

Similarly, the local owners of a small number of dwelling units can survive only if they do most of their own repair work and depend upon a measure of tolerance and cooperation that goes well beyond that of an ordinary economic contract. Those whose property is demolished find both their economic interests and their social relations permanently impaired. In the Addams area the two are inextricably combined.

Nevertheless, it should be emphasized that the present study pertains only to that remnant of the Addams area which is still intact. Certainly this is a rather unusual area with many peculiarities of its own and situated in a unique historical context. Currently it is subject to a variety of social welfare programs, and its future as a residential area is in jeopardy. In addition, it is undergoing a progressive cycle of invasions, with the Mexicans pressing upon the Italians, and the Puerto Ricans and Negroes not far behind. But ethnic invasions, residential uncertainty and social welfare programs are long standing forces in the area. It is, after all, a zone of transition, and change is its most permanent aspect. Indeed, there is every reason to believe that the segmentary structure of the area is itself an adaptation to such abrupt and uncontrollable changes. Broken up into a number of ethnic sections, each of them can manage to survive despite the disappearance of neighboring sections. The flexibility with which they can combine makes it possible for each to become allied with an exceptionally wide range of adjacent territorial units. So long as the territorial unities around them remain equally uncertain, there seems little reason to think that residents in the Addams area have any grounds for giving up their present system of ordered segmentation. [. . .]

For many Chicagoans the Addams area is only an indistinct part of the 'West Side'. At that distance, it is generally labeled an impoverished Negro slum, not only dangerous but also a center of criminal activity. Among Negroes alone, it is often contrasted with the 'South Side', which is adjudged more sophisticated and affluent.

The newspapers and, among those persons who know of the West Side, a smaller number of individuals make a finer distinction by referring to the 'Near West Side'. Here the emphasis shifts from Negroes to Italians. Generally this appelation connotes the 'West Side Bloc', 'The Capone Mob', 'gangs', the need for urban renewal, and Mrs Scala's abortive attempt to save the Italian neighborhood by honoring the memory of Jane Addams. More recently the area has added to its doubtful honors that of being the birthplace of Jack Ruby, the killer of President Kennedy's [alleged] assassin.

Among a more select group of people who live adjacent to the Addams area, it is known simply as 'Taylor Street'. Above all, this name implies a connexion with the Outfit and Italians. It is also known that there are 'gangs' and that 'a lot happens on Taylor Street'. At night it is supposed to be dangerous and inhospitable to outsiders. Occasionally, people say that it is 'mixed' and 'anything can happen'.

Doubtless, all these preconceptions are a sort of myth; and any statistician could point out that most of the residents are not criminals, that pedestrians are usually left unmolested, that local children are seldom arrested, and that the majority of the residents are neither Italian nor Negro. These observations, however, provide most Chicagoans with very little comfort; and they would probably only smile and add that these are only the 'official figures'. Most Chicagoans, of course, do not rely much on official statistics to regulate their entry into various neighborhoods. Statistics always turn every act into a gamble; public stereotypes convey a sense of certainty.

In so far as people from outside the Addams area accept these stereotypes as a reasonable guideline for their own actions, certain consequences follow. At the very least, it means that outsiders avoid the area unless they have to go there during work hours or pass through to get somewhere else. A second consequence is the humiliation brought upon the local population. However, for reasons that may be apparent, this is not too important; Addams area residents have many ways of circuiting or 'neutralizing' these public definitions of themselves. Privately each of them knows that he is neither so despicable nor omnipotent as the general public thinks. What they find far more difficult, however, is to be equally assured that the *other residents* are not so bad as they are said to be. Here they must resort to public signs of consistency, trust and predictability. Four alternatives seem possible.

1. Since public definitions and social signs do not provide a gradation of trustworthy types within the Addams area, the residents may take refuge in those ethnic orbits of trust they brought with them from another region. In this case, the range of trust or suspicion will vary from one ethnic group to another depending upon the public signs they acknowledge. At most, however, they can never exceed the boundaries of a particular ethnic group.

2. Residents may also retreat from all social contacts beyond those of the nuclear family, which, in any case, cannot be avoided. Children are kept off the street, watched every minute, sent to a safe parochial school and warned against strangers. Adults view their neighbors with suspicion and remain circumspect in their admissions. Local events are derided or avoided and, at most, nonrelatives are faced in the confines of a church or other 'safe place'. In the meantime, children may revolt to be with their peers, parents may be regarded as unsociable by their neighbors, and the remainder of the residents may abandon such isolationist fam-

ilies to meet their individual difficulties 'on their own'.

3. Where ethnic and kin unities are insufficient to fill the normative void between them, residents may take things in their own hands and establish a 'personal relation'. In this way people create a safe little moral world that is based on private understandings rather than public rulings. Necessarily, this means a relationship where assumed individual proclivities map out the range of permitted behavior. A most serious limitation, however, is that a personal relation requires a massive exchange of information and cannot be extended beyond the immediate participants. In fact, individuals must be felt out one-by-one without assuming very much about those connected with them. The business of society can hardly wait for such a meticulous examination of its members' individual credentials. Even in the Addams area, where personal relations are probably extended to a maximum, they can include only a minority of those encounters which are unavoidable.

4. Even though the public stereotypes applied to Addams area residents do not identify an acceptable morality, they do offer, for some residents, a certain honor and, for others, a determinate way of defining other people. Thus, some persons may thoroughly embrace one of the images that the wider community provides: 'hood', 'gangster', 'tough guy' or 'big shot'. Others may personally reject those labels, but assume their truth regarding other people. Subsequently, they may either gloat over the wider community's inability to curtail such heroic escapades or simply condemn them outright and avoid them at all times. Either way a certain definition of self and other has been established, and some measure of order has replaced a situation of ambiguity.

These alternatives are only a series of analytical exigencies that can be worked out on paper. In the language of game theory, they are 'pure strategies'; in actual practice most of the residents seem to follow a 'mixed strategy'. There are the 'hoods' who have many friends, show great concern for their families and never miss Mass; the isolates who become sociable when they meet someone with whom they are personally acquainted; the ethnic purists who make an exception of some of the people in other ethnic groups; the sociables who make many people their friends but remain on guard against those who are especially notorious. Still, these patterns are not so compatible that all combinations and permutations are possible. At least on any one encounter, they map out the alternatives that the residents confront moment-to-moment.

The major value of this outline is that it shows how nearly the Addams area resembles a prison community or any other population that is not initially credited with a capacity to behave in an approved social manner. In so far as the residents depend upon the public definition of each other, there is very little basis for trust except through the exercise of brute force or economic sanctions. By relying on these definitions alone they would truly descend to Hobbes's 'war of all against all'. To escape this disorder, they must discover some further set of social signs that indicate those they can or cannot trust. [. . .]

Although the reactions of the wider community have been fundamental to the development and current definition of the Addams area, most of the immediate consequences are realized within more limited bounds. The Addams area is surrounded by several other ethnic neighborhoods (see Figure 1) which have their own history and public standing in the wider community. To the north-east is 'Greek Town', where the remnant of a Greek neighborhood survives in a few restaurants, nightclubs and coffee shops. The residents are mostly Mexican, and Addams area residents usually acknowledge that it is the stronghold of a Mexican 'gang' called the 'Potentates'. Directly to the north, across the Eisenhower Expressway, along Van Buren, there is a small Puerto Rican area, which acts like a Balkan 'buffer state' to fend off the Negroes further north. This is the stronghold of the Van Buren Royals, too insignificant to threaten the Addams area, but sufficent to ward off the Negroes between Van Buren and Madison Street. Thus the Negroes to the north are not considered a problem by the people in the Addams area. Madison Street itself is sufficiently far away that Addams area residents can regard it half humorously and half sympathetically; it is the rialto of derelicts and drunks who are a nuisance but not dangerous. To the north-west is a tiny colony of Southern Whites, so busy fighting among themselves that they are harmless to anyone else. Most Addams area residents do not know they are there.

Directly to the west is a more difficult situation. Beyond Ashland, the medical center stretches for almost a half mile. Within this area there are so many policemen and impersonal bodies of social control that safe passage is almost impossible for anything resembling a gang of 'troublemakers'. On the other side of the medical center is another Italian neighborhood that probably resembled the Addams area before it was invaded by the Mexicans, Negroes and Puerto Ricans. At one time, however, there was no medical center and the Italian community extended from Halsted Street to the railroads (see Figure 1). Even so, my older Italian informants told me they never 'had much to do with each other'. Possibly one of the major thoroughfares (Ashland or Damen) intersected their common interests and created an 'impersonal domain' that divided them. Whatever the reason, the Italians 'over on Western' stand in opposition to those on Taylor Street. In the meantime the sanctity of the medical center keeps them at arm's length. Mostly this is a 'private matter' between the Italians in the two areas; but once, when hostilities seemed sure to advance beyond mere rhetoric, it was suspected that Mexicans, Puerto Ricans and even the Negroes in the Addams area might all join forces with their Italian co-residents. Unfortunately this test between ethnic and territorial loyalties never came to issue; the Italians in the two areas kept hesitating until the issue was 'forgotten' or settled by some other means. Still, many of the Italians boys on Taylor Street are able to recognize the names of their counterparts 'over on Western'. There are, for example, the 'West Os' and 'Roman Spectres'. Collectively, they stand in a vague opposition to the Italian groups in the Addams area.

Directly below the western half of the Addams area is the 'Village', a large block of public housing including several high rise buildings and row houses. As in almost all public housing, nearly all the residents are Negro. There are several named groups in this section who are known to the Negro boys in the Addams area; such as the Village Deacons and the Falcons. As in the case of the Italian groups 'over on Western', the Village boys are assumed to stand in opposition to the Negro boys in the Addams area.

To the east of the Village is Jew Town, a very deteriorated Negro neighborhood. Among the Negro boys in the Addams area, it is best remembered as the stronghold of the Egyptian Vipers as well as a few other less notorious groups, such as the Honchos, and the Red Ambers. The 'guys from Jew Town' are also assumed to stand in collective opposition to the Negro boys in the Addams area. Sometimes Addams area residents combine against the Village and Jew Town by referring to them as the 'people' or 'guys' below Roosevelt. Here, however, the oppositional structure seems to include the supposition that all the residents (Negro and white) might join forces against those below Roosevelt. For reasons that I will point out later, Roosevelt Road seems a powerful boundary that separates likely companions and makes improbable compatriots. It must be emphasized, however, that this opposition between all the residents in the Addams area and those below Roosevelt never took form, although at one time there were hostile preliminaries.

South of the Village and Jew Town is Eighteenth Street. The name, like that of Taylor Street, includes an adjoining residential area as well as the street proper. In the memory of some Addams area residents, this was originally a Slavic neighborhood whose residents some referred to as 'DPs'. Today, however, ethnic invasion has reclassified Eighteenth Street as a Mexican neighborhood. To the Mexican boys in Addams area there are several known gangs that hang out on Eighteenth Street, such as the Athenians and Roughshods. In the minds of the Mexicans these groups may not form a confederation, but certainly they are more likely to favor one another than their fellow nationals in the Addams area. In turn, it is also suspected that the Mexicans in the Addams area are more sympathetic with one another than with anyone else and that they might even be able to enlist the help of some of the Italians, Negroes and Puerto Ricans. This suspicion is more than myth; on two or three occasions between 1961 and 1964 it became a reality.

There are many other areas that some of the residents recognize: Bridgeport, Horner, Rockwell, K Town, Lawndale, Bucktown, Simon City, Thirty Fifth Street, the Casbah, Six Tray, Tray Nine, Chinatown and so forth. Like most Chicagoans, however, the majority of them have only heard of these areas and in actual fact they are of little more concern to Addams area residents than to people in the suburbs. What especially distinguishes Addams area residents is that they must somehow manage to live there despite Eighteenth Street, Jew Town, the Village and the 'guys over on Western'. According to Addams area residents, this is very difficult because all the people in these surrounding sections are 'against them'. Within each of these sections, of course, one can hear somewhat the same complaint: individually, they know themselves to be badly divided; it is only the united stand of the Addams area residents that puts them on the defensive. Perhaps in this way each of them husbands the other's reputation. [. . .]

From a distance all of these antagonisms seem to take on the formal characteristics of a 'segmentary system'. First, each group is a sociospatial unit. Second, inclusion in these groupings is mutually exclusive. Third, opposition is between 'equivalent' units. Fourth, the order by which groups combine preserves the equivalence of oppositional units. While segmentary systems are usually restricted to corporate groups, however, the ones here include groups that are no more than corporate units of responsibility. Addams area residents are a group only in the sense that they are jointly liable for each other's behavior. [. . .]

There is a sense in which Addams area residents and others on the 'Near West Side' assume that spatial unity automatically leads to social unity and concerted action. On the one hand, there is the bifurcation of ethnic groups once they have been separated in physical space. All that divides the Mexicans, Negroes, Italians and Puerto Ricans in the Addams area from their fellow nationals in other areas are roads, vacant lots, and buildings. Yet, once they stand in opposition, they never seem to doubt that each street corner group within a single ethnic group will ally itself with other groups from the same territory. Moreover, there is the suspicion, if not the certainty, that all street corner groups within a territory might join forces irrespective of ethnicity.

By their assumption that residential unity implies social collaboration, inner city residents may help create the situation they imagine. Given their conviction that persons from another area will act in concert, they have little alternative except to go into collusion with their own territorial compatriots. To some extent, of course, this emphasis on territorial unities has its background in a cultural history wherein spatial groupings are one of the most frequent forms of social combination. This general pattern, however, is given credence by still another condition. Addams area residents are forced together in rather intimate and congested confines. Somehow the Mexicans, Puerto Ricans, Negroes and Italians must manage to live together. If one day they joined a group from outside the area against others in their own territory, the following day they might meet their co-residents in the same store, church, playground, youth center or school. They are even more likely to cross each other's pathway at the same street corner, bus stop or beefstand. Much as they may dislike each other, Addams area residents always face the prospect of having to see one another on 'the next day'. By comparison, it is far more comforting to have an enemy from outside the area.

In contrast, people who live in the suburbs or more impersonal residential areas seem relatively indifferent to the location of their enemies. In fact, old and bitter enemies may pass each other without even knowing it. Persons in these areas often carry out their antagonisms by proxy through a series of voluntary and formal organizations and seldom meet their opponents face-to-face. In the Addams area, encounters usually take just the opposite course. Most often the residents carry out their antagonisms face-to-face and are only too well aware of whom their enemies are. Also it is very difficult for them to pretend that their relationship has no history, and an impersonal and 'polite' form of exchange is not only unfamiliar, but a marked deviation from precedent. In any case, one of the antagonists is likely to be accompanied by 'intimates' who know of their mutual grievances and may wonder at such an obvious failure to broach the issue.

In the Addams area this segmentary system of spatial and ethnic units is so well understood that the residents seldom bother to tell you of it. If you ask why it exists, they will usually answer that it is 'only natural' or say 'that's just the way it is'. It would be easy to label this as a myth and dismiss the segmentary system outlined above as a reification. All the same, it is a myth that is shared by all the people of the Addams area. In this sense, it is one of those myths that is taken as information and becomes the basis on which people predicate their action.

G. D. Suttles   327

# 49 Margaret Stacey

Relations between Local Residents and New Immigrants in an English Town

Excerpt from Margaret Stacey, *Tradition and Change: A Study of Banbury*, Clarendon Press, 1960, pp. 165–71.

When the study of the impact of the introduction of the aluminium factory on Banbury was first planned, attention was focused on the distinction between Banburians and immigrants. It seemed likely that there were important tensions between these two groups, even that this division might be the key to the social structure of the town.

There was superficial evidence to suggest this. Immigrants of as much as fifteen or even thirty years' standing, and even those holding public office, when asked for advice or information about the town would point out that they were not Banburians. Thus they suggested the existence of a strong in-group to which, because they were immigrant, they were not admitted. Banburians, on the other hand, commented on 'all those foreigners' who had so altered the town that you no longer 'knew where you were'. 'Before the factory came', a phrase so often repeated by the Banburians, had the air of 'before the flood', with the implication that it was the immigrants who had flooded the town. But, although attention was focused from the beginning on the possibility of tension between Banburian and immigrant, in fact little further evidence of such tensions came to light.

Tensions at the level of individual assimilation to the town were found: the case, for example, of the North-Country woman who, although she took steps to join all the organizations that her Banburian neighbours belonged to and was assiduous in her attendance, had still not been accepted by them fifteen years later. No reason could be found for this rejection except her North-Country origin; no difference of status, politics nor religion existed, nor was she in any way unacceptable personally. Hers was an extreme case. Although other examples of a similar kind were found, the subjects usually being North-Country people, in most cases the evidence related to the early years of their immigration, a phase now passed: 'I thought I should never settle down here.' These cases, when added together, pointed to a major difference in ways and attitudes of life between the North Country and the South, or at all events, Banbury, making for difficulties of assimilation rather than to a hostility between Banburians and immigrants as such.

Other than in these individual case histories, the only overt tension observed between Banburian and immigrant was in the case of housing. Frustrations about housing led to accusations by Banburians of favouritism on the part of the Borough Council towards immigrants and vice versa. There were letters in the local papers and debates in the Council chamber. Division was not on a party political basis. Many comments were made to interviewers on the subject: 'Look at those Geordies, they've only been here three years and they've got one of those new prefabs and our Molly was born here and has had her name down for twelve years for a house and still she hasn't got one. Not fair I reckon.' Immigrants complained that it was unfair to consider whether a man had been born in the town or how long he had lived there when making Council house allocations. Was it not enough that he was living and working in the town and was in need of a house? 'We've been here since before the war and we're still in part of one of those old houses with nowhere proper for the kiddies to sleep, boys and girls all crowded up together, they are, and those people down the road were no worse off nor us yet they've got a new house; just because he was born here and his father before him. It ain't right: I've worked here steady ever since I come.'

Houses were in fact allocated on a points system, so many points for the number of children, present accommodation, length of service in the forces and residence in the town, and so on, with special consideration for serious ill health, and for old people for whom special houses were built. There were, however, so few houses to go round that any housing committee would have found it difficult not only to do justice, but to appear to be just in its selection. So many genuine cases had to be refused for the time being.

The deviation in the proportion of Banburian to immigrant tenants in the Council houses as shown in the schedule inquiry is slightly in the Banburian favour. But the deviation is unlikely to be significant. The proportion of Banburians is a reasonable one to find if Banburians and immigrants have approximately the same housing needs. But this is a difficult matter to assess. Rather more immigrants than Banburians are found in badly overcrowded conditions, in rooms and divided houses. But more Banburians than immigrants are found in the old 'slum houses', some of which are also overcrowded. The figures at least indicate that the Council cannot have been seriously unfair either to Banburian or immigrant. Nevertheless, frustrations were expressed in Banburian immigrant terms.

However, when the quietness and secretness of the English techniques of social rejection are remembered, the fact that a rift between Banburians and immigrants was publicly mentioned only in this one case was not sufficient evidence that tensions did not exist. On the other hand, there was plenty of evidence of interaction between Banburians and immigrants. They were found as friends, belonging to the same clubs, drinking together in the same pubs, and marrying each other.

In these circumstances, particularly intermarriage, it was clear that tensions between Banburians and immigrants could not be of a high order. Nevertheless, some comparable division existed. When a man said, apologetically, 'Well, I'm not really a Banburian, you know', and when Banburians inveighed against 'those foreigners', they were stating a commonly accepted belief in an opposition between Banburians and immigrants and one which was shared by both groups. If there was no direct opposition between the groups then this belief must be the expression of some other existing social fact, some other set of tensions. It was this contradiction, popular belief in a distinction between Banburians and immigrants and in practice co-operation without distinction among them, which led to the emergence of the concept of traditionalism opposed by non-traditionalism.

One report, which the field-workers originally attempted to interpret as a possible indication of tension between Banburians and immigrants, is an example of the initial pointers to this concept. It is the case of the Banburian tradesman who said he would refuse to serve any of his customers seen entering a new chain store. That he should make such a pronouncement, with whatever hope of being able to fulfil it, indicated that he believed in the existence of a group with considerable local loyalty and, moreover, solidarity. It is significant that he should attempt to call upon this loyalty rather than rely upon the quality of his goods and services.

Evidence accumulated to show that there was just such an established group, a group bound together by common history and tradition, with a recognized social structure and having certain common values. This shopkeeper was one of a number of local proprietors who owned long-established factories or shops in the town, concerns which in some cases had passed through several generations of the same family. Many of them had ties of kinship, by blood or marriage, with each other, and more had grown up together in the town. Connexions of this sort were strengthened by a further set of ties, for many concerned themselves with running the affairs of the town, in church or chapel, on public bodies, and in social and sporting activities. A man on one committee was likely to be on at least one other and possibly also a rank-and-file member of yet other associations.

So many cross-threads in personal relationships meant that each was seen as a whole man. His family life was connected with his business life and these again with his religious, political and social lives. To a considerable extent he met the same people in every case, or at least the amount of overlapping was sufficient for his behaviour in one field to become rapidly known in another.

Great value was placed on the importance of maintaining these personal relationships. The successful man was the one who had a sound business, was affluent but not too rich, who gave sufficiently freely of his time and money in the service of the town. The pressure to conform to group standards and to avoid eccentric behaviour was considerable. To maintain your business as a 'sound going concern' was more important than expanding it and possibly making a lot more money. A 'progressive' businessman made enough changes to keep up with the times to keep his business going with adequate returns, but had no desire to be ahead of the times. For economic success would not by itself bring social acceptance.

Conformity, stability, conservation of established institutions and values: these were the key-notes of the society that has been defined as traditional. But within that society analysis showed certain important divisions. The groups which clustered about certain formal associations indicated divisions in the social structure. These groups were associated with cultural differences in so far as each tended to lay greatest stress upon a different traditional value.

So there were within the traditional society the Anglican/Conservative group whose members showed a wide range of social and sporting interests, for whom conviviality and enjoyment of life were important. In contrast was the Free Church/Liberal group, very little concerned with sport, having quieter social activities and much more concerned with cultural pursuits. The two groups held in common the value of service to the town and its people, shown in their joint activity in associations such as Rotary.

These middle-class members of traditional Banbury were followed and supported by the traditional working class. The traditional workers, in many cases also of families long established in the town, had their own networks of informal personal relations. In some cases members of the family had 'always' worked for such-and-such traditional concern. If they were church-goers they often went to a church of the same denomination as their employer, for his acceptance of the interlocking of all sides of his life led him to employ members of his denomination in preference to others. The traditional workers shared the middle-class attitudes about the value and the rightness of 'things as they always have been'. They were not inclined to trade unions or Labour politics, accepting their position and the right of the middle class to lead. They avoided 'meddling in what doesn't concern them'. Consequently they voted Conservative or Liberal and did not themselves attempt to stand for the Council or to run formal associations. They provided the rank-and-file support in business and social life which made it possible for traditional Banbury to carry on. Their support might sometimes be merely negative, an acquiescence with the established order, 'not bothering' about things. But they did not rebel or agitate for change.

Since the traditional society is based on a long-standing network of relationships between families and friends who have lived and worked together for many years, it is not surprising to have found that many traditionalists were Banburians. But the traditional society was not exclusively composed of those born and bred in the town. It had absorbed a number of immigrants, people who came to take up traditional occupations and who were prepared to behave according to the traditional standards and to accept the traditional values. But based as it was on a series of face-to-face relationships this society could only accept a limited number of newcomers at a time. Similarly it could adapt itself to small and gradual technical and social changes. Before the 1930s the town had been able to go on relatively undisturbed, compared that is to the changes which had taken place in other parts of the country.

For this reason, the arrival of the aluminium factory represented an abrupt change. Not only did the factory itself initiate much of the change, but it also became the dramatic symbol of the opposition between old and new. For the new industry was in almost every way in direct opposition to the traditional pattern of Banbury life. Tradition and change ceased to be a matter of a traditional system slowly accepting changes which had filtered through from outside, and became an active opposition within the town itself.

Non-traditionalism, which had begun to emerge before the days of the aluminium factory, was reinforced and extended. There had been since 1919, for example, a small Labour Party supported by Banburians who had rejected the traditional system, at least in some important respects. With the arrival of the aluminium factory this small group was reinforced by numbers of immigrant workers, so that today the active strength of the Labour Party comes principally from immigrants. Many of these came from industrial areas where they had been brought up to Labour and trade-union ideas. They did not accept the traditional status system of Banbury and could not understand the acquiescence of the traditional workers in it, saying they were 'like sheep'. The social isolation of these active trade-union and Labour leaders was shown in chapter 3 [not included here]. Standing right outside the closely interlocking traditional structure, they met its members only on local government or other statutory bodies.

Middle-class immigrants in industry also stood outside the traditional status system. They were concerned with getting promotion in their occupations, a possibility which was controlled by their showing at work and was not affected by their relationships in the town. Local social acceptance was not a major goal. Their network of relationships in the town was narrower than that of their traditional counterparts, but they had business, social and kin connexions scattered over a wider area.

To some extent the wider range of social interests brought in by the immigrants had its reflection in the life of the town. But what appear to be non-traditional developments may merely be the result of increased numbers, quantitative rather than qualitative changes. A larger population may mean that there are enough like-minded people to form this or that club, a dramatic society for example, so that a formal group appears which was not previously identifiable, and informally a new 'set' appears. Such interests may have had their scattered representatives in the smaller traditional society and may not be essentially non-traditional. Nevertheless, although it was not always easy, it was usually possible in practice to identify those groups which were not opposed to traditionalism and those which were non-traditional, for the last have values and attitudes in opposition to traditionalism. The case of the Business and Professional Women's Club when compared with the older Townswomen's Guild was an example of an identifiably non-traditional association.

In sum, it was with the arrival of the immigrants that Banbury felt the full force of non-traditionalism. One important key to the social structure and culture of the town therefore is the opposition of non-traditionalism to traditionalism, an opposition which contains within it some of the problems of immigrant assimilation.

# 50 Valdo Pons

The Relation between a Neighbourhood and its Wider Urban Setting in an African Town

Excerpts from Valdo Pons, *Stanleyville: An African Urban Community under Belgian Administration*, Oxford University Press, 1969, pp. 257–68.

The study of Stanleyville was launched in an attempt to explore and delineate aspects of social relations in an African town about which very little was previously known in any systematic way. Thus the two field investigations on which the book is based were essentially exploratory in nature. The social survey was launched primarily to assemble basic social and demographic data on the total population of the town, and the 'community study' of Avenue 21 was a simple and straightforward attempt to obtain detailed first-hand information on day-to-day life and on the nature of social relations in what was thought to be an ordinary and unexceptional neighbourhood on the periphery of one of the city's main townships. As the two investigations were conducted concurrently, the study of the avenue was inevitably begun with little conception of any but the most readily discernible differences between its neighbourhood and other parts of the town. Casual observation had revealed that the avenue formed part of a quiet area in which there were very few *évolués* as compared to some other parts, and it was equally apparent that the ethnic heterogeneity of the people stood in striking contrast to the homogeneity of the population elsewhere. [. . .] But the nature and extent of a whole series of further differences were much less readily apparent and were for the most part only established as a result of systematic inquiry. Thus in launching the study of Avenue 21 I had no means of knowing that, for example, the sex ratio in the neighbourhood was appreciably higher than in most parts of the town, or that the population of women who were married was well above the mean, or that there was in the tribally heterogeneous population a clear dominance of a certain combination of tribes, or that the area had a rapidly increasing number of tenant households and that these were mainly members of tribes which were poorly represented among the title-holders of dwelling compounds. Still less was I aware that neighbourhoods within the three main townships of the city exhibited any regular ecological patterns, or that tribal representation in these neighbourhoods bore any particular relation to the routes of access to the town from various tribal areas in the hinterland, or that some tribal colonies had such markedly different social and demographic configurations. These and associated features of the demographic and ecological structure of the community were all 'discoveries' which were to a limited extent made through casual observation in the field but which only emerged clearly from the later analysis of the survey data. Initially I thus had little conception of the kind of questions to ask in Avenue 21 if my study was to yield information capable of interpretation as part of an analysis of the system of social relations in the wider community. [. . .]

As my fieldwork developed, however, I was constantly led to assess features of social life in the avenue in relation to impressions gathered in other parts of the town and among members of tribes that were not well represented in the avenue and its immediate environs. The attempt to draw these comparisons led me to a progressive definition of the urban situation as a whole. In particular it pointed to a number of differences between various neighbourhoods and to the seeming individuality in a number of respects of the neighbourhood of Avenue 21. This raised important questions concerning the relation of the avenue to the wider community and concerning the principles of integration operating in the African community as a whole. Could the avenue be seen as a microcosm of the town or as representing any particular sector of it? Or, failing both of these improbable possibilities, to what extent was it a good example of a particular kind of locality standing in a certain functional relation to the town centre and to other kinds of locality? It had from the outset been evident that Avenue 21 and its environs were different from, say, the inner areas of Belge I [one of the main townships] and it seemed clear that a contrast of this kind was related to the differing locations of the two neighbourhoods in relation to the 'European town' as well as to their differing functions in relation to the urban area as a whole. But why should there be any significant differences between Avenue 21 and other peripheral areas? And, in keeping with this line of questioning, why were there such striking differences in a number of respects between two in-lying areas such as the 'fashionable' part of Belge I and 'the Lokele quarter' of Belge II [another of the three main townships]? In more general terms, to what extent could differences between neighbourhoods be attributed to 'natural' forces of urban differentiation, and to what extent were there other important factors at work? It was evident that until these questions could be satisfactorily answered, it would be difficult to assess features of social organization in Avenue 21 in their correct context.

Comparisons between various neighbourhoods in the town were there-fore accorded a high priority in the analysis of the survey data, and the findings were later evaluated in relation to the differences found between the larger tribal colonies. In the light of these comparisons, the seemingly unique combination of features in Avenue 21 and its environs was readily explicable. It became apparent that the nature of any locality in the town was a product of two broad sets of variables which were largely independent of each other. On the one hand, the composition of the population and certain aspects of social relations in a neighbourhood were partly functions of its location in relation to the town centre and of the position it occupied in the over-all ecological structure of the town; on the other hand, neighbourhoods also varied appreciably according to their location in relation to routes of access to the town from the interior. Immigrants coming to town had in the past settled in areas close to their points of entry to the urban area and to a large extent they were still doing so. As a result various neighbourhoods contained markedly different combinations of tribal elements and, since different tribes commonly varied in their histories of urban incorporation, in their rural–urban relations, in their modes of accommodation to urban life, and in their fertilities and related social and demographic characteristics, the particular tribal compositions of some neighbourhoods were closely associated with social features and patterns of behaviour which had themselves become factors of internal differentiation in the community.

Taken in conjunction with the known influence of historical and geographical factors on migration to Stanleyville from various areas of the hinterland, the above observations showed that the processes of urban integration were taking place in an over-all social context characterized by a series of variable factors. Moreover, it was clear that much of the variability derived from elements which were rooted in the past and which frequently stemmed from far beyond the town boundaries. First, there was appreciable diversity in the social, cultural and demographic characteristics of peoples in various rural areas in the hinterland. Secondly, there was significant variation between 'natural areas' that had already developed in the town. Thirdly, the urban population was made up of tribal colonies which displayed marked variations in their general social configurations, and which had to varying extents established themselves within limited neighbourhoods in the town. Fourthly, the very processes of immigration and urban incorporation were taking place within social and economic contexts which varied appreciably for migrants from different parts of the region. Finally, as stressed at the very beginning of the study, the town and its region were developing within an over-all context of unprecedented social and economic expansion, and this very expansion was uneven in its effects on different parts of the region as well as on different parts of the town.

In brief, then, new immigrants coming to Stanleyville were drawn from areas that often differed in nature as well as in the pace of current social and economic change; the histories of migration from village to town of these new arrivals were often appreciably different, some having come to Stanleyville direct and others having spent intervening periods of varying lengths in smaller labour centres; and, on arrival in Stanleyville, they were being dispersed in differentiated neighbourhoods according to processes which were clearly selective in regard to tribe and to geographical area of origin in some cases, and in regard to degree of 'civilization' and to previous experiences in wage-earning centres in others.

According to this view of the town, we would expect the pattern of social relations to vary appreciably in some respects from *one type of urban neighbourhood* to another, while also expecting it to vary in other respects from *one sector of the town* to another. And, indeed, as the analysis developed, it became increasingly clear that some of the differences encountered from one neighbourhood to another formed regular patterns of variation between 'natural areas' that had arisen out of the processes of urban differentiation, whereas others were related both to differences between parent populations and to differing patterns of urban incorporation and of rural–urban relations.

In the absence of intensive studies of other localities we have no basis for detailed comparative analyses of social relations either in different types of neighbourhoods or in different sectors of the town. We can, however, usefully reassess the more striking differences that were noted between the neighbourhood of Avenue 21 and some other areas. First, we saw that the range between the more 'civilized' and the less 'civilized' (or most 'uncivilized') members of the avenue's population was much narrower than in the community as a whole, and also appreciably narrower than in most other neighbourhoods taken on their own. [. . .]

The second difference was related to the first. There were in Avenue 21 and its environs some groupings which had a semblance of formal organization but which were in effect no more than either friendship groups or loose agglomerations of neighbours and near-neighbours. Two examples are the 'club', which amounted to little more than a clique of men who occasionally drank together, and *la réunion*, which was a very loose and amorphous burial association based on one avenue but having no committee, no rules and no meetings. The absence of more fully developed voluntary associations was a striking fact which stood in sharp contrast to the existence in the 'fashionable' areas of Belge I of the larger associations of *évolués* and of many smaller ones of non-*évolués,* as well as to the development even in many less 'fashionable' neighbourhoods of both tribal and non-tribal associations. The difference can be partly attributed to the low status of the inhabitants in Avenue 21 and its environs; in the town as a whole, participation in voluntary associations was typically a feature of 'civilized' life, and it was unusual for persons of low status to be members of formal associations whether of a tribal or a non-tribal kind. But the difference was also undoubtedly related to other aspects of neighbourhood relations in Avenue 21 and its immediate environs. The relative absence of anonymity, the close-knit texture of relations between well-established residents, the widespread networks of personal relations established within the loose frameworks of tribal 'brotherhood' and 'family friendship', and the measure of neighbourhood solidarity that had developed over the years, were all aspects of a situation in which formally constituted voluntary associations would have been rankly incongruous. There were in the area some men – and also a few women – who were members of associations meeting outside the neighbourhood, but they were rare and exceptional. [. . .] This general contrast between the prevalence of voluntary associations in some areas and their absence in the environs of Avenue 21 suggests that, despite the social diversity and the increasingly heterogeneity of the population, the fabric of social relations in the area remained *relatively* uniform and undifferentiated; such social cohesion as there was continued to be predominantly 'communal' rather than 'associational'. The number of inhabitants who did not readily find their social niche through common affinities and pre-existing relations was undoubtedly increasing, but this increase had not as yet led to any fundamental change in the basis of neighbourhood relations.

Thirdly, the neighbourhood of Avenue 21 had few inhabitants with strong rural–urban links and few with large families or with extensive networks of 'real' kinsmen. In this respect it was similar to the inner areas of Belge I, as well as to a number of other neighbourhoods in the town; but it was clearly very different from all areas – whether in-lying or peripheral – where there was a predominance of inhabitants from tribes like the Lokele, Topoke, Bambole and Balengola. Where these and similar tribes were well represented, social control through kinship connexions was undoubtedly much stronger. Avenue 21 and its environs were, however, a clear example of a neighbourhood with a relatively 'weak' system of social control, with a relatively high incidence of 'semi-institutional' relations, and with a high ratio of 'fictitious' to 'real' kinship connexions. This contributed to, and was in part a reflection of, a somewhat distinctive pattern of relations between the sexes. The neighbourhood had a high proportion of married women and the incidence of prostitution and semi-prostitution was low. But it was an area with a high ratio of men to women, with small families, and with a relatively permissive code of sexual morality for women. Marriages were unstable and certain categories of non-marital and extra-marital liaisons were readily given 'semi-institutional' recognition as partnerships with limited rights and obligations. This resulted in the proliferation of 'fictitious' affinal relationships defined through partnerships ranging from explicitly negotiated 'trial marriages' and other well-recognized non-marital unions to much more ephemeral liaisons. And the high incidence of 'fictitious' affines, associated as it was with a high incidence of relations of 'fictitious' brothers, distinguished the neighbourhood not only from areas of the town like 'the Lokele quarter' with its appreciably more stable marriages, larger families and higher ratios of 'real' to 'fictitious' kinship relations, but also from neighbourhoods like the inner areas of Belge I where social life was much affected by associational-type relations, on the one hand, and by the incidence of more specifically commercial and contractual relations on the other.

When these and associated differences between the neighbourhood of Avenue 21 and other areas in the town are considered in conjunction with the differences between the social configurations and patterns of urban incorporation of various tribal colonies, it is evident that an urban way of life was being developed and passed on to new immigrants in a variety of markedly different settings. [. . .]

In originally choosing Avenue 21 for intensive investigation, I had unknowingly begun the study of a neighbourhood where certain processes of urban integration were more pronounced than others. I have no doubt that the particular processes exhibited in Avenue 21 were also, in varying degrees, encountered elsewhere in the town. At the same time, I know that some of the processes common in other areas, and in other sections of the population, were scarcely operating in the neighbourhood of Avenue 21.

# 51 The Community Study as a 'Method'

## (a) M. Stein

The Value of Community Studies

Excerpts from M. Stein, *The Eclipse of Community*, Princeton University Press, 1960, pp. 3–5, 94–9.

American historians who have been writing the history of the past fifty years have access to an important source of data in the many community studies completed by American sociologists during this period. These studies differ from other sources of information about national history in that they describe events occurring at a great distance from the places where national power was concentrated. No picture of the daily round of life in a middle-sized American town during the twenties can be found to improve upon that presented by the Lynds in *Middletown in Transition*. Community studies cannot provide information about the men and events on the national scene that influence historical processes so decisively, but they do describe the effects of these processes on the everyday lives of ordinary men and women. They fill out the historical record by giving the intimate meanings that large-scale changes had for a limited segment of the population.

In doing this, it is clear that they have serious limitations. Thus, a historian would not be likely to assume that the effects of the depression in Muncie, Indiana [the subject of *Middletown*] were comparable to its effects in Detroit, Michigan. The usefulness of a community study as a source of information about national experiences and responses is limited by the extent of its representativeness. These studies actually fall into a kind of limbo between sociology and history. They are usually drawn on for illustrative purposes but rarely incorporated into the narrative interpretations of historians, on the one hand, or into the general theories of sociologists, on the other. Before either sociologists or historians can use these studies to the fullest possible extent, some kind of general framework relating the studies to each other has to be devised.

In formal terms, the purpose of such a framework is to raise low-order generalizations about specific events and processes occurring in one community during a circumscribed time period to a higher level, so that they can be related to other low-order generalizations about similar events occurring in a different community during the same or another time period. In less formal terms, the framework aims at developing an approach to community studies which will discern similar processes at work in different contexts. Or, to put it still another way, the purpose is to devise an approach to community studies in which each investigation becomes a case study illustrating the workings of generalized processes in a specific setting.

The range of variation found among the many community studies in the literature is great, making the task of reconciling them difficult. Aside from obvious differences between the communities in terms of such important dimensions as age, size, economy, regional location, etc., additional problems are introduced by the fact that the field work was conducted at different times and that the talents, training, facilities and interests of the field workers differed widely from study to study. Each research report is a synthesis by the author of several orders of data about a particular community, arranged according to his sense of significant social structures and processes. This synthesis rarely takes into account the relation of the material to other related studies nor do most research reports contain chapters which satisfactorily present generalized conclusions. The community sociologist has been a better ethnographer than a theorist and this is probably as it should be. Weaving the scattered strands of a single community into a coherent picture is in itself a difficult task.

Achieving the formal purpose of this book – that is, the development of a framework for relating disparate community studies to each other – presupposes the substantive purpose which is to develop a theory of American community life. The purposes are closely linked since the perception of relationships between studies rests upon the assumption that similar social forces are at work in the separate communities. Social theories about the forces transforming Western society during the past four centuries converge on three kinds of processes – urbanization, industrialization and bureaucratization, as the central sources of change. Such theorists as Marx, Weber, Durkheim, Simmel and Mannheim may emphasize one or the other, but all recognize the three as being involved in fundamental social change. On the basis of this agreement, and the conviction that all three could be observed at work in American communities, the decision was made to search for their effects as these are reported in the various community studies examined. [. . .]

Even if one assumes that time can be held in abeyance, it is doubtful that the student of any particular American community can reasonably claim to generalize his distinctively sociological findings so as to imply descriptive validity for all or even most American communities. The search for 'representative' communities on the basis of which generalization about all of them or about the society itself can be developed is doomed to failure. Yet Park, the Lynds and Warner all made this assumption about the objects of their research. The point is not that Chicago, Muncie and Newburyport [the subject of Warner's Yankee City series] were representative communities in any statistical sense but rather that they were undergoing processes of structural transformation that affected all American cities and towns to one or another degree, and therefore could be used as laboratories in which to study these representative social processes.

The emphasis in the foregoing chapters on one process in each community – urbanization in Chicago, industrialization in Muncie and bureaucratization in Newburyport – suggests the direction in which this effort at community theorizing will move. While Park was explicit about searching for generalizations about urbanization and Warner was aware of the general implications of his research (though he never explicitly placed it in the framework of a theory of bureaucracy), the Lynds confined themselves more closely to the enormous task of reporting what happened when industrialization hit Middletown. They left to the reader or later theorist the further task of deciding which of the structural changes were likely to accompany industrialization when it occurred in other places.

Unfortunately, sociological readers of the Lynd study have simply not been diligent enough. *Middletown* is now read mainly by undergraduates as a sociological classic of the kind everyone should be familiar with even though its significance is primarily historical. After all, the Lynds describe events that took place between thirty and sixty-five years ago and the real interests of undergraduates, no less than of professional sociologists, are usually in more recent matters. American sociology, unlike its European counterpart, has always displayed impatience with the ineradicable historicity of much sociological data. Why should anyone today be concerned with what happened in an obscure town like Muncie, Indiana, such a long time ago? Muncie itself has undoubtedly changed considerably since then, as the Lynds themselves demonstrated by returning in 1936 to produce *Middletown in Transition,* a book superseding the first volume – or does it?

The question conceals genuine problems. How can generalizations be extracted from material which is probably not representative and which refers to events that occurred long ago? Furthermore, of what use would these generalizations be for understanding that same community now, thirty years later, no less some other community as it was at the time or as it is today? It is safe to assume that even at that time the effects of industrialization on Chicago, with its complex ethnic and class structure, must have been significantly different from the effects of this same process on Muncie.

The problem of generalizing from the community study has long been a matter of concern to sociologists, and one suspects that the apparent failure to resolve it satisfactorily helps to account for the relative neglect of this field during the past fifteen years. Why study communities when one can much more easily study small groups? In spite of the recent proliferation of mechanical gadgets for recording interaction patterns, small groups are still far easier to observe systematically than small communities.

Furthermore, students of small groups can sidestep the problem of generalizability simply by defining their objects of study on a sufficiently high level of abstraction as to eliminate substantive differences of social context from the range of legitimate concerns. Presumably, a small group of miners in a mine can be analytically equated with a small group of soldiers on a battlefield and a small group of students solving a chess problem on the wrong side of a one-way screen. If the researcher is sufficiently ingenious, he can even arrange to examine the formation and dissolution of small groups at his own behest.

The advantages and perhaps the attractiveness of small-group research would seem to lie largely in the readiness with which observational studies can be conducted and findings generalized. In both of these respects, the field of community studies is not nearly as convenient. At its best, however, it offers closeness to human experience and human problems of a kind rarely captured in the confines of the small-groups laboratory. Even the literature appeals to one's appetite for diversity so that the susceptible reader is easily enthralled by the descriptions of the strange social worlds – the slums, the ghetto, the hobo jungles, Bohemia, the Gold Coast and the taxi-dance halls – that Park discovered during his explorations of Chicago. After sufficient immersion in the Lynds's *Middletown*, the people, homes, schools and churches of Muncie acquire an elusive familiarity that renders them clearer than the persisting images of communities in which one may have spent many years.

There is no denying the sheer descriptive appeal of the community study. Susceptibility to this appeal, some feeling for the varieties of styles of living found in complex modern settings, is undoubtedly a real asset for students in this field. Such sensitivity, however, must be balanced by sustained concern with the general implications of this rich observational detail. William Foote Whyte, in *Street Corner Society*, presents as vivid a picture of slum dwellers and slum life as has ever been captured by any journalist or novelist, but the distinctively sociological merit of his work lies in the interpretation of these life patterns in terms of hypotheses about slum social structure, ethnic assimilation and mobility. Novelists, journalists and community sociologists share an interest in describing the life of their times, but we have a special responsibility based on our commitment to developing a reliable body of knowledge. [. . .]

In our effort to develop a somewhat more general theory, specific emphases in each of the sets of studies had to be extracted and conceptualized differently. This necessarily meant leaving much of the data untouched and even 'distorting' some of that which was extracted when conceptualizing it differently than did the original field worker. Yet this is necessary to expose the relationship between the three sets of studies as well as their collective relationship to later research. Such generalization does not permanently damage the original researches, since these are always available to all who would study them. Hopefully, it should make such examination of the sources more fruitful by placing them in a more general context and thereby illuminating the particulars reported in each.

Theorizing from such a vast amount of empirical material as is represented by the three sets of studies already reviewed, as well as from the entire body of American community studies, is a challenging and even frightening task. The person who would do so has to be prepared to omit much that seemed important to the authors of the studies he is working from as well as much that seems important in them to him but which does not yet fit into his evolving theoretical framework. Finding an adequate level of generality is an ever-present problem, as is remaining satisfied with any given level once it has proved useful. This theory attempts to stay as close to the empirical materials as it can while still establishing the relationship of the trends they reveal to the major social processes of our time. Thus, the choice of urbanization, industrialization and bureaucratization as processes shaping American community life was based on the findings of general sociological theorists like Marx, Weber, Durkheim and others. That each of these three sets of studies exemplifies one of the processes as they manifest themselves at the level of the community suggests that the field workers were able to detect major forces of change even though they did not always interpret them with these concepts. [. . .]

Every community study is to be viewed as a case study. We can go even further and maintain that they should all be studies of the effects of basic processes and historical events on changing social patterns. This means that the state of affairs before the change as well as while it is in progress should be carefully specified. Every good community study is a study of transitional processes.

# (b) A. Vidich, J. Bensman and M. Stein

## Reflections on Community Studies

Excerpt from A. Vidich, J. Bensman and M. Stein, *Reflections on Community Studies*, Wiley, 1964, pp. vii–xi.

No one has yet been able to present a formal methodology for the optimum or proper method for the scientific study of the community. This is necessarily so because there is no way to disentangle the research method from the investigator himself. During the research and his personal experience of it, the investigator is led into interests and problems that were initially outside the scope of his imagination, so that only with the passage of time does his own work inevitably become fairly sharply defined.

To the extent that the community sociologist responds to his own personal experience, he develops the techniques, methods and theories necessary to comprehending his particular data. Community sociology at its best always relies on this kind of creative response, so that the great studies, even when the critic might feel they are inadequate or mis-directed, always have the quality of individuality, integrity and dis-covery. By the same token, nothing in the tradition of community studies points in the direction of a general, a historical, all-encompassing theory of society. The complexity of history combined with the particularity of its investigators mitigates against a grand scheme. Intimate contact with the world and its inhabitants usually imposes a certain modesty on the investigator.

Anthropologists constantly use the community study as a standard technique of field research. Those hardy investigators of the primitive and tribal world confront distant and unknown societies whose alien ways of life they have to communicate to their Western readers. Theirs is a straightforward but real problem: how to present an authentic, living portrait of a society. They have no self-consciousness about the com-munity study as a 'method' of investigation or any doubts as to its use-fulness and validity. For them, social reality thrusts itself forward and demands that a way be found for reducing it to words without unduly offending its integrity as they see it. As a result of their endeavors, the anthropologists have produced a rich library of community studies.

The anthropological style of investigation was first applied to the study of an American community when the Lynds went to Muncie, Indiana, in the early 1920s. The Lynds originally were not academic anthropologists or sociologists, but they had a keen eye and an ear for life in the concrete and, most important, a capacity for detaching themselves from the beliefs and values of the local residents. Because they were able to assume the attitude of the outsider (like the anthropologist, who, however, achieves this attitude much easier because he *is* an alien outsider), the Lynds's study of *Middletown* and their later study of *Middletown in Transition* still stand as important case histories in the description and analysis of American society.

Shortly after the publication of *Middletown in Transition*, W. Lloyd Warner, then recently returned from his study of the Australian aborigines, went to Newburyport to conduct a study of its aborigines by the same techniques he had found so useful among the Murngin. From Warner's experience it is clear that his study of Yankee City has been much more than an application of anthropological methods to the study of a modern community. In Warner we have an example of how the investigator's personal research experience influences his image of the city, of sociology, of modern society and of himself. It has probably come as a surprise to Warner himself that he should have come back to the basic problems concerning the symbolic coordination of society, which he posed in his Murngin study, in his latest book on Yankee City, *The Living and the Dead*. The link between *The Murngin* and *The Living and the Dead* is Warner's special intellectual problem, but it is also the fundamental problem of the symbolic integration of society, and herein we find the connexion between Warner's problem, which he has been driven to solve, and a generic problem, which all students of society have faced. A reading of these two books makes social theory itself come alive because the relationship between theory, theorist and reality is visible.

It is clear, however, that Warner's encounter with Yankee City involved more than an anthropological study of a tribal community; Newburyport did not quite fit the tribal model. Class structure, labor, the corporation and the ethnic group did not lend themselves to the ethnographic treatment. Before long Warner found himself embroiled in most of the central issues and problems of modern industrial society, and it is a credit to his intellectual integrity that he faced these problems and made them his own. Because he responded to his reality, we now have a unique and unequaled portrait of an American city which no amount of general theory could ever produce.

But to complete the picture, it was not possible for Warner to ignore the press of his data. Yankee City opened up issues that went far beyond the community, and before long Warner found himself engaged in an examination of the fundamental institutions of American society. *Democracy in Jonesville* and *The Corporation in the Emergent American Society* find Warner grappling with issues central to the fundamental structure of Western institutions. Clearly we have here an example of an investigator whose personal experience is inextricably intertwined with the discovery of the world. Surely a method of investigation which can carry a researcher from *The Murngin* in aboriginal Australia to *The Living and the Dead* in Newburyport is worthy of further examination.

Since the Lynds and Warner, hundreds of studies of communities have been conducted and written. By themselves these studies do not necessarily add up to a description of the 'total' society. In fact, any unfriendly critic can easily point to the lack of theoretical accumulation in the total product produced by the community sociologists, but intramural criticism, especially by sociologists who would like to solve all the problems of life in a single theory, is much less important than detailed efforts aimed at capturing the evolving and disappearing reality as it presents itself to the individualistic observers who try to capture it. Community sociologists have certainly not presented an integrated portrait of the world, but this has not been their objective. They have tried, at best, to capture some segment of an elusive reality which would be true to the world of the observed as seen by the particular perspective of the observer. In so far as the community sociologist is true to his task, his method of investigation remains as a major method in the social sciences.

Critics have pointed out the 'weaknesses' of the community study method as a scientific mode of investigation. They have noted that the community portrait usually rests on the observations of a single person, that the procedures of observation are not systematized, that there is no guarantee that another investigator would produce similar results, that the values of the observer cannot be disentangled from his data and, finally, that there is never any way of knowing if the work is scientifically valid.

But no matter how continuously and intensively the critics have attacked the community studies and their methods, no sooner has the attack been made than there appears another series of frequently independent and unrelated studies which confound the critics. *Middletown, The Yankee City Series, Street Corner Society, Caste and Class in a Southern Town, Deep South, Crestwood Heights, Small Town in Mass Society, The Eclipse of Community, The Living and the Dead*, each has reopened the problems of community inquiry along new and unexpected lines. Moreover, in more recent years the community study method has been applied to mental institutions, prisons, hospitals, schools and almost all other forms of total institutions characteristic of a bureaucratic world. The capacity for the community study to survive and to illuminate contemporary society may well be intrinsic to its scope, its methods and its problems.

Over the past thirty or forty years sociology and anthropology have seen the growth of a wide range of highly complex methods and techniques of research as well as a continuous expansion, proliferation and reformulation of its concepts and basic theories. All of the methodological specialization and complexity of apparatus developed in the interest of creating a scientific anthropology and sociology have given the proponents of these methods a point of departure for denigrating the scientific validity of community studies. After all, statistical methods, computer technology, model building, cross-cultural uniformities, empirical replications, linguistic constructs, theory construction and so forth, are terms whose scientific tone arises from linguistic habit. Thus the proponents of rigorous method and systematic theory have not found it difficult to pronounce the community study 'perhaps acceptable as a branch of humanistic studies, but certainly not to be taken seriously as social science'.

The increased specialization of social science under its newer methodologies has led to a continuous narrowing of the specific problem to which any specific study is addressed. One result of this has been any number of highly specialized, technically perfected studies which, however, are characterized by a paucity of concepts, theories and interpretations capable of presenting any image of the larger society being studied. The development of abstract concepts, complex indices and statistical devices in the more 'scientific' methodologies, and the use of highly 'structured' research 'instruments' has left the analysts using these instruments in the position of having little direct knowledge of the social world they are supposed to survey. Thus the analyst who uses these instruments is unable to present an image of social behavior as it appears in its 'natural setting', because he is not in a position to observe behavior as it is experienced and acted out by the participants described in his study. As a result, as abstract social science progresses, the image of reality which it purports to describe is increasingly lost.

The survival of the community study perhaps can be explained precisely because it has not absorbed too completely the major techniques of the more 'advanced' social sciences. Though more recent studies of the community have tended to focus their attention on selected problems rather than attempts to describe the whole community, they have always shown, no matter how imperfectly, the interrelationship between the various segments of community life. As a result the 'totality' has neither been neglected nor shattered into unrelated segments. Community researchers have been 'functionalists' in the symphonic sense of that term whether they have bothered to use the rhetoric of functionalism or not. As a consequence of the unwillingness of most community researchers to forsake direct observation and direct reporting of the community life, we still have coherent images of the community and social life which are unattainable by other methodologies.

# Part Eight Social Stratification

The central ideas in social stratification are rather closely related to practical social life: one could contrast the use of terms like 'class' and 'status' in sociology with the formal, highly abstract use of the idea of utility in economic theory, where our practical grasp of the meaning of utility is a poor guide to the specialized way it is used by economists. For sociologists, categories like class, estate and caste are not only important because they tend to have major consequences for the income-patterns, access to property and occupations, mortality rates, etc. of the people who are thus categorized. Social categories of this kind are also used by people in labelling themselves and others, in shaping their expectations and ambitions and in interpreting their experiences. For all these reasons the sociologist is interested in patterns of stratification.

These varied concerns, and some overlapping of meaning between the various terms commonly used in the study of social stratification, have resulted in certain persistent complexities in the subject. The Readings have been chosen in part to illustrate some of these, and to demonstrate the need for reducing the scope of ambiguity and inexactness in discussions of the nature and relevance of stratification.

The first two extracts are from broad discussions of two 'pre-industrial' types of stratification, feudal and caste societies. Most of the Readings, however, can be grouped around the two poles of modern stratification theory – Karl Marx on class and Max Weber on status. Reading 63 by T. B. Bottomore gives a brief outline of élitist theory. Certain other Readings in this volume are highly relevant for the understanding of stratification, notably those in education (particularly the extract from Basil Bernstein) and work and industry.

# 52 Marc Bloch

## The Fundamental Characteristics of European Feudalism

Excerpts from Marc Bloch, *Feudal Society*, translated by L. A. Manyon,
Routledge & Kegan Paul, 1961, pp. 443–5. First published in French in 1939.

The simplest way will be to begin by saying what feudal society was not.
Although the obligations arising from blood-relationship played a very
active part in it, it did not rely on kinship alone. More precisely, feudal
ties proper were developed when those of kinship proved inadequate.
Again, despite the persistence of the idea of a public authority superimposed on the multitude of petty powers, feudalism coincided with a
profound weakening of the State, particularly in its protective capacity.
But much as feudal society differed from societies based on kinship as
well as from those dominated by the power of the State, it was their
successor and bore their imprint. For while the characteristic relationships of personal subjection retained something of the quasi-family
character of the original companionage, a considerable part of the political authority exercised by innumerable petty chiefs had the appearance
of a usurpation of 'regalian' rights.

European feudalism should therefore be seen as the outcome of the
violent dissolution of older societies. It would in fact be unintelligible
without the great upheaval of the Germanic invasions which, by forcibly
uniting two societies orginally at very different stages of development,
disrupted both of them and brought to the surface a great many modes
of thought and social practices of an extremely primitive character. It
finally developed in the atmosphere of the last barbarian raids. It involved a far-reaching restriction of social intercourse, a circulation of
money too sluggish to admit of a salaried officialdom and a mentality
attached to things tangible and local. When these conditions began to
change, feudalism began to wane.

It was an unequal society, rather than a hierarchical one – with chiefs
rather than nobles; and with serfs, not slaves. If slavery had not played
so small a part, there would have been no need for the characteristically
feudal forms of dependence, as applied to the lower orders of society. In
an age of disorder, the place of the adventurer was too important, the
memory of men too short, the regularity of social classifications too uncertain, to admit of the strict formation of regular castes.

Nevertheless the feudal system meant the rigorous economic subjection of a host of humble folk to a few powerful men. Having received from earlier ages the Roman *villa* (which in some respects anticipated the manor) and the German village chiefdom, it extended and consolidated these methods whereby men exploited men, and combining inextricably the right to the revenues from the land with the right to exercise authority, it fashioned from all this the true manor of medieval times. And this it did partly for the benefit of an oligarchy of priests and monks whose task it was to propitiate Heaven, but chiefly for the benefit of an oligarchy of warriors. [...]

In feudal society the characteristic human bond was the subordinate's link with a nearby chief. From one level to another the ties thus formed – like so many chains branching out indefinitely – joined the smallest to the greatest. Land itself was valued above all because it enabled a lord to provide himself with 'men' by supplying the remuneration for them. 'We want lands,' said in effect the Norman lords who refused the gifts of jewels, arms and horses offered by their duke. And they added among themselves: 'It will thus be possible for us to maintain many knights, and the duke will no longer be able to do so.'

It remained to devise a form of real property right suitable for the remuneration of services and coinciding in duration with the personal tie itself. From the solution which it found for this problem, Western feudalism derived one of its most original features. While the 'men of service' who surrounded the Slav princes continued to receive their estates as outright gifts, the fief of the Frankish vassal, after some fluctuations of policy, was in theory conceded to him only for the term of his life. For among the highest classes, distinguished by the honourable profession of arms, relationships of dependence had assumed, at the outset, the form of contracts freely entered into between two living men confronting one another. From this necessary personal contact the relationship derived the best part of its moral value. Nevertheless at an early date various factors tarnished the purity of the obligation: hereditary succession, natural in a society where the family remained so strong; the practice of enfeoffment which was imposed by economic conditions and ended by burdening the land with services rather than the man with fealty; finally and above all, the plurality of vassal engagements. The loyalty of the commended man remained, in many cases, a potent factor. But as a paramount social bond designed to unite the various groups at all levels, to prevent fragmentation and to arrest disorder, it showed itself decidedly ineffective.

# 53 Gerald D. Berreman

## Caste Systems

Excerpt from Gerald D. Berreman, 'Stratification, pluralism and interaction: a comparative analysis of caste', in A. V. S. de Reuck and Julie Knight (eds.), *Caste and Race*, J. & A. Churchill for CIBA Foundation, 1967, pp. 46–51.

When viewed comparatively and structurally, caste systems have been customarily described as systems of stratification – unusually rigid, birth-ascribed, permitting of no individual mobility, but nevertheless examples of ranked aggregates of people. To the extent that theories have been employed, concepts applied or hypotheses ventured, they have been derived primarily from the study of stratification. These have not proved inappropriate to the data, but they have been insufficient. As a colleague has remarked, there is a notable sterility – a striking lifelessness – manifest in the application of concepts of stratification to the Indian caste system, and to other caste systems as well. This is a failing not found in studies which define caste primarily in cultural terms. But the virtues of such studies are accompanied by an important limitation: failure to say anything very relevant to man and society outside India, or outside the particular region and the specific groups within that region which have been described.

I wish to suggest here a more comprehensive approach which makes for cross-cultural comparability without sacrificing cultural content. Such an approach uses concepts derived from three bodies of descriptive and analytical literature: studies of stratification, studies of cultural pluralism and studies of social interaction. It is my contention that caste systems are indeed rigid systems of social stratification, but that they are also systems of sociocultural pluralism and that both of these facts are to be understood largely in terms of distinctive patterns of social interaction. By viewing caste systems in this way we lend greater validity and hence greater utility, as well as increased credibility, to comparative studies of these phenomena. We can analyse a broader range of caste systems, caste-like systems and related phenomena than is possible with concepts derived only from stratification theory. We can analyse processes of change in caste systems and changes to or from caste systems. We can describe more satisfactorily the continuum from non-caste to caste organization and the dimensions which define that continuum. In short, to view caste in true perspective we must use the three dimensions: stratification, pluralism and interaction.

Cross-cultural definitions of caste are necessarily highly abstract, for the term may be expected to apply to situations as different as India and the United States, and to groups as diverse as the Burakumin of Japan and the blacksmiths of East Africa. But a definition of caste must also be abstract even if it is to be applied within South Asia to both Swat and Ceylon and, in India, to Brahmans, Nayars and sweepers. Accordingly, my own definition of a caste system is abstract: *a caste system occurs where a society is made up of birth-ascribed groups which are hierarchically ordered and culturally distinct. The hierarchy entails differential evaluation, rewards and association.*

## In society

That a caste system is in a society implies that it is in fact a system. The groups comprising it are differentiated, interacting and interdependent parts of a larger society. Often, and perhaps universally, they are economically interdependent and/or occupationally specialized. Their members view themselves and are viewed by others as being relatively homogeneous elements in a system of differentiated component groups rather than, as in the case of tribes in India, being relatively independent (and mutually unranked) systems in themselves.

## Comprised of groups

That a caste system is comprised of groups implies that each rank in the hierarchy is shared by socially distinct aggregates of people. These people recognize that they comprise discrete, bounded, ranked entities. The size and degree of corporateness of such groups varies widely. The members usually share a group name; always they interact with one another in characteristic ways; always there are symbols of group membership ranging from skin colour to cultural features such as language, occupation, dress, place of residence, and the like. Only members of the group are one's peers. Where group affiliation is relevant, individual attributes are irrelevant.

## Birth ascription

That membership in castes is determined by birth means that an individual is assigned his lifelong and unalterable status according to his parentage – a status which he shares with others of similar birth who are therefore assigned to the same group (caste). A common means of guaranteeing this status is by prescribing endogamous marriage in the caste, and assigning to the child the caste affiliation of its parents. But this method is by no means universal even in India, for caste, like kin-group affiliation, can be assigned unilineally or according to other, more complex, rules based on birth.

## Hierarchy

That a caste system is a hierarchy implies that it is a system of differential evaluation, differential power and rewards, and differential association; in short, a system of institutionalized inequality. This is a sufficiently complex and crucial aspect of the definition to warrant elaboration.

## Differential evaluation

Castes are ranked, ultimately, in terms of differential 'intrinsic worth' ascribed to those who comprise them. This may be expressed in many different idioms: idioms such as purity (as in India), honour (as in Swat) or genetically determined capabilities (as in the United States) – but always those who are high regard themselves as more worthy than those who are low. Those who are low universally question, if not the criteria of rank, then the judgement which relegates them to the low end of the hierarchy. They may take the alleged criteria more literally than do others, or confuse the idiom in which rank is expressed for the criteria by which it is conferred. Thus, they may adopt the attributes and behaviour of those above them on the assumption that these are the bases for status, only to find that (in the short run at least) it is the fact that they were born low rather than that they are dirty or polluted which makes them unworthy and hence low.

Caste systems rank birth-ascribed group membership rather than attributes. Class systems, by contrast, define the rank of their members according to their individual attributes and behaviour. *In a caste system an individual displays the attributes of his caste because he is a member of it. In a class system, an individual is a member of his class because he displays its attributes.* Individual mobility is by definition impossible in a caste system, and possible (although in some systems statistically very unlikely) in a class system.

## Differential rewards

Differential evaluation is accompanied by differential power and other differential rewards contingent upon caste membership: access to goods, services and other valued things. The ability to influence the behaviour of others, the source of one's livelihood, the kind and amount of food, shelter and medical care, of education, justice, esteem and pleasure – all of these things which an individual will receive during his life – and the very length of life itself, are determined in large measure by caste status.

I have elsewhere compared some of the specific rewards and costs of caste status in the Indian village that I studied with those in a Southern town of the United States reported by Dollard.

*Differential association (interaction)*

A caste hierarchy is to a large extent an interactional hierarchy. Social interaction is inherently symbolic – that is, it has meaning. Rank is expressed and validated in interaction between persons; it is manifest in patterns of interpersonal behaviour and in patterns of differential association. Who may be one's friend, one's wife, one's neighbour, one's master, one's servant, one's client, one's competitor, is largely a matter of caste. Every relevant other is a superior, a peer or an inferior, depending upon caste. Only within the caste is status equality found. Between castes any kind of interaction which defies or jeopardizes the rules of hierarchy is taboo even when such behaviour does not directly challenge the official bases (the criteria) of the rank system. Thus, there is always a more or less elaborate etiquette of inter-caste relations which is stringently enforced from within and above. Deference is a group matter, not merely an individual one, for it demonstrates and validates the system of ranked groups. The hierarchical nature of interaction between castes is such as to bestow responsibilities and prerogatives implying different degrees of responsibility, maturity and even humanity to different castes.

It is becoming increasingly evident that castes cannot be defined adequately, at least in any operational sense, without reference to interaction patterns. Bailey, Karve and Leach have defined castes in India as the most extensive kin groups, for they are the maximal limit of the marriage network. Caste membership, like caste ranking, could be empirically determined by observations (or reports) of interaction, since that is the way in which membership is expressed. An interactional definition of a caste system might be: *a system of birth-ascribed groups each of which comprises for its members the maximum limit of status-equal interaction, and between all of which interaction is consistently hierarchical.* A caste might be defined as a network of status-equal interactions in a society characterized by a network of hierarchical interactions among birth-ascribed groups. The interactions referred to could range from informal social encounters to marriage, and could include a wide variety of interactional networks including occupational, economic, political, ritual, friendship, and so on. It is an interesting fact that although castes in India are widely recognized to be networks, no specific caste has been definitively studied or even delimited from this point of view.

# 54 Marx and Engels on Class

## (a) Karl Marx and Friedrich Engels

### Bourgeois and Proletarians

Excerpt from Karl Marx and Friedrich Engels, *The Communist Manifesto*, reprinted in L. S. Feuer (ed.), *Marx and Engels: Basic Writings*, Collins, 1959, pp. 48–9. First published in German in 1848.

The history of all hitherto existing society is the history of class struggles.

Freeman and slave, patrician and plebeian, lord and serf, guild master and journeyman, in a word, oppressor and oppressed, stood in constant opposition to one another, carried on an uninterrupted, now hidden, now open fight, a fight that each time ended either in a revolutionary reconstitution of society at large or in the common ruin of the contending classes.

In the earlier epochs of history we find almost everywhere a complicated arrangement of society into various orders, a manifold gradation of social rank. In ancient Rome we have patricians, knights, plebeians, slaves; in the Middle Ages, feudal lords, vassals, guild masters, journeymen, apprentices, serfs; in almost all of these classes, again, subordinate gradations.

The modern bourgeois society that has sprouted from the ruins of feudal society has not done away with class antagonisms. It has but established new classes, new conditions of oppression, new forms of struggle in place of the old ones.

Our epoch, the epoch of the bourgeoisie, possesses, however, this distinctive feature: it has simplified the class antagonisms. Society as a whole is more and more splitting up into two great hostile camps, into two great classes directly facing each other: bourgeoisie and proletariat.

## (b) Karl Marx

## Historical Tendency of Capitalist Accumulation

Excerpt from Karl Marx, *Capital*, reprinted in L. S. Feuer (ed.), *Marx and Engels: Basic Writings*, Collins, 1959, pp. 205–8. First published in German in 1867.

What does the primitive accumulation of capital, i.e. its historical genesis, resolve itself into? In so far as it is not immediate transformation of slaves and serfs into wage labourers and therefore a mere change of form, it means only the expropriation of the immediate producers, i.e. the dissolution of private property based on the labour of its owner. Private property, as the antithesis to social, collective property, exists only where the means of labour and the external conditions of labour belong to private individuals. But according as these private individuals are labourers or not labourers, private property has a different character. The numberless shades that it at first sight presents correspond to the intermediate stages lying between these two extremes. The private property of the labourer in his means of production is the foundation of petty industry, whether agricultural, manufacturing or both; petty industry, again, is an essential condition for the development of social production and of the free individuality of the labourer himself. Of course, this petty mode of production exists also under slavery, serfdom and other states of dependence. But it flourishes, it lets loose its whole energy, it attains its adequate classical form only where the labourer is the private owner of his own means of labour set in action by himself, the peasant of the land which he cultivates, the artisan of the tool which he handles as a virtuoso. This mode of production presupposes parcelling of the soil and scattering of the other means of production, so also it excludes co-operation, division of labour within each separate process of production, the control over and the productive application of the forces of nature by society and the free development of the social productive powers. It is compatible only with a system of production, and a society, moving within narrow and more or less primitive bounds. To perpetuate it would be, as Pecqueur rightly says, 'to decree universal mediocrity'. At a certain stage of development it brings forth the material agencies for its own dissolution. From that moment new forces and new passions spring up in the bosom of society, but the old social organization fetters them and keeps them down. It must be annihilated; it is annihilated. Its annihilation, the transformation of the individualized and scattered means of production into socially concentrated ones, of the pygmy property of the many into the huge property of the few, the expropriation of the great mass of the people from the soil, from the means of subsistence, and from the means of labour, this fearful and painful expropriation of the mass of the people forms the prelude to the history of capital. It comprises a series of forcible methods, of which we have passed in review only those that have been epoch making as methods of the primitive accumulation of capital. The expropriation of the immediate producers was accomplished with merciless vandalism, and under the stimulus of passions the most infamous, the most sordid, the pettiest, the most meanly odious. Self-earned private property, which is based, so to say, on the fusing together of the isolated, independent labouring individual with the conditions of his labour, is supplanted by capitalistic private property, which rests on exploitation of the nominally free labour of others, i.e. on wage labour.

As soon as this process of transformation has sufficiently decomposed the old society from top to bottom, as soon as the labourers are turned into proletarians, their means of labour into capital, as soon as the capitalist mode of production stands on its own feet, then the further socialization of labour and further transformation of the land and other means of production into socially exploited and, therefore, common means of production, as well as the further expropriation of private proprietors, take a new form. That which is now to be expropriated is no longer the labourer working for himself, but the capitalist exploiting many labourers. This expropriation is accomplished by the action of the immanent laws of capitalistic production itself, by the centralization of capital. One capitalist always kills many. Hand in hand with this centralization, or this expropriation of many capitalists by few, develop, on an ever extending scale, the co-operative form of the labour process, the conscious technical application of science, the methodical cultivation of the soil, the transformation of the instruments of labour into instruments of labour usable only in common, the economizing of all means of production by their use as the means of production of combined, socialized labour, the entanglement of all peoples in the net of the world market, and this, the international character of the capitalistic régime. Along with the constantly diminishing number of the magnates of capital, who usurp and monopolize all advantages of this process of transformation, grows the mass of misery, oppression, slavery, degradation, exploitation; but with this too grows the revolt of the working class, a class always increasing in numbers, and disciplined, united, organized by the very mechanism of the process of capitalist production itself. The monopoly of capital becomes a fetter upon the mode of production which has sprung up and flourished along with and under it. Centralization of the means of production and socialization of labour at last reach a point where they become incompatible with their capitalist integument. This integument is burst asunder. The knell of capitalist private property sounds. The expropriators are expropriated.

The capitalist mode of appropriation, the result of the capitalist mode of production, produces capitalist private property. This is the first negation of individual private property, as founded on the labour of the proprietor. But capitalist production begets, with the inexorability of a law of nature, its own negation. It is the negation of negation. This does not re-establish private property for the producer, but gives him individual property based on the acquisitions of the capitalist era, i.e. on co-operation and the possession in common of the land and of the means of production.

The transformation of scattered private property, arising from individual labour, into capitalist private property is, naturally, a process incomparably more protracted, violent and difficult than the transformation of capitalistic private property, already practically resting on socialized production, into socialized property. In the former case we had the expropriation of the mass of the people by a few usurpers; in the latter we have the expropriation of a few usurpers by the mass of the people.

## (c) Karl Marx

The Class Struggles in France, 1848 to 1850

Excerpts from Karl Marx, *The Class Struggles in France, 1848 to 1850*, reprinted in L. S. Feuer (ed.), *Marx and Engels: Basic Writings*, Collins, 1959, pp. 322–3, 353–4. First published in 1850.

After the July revolution [of 1830], when the liberal banker Laffitte led his godfather, the Duke of Orleans, in triumph to the Hôtel de Ville, he let fall the words: '*From now on the bankers will rule.*' Laffitte had betrayed the secret of the revolution.

It was not the French bourgeoisie that ruled under Louis Philippe, but *one section* of it: bankers, stock-exchange kings, railway kings, owners of coal and iron mines and forests, a part of the landed proprietors that rallied round them – the so-called *finance aristocracy*. It sat on the throne, it dictated laws in the Chambers, it distributed public offices, from cabinet portfolios to tobacco bureau posts.

The *industrial bourgeoisie,* properly so called, formed part of the official opposition, i.e. it was represented only as a minority in the Chambers. Its opposition was expressed all the more resolutely, the more unalloyed the autocracy of the finance aristocracy became, and the more it itself imagined that its domination over the working class was ensured after the mutinies of 1832, 1834 and 1839, which had been drowned in blood. *Grandin*, Rouen manufacturer and the most fanatical instrument of bourgeois reaction in the Constituent as well as in the Legislative National Assembly, was the most violent opponent of Guizot in the Chamber of Deputies. *Léon Faucher*, later known for his impotent efforts to climb into prominence as the Guizot of the French counter-revolution in the last days of Louis Philippe, waged a war of the pen for industry against speculation and its trainbearer, the government. *Bastiat* agitated in the name of Bordeaux and the whole of wine-producing France against the ruling system.

The *petty bourgeois* of all gradations, and the *peasantry* also, were completely excluded from political power. Finally, in the official opposition or entirely outside the *pays légal*, there were the *ideological* representatives and spokesmen of the above classes, their savants, lawyers, doctors, etc. – in a word, their so-called *men of talent*. [. . .]

The most comprehensive contradiction of this constitution, however, consists in the following: the classes whose social slavery the constitution is to perpetuate, proletariat, peasantry, petty bourgeoisie, it puts in possession of political power through universal suffrage. And from the class whose old social power it sanctions, the bourgeoisie, it withdraws the political guarantees of this power. It forces the political rule of the bourgeoisie into democratic conditions, which at every moment help the hostile classes to victory and jeopardize the very foundations of bourgeois society. From the former classes it demands that they should not go forward from political to social emancipation; from the others that they should not go back from social to political restoration.

These contradictions perturbed the bourgeois republicans but little. To the extent that they ceased to be *indispensable* – and they were indispensable only as the protagonists of the old society against the revolutionary proletariat – they fell, a few weeks after their victory, from the position of a *party* to that of a *coterie*. And they treated the constitution as a big *intrigue*. What was to be constituted in it was, above all, the rule of the coterie.

## (d) Karl Marx

## Eighteenth Brumaire of Louis Bonaparte

Excerpt from Karl Marx, *Eighteenth Brumaire of Louis Bonaparte*, reprinted in
L. S. Feuer (ed.), *Marx and Engels: Basic Writings*, Collins, 1959, pp. 377–9.
First published in 1852.

Only under the second Bonaparte does the State seem to have made itself
completely independent. As against civil society, the State machine has
consolidated its position so thoroughly that the chief of the Society of
December 10 suffices for its head, an adventurer blown in from abroad,
raised on the shield by a drunken soldiery, which he has bought with
liquor and sausages, and which he must continually ply with sausage
anew. Hence the downcast despair, the feeling of most dreadful humiliation and degradation that oppresses the breast of France and makes her
catch her breath. She feels dishonoured.

And yet the State power is not suspended in mid-air. Bonaparte represents a class, and the most numerous class of French society at that, the
*small-holding* [*Parzellen*] *peasants*.

Just as the Bourbons were the dynasty of big landed property and just
as the Orleans were the dynasty of money, so the Bonapartes are the
dynasty of the peasants, that is, the mass of the French people. Not the
Bonaparte who submitted to the bourgeois parliament, but the Bonaparte who dispersed the bourgeois parliament is the chosen of the peasantry. For three years the towns had succeeded in falsifying the
meaning of the election of December 10 and in cheating the peasants out
of the restoration of the empire. The election of 10 December 1848 has
been consummated only by the *coup d'état* of 2 December 1851.

The small-holding peasants form a vast mass, the members of which
live in similar conditions but without entering into manifold relations
with one another. Their mode of production isolates them from one
another instead of bringing them into mutual intercourse. The isolation
is increased by France's bad means of communication and by the poverty of the peasants. Their field of production, the small holding, admits
of no division of labour in its cultivation, no application of science and,
therefore, no diversity of development, no variety of talent, no wealth of
social relationships. Each individual peasant family is almost self-
sufficient; it itself directly produces the major part of its consumption,

and thus acquires its means of life more through exchange with nature than in intercourse with society. A small holding, a peasant and his family; alongside them another small holding, another peasant and another family. A few score of these make up a village, and a few score of villages make up a Department. In this way the great mass of the French nation is formed by simple addition of homologous magnitudes, much as potatoes in a sack form a sack of potatoes. In so far as millions of families live under economic conditions of existence that separate their mode of life, their interests and their culture from those of the other classes and put them in hostile opposition to the latter, they form a class. In so far as there is merely a local interconnexion among these small-holding peasants and the identity of their interests begets no community, no national bond and no political organization among them, they do not form a class. They are consequently incapable of enforcing their class interest in their own name, whether through a parliament or through a convention. They cannot represent themselves, they must be represented. Their representative must at the same time appear as their master, as an authority over them, as an unlimited government power that protects them against the other classes and sends them rain and sunshine from above. The political influence of the small-holding peasants, therefore, finds its final expression in the executive power subordinating society to itself.

Historical tradition gave rise to the belief of the French peasants in the miracle that a man named Napoleon would bring all the glory back to them. And an individual turns up who gives himself out as the man because he bears the name of Napoleon, in consequence of the Code Napoléon, which lays down that *la recherche de la paternité est interdite* [research into paternity is forbidden]. After a vagabondage of twenty years and after a series of grotesque adventures the legend finds fulfilment and the man becomes Emperor of the French. The fixed idea of the nephew was realized because it coincided with the fixed idea of the most numerous class of the French people.

# 55 Stanislaw Ossowski

## The Term 'Social Class'

Excerpts from Stanislaw Ossowski, *Class Structure in the Social Consciousness*,
translated by Sheila Patterson, Routledge & Kegan Paul, 1963, pp. 129–31, 182–5.
First published in Polish in 1957.

In its narrower meaning, in which it is opposed to estates and castes,
'class' can be defined either by the negation of the attributes charac-
terizing a caste or an estate or by criteria altogether inapplicable to what
we have in mind when we speak of 'estates' or 'castes'. When, therefore,
we have to do with the denotation of the term 'class' in application to
problems of social structure, I see three possibilities, each of which has
been and is made use of in sociological theories and in different accounts
of the system of social relations, though not always with a distinct conceptual awareness.

1. In the general sense each group which is regarded as one of the basic
components of the social structure may be called a 'class' of the social
structure. I shall be considering the interpretation of the expression 'one
of the basic components of the social structure' in the following chapter
[not included here]. In any case such a comprehensive concept includes
both estate and caste, and also class in the second and third meanings
distinguished here.

2. Of the two specifying versions of the concept of class which I should
like to consider here, the first shows us a social class as a group distinguished in respect of the relations of property. We formulate this
criterion in a quite general way, or rather we indicate only the kind of
criterion involved, because this version, i.e. the economic version of the
concept of social class, may vary in content in different definitions. This
framework allows room for the definitions of both Adam Smith and
Madison, for the age-old division of men into rich, poor and moderately
well-to-do, for the Marxian division of classes according to their relation
to the means of production, and for the economic definition of social
class found in the early American sociologists (Ward, Small, Giddings
and Cooley).

The economic criteria which are involved in the concept of class in all
varieties of this version neither coincide with nor exclude the criteria
which determine the extension of such concepts as estate or caste. Some

caste or estate-systems can at the same time be economic-class systems, but such a coincidence can only be empirically established. In cases where such a coincidence does apply one can speak of the 'class' aspect of caste relations or the 'estate' aspect of the class-system.

In a somewhat different meaning it is also possible to speak of the 'class' aspect of an estate-system or a caste-system even when the co-incidence does not occur, if we assume that between an estate-system and a class-system there holds some more or less complicated causal dependence. This is precisely the Marxian assumption. The view, not form-ulated by the Marxists, that all the historical struggles between estates, which are not separate classes in the economic sense, were in reality disguised class struggles, would correspond to the well-known view about the true nature of the religious conflicts in history.

3. In the second version specifying the concept of class, the class-system is contrasted with group-systems in the social structure in which an indi-vidual's membership of a group is institutionally determined and in which privileges or discriminations result from an individual's ascription to a certain group. In contradistinction to such groups of a caste or estate type, a class in this version is a group of which membership is not assigned by a birth certificate nor any official document, such as a title of nobility or an act of manumission, but is the consequence of social status otherwise achieved. The privileges and discriminations, which in this case require no sanction from any source, are not the effect but the cause of the individual's placement in the capitalist or proletarian class: one is reckoned among the capitalists because one possesses capital, and one belongs to the proletariat because one possesses no other sources of income than the capacity to hire out one's labour. The ideal type of privileges and discriminations that fix an individual's social status re-gardless of the social categories to which this individual may belong are the economic privileges and discriminations found in a system of free competition: property, income, the way in which one works for a living.

In various social systems one can observe two or more co-existing types of the relation of class dependence (using the term class in its widest sense). The two specifying versions of the concept of class are nevertheless most closely connected with an unrestricted capitalist sys-tem. In the former version, however, a class can at the same time be a caste or an estate, whereas in the latter these concepts are mutually exclusive. In contradistinction to groups whose composition and privi-leges have the sanction of political or religious institutions, a social class in the latter version comes into being 'spontaneously', by the force of events.

This is the usual way in which the term 'class' is used by contemporary sociologists of a non-Marxist persuasion. Hence we find the terms 'caste' and 'class' contrasted in dictionaries of the social sciences, and hence such titles as 'caste and class in a Southern Town'.

Incidentally we should note that, as seen from the viewpoint of the third conception, social classes, in the sense of so-called 'high society' and in general classes in a scheme of synthetic gradation, should be regarded as a sort of synthesis of caste and class – at least in societies where some estate traditions survive.

Because of the absence of terminological distinctions, 'class' has different meanings in different contexts. It means one thing when one speaks of the 'overlapping of a caste and a class structure', and something else when we speak of the 'history of class societies' or the 'history of the class struggle'. In these cases the meaning of the term is determined by its context. This may not evoke misunderstandings as to the denotation of the term, but it does imply the risk mentioned above. Moreover the burdening of the term 'class' with an ambiguous content makes it more difficult to analyse the structure of modern societies with nationalized means of production. [. . .]

In our own world the relations of ownership to the means of production are still a factor of immense significance in the formation of human relations; without the Marxian insight into social life it would be virtually impossible to conduct an incisive analysis of the changes which are taking place in the modern world. But the scope of the applicability of the Marxian criterion has undergone important changes.

The inadequacy of the classic Marxist–Leninist conception of class for analysing the social structure of countries in which the means of production have been nationalized has found one form of expression in Stalin's conception of non-antagonistic classes, and another in the discussions about the systems of privileges enjoyed by particular groups in these countries.

The Marxian criterion of social class has also lost some of its adequacy in relation to the capitalist countries. Here I am not by any means referring only to the Fascist countries, where the large-scale application of the means of compulsion [was normal but also to] countries in which the principles of economic liberalism are respected. Such changes are seen at their most effective in the United States.

According to Marx and Engels the development of capitalism was to be accompanied by a rapid process of economic polarization and by the disappearance of the middle class. The envisaged polarization did not occur, but it is by no means easy to say whether the process of disappearance of the middle class predicted by Marx is actually occurring in the world's most advanced capitalist country. The old American middle class which formed so large a part of the United States population in de Tocqueville's period, and which in his view was the guarantee of American democracy, was that of the property owners who work in their own establishments. This class has in fact shrunk rapidly, in line with Marx's prediction, although not so rapidly as might have been expected in view of the violent rate of the accumulation of capital. Simultaneously, however, a new middle class has been rising, a class of civil servants, trade union officials, local government officers, a class of technicians, white-collar workers and minor executives in the large industrial establishments.

The rapid rise of this new class shows up strikingly in statistical returns and is changing the whole social structure of the United States. In the time of de Tocqueville and Marx it was too insignificant to be differentiated as a separate class, and it was not included in the framework of the classical Marxian division. It was a marginal group. Now this marginal group among the classes of the Marxian scheme has so increased in size in contemporary America that it is impossible not to regard it as a class, especially when we consider general trends of development in the United States. This new class, which has a corresponding group in the 'stratum' of non-manual white-collar workers in state and local government and in party offices in the U.S.S.R. is, it would seem, even characterized by its own social attitudes and its own subculture.

Thus the answer to the question whether the Marxian forecast about the fate of the middle class is being fulfilled in the United States depends on the interpretation of the term 'middle class'; in Marx's day this term did not involve such difficulties.

The well-known conflicts between medium and large property owners which occurred in the United States in the Rooseveltian era also suggest certain new reflections about the criterion of social class. The owners of medium-sized property whom Roosevelt's legislation was intended to defend against the large property owners were in fact businessmen or firms disposing of hundreds of thousands of dollars, or even 'small millionaires' threatened by the great concerns and the multi-millionaires. This bitter 'class struggle' which so absorbed American society – and was of great significance for the American social structure – can be presented only within the framework of a scheme of gradation, and not of a scheme of intersecting dichotomies.

There are other reasons why the nineteenth-century conception of social class, in both the liberal and the Marxian interpretations, has lost much of its applicability in the modern world. In situations where changes of social structure are to a greater or lesser degree governed by the decision of the political authorities, we are a long way from social classes as interpreted by Marx, Ward, Veblen or Weber, from classes conceived of as groups determined by their relations to the means of production or, as others would say, by their relations to the market. We are a long way from classes conceived of as groups arising out of the spontaneous activities of individuals or at the most of spontaneously created class organizations. In situations where the political authorities can overtly and effectively change the class structure; where the privileges that are most essential for social status, including that of a higher share in the national income, are conferred by a decision of the political authorities; where a large part or even the majority of the population is included in a stratification of the type to be found in a bureaucratic hierarchy – the nineteenth-century concept of class becomes more or less an anachronism, and class conflicts give way to other forms of social antagonism.

The planned direction of changes in the social structure and the direct dependence of the economic status of the majority of the population on the state authorities are features that are characteristic of contemporary socialist societies. They are not however confined to these societies. In an interesting paper on 'Changes in patterns of stratification attendant on attainment of political independence', presented at the Third World Congress of Sociology at Amsterdam in 1956, Dr S. N. Eisenstadt discussed the role of the political authorities in the formation of social stratification in countries which have just achieved their independence, and in particular in former colonial countries. We can also look for more striking examples. Whereas in his own day, Roosevelt's New Deal was regarded in certain circles as an attack on the old American traditions, today the immense national budget of the United States permits infinitely thorough-going intervention by the political authorities in the economic life of the country and enables them to exert considerable influence on the distribution of the national income and the system of class relations.

# 56 G. D. H. Cole

British Class Structure in 1951

Excerpts from G. D. H. Cole, *Studies in Class Structure*, Routledge & Kegan Paul, 1955, pp. 149–51, 185–7.

In dealing with the assessment of class there are at least three different ways of setting out. Class can be regarded, as the Marxists among many others regard it, as an objective phenomenon, so that, subject to marginal exceptions, each individual can be put into a definite class-pocket in terms of one or more defined characteristics of his situation in society. The chosen criterion may be his relation to the 'process of production' or the size of his income or possibly the age at which he left school or some other objective characteristic – or perhaps a combination of several such characteristics. If, however, more than one criterion is used, subjectivity is bound to enter in, for it becomes necessary, when different criteria lead to different conclusions, to decide to which the primary importance is to be allowed. The second way of approach is the directly subjective – that of asking each person to say to what class he holds himself to belong, and accepting the answers as valid. One trouble about this method is that the answers may be much affected by the terms in which the questions are put – as in the well-known instances in which the substitution of 'lower' for 'working' as the name given to the class to be distinguished from 'upper' and 'middle' has notoriously influenced the replies. The third method – much the hardest to apply in practice – is that of estimating a person's class by finding out the views of his friends and neighbours; for this involves very elaborate questioning, is open to the same difficulty in respect of the names given by the investigators to the various classes, and in addition gives rise to awkward problems when friends and neighbours differ in their assessments. In theory, I suppose, the investigator could start without making any suggestions about class-names or categories; but if he did he would be confronted with a set of answers which would be too discordant to be added up and would be rendered largely meaningless because the answerers would have widely different notions about the meaning to be given to a question about class unaccompanied by any elucidation of the sense in which the word was being used.

These difficulties are so well known that there is no need to discuss them in any detail in the present study. My purpose here is to take the recently published data for the British Census of 1951, and to see what light can be derived from them concerning the present class structure of British society. The preliminary reports in question, it should be pointed out, are based, not on the full examination of the Census schedules, but on a random sample of 1 per cent of the total. They may therefore not yield precisely correct results, especially in relation to some of the smaller groups; but they are not likely to be so much out as to invalidate any important conclusions that can be derived from them. Their serious shortcoming, from the standpoint of their use in considering class structure, is first that they rest on a list of occupations which is in some respects inadequate because it groups too many categories together, and secondly that the assignment to a particular class is made, not for each individual, but for each occupational group as a whole, so that, for example, all 'farmers' constitute a single group irrespective of the importance of their holdings, and 'managers' are picked out as a separate category only for some occupations, whereas in others they are mixed up with 'operatives' and in others are included in a residuary category of 'managers' in general, without assignment to a particular line of business.

The Census authorities, in dealing with the problem of class, work mainly on the basis of an arbitrary division of the occupied population into five 'social classes' placed one below another in a descending order. The top class is composed mainly of the higher professions and of such persons as can be grouped together under the heading of higher 'managers' or directors of business enterprise. It includes all ministers of religion, officers in the armed forces, lawyers, professional scientists, authors, journalists and medical doctors; but it excludes all teachers and all artists, as both these groups are relegated to class II because they consist mainly of less well paid professionals. In other words, the whole of each name-group is assigned to the same class, and the possibility of breaking up a group depends on it having been given a distinct name for the purpose of enumeration in the Census. Thus, higher civil servants are distinguished from middle civil servants, and put in class I, because there are definite grade names for the two categories, whereas there are no such formal names for the higher and lower administrative and managerial groups in the majority of occupations. In the present sample survey all railway officials are put in class II, whereas some road transport officials are assigned to class I; and so on.

Class II in the Census classification is made up largely of shopkeepers and farmers, to whom are added the secondary professions, such as teaching and nursing, and a substantial number of managerial groups not deemed worthy of inclusion in class I.

With class III, by far the largest, the Census enters on much more debatable ground. Into this class are put, as far as possible, all foremen and supervisory workers, clerks, shop assistants, typists and blackcoated workers, together with all manual workers who are regarded as belonging to predominantly skilled trades. The conception of skill is here extended not only to jobs which are learnt by some form of apprenticeship or formal learnership, but also to a great many trades in which there is no clear dividing line between craftsmen and semi-skilled workers. The effect is to create an enormous middle group, which in my analysis I have done my best to break up by separating off, where I could, the supervisory and non-manual workers on the one hand and the manual operatives on the other, forming two class-groups standing, not one above the other, but broadly at the same social class level. These I have called IIIA and IIIB.

Class IV is meant to consist of semi-skilled workers, standing between the 'skilled', in the broad sense given to the term in the Census, and the unskilled workers, who are in some cases labourers permanently attached to a particular industry or occupation and in others a floating group of more or less casual workers. This unskilled category makes up class V. [. . .]

This study has left in the background certain important theoretical questions which arise in connexion with any attempt to relate the concepts of occupation and social class. In some cases the description of a man's occupation carries with it a clear statement of his position in the class structure – for example, agricultural labourer, railway porter, or enginedriver, mule-spinner, compositor, dock labourer, shop assistant, bank clerk, university professor, chartered accountant, mine manager, postman, riveter, bishop, police magistrate, admiral, dustman, midwife. Even within these occupational groups there are differences of status, as well as of income; but in using these words, we do at least give a broad categorization of class as well as of occupation. Many occupational terms, however, fail to carry any clear indication of class. This is the case not only where they are not specific enough – for example, manager or labourer or clerk, without any further indication – but also where the same word is habitually used in different senses or where an occupation ranges over a number of social classes but cannot be satisfactorily broken up to indicate the differences in terms of any qualifying occupational description. Baker or butcher or tailor may mean either a shopkeeper or a journeyman employed at a wage in manual labour; engineer may mean either a professional belonging to one of the great engineering institutes – civil, mechanical, etc. – or a skilled metal-working mechanic. The other type of difficulty – that of an occupation whose members may belong to widely different social classes – can be illustrated by many examples. The stationmaster of a big railway junction and the station-master of a small country station cannot be assigned to the same social class: nor can all shopkeepers (or all grocers, or drapers, or tobacconists), or all farmers, or all journalists, or all artists, or all teachers. Brokers, agents and works managers are other instances of widely varying occupations which it is difficult to break up into social class groups.

The theoretical interest of this problem arises chiefly in relation to the Marxist theory of classes, which insists that class depends on relation to the means of production. Marx used this principle, first, to categorize the opposed classes of *bourgeois*, or capitalists, and proletarians, and secondly to distinguish from both what he called the *petite bourgeoisie*. Both *bourgeois* and proletariat were related, in Marx's characterization, to the development of modern economic techniques – mechanization and large-scale production; whereas the *petite bourgeoisie* and the peasants were regarded by him as essentially related to obsolescent forms of economic structure. Marx took little account in his theory of the growing body of salary-earning technicians and administrators who, at the lower levels of these groups, were coming to constitute a new and quite different *petite bourgeoisie* interposed between the capitalists and the proletariat. These he regarded as hirelings of the capitalists, identified with their class-interests. Yet they clearly earned their livings in a different way, in the form of salaries which had more in common with wages than with profits. Nor did Marx take much account of the growing diffusion of shareholding interest in joint stock enterprise, though this made partners of the active capitalists not only many passive livers upon unearned incomes but also many active managerial and professional workers whose returns on investments only supplemented their principal sources of income.

Critics of Marxism have often argued, on the strength of these and other gaps or defects in the Marxian theory, that the entire attempt to link class and occupational categories together is mistaken. Some of them have put forward theories of class as an essentially social, or 'prestige', category, having little or no connexion either with occupation or with the relation of occupational groups to the means of production. This, however, is to lean over much too far in the opposite direction. It is undoubtedly possible to assign to definite positions in terms of class status the vast majority of those who belong to a large number of occupational groups, though not to all; and there is no good reason for refusing to do this because it cannot be done for every group. It is no doubt true that even within such groups as dock labourers or mule-spinners or chartered accountants or doctors of medicine there are substantial differences in class status, related in part to differences of income and in part to the prestige of particular types of job. But that does not prevent the great majority of persons in each of these groups from being assignable, with sufficient precision, to a single class.

# 57 Seymour M. Lipset and Hans L. Zetterberg

Social Mobility in Industrial Societies

Excerpts from Seymour M. Lipset and Hans L. Zetterberg, 'Social mobility in industrial societies', in Seymour M. Lipset and Reinhard Bendix (eds.), *Social Mobility in Industrial Society*, University of California Press, 1959, pp. 11–75.

Widespread social mobility has been a concomitant of industrialization and a basic characteristic of modern industrial society. In every industrial country, a large proportion of the population have had to find occupations considerably different from those of their parents. During the nineteenth century, the proportion of the labor force in urban occupations increased rapidly, while the proportion in agriculture decreased.

In the twentieth century the West has been characterized by a rapid growth of trade and of service industries, as well as of bureaucracy in industry and government; more people have become employed in white-collar work, and the comparative size of the rural population has declined even more rapidly than before. These changes in the distribution of occupations from generation to generation mean that no industrial society can be viewed as closed or static.

This apparently simple statement runs counter to widely held impressions concerning the different social structures of American and Western European societies. According to these impressions, America has an 'open society' with considerable social mobility, but the countries of Western Europe (specifically England, France, Italy, Germany, the Low Countries and the Scandinavian nations) have societies that are 'closed', in the sense that the children of workers are forced to remain in the social position of their parents. This judgement reflects earlier European beliefs. In the age of the French Revolution, America appeared to be a land free from traditional institutions and historical legacies: the country of the future, Hegel called it, where each man was master of his fate just as American democracy itself was the product of human reason. This notion has been reiterated in many analyses, all contrasting American and European societies.

For the most part these discussions deal with the differences between democratic and autocratic institutions; but they also express assumptions about contrasting patterns of social mobility. Sometimes the political and social aspects of the contrast between America and Europe have been linked as cause and effect: differences in political institutions and values have been cited as evidence for the assertion that the society of America is 'open', those of Europe 'closed'; and the supposedly greater rate of social mobility in American society has been viewed as a major reason for the success of American democracy. For example, some fifty years ago Werner Sombart referred to the opportunities abundant in America as the major reason why American workers rejected the Marxist view that there is little opportunity under capitalism, while European workers accepted it because their opportunities were more restricted. Such judgements as Sombart's were, however, no more than inferences based on the general contrast between the American tradition which proclaimed the goal of opportunity for all and the European emphasis upon social stability and class differences. For as a matter of fact, it is not really clear whether the different political orientation of the American and European worker reflects different opportunities for social mobility or only a difference in their ethos!

The questions implicit in these alternative interpretations can be answered today with somewhat more assurance than was possible even two decades ago because of recent research in social mobility. In this chapter we attempt to summarize the findings available for a number of countries. Since our object is to assemble a large amount of empirical evidence, it will be useful to state at the outset that *the over-all pattern of social mobility appears to be much the same in the industrial societies of various Western countries*. This is startling – even if we discount the mistaken efforts to explain differences in political institutions by reference to different degrees of social mobility in the United States and in Western Europe. Further, although it is clear that social mobility is related in many ways to the economic expansion of industrial societies, it is at least doubtful that the rates of mobility and of expansion are correlated. Since a number of the countries for which we have data have had different rates of economic expansion but show comparable rates of social mobility, our tentative interpretation is that the social mobility of societies becomes relatively high once their industrialization, and hence their economic expansion, reaches a certain level. [. . .]

Several different processes inherent in all modern social structures have a direct effect on the rate of social mobility, and help account for the similarities in rates in different countries: (a) changes in the number of available vacancies; (b) different rates of fertility; (c) changes in the rank accorded to occupations; (d) changes in the number of inheritable status-positions; and (e) changes in the legal restrictions pertaining to potential opportunities. [. . .]

Although it appears that the *amount* of social mobility is largely determined by the more or less uniform structural changes of industrialized societies and is therefore much the same in all such societies, it should be emphasized that the *consequences* of that mobility have been most diverse. To take an extreme example: if a Negro in South Africa obtains a nonmanual position, he is a ready candidate for leadership in a movement of radical protest. But if a white American from a working-class family makes the same move, he usually becomes politically and socially conservative. Perhaps the most important key to an explanation of such varying consequences of mobility across the line between manual and nonmanual occupations, is the concept of *status discrepancies*. Every society may be thought of as comprising a number of separate hierarchies – e.g. social, economic, educational, ethnic, etc. – each of which has its own status structure, its own conditions for the attainment of a position of prestige within that structure. There are likely to be a number of discrepancies among the positions in the different hierarchies that every person occupies simultaneously for, as Georg Simmel pointed out, every person maintains a unique pattern of group affiliations. Mobility merely adds to these discrepancies by creating or accentuating combinations of a high position in one rank and a low one in another; for example, a high position in an occupation combined with a low ethnic status, or a high position in the social-class hierarchy (based on the status of people with whom one associates) combined with a low income.

The few analyses of the psychological dimension of this problem that have been made indicate that status discrepancies may cause difficulties in personal adjustment because high self-evaluations in one sphere of life conflict with low ones in another. Durkheim, for example, suggested that both upward and downward mobility result in increased suicide rates by increasing the number of persons who find themselves in an *anomic* situation, one in which they do not know how to react to the norms involved. Studies of mental illness have suggested that people moving up in America are more likely to have mental breakdowns than the non-mobile. [. . .]

In effect, the principal impression which may be derived from the summary of mobility studies around the world is that no known complex society may be correctly described as 'closed' or static. Although the paths of mobility and the extent to which the mobile may enter or leave different strata are not the same in all such societies, the number of persons in each who are able to rise above the position of their parents is large enough to refute the statement that 'class barriers are insurmountable'. There is now more evidence to document this than has ever existed before, thanks to the researches of sociologists in many lands, but the conclusion is not so new or startling as it might seem – as witness the

American saying, 'Three generations from shirt-sleeves to shirt-sleeves', the German proverb which refers to 'the third critical generation', the old Lancashire maxim, 'Clogs to clogs in three generations', and the Chinese saying that 'a family may rise from rags to riches in three generations and go back to rags in the next three'. Although the materials which we have examined here give us no good basis for generalizing about nonindustrial societies, there is much evidence from historians of Western society as well as from contemporary students of basically non-industrial societies that such societies have also been characterized by considerable mobility. The difference between the pace of mobility in China and the Western world that these maxims suggest in their contrast between six and three generations as the length of the cycle may reflect the difference between nonindustrial and industrial societies. Both have considerable mobility. But industrial societies have more frequent and especially *more rapid* movement.

# 58 Seymour M. Lipset

Classes and Parties in American Politics

Excerpts from Seymour M. Lipset, *Political Man: The Social Bases of Politics*, Heinemann (Mercury Books edn.) 1963, pp. 285–307. First published by Doubleday in 1959.

It often comes as a shock, especially to Europeans, to be reminded that the first political parties in history with 'labour' or 'working man' in their names developed in America in the 1820s and 1830s. The emphasis on 'classlessness' in American political ideology has led many European and American political commentators to conclude that party divisions in America are less related to class cleavages than they are in other Western countries. Polling studies, however, belie this conclusion, showing that in every American election since 1936 (studies of the question were not made before then), the proportion voting Democratic increases sharply as one moves down the occupational or income ladder. In 1948 almost 80 per cent of the workers voted Democratic, a percentage which is higher than has ever been reported for left-wing parties in such countries as Britain, France, Italy and Germany. Each year the lower-paid and less skilled workers are the most Democratic; even in 1952, two-thirds of the unskilled workers were for Stevenson, though the proportion of all manual workers backing the Democrats dropped to 55 per cent in that year – a drop-off which was in large measure a result of Eisenhower's personal 'above the parties' appeal rather than a basic swing away from the Democratic party by the lower strata.

*Table 1* Per Cent Republican Voting or Voting Preference among Occupational Groups and Trade-Union Members

|  | 1940 | 1948 | 1952 | 1954 | 1956 |
|---|---|---|---|---|---|
| Business and professional | 64 | 77 | 64 | 61 | 68 |
| White-collar workers | 52 | 48 | 60 | 52 | 63 |
| Manual workers (skilled and unskilled) | 35 | 22 | 45 | 35 | 50 |
| Farmers | 46 | 32 | 67 | 56 | 54 |
| Trade-union members | 28 | 13 | 39 | 27 | 43 |

In general, the bulk of the workers, even many who voted for Eisenhower in 1952 and 1956, still regarded themselves as Democrats, and the results of the 1954 and 1958 congressional elections show that there has been no shift of the traditional Democratic voting base to the Republicans. Two-thirds of the workers polled by Gallup in 1958 voted for a Democrat for Congress.

The same relationship between class, considered now as a very general differentiating factor, and party support exists within the middle and upper classes. The Democrats have been in a minority among the nonmanual strata and, except among the intellectual professions, the Democratic proportion of the nonmanually occupied electorate declines inexorably with income and occupational status to the point where, according to one study, only 6 per cent of the heads of corporations with more than 10,000 employees are Democrats. Perhaps the best single example of the pervasiveness of status differences as a factor in American politics is the political allegiances of the chief executives of major American corporations. This study, done in 1955 by the Massachusetts Institute of Technology's Center for International Studies, and based on interviews with a systematic sample of one thousand such men, found that even within this upper economic group, the larger the company of which a man was an officer, the greater the likelihood that he was a Republican (see Table 2).

*Table 2*  Relationship between Size of Firm and Political Party
Allegiances of Corporation Executives – 1955

| Size of firm | Republican % | Democratic % | Independent % |
| --- | --- | --- | --- |
| More than 10,000 workers | 84 | 6 | 10 |
| 1000–9999 | 80 | 8 | 12 |
| 100–999 | 69 | 12 | 19 |

Consistent with these findings are the popular images of typical supporters of each party. The Gallup Poll, shortly before the 1958 congressional elections, asked a nation-wide sample what their picture of the typical Democrat was, and received these answers most frequently: 'middle class ... common people ... a friend ... an ordinary person ... works for his wages ... average person ... someone who thinks of everybody'. The typical Republican, in contrast, is 'better class ... well-to-do ... big businessman ... money voter ... well-off financially ... wealthy ... higher class'. [...]

The importance of class factors should not, however, cause us to over-look the fact that in the United States, as in every other democratic country, a large minority of the workers and a small section of the middle classes deviate from the dominant class tendency. One of the necessary conditions for a viable two-party system is that both parties hover around the 50 per cent mark. Hence in every industrialized country the conservative parties must win working-class support; and in the United States and Britain, the Republican and Conservative parties have necessarily accepted many of the reforms enacted by their adver-saries. Actually the conservatives' gradual shift to the left is endemic in the sheer demography of democratic politics – the poor will always be in the majority.

The preponderance of 'poorer' people also means that the con-servatives must always attempt to reduce the saliency of class issues in politics. It is clearly to the advantage of the parties of the left for people to vote consciously in terms of class. Consequently, the Republicans always seek to emphasize non-class issues, such as military defence, foreign policy, corruption, and so forth. [. . .]

The current spirit of 'moderation' in politics seems at first glance to belie the thesis that class factors have become more significant in dis-tinguishing between the supporters of the two parties, but in reality it does not. There are two basic underlying processes which account for the present shift towards the centre on the part of both parties. One, which has been stressed by many political commentators, is the effect of the pro-longed period of prosperity the country has enjoyed and the resultant increase in the entire population's standard of living. It has been argued that the lower-class base to which the Democratic party appeals is de-clining numerically, and therefore the party cannot advocate reform measures if it desires to win. But at least as important as the change in economic conditions is the effect on the ideological 'face' of both parties of being in or out of office. The policies of the 'out' party are largely set by its representatives in the House and Senate. Thus the Democrats in opposition, as at present, are led by conservative or centrist Southerners, while the Republican leadership in Congress veers most sharply to the right when the Democrats hold the presidency.

A Democratic President is invariably to the left of the Democratic congressional leadership, since he is basically elected by the large urban industrial states where trade unions and minority groups constitute the backbone of the party, while the Southerners continue to sway the con-gressional Democratic contingent. Similarly, a Republican President under current conditions must remain to the left of his congressional supporters, since he, too, must be oriented towards carrying or retaining the support of the industrial, urban and, therefore, more liberal sections of the country, while most Republican Congressmen are elected in 'safe' conservative districts. So when the Republicans hold the presidency, they move to the left as compared to their position in opposition, while the Democrats, shifting from presidential incumbency to congressional opposition, move to the right. This shift produces a situation in which the policies of the two parties often appear almost indistinguishable.

# 59 R. M. Titmuss

The Rich

Excerpts from R. M. Titmuss, *Income Distribution and Social Change*, Allen & Unwin, 1962, pp. 50–52, 188–9.

To study the rich and the sources of power in society is not the kind of activity which comes easily to social workers attempting to understand the human condition. Traditionally, they have been concerned with the poor and the consequences of poverty and physical handicap. They have thus tended to take – perhaps were compelled to take – a limited view of what constituted poverty. It was a view circumscribed by the immediate, the obvious and the material; a conception of need shaped by the urgencies of life daily confronting those they were seeking to help. In so far as they looked at relativities and inequalities in society – which they seldom did – they restricted their studies to the day-to-day differences in levels of expenditure on the more obvious or more blatant necessities of life. Daily subsistence was both the yardstick and the objective.

Far-reaching changes affecting the structure and functions of social institutions; general improvements in material standards of living; and the growth of knowledge about the causes and consequences of social ills in the modern community, are now forcing on us the task of re-defining poverty. Subsistence is no longer thought to be a scientifically mean-ingful or politically constructive notion. We are thus having to place the concept of poverty in the context of social change and interpret it in relation to the growth of more complex and specialized institutions of power, authority and privilege. We cannot, in other words, delineate the new frontiers of poverty unless we take account of the changing agents and characteristics of inequality. How then is poverty to be measured today and on what criteria, secular, social and psychological?

Each generation has to undertake anew this task of re-interpretation if it wishes to uphold its claim to share in the constant renewal of civilized values. Yet the present generation, it must be conceded, has been some-what tardy in accepting this obligation. It has been too content to use the tools which were forged in the past for measuring poverty and in-equality.

These tools are now too blunt, insensitive and inadequate. They do not go deep enough. These also are the lessons thrown up by this particular study of one of the primary sources of knowledge about the distribution of incomes. They yield a surface view of society which is increasingly at variance with other facts and with the evidence of one's eyes.

What, it may be asked, has prevented us from sharpening these tools of inquiry and applying them with more precision to contemporary Britain? Three by no means inclusive reasons may be provocatively advanced.

First it may be said that modern societies with a strongly rooted and relatively rigid class structure do not take kindly to self-examination. The major stimulus to social inquest in Britain during the present century has come from the experience of war. On each occasion this experience was sufficiently mortifying to weaken temporarily the forces of inertia and resistance to change. In the absence of such stimuli in the future, we may have quite consciously to invent and nourish new ways and means of national self-examination. This task may be harder to discharge in the face of rising standards of living and the growing influence of the mass media of complacency. Perhaps the most powerful challenge of all will come from the notion that economic growth will solve all our social problems involving choice, distribution and priorities.

Secondly, it becomes clearer as we learn to distinguish between the promise of social legislation and its performance that the present generation has been mesmerized by the language of 'The Welfare State'. It was assumed too readily after 1948 that all the answers had been found to the problems of health, education, social welfare and housing, and that what was little more than an administrative tidying-up of social security provisions represented a social revolution. The origins and strength of this climate of opinion – some illustrations of which are given later – will no doubt continue to puzzle historians for a long time to come.

Thirdly, and concomitantly, the 1950s saw the spread of the idea that some natural built-in 'law' was steadily leading to a greater equality of incomes and standards of living. It followed implicitly from this theory that further economic growth would hasten the operation of the natural law of equalization. This was not a new thesis; Marshall had stated it hopefully over seventy years ago: 'the social and economic forces already at work are changing the distribution of (income) for the better; ... they are persistent and increasing in strength; and ... their influence is for the greater part cumulative'. [. . .]

Some investigators of income distribution have projected their conclusions into the future by suggesting that in the economic expansion of 1938–57 there was, on the basis of evidence derived from the Board of Inland Revenue data, some sort of permanent and built-in bias towards greater equality of incomes. It should, however be pointed out that there is now little scope for the further employment of wives and mothers (probably none at all if the trend of fertility in recent years continues its upward path); nor can we repeat all over again a reduction in unemployment of two to three millions; nor the remarkable reductions in differential mortality under the age of 60 since 1938.

The phenomenal rise since 1938 in the amount of marriage and in the number of earlier marriages is one of the major factors in producing a statistical illusion of greater income equality. It is, nevertheless, a cause for surprise that the full significance of one of the most remarkable social changes of recent decades has been virtually ignored by practically all those who have commented on the income distribution statistics. Large numbers of girls and young women, formerly appearing as low value income units, disappeared completely from the statistics. Many reappeared later to inflate for a time the value of the units for married couples. But here again there are limits – which we are now rapidly approaching – to any further increase in the amount of marriage over the age of twenty-one. Even the trend from single residential domestics in the 1930s to married non-residential charwomen in the 1950s can help in this process of statistical deception. But it cannot continue to help indefinitely.

We may now consider some of the possible effects of these factors specifically in relation to the top 1 to 5 per cent of incomes in 1938 and 1955–8. It is likely that these groups contained in the latter years, absolutely and relatively:

1. More single income units represented by more elderly and wealthy widows due to the lengthening expectation of life among social class I women (of all estates exceeding £50,000 in net capital value in Great Britain in 1958–9 33 per cent were left by women). These units, though high in value, would not be as high as the units which would have been included if the husbands had survived and had not split both capital and income before death among their families.

2. More single income units represented by more divorced men and women in social class I relative to divorce rates in social classes IV–V.

3. Proportionately fewer employed married women relative to the increase in the employment of wives and men in income ranges below £1000.

4. More wives with 'professional earnings and profits' (and possibly separately assessed) relative to 1938 and relative to lower income ranges. The sample census of 1954–5 threw up some remarkable figures in this connexion. Of 43,500 married couple units in the income range £5000 and

over, 41 per cent of the wives (of all ages) had professional earnings and profits. In the income range £2500–£4999 the proportion was 44 per cent for 128,000 units. For all married couple units above the exemption limit (11, 923,000 including those in the ranges £2500 and over) the proportion was only 10 per cent.

5. More units reduced in value as a result of the operation of irrevocable settlements, discretionary trusts, family and educational trusts and gifts *inter vivos* in favour of children, grandchildren and other kin or 'life tenants' by parents, grandparents and other relatives by blood and marriage. These processes are also likely to create among child and other beneficiaries below the surtax level more single income units. The splitting and spreading of top incomes over time and on a kinship basis probably causes more bunching of incomes in the distribution as a whole. The object of giving as much income as possible to each member without attracting higher rates of tax is likely to have this effect. Consequently, some units will be raised from lower ranges: others will be newly created; for example, more children and young people, previously nil income-receivers or whose small incomes were aggregated for statistical purposes with parental incomes, appear as middle-range income units in their own right. Some evidence in support of this thesis is to be found in the study of 'The distribution of personal wealth in Britain' by Lydall and Tipping (*Oxf. Instit. stat. Bull.*, vol. 23, 1961). One of their significant conclusions, in analysing estate duty returns for 1951–6, was that the greatest degree of concentration of wealth is to be found amongst the youngest adults (age 20–24). While the average net capital held by those with more than £2000 varied from nearly £16,000 per person for those aged 20–24 to less than £10,000 per person for those in the age groups 45–74 (and about £11,000 for the 75s and over), the average for all holdings ranged from £330 per person in the group 20–24 to £2310 for the 75s and over. The evidence in later chapters suggests that this deliberate redistribution within families of larger fortunes has markedly increased since 1938.

6. More units reduced in value as a result of deliberate reductions of high salaries to spread income into retirement and pay less tax over the life span as a whole.

7. More units reduced in value so as to acquire the right to tax-free lump sums of up to £40,000 or more on actual or nominal retirement.

8. More units reduced in value as a result of higher expense accounts compensating for lower salaries, fees and earnings.

9. More units reduced in value as a result of some part of fees, salaries and earnings being translated into or exchanged for income in kind (not

taxable or taxable at lower values) for the earner, his wife and/or children and other relatives.

10. More units reduced in value as a result of lower fees, salaries and earnings being compensated with bonus shares carrying tax-free capital gains and tax-free gains on retirement.

11. More units reduced in value as a result of compensation for real or contrived severance of employment thus transforming income into capital.

Again, this list by no means exhausts the subject of the ways in which current income may be split or spread or transformed into capital for oneself or for others.

# 60 H. Pelling

The Organization of the Working Class

Excerpt from H. Pelling, *A History of British Trade Unionism*, Penguin Books, 1963, pp. 89–92.

The years from the 1880s to the 1920s, which are now to be considered, form a much shorter period than that which we have surveyed in the preceding four chapters [not included here]. But they saw a great growth of unionism, as well as many changes in its character which remain important today. They must therefore be examined in some detail.

It is true that the rate of growth of industrial production was already slowing down in the last quarter of the nineteenth century, the years of the so-called 'Great Depression'. There was a rapid growth of competition in international trade, owing to the industrialization of the United States, Germany and other countries, and British manufacturers were faced with declining profits and the need to search for fresh markets. But although agriculture suffered a real decline in these years, industry as a whole was able to find new outlets for its products, often in the remoter parts of the world that were now for the first time being colonized or developed. The early part of the twentieth century was a period of fair prosperity and expansion for British industry, although in the development of new inventions and processes it was clear that other countries were often in the lead. It was only after the First World War, in the 1920s, that the staple export trades of coal and cotton fell into continuous difficulty, and serious unemployment became a constant feature of the economy.

It is in these years of the late nineteenth and early twentieth centuries that we can most safely speak of a comparatively homogeneous 'working class', as indeed contemporaries were now willing to do. This was to some extent a result of the further growth of the factory system, which now tended to reduce the differential of skill and to demand large numbers of semi-skilled workers, employed in factories by the hundred or thousand. Developments in the mining industry – the sinking of deeper shafts and the increase in the size of pits – moved in the same direction; and this was the period of the dominance of the miners' unions in the counsels of the TUC and its Parliamentary Committee. In part, the growth of working-class cohesion was due to the effect of better transport facilities and to the constant expansion of the cities and towns by migration from the countryside. In part also it owed something to the gradual improvement in living standards, especially in those of the unskilled labourer, who benefited in the years of the 'Great Depression' from the declining price in foodstuffs if not from money-wage increases. State education, introduced in 1870 and made free in 1891, gradually assured a general minimum of literacy and gave the children of all manual workers a common background of early experience and training which was not shared by the children of the middle class. The Reform Acts made all alike conscious of their political opportunities, and encouraged some of the politicians to look with more favour on the extension of unionism to the unskilled. The result was, from the 1880s, the permanent establishment for the first time of unions of unskilled workers, which in due course rose to equal and to surpass in size the societies of the artisans.

But while the working class was becoming more homogeneous, in many ways the social distance between its better-off elements, on the one hand, and the middle class, on the other, grew wider than before. The divisive effect of the system of education was one factor; another was the growth in the scale of industry and commerce in many of its departments. More and more family firms were converted into limited-liability companies, in which the old personal contact between employer and worker was lost. So too, as cities and towns grew in size and as local train and tram services improved, there developed an increasing separation of the classes by residential area: those who could afford the housing costs and the fares moved to 'select' suburbs, where they were out of sight of industry and manual workers alike. To an increasing degree, their knowledge of working-class conditions, if they had any, was derived at second hand from the reports of social investigators.

In spite of the formal legalization of unions in the 1870s, therefore, the union leaders found that they had to wage constant struggles in order to retain their place in a society which regarded their exclusion from all places of responsibility as natural and inevitable. Although there were always exceptions, in general the political parties, the civil service and the legal profession could not as yet understand working-class aspirations or recognize that trade unions demanded more than the mere right to exist – that they sought to play a major role in the country's future. Even if it had not been for the existence of a new generation of union leaders influenced by Socialism and impatient with the old political parties, the hostility of the law to trade-union claims might well have impelled the unions to form a political party of their own. As it was, the Labour Party represented a powerful combination of social forces which, after it had come into existence, could not be prevented from gradually causing the disintegration of the existing structure of Parliamentary politics. In the meantime, while this process was taking place, the unions showed their growing strength in ever larger and more extensive strike action, on several occasions in the new century threatening a virtual disruption of the economic life of the country.

The First World War showed even more clearly the reality of the unions' industrial power; temporarily, it won their leaders some of the national recognition that they had long been claiming. It also caused an immense extension of the machinery of government, which required the close co-operation of the unions to ensure smooth working. But the end of the war brought a rapid dismantling of this machinery, and the reversion of the unions and their political arm to a role of opposition and hostility to the government of the day. The short-lived Labour Government of 1924, heavily defeated at a general election after only a few months, could hardly do anything to ease the general sense of frustration in the union ranks. The industrial power of the unions, increasingly easy to mobilize but unharnessed to constructive purposes, was bound to come into conflict with the State. The result was the General Strike of 1926 – which showed once and for all that the only alternative to social revolution lay in a more effective partnership between the unions and the Government, whatever its political complexion.

# 61 Max Weber on Class and Status

## (a) Max Weber

## Social Status

Excerpt from Max Weber, *The Theory of Social and Economic Organizations*, translated by A. M. Henderson and Talcott Parsons, revised and edited by Talcott Parsons, Oxford University Press, Inc., 1947. Reprinted in Hans H. Gerth and C. Wright Mills (eds.), *From Max Weber: Essays in Sociology*, Routledge & Kegan Paul, 1948, p. 428. First published in German in 1922.

The term of 'social status' will be applied to a typically effective claim to positive or negative privilege with respect to social prestige so far as it rests on one or more of the following bases: (a) mode of living, (b) a formal process of education which may consist in empirical or rational training and the acquisition of the corresponding modes of life, or (c) on the prestige of birth, or of an occupation.

The primary practical manifestations of status with respect to social stratification are connubium, commensality and often monopolistic appropriation of privileged economic opportunities and also prohibition of certain modes of acquisition. Finally, there are conventions or traditions of other types attached to a social status.

Stratificatory status may be based on class status directly or related to it in complex ways. It is not, however, determined by this alone. Property and managerial positions are not as such sufficient to lend their holder a certain social status, though they may well lead to its acquisition. Similarly, poverty is not as such a disqualification for high social status though again it may influence it.

Conversely, social status may partly or even wholly determine class status, without, however, being identical with it. The class status of an officer, a civil servant and a student as determined by their income may be widely different while their social status remains the same, because they adhere to the same mode of life in all relevant respects as a result of their common education.

## (b) Max Weber

## Class and Market Situation

Excerpts from Max Weber, 'Class, status, party', published posthumously in
Hans H. Gerth and C. Wright Mills (eds.), *From Max Weber: Essays in Sociology*,
Routledge & Kegan Paul, 1948, pp. 181–94. First published in 1922–3.

In our terminology, 'classes' are not communities; they merely represent possible, and frequent, bases for communal action. We may speak of a 'class' when (a) a number of people have in common a specific causal component of their life chances, in so far as (b) this component is represented exclusively by economic interests in the possession of goods and opportunities for income, and (c) is represented under the conditions of the commodity or labour markets. (These points refer to 'class situation', which we may express more briefly as the typical chance for a supply of goods, external living conditions and personal life experiences, in so far as this chance is determined by the amount and kind of power, or lack of such, to dispose of goods or skills for the sake of income in a given economic order. The term 'class' refers to any group of people that is found in the same class situation.)

It is the most elemental economic fact that the way in which the disposition over material property is distributed among a plurality of people, meeting competitively in the market for the purpose of exchange, in itself creates specific life chances. According to the law of marginal utility this mode of distribution excludes the non-owners from competing for highly valued goods; it favours the owners and, in fact, gives to them a monopoly to acquire such goods. Other things being equal, this mode of distribution monopolizes the opportunities for profitable deals for all those who, provided with goods, do not necessarily have to exchange them. It increases, at least generally, their power in price wars with those who, being property-less, have nothing to offer but their services in native form or goods in a form constituted through their own labour, and who above all are compelled to get rid of these products in order barely to subsist. This mode of distribution gives to the propertied a monopoly on the possibility of transferring property from the sphere of use as a 'fortune', to the sphere of 'capital goods'; that is, it gives them the entrepreneurial function and all chances to share directly or indirectly in returns on capital. All this holds true within the area in which pure market conditions prevail. 'Property' and 'lack of property' are, therefore, the basic categories of all class situations. It does not matter whether these two categories become effective in price wars or in competitive struggles.

Within these categories, however, class situations are further differentiated: on the one hand, according to the kind of property that is usable for returns; and, on the other hand, according to the kind of services that can be offered in the market. Ownership of domestic buildings; productive establishments; warehouses; stores; agriculturally usable land, large and small holdings – quantitative differences with possibly qualitative consequences – ; ownership of mines; cattle; men (slaves); disposition over mobile instruments of production, or capital goods of all sorts, especially money or objects that can be exchanged for money easily and at any time; disposition over products of one's own labour or of others' labour differing according to their various distances from consumability; disposition over transferable monopolies of any kind – all these distinctions differentiate the class situations of the propertied just as does the 'meaning' which they can and do give to the utilization of property, especially to property which has money equivalence. Accordingly, the propertied, for instance, may belong to the class of rentiers or to the class of entrepreneurs.

Those who have no property but who offer services are differentiated just as much according to their kinds of services as according to the way in which they make use of these services, in a continuous or discontinuous relation to a recipient. But always this is the generic connotation of the concept of class: that the kind of chance in the *market* is the decisive moment which presents a common condition for the individual's fate. 'Class situation' is, in this sense, ultimately 'market situation'. The effect of naked possession *per se*, which among cattle breeders gives the non-owning slave or serf into the power of the cattle owner, is only a forerunner of real 'class' formation. However, in the cattle loan and in the naked severity of the law of debts in such communities, for the first time mere 'possession' as such emerges as decisive for the fate of the individual. This is very much in contrast to the agricultural communities based on labour. The creditor–debtor relation becomes the basis of 'class situations' only in those cities where a 'credit market', however primitive, with rates of interest increasing according to the extent of dearth and a factual monopolization of credits, is developed by a plutocracy. Therewith 'class struggles' begin.

Those men whose fate is not determined by the chance of using goods or services for themselves on the market, e.g. slaves, are not, however, a 'class' in the technical sense of the term. They are, rather, a 'status group'. [. . .]

Every class may be the carrier of any one of the possibly innumerable forms of 'class action', but this is not necessarily so. In any case, a class does not in itself constitute a community. To treat 'class' conceptually as having the same value as 'community' leads to distortion. That men in the same class situation regularly react in mass actions to such tangible situations as economic ones in the direction of those interests that are most adequate to their average number is an important and after all simple fact for the understanding of historical events. Above all, this fact must not lead to that kind of pseudoscientific operation with the concepts of 'class' and 'class interests' so frequently found these days, and which has found its most classic expression in the statement of a talented author, that the individual may be in error concerning his interests but that the 'class' is 'infallible' about its interests. Yet, if classes as such are not communities, nevertheless class situations emerge only on the basis of communalization. The communal action that brings forth class situations, however, is not basically action between members of the identical class; it is an action between members of different classes. Communal actions that directly determine the class situation of the worker and the entrepreneur are: the labour market, the commodities market and the capitalistic enterprise. But, in its turn, the existence of a capitalistic enterprise presupposes that a very specific communal action exists and that it is specifically structured to protect the possession of goods *per se*, and especially the power of the individuals to dispose, in principle freely, over the means of production. The existence of a capitalistic enterprise is preconditioned by a specific kind of 'legal order'. Each kind of class situation, and above all when it rests upon the power of property *per se*, will become most clearly efficacious when all other determinants of reciprocal relations are, as far as possible, eliminated in their significance. It is in this way that the utilization of the power of property in the market obtains its most sovereign importance. [. . .]

In contrast to classes, *status groups* are normally communities. They are, however, often of an amorphous kind. In contrast to the purely economically determined 'class situation' we wish to designate as 'status situation' every typical component of the life fate of men that is determined by a specific, positive or negative, social estimation of *honour*. This honour may be connected with any quality shared by a plurality and, of course, it can be knit to a class situation: class distinctions are linked in the most varied ways with status distinctions. Property as such is not always recognized as a status qualification, but in the long run it is, and with extraordinary regularity. In the subsistence economy of the organized neighbourhood, very often the richest man is simply the chieftain. However, this often means only an honorific preference. For example, in the so-called pure modern 'democracy', that is, one devoid of any expressly ordered status privileges for individuals, it may be that only the families coming under approximately the same tax class dance with one another. This example is reported of certain smaller Swiss cities. But status honour need not necessarily be linked with a 'class situation'. On the contrary, it normally stands in sharp opposition to the pretensions of sheer property.

Both propertied and property-less people can belong to the same status group, and frequently they do with very tangible consequences. This 'equality' of social esteem may, however, in the long run become quite precarious. The 'equality' of status among the American 'gentlemen', for instance, is expressed by the fact that outside the subordination determined by the different functions of 'business', it would be considered strictly repugnant – wherever the old tradition still prevails – if even the richest 'chief', while playing billiards or cards in his club in the evening, would not treat his 'clerk' as in every sense fully his equal in birthright. It would be repugnant if the American 'chief' would bestow upon his 'clerk' the condescending 'benevolence' marking a distinction of 'position', which the German chief can never dissever from his attitude. This is one of the most important reasons why in America the German 'clubby-ness' has never been able to attain the attraction that the American clubs have.

In content, status honour is normally expressed by the fact that above all else a specific *style of life* can be expected from all those who wish to belong to the circle. Linked with this expectation are restrictions on 'social' intercourse (that is, intercourse which is not subservient to economic or any other of business's 'functional' purposes). These restrictions may confine normal marriages to within the status circle and may lead to complete endogamous closure. As soon as there is not a mere individual and socially irrelevant imitation of another style of life, but an agreed-upon communal action of this closing character, the 'status' development is under way.

In its characteristic form, stratification by 'status groups' on the basis of conventional styles of life evolves at the present time in the United States out of the traditional democracy. [. . .]

With some over-simplification, one might say that 'classes' are stratified according to their relations to the production and acquisition of goods; whereas 'status groups' are stratified according to the principles of their *consumption* of goods as represented by special 'styles of life'.

An 'occupational group' is also a status group. For normally, it successfully claims social honour only by virtue of the special style of life which may be determined by it. The differences between classes and status groups frequently overlap. It is precisely those status communities most strictly segregated in terms of honour (viz. the Indian castes) who today show, although within very rigid limits, a relatively high degree of indifference to pecuniary income. However, the Brahmins seek such income in many different ways.

As to the general economic conditions making for the predominance of stratification by 'status', only very little can be said. When the bases of the acquisition and distribution of goods are relatively stable stratification by status is favoured. Every technological repercussion and economic transformation threatens stratification by status and pushes the class situation into the foreground. Epochs and countries in which the naked class situation is of predominant significance are regularly the periods of technical and economic transformations. And every slowing down of the shifting of economic stratifications leads, in due course, to the growth of status structures and makes for a resuscitation of the important role of social honour.

# 62 Theodore Caplow

The Measurement of Occupational Status

Excerpts from Theodore Caplow, *The Sociology of Work*, University of Minnesota Press, 1954, pp. 30–31, 42–8.

Occupational position is an important factor in the determination of individual prestige and in the allocation of social privileges. There appears to be a consistent tendency for occupational identification to displace such other status-fixing attributes as ancestry, religious office, political affiliation and personal character. Each of the three general trends which can be discerned in modern industrial society (aggregation, differentiation, rationalization) seems to lead toward increasing emphasis on the importance of the occupational label.

One of the consequences of *aggregation* is the substitution of formal organizations for informal groupings and the substitution of regulatory mechanisms for the voluntary coordination of human activities. The village type of community, in which most human history has been enacted, identifies individuals in terms of their total life histories, which in turn form part of larger family histories. In the village community, status is always hereditary to some extent, and all the segments of an individual's personality enter into the definition of his role. The metropolitan community is driven by its own complexity to associate each status with a particular economic function. The urban dweller tends to define his own relationship to his fellows in functional terms, since other means of identification with the community are attenuated. Then, too, the separation of home from workplace and the necessity for casual interaction with many unrelated people require various shorthand methods for recognizing others, of which occupational designations are the most convenient, after sex, age and race.

The large working unit presents a parallel situation, also characterized by anonymity and impersonality. Thus bureaucratic structures come to rely more and more upon formal position. The uniform, not the man, is saluted; duties are ascribed to the office rather than the officeholder, and people are designated by position rather than by name.

*Differentiation* narrows the scope of the individual's activity and introduces complexities into the social order which are hidden from the view of all but the specialists concerned. The requirements of each occupation, the importance or responsibility of its functions, and the evaluation of performance come to be more and more esoteric. The layman cannot judge the competence of a physician or of a coremaker, and is therefore forced to respond primarily to an occupational label rather than to a set of individual characteristics.

Both *aggregation* and *differentiation* destroy the continuity of the individual's life history, as seen by his fellows. The shift from a status system based upon family background and personal history to one based upon occupational function is inevitable. Private histories evaporate in the mobile and impersonal urban environment.

Moreover, as *rationalization* proceeds and the assignment of occupational functions becomes 'scientific', 'appropriate' and 'efficient', it comes to be assumed that the occupational label is a fair index of intelligence, ability, character and personal acceptability. The modern reliance upon occupation as the measure of a man takes for granted the existence of high correlations between occupational position and all other attributes. That these correlations are probably exaggerated is beside the point; the general belief in their existence is a pervasive element in social interaction. [...]

### Socio-economic scales

The Centers scale, the Beckman classification and the census classification itself when used as a status scale are based on a number of widely held assumptions. These are roughly defined, but extremely important. Among the assumptions are these:

1. White-collar work is superior to manual work.
2. Self-employment is superior to employment by others.
3. Clean occupations are superior to dirty ones.
4. The importance of business occupations depends upon the size of the business, but this is not true of agricultural occupations.
5. Personal service is degrading, and it is better to be employed by an enterprise than be to employed in the same work by a person. [...]

The urban blue-collar occupations include two conspicuous groups: machine operators in factories and artisans in the conventional trades. Union activity in the United States has been centred in these two groups. Each of them presents certain characteristic problems to the scalemaker.

The income of artisans is highly variable over the business cycle. At the depth of the Depression, it seldom exceeded the going minimum factory wage and the distinction between artisans and factory hands tended to blur out. Throughout the decade of the 1940s, it compared favorably both in amount and in stability with the income of the lower professional groups, and exceeded on the average the income of minor proprietors. With this increase in income level came a corresponding increase in prestige and respectability. This was something more than a reflection of disposable wages. To the extent that craft organizations were able to control recruiting and to maintain a partial monopoly of the trade, journeymen were in effect proprietors, disposing of rights and privileges readily convertible into money. Moreover, the organization of the building trades is such that there is no clear distinction between proprietors and workers. In many places, a subcontractor must, by custom or regulation, be a qualified artisan, and in many private employments foremen are selected from the crew of artisans and maintain their union status. A substantial number of small-home builders, for example, are carpenters, or journeymen of other building trades, who are permanently identified with their craft, but whose general social position reflects a high level of economic well-being and local influence.

Factory machine operators are, on the whole, the most homogeneous of the large occupational groups. With the increasing bureaucratization of the factory, there come to be a considerable number of skilled jobs which are specific to a given industry, to a given plant, or even to a given operation, and which cannot be casually classed as semiskilled without doing violence to the facts. Many of them, in inspection and quality control, for example, are literally white-collar jobs, without clerical function. The average tenure of employment in factory jobs is very short, and probably only a minority of all semiskilled industrial employees are identified with an occupation in the same sense that craftsmen or professionals are so connected. In certain industries a large proportion of all factory employees are in the marginal categories of the labor force: married women, adolescents, farmers. Since factory income is in these cases a supplementary income, classification in the semiskilled group will not correctly reflect the position of these workers in the community. [. . .]

It would seem that the relative rank of manual occupations is fixed by the usual complex of factors: pecuniary value, potential upward mobility, functional status, responsibility, ascribed intelligence level and historical connotations. Admittedly, the outcome of this calculation is generally less favorable to the manual occupations than to those which involve only the manipulation of symbols. Admittedly, too, social class factors, the remnants of the ideology of the landowning aristocracy, and the conditions of industrial employment, all contribute to attach a certain negative weight to work done in overalls. The fact remains that the white-collar occupations enjoy no general and categorical superiority over the blue-collar occupations with respect to any important social index, and that blue-collar occupations can easily be sorted by skill. [. . .]

## Importance of size of business

The statement that the rank of business occupations depends upon the size of the business embodies a half-truth which is particularly difficult to revise into a whole truth. The size of an enterprise always has some influence on the roles of its members. This is sometimes positive and sometimes negative. Department stores are appropriately graded in order of size, but country clubs are not. The largest wheat farm and the smallest have many things in common, but owning one is not the same thing as owning the other. Any change in organizational size is likely to be accompanied by a fairly complex series of consequences, whose nature depends more upon the specific situation than upon any general principles.

We do not have adequate statistics on the origin or even on the distribution of high incomes, but it would appear that most very high incomes are derived from small enterprises, where the owner's or manager's share is not limited by bureaucratic considerations. It would also seem that the authority of a supervisor over a given number of employees is likely to bring more recognition in a relatively small company than in a very large one. On the other hand, identification with certain organizations confers advantages automatically. In communities dominated by a single company or group of companies, mere employment by them may constitute membership in a favored class.

When we add to these somewhat contradictory considerations the fact that the distribution of functions within large and small organizations is often entirely different (who corresponds to the editor of a country weekly on the staff of a metropolitan daily?), it is quite obvious that no summary generalization will cover the matter. Perhaps the most useful statement is that very small organizations (school systems or smelters will do equally well for examples) usually lack of prestige, that large organizations always enjoy some prestige, but that the proudest group is likely to be middle-sized. Needless to say, this is not an easy state of affairs to scale.

# 63 T. B. Bottomore

Élites and Society

Excerpts from T. B. Bottomore, *Élites and Society*, Basic Books and Watts, 1964, pp. 6–7, 105–7.

The conceptual scheme which Mosca and Pareto have handed down comprises the following common notions: in every society there is, and must be, a minority which rules over the rest of society; this minority – the 'political class' or 'governing élite', composed of those who occupy the posts of political command and, more vaguely, those who can directly influence political decisions – undergoes changes in its membership over a period of time, ordinarily by the recruitment of new individual members from the lower strata of society, sometimes by the incorporation of new social groups, and occasionally by the complete replacement of the established élite by a 'counter-élite', as occurs in revolutions. This phenomenon, the 'circulation of élites', will be examined more fully in a later chapter [not included here]. From this point, the conceptions of Pareto and Mosca diverge. Pareto insists more strongly upon the separation between rulers and ruled in every society, and dismisses the view that a democratic political system differs from any other in this respect. He explains the circulation of élites in mainly psychological terms, making use of the idea of residues (sentiments) which he has set out at great length in the earlier parts of *The Mind and Society*. Mosca, on the other hand, is much more aware of the heterogeneity of the élite, the higher stratum of the political class, itself; of the interests of social forces which are represented in it; and, in the case of modern societies, of its intimate bonds with the rest of society, principally through the lower stratum of the political class, the 'new middle class'. Thus Mosca also allows that there is a difference between modern democracies and other types of polity, and to some extent he recognizes that there is interaction between the ruling minority and the majority, instead of a simple dominance by the former over the latter. Finally, Mosca explains the circulation of élites sociologically as well as psychologically, in so far as he accounts for the rise of new élites (or of new elements in the élites) in part by the emergence of social forces which represent new interests (e.g. technological or economic interests) in the society. [. . .]

The criticism of democratic theories of politics which Mosca and Pareto formulated in the theory of élites began with the observation that in every society there is a minority which effectively rules. This criticism could be met – as Mosca himself saw – while acknowledging the fact that a governing élite is necessary in every society, by arguing that the distinctive feature of democracy, as a form of government, is that it permits élites to form freely and establishes a regulated competition between élites for the positions of power. This conception of democracy as a political system in which political parties compete for the votes of a mass electorate, implies further that the élites are relatively 'open' and are recruited on the basis of merit (i.e. there is presumed to be a continuous and extensive circulation of élites), and that the mass of the population is able to participate in ruling society at least in the sense that it can exercise a choice between the rival élites. [. . .]

The reconciliation between the idea of élites and the idea of democratic government has proceeded apace during the twentieth century, as Mannheim's own work bears witness, and it has been assisted by a number of favourable circumstances. One of these is the general enhancement of the importance of leadership which has resulted from large-scale warfare, from international rivalry in economic growth and from the rise and development of new nations; all of which has turned men's thoughts away from the dangers of élite rule towards the need for efficient and enterprising élites. Another circumstance which has lent support to the competition model of democracy is the contrast between the consequences of élite rule in one-party states, and the experiences of those democratic societies in which there is competition for power among several political parties, none of which aims to bring about a radical change in the social structure. Furthermore, this model has also a scientific appeal, by reason of the analogy which it presents to the model of economic behaviour in a free enterprise system, and of the promise which it thus holds out of an analysis of political behaviour as exact and rigorous, if also as limited, as economic analysis. The analogy was stated plainly by Schumpeter who also went on to argue, more generally, that modern democracy arose with the capitalist economic system and is causally connected with it. The view is conveyed succinctly in the remark made by a successful politician, which Schumpeter quotes: 'What businessmen do not understand is that exactly as they are dealing in oil so I am dealing in votes.' More recently, this conception of democracy as a competition for votes between political parties has been presented in more elaborate forms, as for example in the 'economic theory of democracy' of A. Downs, who summarizes his theory in the following terms: 'Our main thesis is that parties in democratic politics are analogous to entrepreneurs in a profit-seeking economy. So as to attain their private ends, they formulate whatever policies they believe will gain the most votes, just as entrepreneurs produce whatever products they believe will gain the most profits for the same reasons.' Another example of the use of this model is to be found in the tentative efforts to apply the theory of games to political behaviour, i.e. to apply to the activities of political parties a mathematical scheme which is extensively used in analysing the behaviour of business enterprises.

# Part Nine The Problem of Order

The Readings in this Part present a debate over the sociological worth of the assumption that society is ordered around a 'value consensus', that the regulation of social life stems from a commonly accepted moral order.[1] The work of Talcott Parsons (Reading 64) – whose own efforts to articulate a general theory of society on the basis of just such an assumption are discussed in several of the selections – presents the case for consensus theory by criticizing alternative solutions to the problem of social order. He reveals the difficulties which confront Hobbes in attempting to solve the problem, and outlines Durkheim's arguments against Spencer's theory that social solidarity derives from contractual relationships between the members of society. That social order cannot be explained either on the basis of the pursuit of self-interest by the members of society, or as an outcome of a 'social contract', is taken by Parsons to be sufficient warrant for assuming that it is moral concensus which binds men together in society.

Parsons's substantive analyses of social order are too complex to permit condensation; the way in which consensus theory may be used to analyse social life is, therefore, illustrated in Edward Shils's brilliant and lucid discussion of the social 'location' of dominant values (Reading 65) Although Shils's arguments differ from those of Parsons they are fairly typical of those advanced by consensus theorists.

Both David Lockwood (Reading 66) and John Rex (Reading 67) take issue with Parsonian perspectives: Lockwood, in his examination of one of Parsons's major works, *The Social System*, attempts to show how elements derived from the Marxian tradition of social theory – in particular, the notion of interests – can lead us to a deeper understanding of social life than may be obtained from consensus theory, whilst Rex outlines the structure of a conflict theory of society which is intended as a direct alternative to the Parsonian scheme. Neither author argues for a total neglect of common values but each suggests that the significance of values is considerably less than Parsons is prepared to admit and, per-

[1] For a definition and discussion of value consensus, see the comparison volume *Introducing Sociology*, ch. 8 (ed. P. Worsley, Penguin Books, 1970).

haps, far less important in accounting for social order than is power.

These criticisms of Parsons's views were developed at a time when he had written scarcely a word on the topic of power, but during the latest phase of his work, throughout the last decade, Parsons has made power a central issue in his work. Anthony Giddens (Reading 68) examines these recent developments in Parsonian thought and concludes that although they do make an important contribution, they are still open to the kind of criticisms made by Rex and Lockwood.

We turn next to a specific problem – that of deviance. Robert K. Merton's anomie theory of deviance remains the most complete and successful attempt to account for deviant behaviour from within consensus theory; we include here one of its earliest and most succinct formulations (Reading 69). The critics of Merton's position have developed their objections within a very different tradition of thought from that which inspires Lockwood and Rex; they do not object to an emphasis upon values but they oppose the interpretation which consensus theorists often give of the relationship between values and social order. Consensus theorists, as Turner (Reading 70) argues in general terms, and as Lemert (Reading 71) argues in relation to Merton's theory, assume that the identification of a moral order is sufficient to account for social order and thus fail to examine the way in which this moral order is created and sustained in interpersonal interactions; further, consensus theorists tend to treat the moral order as precise and clear when, in fact, it is more commonly ambiguous, uncertain and unspecified.

# 64 Talcott Parsons

## (a) Hobbes and the Problem of Order

Excerpt from Talcott Parsons, *The Structure of Social Action*, Free Press, 1949, pp. 89–94. First Published in 1937.

For present purposes the basis of Hobbes's social thinking lies in his famous concept of the state of nature as the war of all against all. Hobbes is almost entirely devoid of normative thinking. He sets up no ideal of what conduct should be, but merely investigates the ultimate conditions of social life. Man, he says, is guided by a plurality of passions. The good is simply that which any man desires. But unfortunately there are very severe limitations on the extent to which these desires can be realized, limitations which according to Hobbes lie primarily in the nature of the relations of man to man.

Man is not devoid of reason. But reason is essentially a servant of the passions – it is the faculty of devising ways and means to secure what one desires. Desires are random, there is 'no common rule of good and evil to be taken from the nature of the objects themselves'. Hence since the passions, the ultimate ends of action, are diverse there is nothing to prevent their pursuit resulting in conflict.

In Hobbes's thinking, the reason for this danger of conflict is to be found in the part played by power. Since all men are seeking to realize their desires they must necessarily seek command over means to this realization. The power a man has is in Hobbes's own words simply 'his present means to obtain some future apparent good'. One very large element of power is the ability to command the recognition and services of other men. To Hobbes this is the most important among those means which, in the nature of things, are limited. The consequence is that what means to his ends one man commands another is necessarily shut off from. Hence power as a proximate end is inherently a source of division between men.

Nature hath made men so equal in the faculties of body and mind, that though there be found one man sometimes manifestly stronger in body or of quicker mind than another, yet when all is reckoned together the difference between man and man is not so considerable as that one man can thereupon claim to himself any benefit, to which another may not pretend as well as he. ... From this equality of ability ariseth equality of hope in the attaining of our ends. And therefore if any two men desire the same thing which never-theless they cannot both enjoy, they become enemies; and in the way to their end endeavour to destroy or subdue one another.

In the absence of any restraining control men will adopt to this im-mediate end the most efficient available means. These means are found in the last analysis to be force and fraud. Hence a situation where every man is the enemy of every other, endeavouring to destroy or subdue him by force or fraud or both. This is nothing but a state of war.

But such a state is even less in conformity with human desires than what most of us know. It is in Hobbes's famous words a state where the life of man is 'solitary, poor, nasty, brutish and short'. The fear of such a state of things calls into action, as a servant of the most fundamental of all the passions, that of self-preservation, at least a modicum of reason which finds a solution of the difficulty in the social contract. By its terms men agree to give up their natural liberty to a sovereign authority which in turn guarantees them security, that is immunity from aggression by the force or fraud of others. It is only through the authority of this sovereign that the war of all against all is held in check and order and security maintained.

Hobbes's system of social theory is almost a pure case of utilitarian-ism. The basis of human action lies in the 'passions'. These are discrete, randomly variant ends of action: 'There is no common rule of good and evil to be taken from the nature of the objects themselves.' In the pursuit of these ends men act rationally, choosing, within the limitations of the situation, the most efficient means. But this rationality is strictly limited, reason is the 'servant of the passions', it is concerned only with questions of ways and means.

But Hobbes went much farther than merely defining with extra-ordinary precision the basic units of a utilitarian system of action. He went on to deduce the character of the concrete system which would result if its units were in fact as defined. And in so doing he became involved in an empirical problem which has not yet been encountered, as the present discussion so far has been confined to defining units and noting merely their logical relations in utilitarian thought – the problem of *order*. This problem, in the sense in which Hobbes posed it, constitutes the most fundamental empirical difficulty of utilitarian thought. It will form the main thread of the historical discussion of the utilitarian sys-tem and its outcome.

Before taking up his experience with it, two meanings of the term which may easily become confused should be distinguished. They may be called normative order and factual order respectively. The antithesis of the latter is randomness or chance in the strict sense of phenomena conforming to the statistical laws of probability. Factual order, then, connotes essentially accessibility to understanding in terms of logical theory, especially of science. Chance variations are in these terms impossible to understand or to reduce to law. Chance or randomness is the name for that which is incomprehensible, not capable of intelligible analysis.

Normative order, on the other hand, is always relative to a given system of norms or normative elements, whether ends, rules or other norms. Order in this sense means that process takes place in conformity with the paths laid down in the normative system. Two further points should, however, be noted in this connexion. One is that the breakdown of any given normative order, that is a state of chaos from a normative point of view, may well result in an order in the factual sense, that is a state of affairs susceptible to scientific analysis. Thus the 'struggle for existence' is chaotic from the point of view of Christian ethics, but that does not in the least mean that it is not subject to law in the scientific sense, that is to uniformities of process in the phenomena. Secondly, in spite of the logically inherent possibility that any normative order may break down into a 'chaos' under certain conditions, it may still be true that the normative elements are essential to the maintenance of the *particular* factual order which exists when processes are to a degree in conformity with them. Thus a social order is always a factual order in so far as it is susceptible of scientific analysis, but it is one which cannot have stability without the effective functioning of certain normative elements.

As has been shown, two normative features play an essential role in the utilitarian scheme, ends and rationality. Thus, for Hobbes, given the fact that men have passions and seek to pursue them rationally, the problem arises of whether, or under what conditions, this is possible in a social situation when there is a plurality of men acting in relation to one another. Given one other fact, which Hobbes refers to as the 'equality of hope', the problem of order in the normative sense of a degree of an attainability of ends, of satisfaction of the passions, becomes crucial. For under the assumption of rationality men will seek to attain their ends by the most efficient means available. Among their ends is empirically found to be attainment of the recognition of others. And to them under social conditions the services of others are always and necessarily to be found among the potential means to their ends. To securing both of these, recognition and service, whether as ultimate or proximate ends, the most immediately efficient means, in the last analysis, are force and fraud. In the utilitarian postulate of rationality there is nothing whatever to exclude the employment of these means. But the effect of their unlimited employment is that men will 'endeavour to destroy or subdue one another'. That is, according to the strictest utilitarian assumptions, under social conditions, a complete system of action will turn out to be a 'state of war' as Hobbes says, that is, from the normative point of view of the attainment of human ends, which is itself the utilitarian starting point, not an order at all, but chaos. It is the state where any appreciable degree of such attainment becomes impossible, where the life of a man is 'solitary, poor, nasty, brutish and short'.

The point under discussion here is not Hobbes's own solution of this crucial problem, by means of the idea of a social contract. This solution really involves stretching, at a critical point, the conception of rationality beyond its scope in the rest of the theory, to a point where the actors come to realize the situation as a whole instead of pursuing their own ends in terms of their immediate situation, and then take the action necessary to eliminate force and fraud, and purchasing security at the sacrifice of the advantages to be gained by their future employment. This is not the solution in which the present study will be interested. But Hobbes saw the problem with a clarity which has never been surpassed, and his statement of it remains valid today. It is so fundamental that a genuine solution of it has never been attained on a strictly utilitarian basis, but has entailed either recourse to a radical positivistic expedient or breakdown of the whole positivistic framework.

Before leaving Hobbes it is important to elaborate a little further the reasons for the precariousness of order so far as the utilitarian elements actually dominate action. This precariousness rests, in the last analysis, on the existence of classes of things which are scarce, relative to the demand for them, which, as Hobbes says, 'two [or more] men desire' but 'which nevertheless they cannot both enjoy'. Reflection will show that there are many such things desired by men either as ends in themselves or as means to other ends. But Hobbes, with his characteristic penetration, saw that it was not necessary to enumerate and catalogue them and to rest the argument on such a detailed consideration, but that their crucial importance was inherent in the very existence of social relations themselves. For it is inherent in the latter that the actions of men should be potential means to each other's ends. Hence as a proximate end it is a direct corollary of the postulate of rationality that all men should desire and seek power over one another. Thus the concept of power comes to occupy a central position in the analysis of the problem of order. A purely utilitarian society is chaotic and unstable, because in the absence of limitations on the use of means, particularly force and fraud, it must, in the nature of the case, resolve itself into an unlimited struggle for power; and in the struggle for the immediate end, power, all prospect of attainment of the ultimate, of what Hobbes called the diverse passions, is irreparably lost.

If the above analysis is correct one might suppose that Hobbes's early experiments with logical thinking on a utilitarian basis would have brought that type of social thought to a rapid and deserved demise. But such was very far from being the case, indeed in the eighteenth and nineteenth centuries it enjoyed a period of such vogue as to be considered almost among the eternal verities themselves. But this was not because the Hobbesian problem was satisfactorily solved. On the contrary, as so often happens in the history of thought, it was blithely ignored and covered up by implicit assumptions.

## (b) The Non-Contractual Elements in Contract

Excerpts from Talcott Parsons, *The Structure of Social Action*, Free Press, 1949, pp. 311–16. First published in 1937.

Spencer's contractual relation is the type case of a social relationship in which only the elements formulated in 'utilitarian' theory are involved. Its prototype is the economic exchange relationship where the determinant elements are the demand and supply schedules of the parties concerned. At least implicit in the conception of a system of such relationships is the conception that it is the mutual advantage derived by the parties from the various exchanges which constitutes the principal binding, cohesive force in the system. It is as a direct antithesis to this deeply imbedded conception of a system of 'relations of contract' that Durkheim wishes his own 'organic solidarity' to be understood.

The line which Durkheim's criticism takes is that the Spencerian, or more generally utilitarian, formulation fails to exhaust, even for the case of what are the purely 'interested' transactions of the market place, the elements which actually are both to be found in the existing system of such transactions, and which, it can be shown, must exist, if the system is to function at all. What is omitted is the fact that these transactions are actually entered into in accordance with a body of binding rules which are not part of the *ad hoc* agreement of the parties. The elements included in the utilitarian conception are, on the contrary, all taken account of in the terms of agreement. What may, however, be called the 'institution' of contract – the rules regulating relations of contract – has not been agreed to by the parties but exists prior to and independently by any such agreement.

The content of the rules is various. They regulate, in the first place, what contracts are and what are not recognized as valid. A man cannot, for instance, sell himself or others into slavery. They regulate the means by which the other party's assent to a contract may be obtained; an agreement secured by fraud or under duress is void. They regulate various consequences of a contract once made, both to the parties themselves and to third persons. Under certain circumstances a party may be enjoined from enforcing a contract quite legally made, as when the holder of a mortgage is sometimes prohibited from foreclosing when interest payments are not made. Similarly one party may be forced to assume obligations which were not in his contract. They regulate, finally, the procedure by which enforcement in the courts is obtainable. In a society like our own this nexus of regulations is exceedingly complex.

For convenience Durkheim lays the principal stress on the body of rules which are formulated in law and enforceable in the courts. But this must not be allowed to lead to misunderstanding of his position. Even Spencer recognized the necessity for some agency outside the contracting parties themselves to enforce contracts. But on the one hand, Spencer and the other individualistic writers have laid their principal stress on enforcement of the terms of agreements themselves, whereas Durkheim's main stress is on the existence of a body of rules which have not been the object of any agreement among the contracting parties themselves but are socially 'given'. If they wish to enter into relations of contract it is only under the conditions laid down in these rules and with the consequences with reference both to eventual rights and to obligations which they define that they may do so at all. Of course if the rules were not to some degree enforced, they would be unimportant, but it is on their independence of the process of *ad hoc* agreement that Durkheim lays his emphasis. Secondly, while he discusses mainly legal rules, he is careful to point out that these stand by no means alone, but are supplemented by a vast body of customary rules, trade conventions and the like which are, in effect, obligatory equally with the law, although not enforceable in the courts. This shading off of law into trade practice indicates that this body of rules is much more closely integrated with the contractual system itself than the individualists would be ready to grant. The latter tended to think of the role of society in these matters as represented by the state, as one of only occasional intervention to straighten out a difficulty in a machinery which normally functioned quite automatically without 'social' interference.

Why is this body of rules of contract important? In the first place,

Durkheim notes that the possible consequences of the relations entered into by agreement, both to the parties themselves and to others, are so complex and remote that, if they all had to be thought out *ad hoc* and agreed to anew each time, the vast body of transactions which go on would be utterly impossible. As it is, it is necessary only to agree formally to a very small part of these matters; the rest is taken care of by the recognized rules.

But the most important consideration of all is that the elements formulated in the utilitarian theory contain no adequate basis of order. A contractual agreement brings men together only for a limited purpose, for a limited time. There is no adequate motive given why men should pursue even this limited purpose by means which are compatible with the interests of others, even though its attainment as such should be so compatible. There is a latent hostility between men which this theory does not take account of. It is as a framework of order that the institution of contract is of primary importance. Without it men would, as Durkheim explicitly says, be in a state of war. But actual social life is not war. In so far as it involves the pursuit of individual interests it is such interests, pursued in such a manner as greatly to mitigate this latent hostility, to promote mutual advantage and peaceful cooperation rather than mutual hostility and destruction. Spencer and others who think like him have entirely failed to explain how this is accomplished. And in arriving at his own explanation Durkheim first points to an empirical fact: this vast complex of action in the pursuit of individual interests takes place within the framework of a body of rules, independent of the immediate individual motives of the contracting parties. This fact the individualists have either not recognized at all, or have not done justice to. It is the central empirical insight from which Durkheim's theoretical development starts, and which he never lost.

It is clear that what Durkheim has here done is to reraise in a peculiarly trenchant form the whole Hobbesian problem. There are features of the existing 'individualistic' order which cannot be accounted for in terms of the elements formulated in utilitarian theory. The activities that the utilitarians, above all the economists, have in mind can take place only within a framework of order characterized by a system of regulatory rules. Without this framework of order it would degenerate into a state of war. On this fundamental critical ground Durkheim is clear and incisive, and in this respect he never in the least altered his position. Nor did he ever abandon the basic empirical insight just mentioned, the importance of a system of regulatory, normative rules. His difficulties appeared in confronting the problem of how to fit this insight, dependent as it was on his critical position, into a conceptual scheme which would be scientifically satisfactory, yet not share the fallacies of the scheme under-lying the position he had criticized.

The solution to which Hobbes turned was, as has been seen, that of the *deus ex machina*. The sovereign, standing entirely outside the system, forcibly kept order by the threat of sanctions. Even in the most opti-mistic of the individualistic writers short of anarchism there is at least a glimmer of the Hobbesian solution in the place reserved to the state in the enforcement of contracts. It has already been noted that Durkheim's thinking was not tending in these channels. While not inclined to de-preciate the role of the state, neither was he inclined to the radical dual-ism of state versus the nexus of individual interests which characterized the whole utilitarian tradition. The fact that for him the system of rules of contract shaded off from formal law into informal trade practice, while yet maintaining its regulatory character, its independence of im-mediate individual interests, made the rigidity of such a dichotomy im-possible. [...]

In so far as the problem of order in Hobbes's sense was the logical starting point of Durkheim's study, and his approach to it was through a critique of orthodox utilitarian interpretations of a system of relations of contract, it is not difficult to understand how the division of labor and the problem of social differentiation became involved. For, especially to the classical economists, the division of labor is one of the prime features of an individualistic society. Without specialization there would be on a utilitarian basis no society at all, since it is the mutual advantages of exchange which constitute the main motive for abandoning the state of nature and entering into social relationships.

# 65 Edward Shils

Centre and Periphery

Edward Shils, 'Centre and periphery', in *The Logic of Personal Knowledge: Essays Presented to Michael Polanyi*, Routledge & Kegan Paul, 1961, pp. 117–30.

Society has a centre. There is a central zone in the structure of society. This central zone impinges in various ways on those who live within the ecological domain in which the society exists. Membership in the society, in more than the ecological sense of being located in a bounded territory and of adapting to an environment affected or made up by other persons located in the same territory, is constituted by relationship to this central zone.

The central zone is not, *as such*, a spatially located phenomenon. It almost always has a more or less definite location within the bounded territory in which the society lives. Its centrality has, however, nothing to do with geometry and little with geography.

The centre, or the central zone, is a phenomenon of the realm of values and beliefs. It is the centre of the order of symbols, of values and beliefs, which govern the society. It is the centre because it is the ultimate and irreducible; and it is felt to be such by many who cannot give explicit articulation to its irreducibility. The central zone partakes of the nature of the sacred. In this sense, every society has an 'official' religion, even when that society or its exponents and interpreters, conceive of it, more or less correctly, as a secular, pluralistic and tolerant society. The principle of the Counter-Reformation: *Cuius regio, ejus religio*, although its rigor has been loosened and its harshness mollified, retains a core of permanent truth.

The centre is also a phenomenon of the realm of action. It is a structure of activities, of roles and persons, within the network of institutions. It is in these roles that the values and beliefs which are central are embodied and propounded.

The larger society appears, on a cursory inspection and by the methods of inquiry in current use, to consist of a number of interdependent subsystems – the economy, the status system, the polity, the kinship system and the institutions which have in their special custody the cultivation of cultural values, e.g. the university system, the ecclesiastical system, etc. Each of these subsystems itself comprises a network of organization which are connected, with varying degrees of affirmation, through a common authority, overlapping personnel, personal relationships, contracts, perceived identities of interest, a sense of affinity within a transcendent whole and a territorial location possessing symbolic value. (These subsystems and their constituent bodies are not equally affirmative *vis-à-vis* each other. Moreover the degree of affirmation varies through time, and is quite compatible with a certain measure of alienation within each élite and among the élites.)

Each of these organizations has an authority, an élite, which might be either a single individual or a group of individuals, loosely or closely organized. Each of these élites makes decisions, sometimes in consultation with other élites and sometimes, largely on its own initiative, with the intention of maintaining the organization, controlling the conduct of its members and fulfilling its goals. (These decisions are by no means always successful in the achievement of these ends, and the goals are seldom equally or fully shared by the élite and those whose actions are ordained by its decisions.)

The decisions made by the élites contain as major elements certain general standards of judgement and action, and certain concrete values, of which the system as a whole, the society, is one of the most preeminent. The values which are inherent in these standards, and which are espoused and more or less observed by those in authority, we shall call the *central value system* of the society. This central value system is the central zone of the society. It is central because of its intimate connexion with what the society holds to be sacred; it is central because it is espoused by the ruling authorities of the society. These two kinds of centrality are vitally related. Each defines and supports the other.

The central value system is not the whole of the order of values and beliefs espoused and observed in the society. The value systems obtaining in any diversified society may be regarded as being distributed along a range. There are variants of the central value system running from hyperaffirmation of some of the components of the major, central value system to an extreme denial of some of these major elements in the central value system; the latter tends to but is not inevitably associated with, an affirmation of certain elements denied or subordinated in the central value system. There are also elements of the order of values and beliefs which are as random with respect to the central value system as the value and beliefs of human beings can be.

The central value system is constituted by the values which are pursued and affirmed by the élites of the constituent subsystems and of the organizations which are comprised in the subsystems. By their very possession of authority, they attribute to themselves an essential affinity with the sacred elements of their society, of which they regard themselves as the custodians. By the same token, many members of their society attribute to them that same kind of affinity. The élites of the economy affirm and observe certain values which should govern economic activity. The élites of the polity affirm and observe certain values which should govern political activity. The élites of the university system and the ecclesiastical system affirm and practice certain values which should govern intellectual and religious activities (including beliefs). On the whole, these values are the values embedded in current activity. The ideals which they affirm do not far transcend the reality which is ruled by those who espouse them. The values of the different élites are clustered into an approximately consensual pattern.[1]

One of the major elements in any central value system is an affirmative attitude towards established authority. This is present in the central value systems of all societies, however much these might differ from each other in their appreciation of authority. There is something like a 'floor', a minimum of appreciation of authority in every society, however liberal that society might be. Even the most libertarian and equalitarian societies that have ever existed possess at least this minimum appreciation of authority. Authority enjoys appreciation because it arouses sentiments of sacredness. Sacredness by its nature is authoritative. Those persons, offices or symbols endowed with it, however indirectly and remotely, are therewith endowed with some measure of authoritativeness.

The appreciation of authority entails the appreciation of the institutions through which authority works and the rules which it enunciates. The central value system in all societies asserts and recommends the appreciation of these authoritative institutions.

Implicitly, the central value system rotates on a centre more fundamental even than its espousal by and embodiment in authority. Authority is the agent of *order*, an *order* which may be largely embodied in authority or which might transcend authority and regulate it, or at least provide a standard by which existing authority itself is judged and even claims to judge itself. This order, which is implicit in the central value system, and in the light of which the central value system

1. The degree of consensuality differs among societies and times. There are societies in which the predominant élite demands a complete consensus with its own more specific values and beliefs. Such is the case in modern totalitarian societies. Absolutist régimes in past epochs, which were rather indifferent about whether the mass of the population was party to a consensus, were quite insistent on consensus among the élites of their society.

Edward Shils   417

legitimates itself, is endowed with dynamic potentialities. It contains, above all, the potentiality of critical judgement on the central value system and the central institutional system. The dynamic potentiality derives from the inevitable tendency of every concrete society to fall short of the order which is implicit in its central value system.

Closely connected with the appreciation of authority and the institutions in which it is exercised, is an appreciation of the *qualities* which qualify persons for the exercise of authority or which are characteristic of those who exercise authority. These qualities, which we shall call secondary values, can be ethnic, educational, familial, economic, professional; they may be ascribed to individuals by virtue of their relationships or they may be acquired through study and experience. But whatever they are, they enjoy the appreciation of the central value system simply because of their connexion with the exercise of authority. (Despite their ultimately derivative nature, each of them is capable of possessing an autonomous status in the central zone, in the realm of the sacred; consequently, severe conflicts can be engendered.)

The central value system thus comprises secondary as well as primary values. It legitimates the existing distribution of roles and rewards to persons possessing the appropriate qualities which in various ways symbolize degrees of proximity to authority. It legitimates these distributions by praising the properties of those who occupy authoritative roles in the society, by stressing the legitimacy of their incumbency of those roles, and the appropriateness of the rewards they receive. By implication, and explicitly as well, it legitimates the smaller rewards received by those who live at various distances from the circles in which authority is exercised.

The central institutional system may thus be described as the set of institutions which is legitimated by the central value system. Less circularly, however, it may be described as those institutions which, through the radiation of their authority, give some form to the life of a considerable section of the population of the society. The economic, political, ecclesiastical and cultural institutions impinge compellingly at many points on the conduct of much of the population in any society through the actual exercise of authority and the potential exercise of coercion, through the provision of persuasive models of action, and through a partial control of the allocation of rewards. The kinship and family systems, although they have much smaller radii, are microcosms of the central institutional system, and do much to buttress its efficacy.

The existence of a central value system rests, in a fundamental way, on the need which human beings have for incorporation into something which transcends and transfigures their concrete individual existence. They have a need to be in contact with symbols of an order which is larger in its dimensions than their own bodies and more central in the 'ultimate' structure of reality than is their routine everyday life. Just as friendship exists because human beings must transcend their own self-limiting individuality in personal communion with another personality, so membership in a political society is a necessity of man's nature. There is need to belong to a polity just as there is a need for conviviality. Just as a person shrivels, contracts and corrupts when separated from all persons or from those persons who have entered into a formed and vital communion with him, so the man with political needs is crippled and numbed by his isolation from a polity or by his membership in a political order which cannot claim his loyalty.

The need for personal communion is a common quality among human beings who have reached a certain level of individuation. Those who lack the need and the capacity impress us by their incompleteness. The political need is not so widely spread or highly developed in the mass of the population of any society as the need and capacity for conviviality. Those who lack it impress by their 'idiocy'. Those who possess it add the possibility of civility to the capacity for conviviality which we think a fully developed human being must possess.

The political need is of course nurtured by tradition but it cannot be accounted for by the adduction of tradition. The political need is a capacity like certain kinds of imagination, reasoning, perceptiveness or sensitivity. It is neither instinctual nor learned. It is not simply the product of the displacement of personal affects on to public objects, although much political activity is impelled by such displacement. It is not learned by teaching or traditional transmission, though much political activity is guided by the reception of tradition. The pursuit of a political career and the performance of civil obligations gains much from the impulsion of tradition. None the less, tradition is not the seed of this inclination to attach oneself to a political order.

The political need, which may be designated as the need for civility, entails sensitivity to an order of being where 'creative power' has its seat. This creative centre which attracts the minds of those who are sensitive to it is manifested in authority operating over territory. Both authority and territory convey the idea of potency, of 'authorship', of the capacity to do vital things, of a connexion with events which are intrinsically important. Authority is thought, by those with the political or civil need, to possess this vital relationship to the centre from which a right order emanates. Those who are closely and positively connected with authority, through its exercise or through personal ties, are thought, in consequence of this connexion, to possess a vital relationship to the centre, the locus of the sacred, the order which confers legitimacy. Land – 'territoritiality' – has similar properties, and those who exercise authority through control of land have always been felt to enjoy a special status in relation to the core of the central value system. Those who live within given territorial boundaries come to share in these properties and thus become the objects of political sentiments. Residence within certain territorial boundaries, and rule by common authority are the properties which define citizenship and establish its obligations and claims.

It must be stressed that the political need is not by any means equally distributed in any society, even the most democratic. There are human beings whose sensitivity to the ultimate is meagre, although there is perhaps no human being from whom it is entirely absent. Nor does sensitivity to remote events which are expressive of the centre always focus on their manifestations in the polity.

Apolitical scientists who seek the laws of nature but are indifferent, except on grounds of prudence, to the laws of society are one instance of this uneven development of sensitivity to ultimate things. Religious persons who are attached to transcendent symbols without embodiment in civil polity or in ecclesiastical organization represent another variant. In addition to these, there are very many persons whose sensitivity is exhausted long before it reaches so far into the core of the central value system. Some have a need for such contact only in crises and on special periodic occasions, at the moment of birth or marriage or death, or on holidays. Like the intermittent, occasional and unintense religious sensibility, the political sensibility, too, can be intermittent and unintense. It might come into operation only on particular occasions, e.g. at election time, or in periods of severe economic deprivation or during a war or after a military defeat. Beyond this there are some persons who are never stirred, who have practically no sensibility as far as events of the political order are concerned.

Finally, there are persons, not many in any society but often of great importance, who have a very intense and active connexion with the centre, with the symbols of the central value system, but whose connexion is passionately negative. Equally important are those who have a positive but no less intense and active connexion with the symbols of the centre, a connexion so acute, so pure and vital that it cannot tolerate any falling short in daily observance such as characterizes the élites of the central institutional system. These are often the persons around whom a sharp opposition to the central value system and even more to the central institutional system is organized. From the ranks of these come prophets, revolutionaries, doctrinaire ideologists for whom nothing less than perfection is tolerable.

The need for established and created order, the respect for creativity and the need to be connected with the 'centre' do not exhaust the forces which engender central value systems. To fill out the list, we must consider the nature of authority itself. Authority has an expansive tendency. It has a tendency to expand the order which it represents towards the saturation of territorial space. The acceptance of the validity of that order entails a tendency towards its universalization within the society over which authority rules. Ruling indeed consists in the universalization within the boundaries of society, of the rules inherent in the order. Rulers, simply out of their possession of authority and the impulses which it generates, wish to be obeyed and they wish to obtain assent to the order which they symbolically embody. The symbolization or order in offices of authority has a compelling effect on those to whom authority is directed; it has an even more compelling effect on those who occupy those offices.

In consequence of this, rulers seek to establish a universal diffusion of the acceptance and observance of the values and beliefs of which they are the custodians through incumbency in those offices. They use their powers to punish those who deviate and to reward with their favour those who conform. Thus, the mere existence of authority in society imposes a central value system on that society.[2]

Not all persons who come into positions of authority possess the same responsiveness to the inherently dynamic and expansive tendency in authority. Some are more attuned to it; others are more capable of resisting it. Tradition, furthermore, acts as a powerful brake upon expansiveness, as does the degree of differentiation of the structure of élites and of the society as a whole.

The central institutional system, probably even in revolutionary crises, is the object of a substantial amount of consensus. The central value system which legitimates the central institutional system is widely shared, but the consensus is never perfect. There are differences within even the most consensual society about the appreciability of authority, the

2. I would regret an easy misunderstanding to which the sentences above might give rise. There is much empirical truth in the common observations that rulers 'look after their own', that they are only interested in remaining in authority, in reinforcing their possession of authority and in enhancing their security of tenure through the establishment of a consensus built around their own values and beliefs. None the less these observations seem to me to be too superficial. They fail to discern the dynamic property of authority as such, and particularly of authority over society.

institutions within which it resides, the élites which exercise it and the justice of its allocation of rewards.

Even those who share in the consensus, do so with different degrees of intensity, whole-heartedness and devotion. As we move from the centre of society, the centre in which authority is possessed, to the hinterland or the periphery, over which authority is exercised, attachment to the central value system becomes attenuated. The central institutional system is neither unitary nor homogeneous, and some levels have more majesty than others. The lower one goes in the hierarchy, or the further one moves territorially from the locus of authority, the less likely is the authority to be appreciated. Likewise, the further one moves from those possessing the secondary traits associated with the exercise of authority into sectors of the population which do not equally possess those qualities, the less affirmative is the attitude towards the reigning authority, and the less intense is that of affirmation which does exist.

Active rejection of the central value system is, of course, not the sole alternative to its affirmation. Much more widespread, in the course of history and in any particular society, is an intermittent, partial and attenuated affirmation in the central value system.

For the most part, the mass of the population in pre-modern societies has been far removed from the immediate impact of the central value system. It has possessed its own value systems which were *occasionally* and *fragmentarily* articulated with the central value system. These pockets of approximate independence have not, however, been completely incompatible with isolated occasions of articulation and of intermittent affirmation. Nor have these intermittent occasions of participation been incompatible with occasions of active rejection and antagonism to the central institutional system, to the élite which sits at its centre, and to the central value system which that élite puts forward for its own legitimation.

The more territorially dispersed the institutional system, the less the likelihood of an intense affirmation of the central value system. The more inegalitarian the society, the less the likelihood of an intense affirmation of the central value system, especially where, as in most steeply hierarchical societies, there is a large and discontinuous gap between those at the top and those below them. Indeed, it might be said that the degree of affirmation inevitably shades off from the centre of the exercise of authority and of the promulgation of values.

As long as societies were loosely coordinated, as long as authority lacked the means of intensive control and as long as much of the economic life of the society was carried on outside any market or almost exclusively in local markets, the central value system invariably became attenuated in the outlying reaches. With the growth of the market, and the administrative and technological strengthening of authority, contact with the central value system increased.

When, as in modern society, a more unified economic system, political democracy, urbanization and education have brought the different sections of the population into more frequent contact with each other and created even greater mutual awareness, the central value system has found a wider acceptance than in other periods of the history of society. At the same time these changes have also increased the extent, if not the intensity, of active 'dissensus' or rejection of the central value system.

The same objects which previously engaged the attention and aroused the sentiments of a very restricted minority of the population have in modern societies become concerns of much broader strata of the population. At the same time that increased contact with authority has led to a generally deferential attitude, it has also run up against the tenacity of prior attachments and a reluctance to accept strange gods. Class conflict in the most advanced modern societies is probably more open and more continuous than in pre-modern societies but it is also more domesticated and restricted by attachments to the central value system.[3]

The old gods have fallen, religious faith has become much more attenuated in the educated classes and suspicion of authority is much more overt than it has ever been. None the less in the modern societies of the West, the central value system has gone much more deeply into the heart of their members than it has ever succeeded in doing in any earlier society. The 'masses' have responded to their contact with a striking measure of acceptance.

The power of the ruling class derives from its incumbency of certain key positions in the central institutional system. Societies vary in the extent to which the ruling class is unitary or relatively segmental. Even where the ruling class is relatively segmental, there is, because of centralized control of appointment to the most crucial of the key positions or because of personal ties or because of overlapping personnel, some sense of affinity which, more or less, unites the different sectors of the élite.

3. Violent revolutions and bloody civil wars are much less characteristic of modern societies than of pre-modern societies. Revolutionary parties are feeble in modern societies which have moved towards widespread popular education, a greater equality of status, etc. The strength of revolutionary parties in France and Italy is a measure of the extent to which French and Italian societies have not become modernized. The inertness, from a revolutionary point of view, of their rank and file is partially indicative of the extent to which, despite their revolutionary affiliations, the working class has become assimilated into the central value system of their respective societies.

This sense of affinity rests ultimately on the high degree of proximity to the centre which is shared by all these different sectors of the ruling class. They have, it is true, a common vested interest in their position. It is not, however, simply the product of a perception of a coalescent interest; it contains a substantial component of mutual regard arising from a feeling of a common relationship to the central value system.

The different sectors of the élite, even in a highly pluralistic society where the élite is relatively segmental in its structure, are never equal. One or two usually predominate, to varying degrees, over the others, even in situations where there is much mutual respect and a genuine sense of affinity. Regardless, however, of whether they are equal or unequal, unitary or segmental, there is usually a fairly large amount of consensus among the élites of the central institutional system. This consensus has its ultimate root in their common feeling for the transcendent order which they believe they embody or for which they think themselves responsible.

The mass of the population in all large societies stand at some distance from authority. This is true both with respect to the distribution of authority and the distribution of the secondary qualities associated with the exercise of authority.

The functional and symbolic necessities of authority require some degree of concentration. Even the most genuinely democratic society, above a certain very small size, requires some concentration of authority for the performance of elaborate tasks. It goes without saying that non-democratic societies have a high concentration of authority. Furthermore, whether the society is democratic or oligarchical, the access to the key positions in the central institutional system tends to be confined to persons possessing a distinctive constellation of properties, such as age, educational, ethnic, regional and class provenance, etc.

The section of the population which does not share in the exercise of authority and which is differentiated in secondary properties from the exercisers of authority, is usually more intermittent in its 'possession' by the central value system. For one thing, the distribution of sensitivity to remote, central symbols is unequal, and there is a greater concentration of such sensitivity in the élites of the central institutional system. Furthermore, where there is a more marginal participation in the central institutional system, attachment to the central value system is more attenuated. Where the central institutional system becomes more comprehensive and inclusive so that a larger proportion of the life of the population comes within its scope, the tension between the centre and the periphery, as well as the consensus, tends to increase.

The mass of the population in most pre-modern and non-Western societies have in a sense lived *outside* society and have not felt their remoteness from the centre to be a perpetual injury to themselves. Their low position in the hierarchy of authority has been injurious to them, and the consequent alienation has been accentuated by their remoteness from the central value system. The alienation has not however been active or intense, because, for the most part, their convivial, spiritual and moral centre of gravity has lain closer to their own round of life. They have been far from full-fledged members of their societies and they have very seldom been citizens.

Among the most intensely sensitive or the more alertly intelligent, their distance from the centre accompanied by their greater concern with the centre, has led to an acute sense of being on 'the outside', to a painful feeling of being excluded from the vital zone which surrounds 'the centre' of society (which is the vehicle of 'the centre of the universe'). Alternatively these more sensitive and more intelligent persons have, as a result of their distinctiveness, often gained access to some layer of the centre by becoming school-teachers, priests, administrators. Thus they have entered into a more intimate and more affirmative relationship with the 'centre'. They have not in such instances, however, always overcome the grievance of exclusion from the most central zones of the central institutional and value systems. They have often continued to perceive themselves as 'outsiders', while continuing to be intensely attracted and influenced by the outlook and style of life of the centre.

Modern large-scale society rests on a technology which has raised the standard of living and which has integrated the population into a more unified economy. In correspondence with these changes, it has witnessed a more widespread participation in the central value system through education, and in the central institutional system through the franchise and mass communication. On this account, it is in a different position from all pre-modern societies.

In modern society, in consequence of its far greater involvement with the central institutional system, especially with the economy and the polity, the mass of the population is no longer largely without contact with the central value system. It has, to an unprecedented extent, come to feel the central value system to be its own value system. Its generally heightened sensitivity has responded to the greater visibility and accessibility of the central value system by partial incorporation. Indeed, although, compared with the élite, its contact is still relatively intermittent and unintense, that enhanced frequency and intensity are great universal-historical novelties. They are nothing less than the incorporation of the mass of the population into society. The 'process of civilization' has become a reality in the modern world.

To a greater extent than ever before in history the mass of the population in modern Western societies feel themselves to be 'part' of their society in a way in which their ancestors never did. Just as they have become 'alive' and hedonistic, more demanding of respect and pleasure, so, too, they have become more 'civilized'. They have come to be parts of the civil society with a feeling of attachment to that society and a feeling of moral responsibility for observing its rules and for sharing in its authority. They have ceased to be primarily objects of authoritative decisions by others; they have become to a much greater extent, acting and feeling subjects with wills of their own which they assert with self confidence. Political apathy, frivolity, vulgarity, irrationality and responsiveness to political demagogy are all concomitants of this phenomenon. Men have become citizens in larger proportions than ever before in the large states of history, and probably more, too, than in the Greek city states at the height of the glory of their aristocratic democracies.

The emergence of nationalism, not just the fanatical nationalism of politicians, intellectuals and zealots, but as a sense of nationality and an affirmative feeling for one's own country, is a very important aspect of this process of the incorporation of the mass of the population into the central institutional and value systems. The more passionate type of nationalism is an unpleasant and heroic manifestation of this deeper growth of civility.

None the less this greater incorporation carries with it also an inherent tension. Those who participate in the central institutional and value systems – who feel sufficiently closer to the centre now than their forebears ever did – also feel their position as outsiders, their remoteness from the centre, in a way in which their forebears probably did not feel it.

Parallel with this incorporation of the mass of the population into society – halting, spotty and imperfect as this incorporation is – has gone a change in the attitudes of the ruling classes of the modern states of the West. (In Asia and Africa, the process is even more fragmentary, corresponding to the greater fragmentariness of the incorporation of the masses into those societies.) In the modern Western states, the ruling classes have come increasingly to acknowledge the dispersion, into the wider reaches of the society, of the *charisma* which informs the 'centre'. The qualities which account for the expansiveness of authority have come to be shared more widely in the population, quite far from the 'centre' where reside the incumbents of the position of authority. In the eyes of the élites of the modern states of the West, the mass of the population have somehow come to share in the vital connexion with the 'order' which inheres in the central value system and which was once thought to be in the special custody of the ruling classes.

The élites are, of course, more responsive to sectors of society which have voting power, and therewith, legislative power, and which possess agitational and purchasing powers as well. These would make them simulate respect for the populace even where they did not feel it. None the less, mixed with this simulated respect, is also a genuine respect for the mass of the population as bearers of a true individuality and a genuine, even if still limited appreciation of their intrinsic worth as fellow-members of the civil society and, in the deepest sense, vessels of the *charisma* which lives at the 'centre' of society.

There is a limit to consensus. However comprehensive the spread of consensus, it can never be all embracing. A differentiated large-scale society will always be compelled by professional specialization, tradition, the normal distribution of human capacities and an inevitable anti-nomianism to submit to inequalities in participation in the central value system. Some persons will always be a bit closer to the centre, some will always be more distant from the centre.

None the less, the expansion of individuality attendant on the growth of individual freedom, and opportunity and the greater density of communications have contributed greatly to narrowing the range of inequality. The peak at the centre is no longer so high, the periphery is no longer so distant.

The individuality which has underlain the entry into the consensus around the central value system might in the end also be endangered by it. Liberty and privacy live on islands in a consensual sea. When the tide rises they may be engulfed. This is another instance of the dialectical relationships among consensus, indifference and alienation, but further consideration must be left for another occasion.

# 66 David Lockwood

## Some Remarks on 'The Social System'

David Lockwood, 'Some remarks on "The Social System"',
*British Journal of Sociology*, vol. 7, 1956, pp. 134–43.

In the 'statement of general sociological theory' which is *The Social System* (Parsons, 1952), Professor Parsons has attempted to sift and summarize in systematic form the significant lessons of past thinking in sociology and set out a programme for the future. This enterprise is the product of a steady and consistent growth reaching back some twenty years to his initial study of eminent sociological theorists in *The Structure of Social Action*. The intention of the present essay, however, is not to give an exposition of the Parsonian system of sociology, but to develop in some detail specific criticisms which might be levelled against his conceptualization of the dynamics of social systems and, more particularly, of societies. To treat of such a large subject within so small a space is no doubt unwise in one sense; in another it is an incentive to delineate more sharply what is at issue. In particular, emphasis will be placed on the non-normative elements of social action which seem to constitute a set of variables which Parsons has ignored by concentrating on the normative elements of social structure and process. This omission may be interpreted as an accomplishment since it is the means of giving sociology a more definite status as a special social science; but whether it is a position that can be maintained in practice without inconsistency is open to severe doubt, or so it seems to the writer. This much of the vein of criticism may be anticipated.

In this section are to be considered those propositions put forward in *The Social System* and elsewhere which illustrate Parsons's analysis of social dynamics. It is impossible to do justice in so short a space to the elaborate development and application of the conceptual scheme, of which the following outline is a mere skeleton. Thus most of what is subsequently said is not in criticism of what has been substantively accomplished within a given framework, but rather questions the appropriateness of the framework that is given. In so far as misunderstanding has not occurred, the criticism concerns what has not, rather than what has been done.

For Parsons, the social system is a system of action. It is made up of the interactions of individuals. Of special concern to sociology is the fact that such interactions are not random but mediated by common standards of evaluation. Most important among these are moral standards, which may be called norms. Such norms 'structure' action. Because individuals share the same 'definition of the situation' in terms of such norms, their behaviour can be intermeshed to produce a 'social structure'. The regularity, or patterning, of interaction is made possible through the existence of norms which control the behaviour of actors. Indeed, a stabilized social system is one in which behaviour is regulated in this way and, as such, is a major point of reference for the sociological analysis of the dynamics of social systems. It is necessary in sociology, as in biology, to single out relatively stable points of reference, or 'structural' aspects of the system under consideration, and then to study the processes whereby such structures are maintained. This is the meaning of the 'structural-functional' approach to social-system analysis. Since the social system is a system of action, and its structural aspects are the relatively stable interactions of individuals around common norms, the dynamic processes with which the sociologist is concerned are those which function to maintain social structures, or, in other words, those processes whereby individuals come to be motivated to act in comformity with normative standards.

The equilibrium of social systems is maintained by a variety of processes and mechanisms, and their failure precipitates varying degrees of disequilibrium (or disintegration). The two main classes of mechanisms by which motivation is kept at the level and in the direction necessary for the continuing operation of the social system are the mechanisms of socialization and social control (Parsons, 1952).

The mechanism of socialization is the process by which individuals come to incorporate the normative standards of the society into their personalities; the process of social control is concerned with the regulation of the behaviour of adults who have undergone socialization and are yet motivated to nonconformity.

Although sociological analysis focuses on the dynamic processes which tend to stabilize the social system, 'if theory is *good theory*, there is no reason whatever to believe that it will not be *equally* applicable to the problems of change and to those of process within a stabilized system'. Or again, so far as the social system is concerned, the 'obverse of the analysis of the mechanisms by which it is maintained is the analysis of the forces which tend to alter it. *It is impossible to study one without the other*. ... In principle, propositions about the factors making for the maintenance of the system are at the same time propositions about those making for change.' In the most general terms, then, the two major threats to a given social system are infants who have not been socialized, and individuals who are motivated to deviance or nonconformity. Since the first of these requires no special sociological explanation as a source of instability, interest must focus on the nature of deviance. Here Parsons is not so much concerned with the sources of deviance as with the modes of deviant reactions in terms of the personality mechanisms involved. Pressures making for deviance are regarded as being a matter for investigation in each empirical situation as it arises. In general, there are no social processes, corresponding to those stabilizing mechanisms outlined above, which systematically make for deviance and social change.

Although it would be tempting to begin the criticism of such a conceptual scheme by questioning the validity of some particular assumption, such as the existence of a common value system, or the meaning given to the concept of social structure, it is more rewarding to begin by asking a rather more general question. It is true to say that in principle the concepts with which we try to analyse the dynamics of social systems ought to be equally applicable to the problems of stability and instability, continuance and change of social structures; but this does not necessarily hold true of a particular conceptual scheme such as the one outlined above. It would not hold unless general concepts had been developed which would enable us to take any concrete social system and grasp the balance of forces at work in it. We may ask, therefore, is there anything about the framework just described which would suggest that a certain class of variables, vital to an understanding of the general problem – why do social structures persist and change – has in fact been ignored?

I believe there is. The first point of note in this connexion is that Parsons' array of concepts is heavily weighted by assumptions and categories which relate to the role of *normative* elements in social action, and especially to the processes whereby motives are structured normatively to ensure social stability. On the other hand, what may be called the *substratum* of social action, especially as it conditions interests which are productive of social conflict and instability, tends to be ignored as a general determinant of the dynamics of social systems. For the moment, the substratum of social action may be defined as the factual disposition of means in the situation of action which structures differential *Lebenschancen* and produces interests of a non-normative kind – that is, interests other than those which actors have in conforming with the normative definition of the situation. Although, according to Parsons, such interests must be integrated with the normative patterns governing behaviour in a stabilized social system, it is inherent in the conception of deviance and social instability that non-normative interests have to be treated as a discrete and independent category in sociological analysis. What then is the status of these non-normative elements in the analysis of social action? Is it useful to distinguish between norm and substratum as general points of reference in dynamic analysis? If so, why has Parsons given conceptual priority to the normative structuring of action?

Let us look at the genesis of Parsons's own concern with the normative regulation of conduct. It is the famous Hobbesian problem of order. 'If any two men desire the same thing, which nevertheless they cannot both enjoy, they become enemies; and in the way to their end, which is principally their own conservation, and sometimes their delectation only, endeavour to destroy, or subdue one another.' Relationships of power and social conflict are inherent in the scarcity of means in society. The notions of power and conflict are mutually implicative: power is involved as men seek their interests against the opposition of others; and a division of interests is implicit in the relationships of power that obtain. If conflict is thus endemic in the scarcity of means and the struggle to acquire them, in the fact that the means which one man holds give him power over another man to whom they are also necessary, how then is social order possible? The answer which emerges from *The Structure of Social Action,* the proposition which is at the core of Parsons's subsequent sociology, is that order is possible through the existence of common norms which regulate 'the war of all against all'. The existence of the normative order, therefore, is in one very important sense inextricably bound up with potential conflicts of interest over scarce resources. This functional dependence of norm on conflict, however, does not correspond to an actual succession from a state of nature to a state of civil society: the relation is analytical, not historical. In the present context it is fundamental to the subsequent argument that the presence of a normative order, or common value system, does not mean that conflict has disappeared, or been resolved in some way. Instead, the very existence of a normative order mirrors the continual potentiality of conflict. To be sure, the degree of conflict in the social system is always a matter for empirical investigation; but so is the existence of a common value system. Indeed, the varying degrees of acceptance of, or alienation from, the dominant values of the society may be regarded in large measure as reflecting the divisions of interest resulting from differential access to scarce resources. Most important of all, it would seem to follow quite naturally from this situation that when we talk of the stability or instability of a social system, we mean more than anything else the success or failure of the normative order in regulating conflicts of interest. Therefore, in an adequate view of social dynamics it is necessary to conceptualize not only the normative structuring of motives but also the structuring of interests in the substratum. In other words, it is necessary to know about the forces generated by norm *and* substratum if we wish to understand why patterns of behaviour persist or change.

The step from Hobbes to Marx in this matter is a short one. The introduction of the division of labour transforms the war of all against all into the war of one class against another. Marx agrees with Hobbes that conflict is endemic in social interaction (except in communist society), and goes one step further and asserts that interests of a non-normative kind are not random in the social system, but systematically generated through the social relations of the productive process. This, as Parsons himself has acknowledged, is Marx's fundamental insight into the dynamics of social systems. In a given society, so runs the recommendation, if we wish to understand the balance of forces working for stability or change we must look not only to the normative order, but also and principally to the factual organization of production, and the powers, interests, conflicts and groupings consequent on it. Here are two notions of 'social structure', both characterized by 'exteriority' and 'constraint', the one *de jure,* the other *de facto.* Marx's own analysis tended to focus on the latter meaning. And what emerges from his thinking is a view of the social system and its operation startlingly different from the framework provided by the Parsonian theory. To pursue this theme a little further, it is not accidental for instance that the process of *exploitation* in the Marxian theory represents a radical conceptual antithesis to the social process which has a central place in Parsons's analysis: that of *socialization.* It is not accidental again that a societal typology is based in the first case on the forms of ownership and control of productive means, in the second on the dominant value patterns of the society. Social stratification for Marx is the differentiation of competing economic interest groups in the society on the basis of productive relations; for Parsons it is the differentiation of individuals in terms of social superiority and inferiority on the basis of the dominant value system of the society. It is unnecessary to multiply instances, for in the almost polar opposition of the two sociological systems we witness the logical outcome of fundamentally different abstractions from the nature of social action. One centres on the phenomenon of social conflict and the constraint of the factual social order; the other on that of social solidarity and the constraint of the normative social order. Both theories, moreover, claim generality, both purport to be concerned with social dynamics. Such a conceptual dichotomy can only be reconciled with these claims if it is recognized that a general theory of social systems which conceptualizes one aspect of social structure and process is of necessity a particular theory. Parsons's claim that to study the forces making for stability is at the same time to grasp those making for instability and change, does not hold in his own analysis because of a selective emphasis on the normative elements of social action. The only other explanation is that the alternative system of generalized concepts is intellectually dispensable. The question here is not whether Marx was wrong or right in his specific empirical predictions (in most of them he appears nowadays to have been falsified), but whether the categories with which he approached social reality as a sociologist are generally relevant to our understandings of social process. Is it possible to understand the nature of twentieth-century American society in terms of its 'universalistic-achievement' value pattern without mentioning the changes which its capitalist institutions are undergoing? And if the frustrated dependency needs of the middle-class male caught up in a competitive world produce 'one of the focal points of strain in American society', are the relations between unions and business corporations which Professor Lindblom has recently analysed of no account in the dynamics of that fateful social system?

Such questions, it is submitted, can only be asked because of the bifurcation of sociological analysis represented by the conceptual schemata just discussed. On the one hand, it is suggested that society is unthinkable without some degree of integration through common norms and that sociological theory should deal with the processes whereby this order is maintained. On the other, society is held to be unthinkable without some degree of conflict arising out of the allocation of scarce resources in the division of labour, and sociological analysis is given the task of studying the processes whereby divisions of interest are structured and expressed. The latter view, which seems to be the general import of the Marxian sociology, does not necessarily imply that resources refer only to productive means, or that conflict is necessary and not contingent. In the expansion of these points it may also be shown that there is no real rivalry between the two sociological systems, but that they are on the contrary complementary in their emphases.

It is unnecessary to argue that all conflicts, interests, facilities and powers are 'economic' in the sense of being related to the ownership of productive means, in order to appreciate that some such generic concepts are indispensable in analysing the dynamics of social systems. The Marxian system of economic materialism is a specific case of a more general sociological materialism which has never been given anything like the careful analysis to which Parsons has subjected the concept of the normative. The division of labour may be generalized into a category that stands for the factual disposition and organization of socially effective means, and need not be equated simply with the division of functions, powers and interests associated with productive means. In this connexion it has been pointed out that part of Weber's work can be seen as an attempt to 'round out' Marx's economic materialism by a political and military materialism. This kind of distinction is a necessary refinement in the sociological understanding of the substratum of social action. It would be difficult, for instance, to make sense of the type of social system which Hintze calls *Frühfeudalismus* and Bloch *le premier âge féodal,* without reference to the importance of military means and virtuosity for the differentiation of functions, the distribution of social power and, indeed, for the acquisition and holding of productive means. Similarly, the organization of political power in modern industrial societies cannot realistically be regarded as a mere reflection of conventionally visualized 'property power' but is seen to be an increasingly autonomous force. In short, the interdependencies of the various types of power structures, and the groupings and interests they produce, call for sociological investigation in each type of social structure and cannot be reduced to any simple formula.

That conflict is no more inevitable than order should be evident from the foregoing discussion of norm and substratum as the basic variables in the situation of action. Every social situation consists of a normative order with which Parsons is principally concerned, and also of a factual order, or substratum. Both are 'given' for individuals; both are part of the exterior and constraining social world. Sociological theory is concerned, or should be, with the social and psychological processes whereby social structure in this dual sense conditions human motives and actions. The existence of a normative order in no way entails that individuals will act in accordance with it; in the same way the existence of a given factual order in no way means that certain kinds of behaviour result. The gap between the elements of 'givenness' in this situation and individual or group action is one that is to be bridged only by the sociological appreciation of the way in which motives are structured, normatively and factually.

It is evident, then, that the distinction between order and conflict is one that needs only to be maintained in so far as it illustrates the dimensions of the present problem. Order and conflict are states of the social system, indices of its operation, and to talk of the determinants of order should therefore be to talk of the determinants of conflict. It is only because the problem of order has become bound up with the functioning of the normative system in Parsons's work, that it is necessary to press for the analysis of conflict as a separate task, and especially for the recognition of those aspects of conflict which are non-normative. Just as the problem of order is not just a function of the existence of a normative order and the social mechanisms which procure motivation to conform with it but also of the existence of a social substratum which structures interests differentially in the social system, so the problem of conflict is not reducible to the analysis of the division of labour and the group interests consequent on it. It is rather that both conflict and order are a function of the interaction of norm and substratum. Certain kinds of normative order are more conducive to the development of conflict than others. For instance, the labour–capital conflict in its classical manifestation arose out of the actual situation of the classes under capitalistic production, but it was greatly intensified and sharpened by the existence of a dominant value system, the cardinal features of which, 'freedom' and 'opportunity', contrasted radically with the factual order of events. The generation of conflict, which may be taken as an index of social instability, is never a simple matter of a conflict of material interest but also involves the normative definition of the situation.

To summarize the argument so far. Parsons's claim to have provided a set of general sociological concepts for the analysis of the dynamics of social systems has been questioned on the ground that his conceptual scheme is highly selective in its focus on the role of the normative order in the stabilization of social systems. In order to demonstrate this selectivity it was shown that beginning with the same basic 'problem of order' it was possible to derive an entirely different system of concepts which is oriented to the role of the factual order, or substratum, in the production of social conflict and social instability. At the same time, it is fairly obvious that the two conceptual schemata, though leading to the study of quite different empirical problems, are not theoretically incompatible but rather complementary, in principle at least, within a broader sociological approach.

There is one explanation for the analytical precedence which Parsons gives to the normative structuring of social action which cannot be ignored. That is the argument that sociology should not concern itself with the dynamics of the social system as a whole, but only with some aspect thereof. To this view it is now profitable to turn.

That sociology should deal with a particular set of problems within the theory of social system is the position taken by Parsons in his discussion of the division of labour between the social sciences. Here sociology is defined as having to do with the process of institutionalization of normative patterns: 'that aspect of the theory of social systems which is concerned with the phenomena of institutionalization of patterns of value-orientation in the social system, and of changes in the patterns, with conditions of conformity with and deviance from a set of such patterns, and with motivational processes in so far as they are involved in all of these'. The sphere of 'power', economic and political, precisely the factual social order, is delivered for safe keeping to the economist and political scientist.

The definition of sociology which Parsons sets forth is apparently consistent with his preoccupation with the role of normative factors in social action. It provides a reasoned basis for the actual selectivity of his theoretical system. But is there consistency here; does not his very view of the scope of sociology lead to a recognition of the essential limitations of this preoccupation and selectivity? It has already been noted that the problem of conformity or nonconformity of actors with a common value pattern resolves itself into a consideration of the constraint exercised on the actors by the normative and factual orders and the processes associated with them. It is not only the continual pressure of normative expectations exerted through the processes of socialization and social control, but also the range of differential opportunities created by the division of labour, that form the effective social environment of action. Therefore, if 'changes in the patterns' are to be accounted for sociologically, how is this possible without making the analysis of power and means an integral part of the explanation? To take an obvious, but massive example: how is the growth of collectivistic values within the dominant individualistic ethos of British capitalism to be explained without including the systematic operation of this set of factors? Or again, within this wider change of values, the trade-union movement appears at its inception as a 'group of deviantly motivated individuals' to use the terminology of *The Social System*. Yet is the structuring of this deviant motivation to be adequately comprehended by a system of sociological explanation so limited as the one we find in this book? In the analysis of actual processes of social change all the difficulties that beset a sociology whose theoretical core has developed from a concern with the normative basis of social stability become apparent. Any study of social change, defined even in terms of change in institutionalized value patterns, must be based on concepts which can inter-relate the realistic and normative structure of the situation with the resultant actions of individuals and groups. In any given society, the potentialities of change are not random but systematically related to the balance of indulgence and deprivation among different social groups as this is determined by the types of normative patterns defining expected behaviour, and the types of division of labour distributing factual opportunities to realize ends. If these are elementary and readily acceptable propositions, they only serve to show that sociological analysis, even if it is formally defined as being concerned with a seemingly specialized aspect of the theory of social systems, cannot in fact avoid the role of a synthesizing discipline. In particular, sociology cannot avoid the systematic analysis of the phenomenon of 'power' as an integral part of its conceptual scheme.

What is fundamentally at issue here is the form of inquiry peculiar to sociology. This should be made quite clear. There has long existed a divergence beween those who favour sociology as a special social science, and those who believe that sociology should be a synthetic discipline utilizing the data of the other social sciences to gain a view of the interdependence of elements of social systems. The latter view has been dominant in Europe on the whole. The definitions of sociology as 'an attempt to find out what are the basic phenomena and relationships of society in all its aspects: political, legal, literary, artistic, economic, etc.; what are the relationships between these various aspects of social life and in what ways do they interact upon each other', or as a discipline, which 'utilizing the results arrived at by the specialists is concerned more particularly with their interrelations and seeks to give an interpretation of social life as a whole', do not delve too deeply into the precise relations between the social sciences, but at the same time point to a mode of inquiry which is immediately recognizable as characteristically sociological. The status of sociology in this definition is no doubt embarrassing, its frontiers indistinct, but its identity unmistakable. The fact that economists had written on the division of labour and explored its consequences for economic action, did not preclude its entirely different treatment at the hands of Durkheim, Marx and Weber. At the present time, this sociological mode of investigation is recognizable in a concern with the sources of cohesion and conflict in modern welfare industrialism. Such interests, it is true, are not easily to be gratified without excursions into the special fields of law, economics and politics.

This view of sociology as dealing with the interdependence of the various aspects of social organization seems to be congruent with the more abstract definition suggested in this paper, that sociology has to do with the interplay of norm and substratum in relation to the problem of stability and change of social systems. As I see it, and here I draw on the distinctions made above, Parsons's concern with the normative and his definition of sociology as a discipline exploring the dynamics of the normative, is in one way an attempt, whether intentional or unintentional, to make the status of sociology less ambiguous by making it a special social science. But this confinement, which has a definite conceptual expression, seems to break down, both on a theoretical and an empirical level, when the problems of social stability and change are tackled.

I have no wish to deny that the sociological mode of inquiry should be made explicit by the formulation of particular sociological theories. Indeed, the process of theoretical development in sociology is one by which different factors and their inter-relationships are identified and evaluated. To this development, Professor Parsons's contribution has been, and continues to be, one to which all must be indebted. This is especially true of his insistence on the necessary integration of psychological and sociological thinking around the problems of social dynamics. His claim to have provided a 'statement of general sociological theory' is less acceptable however, because it seems to have sought to clarify the status of sociology at the expense of confining it within a conceptual mould in which it does not happily fit.

*Reference*
PARSONS, T. (1952), *The Social System*, Tavistock and Free Press.

# 67 John Rex

Power, Conflict, Values and Change

Excerpts from John Rex, *Key Problems in Sociological Theory*, Routledge & Kegan Paul, 1961, pp. 110–14, 129–34.

## Norms and the balance of power

It is true, of course, that patterns of social relations do not always entirely fit in with the interests which men pursue. Thus industrialization is sometimes inhibited by the survival of a *Gemeinschaft* mentality among a people which lingers on as a habit. Thus we might admit that to some extent the value system of the society in the sense in which Parsons writes of it is an independent variable of which we must take account. But Parsons goes much further than this. For him the interests which can be pursued and the facilities which are available for use by particular individuals and classes are dependent upon the value system in operation.

Thus we are told that 'every social system must have mechanisms for the allocation of possession of facilities, because their possession is desirable and they are inherently limited in supply relation to demand'. And the sources of this scarcity apart from the fact that there simply are not enough to go round in some cases are said to be relational. But what this means is that some people have more power than others.

Now we might expect this to lead to a discussion of the struggle for power in social systems. But in Parsons the discussion does not take this course. The scarcity of facilities imposed by the unequal distribution of power is something to which the social system has to be adapted and the value patterns ensure the perpetuation of a particular system of allocation of facilities and power. Thereafter discussion of power drops into the background and the system is discussed as though it were integrated purely in terms of value patterns.

There is a very important point here. If we had started our analysis of social systems by positing some measure of rejection by 'alter' of 'ego's' expectations and hence some measure of conflict, it would have been obvious that to some extent ego would try to compel alter to conform to his expectations. It would also have been obvious that alter's eventual behaviour would have been determined by the sort of balance of power prevailing. No doubt the more fortunate party would also have produced moral rationalizations of the situation. But the actual situation would have been produced not by a normative system, but by the balance of power and the eventual agreement of the parties.

Thus, even if it is admitted that social integration is in part dependent upon value systems, there is also a substructure to social order which is determined by the struggle for power and the balance of power. Any complete account of a social system must describe the nature of this power. Moreover, as Wright Mills has pointed out, there are many transitional points between actual coercion and legitimate rule or rule by consent. For 'among the means of power that now prevail is the power to manage and manipulate the consent of men.' No doubt sociologists will always show their bias here and what one calls 'manipulation', another will call 'consent to common norms'. But the point to notice about Parsons is precisely that, in subordinating the questions of power to the question of normative order, he shows a markedly conservative bias.

The practical implications of this point are clearly illustrated in a field such as that of industrial sociology. Anyone with experience of industrial relations knows that the actual relations prevailing between employers and employees are determined by a contract which ends a period of negotiations in which both sides are likely to deploy their power in threatening strikes and lock-outs. Yet very often industrial sociology ignores all this and discusses the social relations of a factory as though they were akin to those of village community, in terms of some sort of value system which is supposed to be accepted by both sides.

Of course there are some fields of sociological study like industrial sociology where the power element in social relations is far more evident than in other cases. But we quote this extreme case in order to emphasize that the pursuit of ends which, from the point of view of the system as a whole, are 'random', does go on, and that if the pursuit of these ends finds no sanction in the norms of the society it may yet continue and be backed by force instead of moral or social authority. And between the sanction of force and that of the social norms there are many intermediate points.

We need not return to a Hobbesian or a utilitarian position in order to say this. What we are asserting is the need for a theory such as Parsons suggested which avoids the pitfalls of both positivism in its various forms, on the one hand, and idealism, on the other. By concentrating solely on the normative aspects of action Parsons produces a theory which is differentiated from idealism only by the fact that he recognizes that the norms affect human conduct only voluntarily, that is to say that they may or may not be obeyed. But once he has shown that they are subjectively experienced in a different way from other factors, he goes on to describe these norms as though they were themselves the social structure.

What we want is a theory which finds a place for both normatively oriented action and action which can be understood as governed by something like scientific knowledge of the relation between means and ends. We also need to recognize that some of the ends which the actors in our system pursue may be random ends from the point of view of the system or actually in conflict with it. If there is an actual conflict of ends, the behaviour of actors towards one another may not be determined by shared norms but by the success which each has in compelling the other to act in accordance with his interests. Power then becomes a crucial variable in the study of social systems.

## The outlines of a conflict model of social systems

The most useful way to conclude this chapter will be to set out the main lines of a model which would be useful in analysing the sort of modern industrial society with which we have most frequently to deal, and showing the place that values have in that model. In the first place we should seek to show what ends were pursued by individuals and groups within the society. It would then become evident that we were faced neither with Hobbes's state of nature nor with a state of perfect harmony. We should find that many members of the society had what MacIver calls 'like and common interests' and that these tend to form up into groups. Between the groups there would be a conflict situation. Our model would then seek to describe the structure of the groups and the relations between them.

Looking first at the structure of the separate groups we should expect to find some commonly accepted definition of the group's aims, to achieving which the actions of individual members would be directed. Many of these actions could be directly understood as means to the achievement of the group's end (i.e. 'appropriate' means as defined by empirical science). Other actions and relationships might not have this direct relationship to the group's aims and might be subjectively experienced as normatively controlled by the members. They might, however, have an indirect relationship through the contribution which they make to group solidarity, i.e. to the prevention of internal conflict. We should also allow for the fact that certain acts might be related to the group ends not as the scientifically appropriate means but as appropriate in terms of what we called 'ritual rules' of the group. These might be derived from the mythology and ideology of the group. We mention these actions as a separate category from those which contribute to group solidarity, even though they may be the same actions, because it has to be shown empirically that they have this effect. In any case there would be two separate points to be made, firstly that there are certain actions which are related to the group's ends in ways other than those which were deemed appropriate in the light of scientific knowledge, and secondly that these actions contributed to group solidarity.

In describing the group situation we should include the formal aspect of role expectations in the social relations among individuals. But we should also describe the content of the group roles. The object of the group model as a whole would be to show the connexion between actions, roles and relations of group members and the group's aims.

As between groups, we should first make clear the points of conflict in their separate aims. We might find that the conflict was a total one or we might find that there were areas of agreement including agreement as to how the conflict might be carried on. But, given that there was a conflict of aims, we should expect each group to seek to enforce upon the other behaviour which at worst did not interfere with and at best actually promoted the achievement of its own aims. If each group did this there would be some sort of power contest using various forms of power and some sort of conflict would ensue until each side recognized that compliance to a certain degree was more profitable than a continuance of the conflict. Provided the balance of power remained stable after agreement had been reached the agreement might be elaborated to provide agreed norms for the behaviour of the members of both groups. But it is also possible that only an uneasy compromise might be arrived at, in which case both sides would remain prepared for a resumption of the conflict. In this case the norms of each separate group might remain unaffected by the truce.

One would also expect that during a period of conflict or truce an ideological battle would continue. Even where conflict is total, there are nearly always common traditions to which appeal can be made and the aim of the ideological argument would be to show that the group's aims were more consistent with the common traditions than those of its opponents. But this is not necessarily to say that the groups in conflict actually have shared values. They may have. But the sole reason for the survival of the common tradition may be that it is necessary for the conduct of the ideological battle.

Thus an alternative model for the analysis of social systems, which includes rational scientific as well as normatively oriented action, and conflict as well as consensus, is perfectly possible without our slipping back into the oversimplifications of positivism which Parsons rightly criticizes. Parsons's own model involves a continually narrowing focus of interest, firstly on the normative elements of social systems, secondly on the special case of complete integration or 'institutionalization' and, third-ly on the formal aspects of the norms. As a specialized study of one analytically separable element of social systems it has real value. But for the analysis of modern industrial societies and plural societies brought into being by culture contacts it is quite inadequate. For these, the main areas of interest of modern sociology, a model which gives a greater place to action of a rational-scientific kind and to conflict is essential. [...]

The main lines of our conflict model for the analysis of social systems are now fairly clear. They may be summarized as follows:

1. Instead of being organized around a consensus of values, social systems may be thought of as involving conflict situations at central points. Such conflict situations may lie anywhere between the extremes of peaceful bargaining in the market place and open violence.

2. The existence of such a situation tends to produce not a unitary but a plural society, in which there are two or more classes, each of which provides a relatively self-contained social system for its members. The activities of the members take on sociological meaning and must be explained by reference to the group's interests in the conflict situation. Relations between groups are defined at first solely in terms of the conflict situation.

3. In most cases the conflict situation will be marked by an unequal balance of power so that one of the classes emerges as the ruling class. Such a class will continually seek to gain recognition of the legitimacy of its position among the members of the subject class and the leaders of the subject class will seek to deny this claim and to organize activities which demonstrate that it is denied (e.g. passive resistance).

4. The power situation as between the ruling and subject classes may change as a result of changes in a number of variable factors which increase the possibility of successful resistance or actual revolution by the subject class. Amongst these variable factors are leadership, the strength of the members' aspirations, their capacity for organization, their possession of the means of violence, their numbers and their role in the social system proposed by the ruling class.

5. In the case of a dramatic change in the balance of power the subject class may suddenly find itself in a situation in which it cannot merely impose its will on the former ruling class, but can actually destroy the basis of that class's existence. New divisions within the revolutionary class may open up, but these may be of an entirely different kind from those which existed in the previous conflict situation.

6. The social institutions and culture of the subject class are geared to, and explicable in, terms of the class's interest in the conflict situation. So far as its long-term aims are concerned, these tend to be expressed in vague and Utopian forms. When the subject class comes to power its actual practices will still have to be worked out. But it is likely that they will be justified and even affected by the morality of conflict and by pre-revolutionary charters and Utopias.

7. A change in the balance of power might lead not to complete revolution, but to compromise and reform. In this case new institutions might arise which are not related simply to the prosecution of the conflict, but are recognized as legitimate by both sides. Such a truce situation might in favourable circumstances give rise to a new unitary social order over a long period, in which limited property rights and limited political power are regarded as legitimately held by particular individuals. But such situations are inherently unstable because any weakening of the countervailing power of the formerly subject class would lead the former ruling class to resume its old ways and the maintenance of this power could easily encourage the subject class to push right on to the revolutionary alternative.

These points would appear to provide a useful framework in terms of which many important contemporary social situations might be analysed. The classification of basic conflict situations, the study of the emergence and structure of conflict groups, the problem of the legitimation of power, the study of the agencies of indoctrination and socialization, the problem of the ideological conflicts in post-revolutionary situations and in situations of compromise and truce, the study of the relations between norms and systems of power – all these have their place within it.

The model has been developed, of course, in relation to the study of total social systems and with special emphasis upon their overtly political aspects. But it is by no means without relevance to the design of research into problems of particular institutions and social segments. There are, as Dahrendorf was right to point out, always conflicts or potential conflicts between those exercising authority and those over whom it is exercised whatever the institutional context, and wherever such conflicts occur the model suggested is relevant for at least a partial analysis of the problems of the institutions concerned. Sometimes it may serve to supplement the model of a stable system. On other occasions when the conflict is central to the life of the institution it may actually displace it entirely. [. . .]

## Conflict and change

We have devoted almost the whole of this chapter [see *Key Problems in Sociological Theory*] to discussing the question of conflict, rather than that of social change, because the sort of theory of conflict which we have suggested *is* a theory of change. There are, however, one or two further points which should be made in connexion with the latter topic.

The first of these is that all forms of functionalist theory as it is usually understood are logically debarred from being able to put forward any sociological theory of change. This is because the whole functionalist effort is devoted to showing why things are as they are. They are as they are because they are demanded by the needs of the social structure. And because the social structure is itself thought of as being something un-problematic, there is no question of its changing. Hence there are only three possibilities of tacking a theory of change on to the theory of stable social systems. All may be stated in terms of the organic analogy.

The first would be a theory of random mutations and natural selec-tion. This has quite rightly not been taken seriously except perhaps by Sumner, partly because the notion of randomness taken by itself is a virtual denial of the applicability of scientific explanations, and partly because it leaves unsolved the question of the standards in terms of which natural selection takes place.

The second alternative rests upon making these standards clear. The analogy with biology suggests at once that the secret is to be found in the notion of adaptation to environment and much sociological writing about change has been concerned with changes in the social system consequent upon changes in the environment of the system. The 'environ-ment' includes not only the physical environment but all those factors which are not explicable in terms of the variables of the system. Thus there have been attempts made to explain change in society as an adap-tation of the system to such factors as technological change, culture contact, growing moral sensitivity and many other factors.

What functionalism has difficulty in explaining is change arising within the system itself rather than in the environment. The third appli-cation of the biological analogy, however, is an attempt to explain change in these terms. It is the idea that social, like organic systems, may be thought of as 'growing'. This is the one possibility of change within the system that the organic analogy leaves open. The difficulty, how-ever, is that, even in biology itself, growth is not something which is properly understood in general theoretical terms. Parsons makes this point when he says:

It is quite possible, indeed common, to know that certain processes of change do in fact typically take place under certain conditions without being able to deduce the pattern of the processes and their outcome from knowledge of the laws of the system. It is also possible to have considerable knowledge about variations in conditions and a variety of scientific consequences of such variations for the system. A familiar example of this type of knowledge is knowledge of the outline of the biological cycle. There is, in biological science, no general theory of the life cycle, by which growth, its cessation at maturity, senescence and finally death can be systematically explained in terms of general laws.

Thus it does not add anything to our knowledge of the causes of change to describe it in terms of birth, growth, senescence, etc., in the way which such writers as Toynbee do. At least there is no scientific theory of change here. There may be some metaphysical theory implied, but, if we reject this as irrelevant, we are merely back where we started confronted with the *empirical* fact of change.

Nor is the problem solved by those writers who forsake the idea of the organism for that of equilibrium. Many of them have spoken of a 'moving' equilibrium. But this is essentially a contradiction in terms. Either a system is in equilibrium or it is moving from one equilibrium to another. It cannot be both things at the same time. Thus the notion of a moving equilibrium remains as a central paradox in such sociological theory.

The action frame-of-reference provides us with much more scope for the development of a theory of change. For it explicitly includes the notion of ends and hence of a possible conflict of ends. But we should none the less be cautious about how much we claim for our conflict theory as a theory of change. In particular we should be cautious about claims which are made about laws of change and development.

The case of Marxist social and political theory is of particular interest here, because it has always taken its stand on the Hegelian point that we should study things in process rather than as static entities. Engels, for instance, speaks of Hegel's 'great basic thought that the world is not to be comprehended as a complex of ready-made things, but as a complex of processes in which things apparently stable go through an uninterrupted process of coming into being and passing away'. And, the Hegelian notion of dialectical change becomes even more relevant when we apply it to society than when it is applied in the physical sciences, for such change is dialectical in the original sense of the term. The model which we have suggested is based on the idea of an argument, albeit a practical rather than a theoretical one, and it would not be stretching the meaning of the terms too far to identify the proposals for social organization of one social class as thesis, those of the other as antithesis and the actual outcome of the conflict as synthesis. Marx seems indeed to have shown great insight in identifying the dialectic with the class struggle. Our model sets out in detail the implications of his doing so.

What we have to beware of, however, is the suggestion that knowledge of thesis and antithesis is sufficient to give us knowledge of what the synthesis must be. Even if we understand the social system of a subject class during the phase of conflict we do not know how it will organize society in a post-revolutionary situation. Therefore it is misleading to use such images as that of the germ of the new society being present in the womb of the old. It is not. All that a revolution settles is that the formerly subject group will be able to create a new social order. It does not entirely settle the question of what that social order will be like.

At the moment, then, all that our theoretical model does is to suggest areas of investigation. We should be concerned to understand the nature of the conflicting interests at the heart of a social system and we should also study the changing balance of power between interest groups and the ideologies in terms of which their actions are justified in various situations (i.e. where there is a ruling class in power, where there is a truce situation, where there has been a successful revolution and so on). All these factors would be relevant to understanding the new synthesis or social order. But until we have a great deal more empirical material we shall not be able even to begin speculating as to why a particular synthesis emerges from a particular sort of conflict.

None the less the importance of our conflict model lies in this, that it does not exclude change because of the nature of its concepts. It is implicit in the way in which the facts are conceptualized, when such a model is applied to them, that change is expected to take place. This is precisely what the model of an organism or an equilibrium excludes. Thus we have a way of formulating sociological theory which not only explains structure and process within a closed system, but which also explains the changes which occur from one system to another.

# 68 Anthony Giddens

'Power' in the Recent Writings of Talcott Parsons

Anthony Giddens, '"Power" in the recent writings of Talcott Parsons', *Sociology*, vol. 2, 1968, pp. 257–70.

Sociology is an extremely variegated discipline. Differences of theoretical outlook and methodology split it into numerous competing traditions and schools of thought. Any mode of classifying sociological theories is therefore partly arbitrary. But there is one general dichotomy between 'approaches' to general sociological theory which is perhaps at the present time more significant than any other. The origins of this dichotomy can easily be discerned in political dilemmas discussed by the classical social thinkers, and is still today more or less directly linked with a definite political value-orientation. The first 'approach', variously labelled 'structural functionalism', 'integration theory' or 'value theory', has over the past quarter of a century been prominent in Western sociology in general, and dominant in American sociology in particular. The second, now often called 'coercion' or 'conflict' theory, is strongly represented in the work of European sociologists, especially in the writings of those affiliated to one or other of the branches of Marxism.

Talcott Parsons is certainly the most eminent contemporary representative of the first 'approach', and as such has been consistently attacked for his 'conservatism' and failure to explain key aspects of social conflict and change. But, many, perhaps the majority, of these critiques have been couched as discussions of 'functionalism' at a very high level of abstraction. Where critics have been more specific, however, they have focused especially on Parsons's neglect of 'conflict groups' and 'non-normative interests' in the determination of social action. And there can be no doubt that one main pivot of the debate between value and coercion theory concerns the nature and sources of *power* in society. It is, therefore, of considerable interest that Parsons should have devoted a number of his recent writings to a discussion of power and related phenomena, explicit reference to which is conspicuous by its relative absence in the bulk of his earlier works.

Parsons's recent work on power involves a conscious modification of his previous views, where he accepted what he calls the 'traditional' view of power. This newer theory of power is an attempt to develop a set of concepts which will overcome what he sees as important defects in the 'traditional' notion. One of the first places where Parsons explicitly confronted these issues was in a review article of C. Wright Mills's *The Power Élite,* published in 1957. There Parsons proffered a variety of criticisms of Mills's book, but also took issue with the conception of power which he saw as underlying Mills's work. Mills's thesis, Parsons argued, gains weight from a 'misleading and one-sided' view of the nature of power, which Parsons labelled the 'zero-sum' concept of power. That is, power is conceived to be possessed by one person or group to the degree that it is not possessed by a second person or group over whom the power is wielded. Power is thus defined in terms of mutually exclusive objectives, so that a party is conceived to hold power in so far as it can realize its own wishes at the expense of those of others. In terms of game theory, from which the phrase 'zero-sum' is taken, to the degree that one party wins, the other necessarily loses. According to Parsons, this tends to produce a perspective from which all exercise of power appears as serving sectional interests. Parsons then went on to suggest that power is more adequately conceived by analogy with a non-zero-sum game: in other words, as a relation from which both sides may gain.

Power, Parsons proposed, can be seen as being 'generated' by a social system, in much the same way as wealth is generated in the productive organization of an economy. It is true that wealth is a finite quantity, and to the degree that one party possesses a proportion of a given sum of money, a second party can only possess the remainder; but the actual amount of wealth produced varies with the structure and organization of different types of economy. In an industrial society, for example, there is typically more for all than in an agrarian one. Power similarly has these two aspects, and it is the collective aspect which is most crucial, according to Parsons, for sociological analysis. Parsons summed up his objections to Mills's views as follows:

To Mills, power is not a facility for the performance of function in, and on behalf of, the society as a system, but is interpreted exclusively as a facility for getting what one group, the holders of power, wants by preventing another group, the 'outs' from getting what it wants.

What this conclusion does is to elevate a secondary and derived aspect of a total phenomenon into the central place (Parsons, 1960, p. 221).

Much of the substance of Parsons's later writings on power consists of a reaffirmation of this position, and an elaboration of the analogy between power and money. The parallels which Parsons develops between the two are based upon the supposition that each has a similar role in two of the four 'functional subsystems' of society which Parsons has distinguished in previous works. Power has a parallel function in the polity (goal-attainment subsystem) to that of money in the economy (adaptive subsystem). The main function of money in the modern economy is as a 'circulating medium': that is, as a standardized medium of exchange in terms of which the value of products can be assessed and compared. Money itself has no intrinsic utility; it has 'value' only in so far as it is commonly recognized and accepted as a standard form of exchange. It is only in primitive monetary systems, when money is made of precious metal, that it comes close to being a commodity in its own right. In a developed economy, precious metal figures directly only in a very small proportion of exchange transactions. The sense in which the economy is 'founded' upon its holdings of gold is really a symbolic and an indirect one, and gold forms a 'reserve' to which resource is made only when the stability of the economy is for some reason threatened.

Power is conceived by Parsons as a 'circulating medium' in the same sense, 'generated' primarily within the political subsystem as money is generated in the economy, but also forming an 'output' into the three other functional subsystems of society. Power is defined, therefore, as 'generalized capacity to serve the performance of binding obligations by units in a system of collective organization when the obligations are legitimized with reference to their bearing on collective goals'. By 'binding obligations' Parsons means the conditions which those in power, and those over whom power is exercised, are subject to through the legitimation which allows them that power; all power involves a certain 'mandate', which may be more or less extensive, which gives power-holders certain rights and imposes on them certain obligations towards those who are subject to their power. The collective goals rest upon the common value-system, which sets out the major objectives which govern the actions of the majority in a society. Thus American society is, according to Parsons, characterized by the primacy of values of 'instrumental activism', which entails that one main 'collective goal' of the society is the furtherance of economic productivity.

Just as money has 'value' because of common 'agreement' to use it as a standardized mode of exchange, so power becomes a facility for the achievement of collective goals through the 'agreement' of the members of a society to legitimize leadership positions – and to give those in such positions a mandate to develop policies and implement decisions in the furtherance of the goals of the system. Parsons emphasizes that this conception of power is at variance with the more usual 'zero-sum' notion which has dominated thinking in the field. In Parsons's view, the net 'amount' of power in a system can be expanded 'if those who are ruled are prepared to place a considerable amount of trust in their rulers.' This process is thought of as a parallel to credit creation in the economy. Individuals 'invest' their 'confidence' in those who rule them – through, say, voting in an election to put a certain government in power; in so far as those who have thus been put into power initiate new policies which effectively further 'collective goals', there is more than a zero-sum circular flow of power. Everybody gains from this process. Those who have 'invested' in the leaders have received back, in the form of the effective realization of collective goals, an increased return on their investment. It is only if those in power take no more than 'routine' administrative decisions that there is no net gain to the system.

Power is thus for Parsons directly derivative of authority: authority is the institutionalized legitimation which underlies power, and is defined as 'the institutionalization of the rights of "leaders" to expect *support* from the members of the collectivity'. By speaking of 'binding obligations', Parsons deliberately brings legitimation into the very definition of power, so that, for him, there is no such thing as 'illegitimate power'. As Parsons expresses it:

The threat of coercive measures, or of compulsion, without legitimation or justification, should not properly be called the use of power at all, but is the limiting case where power, losing its symbolic character, merges into an intrinsic instrumentality of securing compliance with wishes, rather than obligations (Parsons, 1963, p. 250).

In line with his general approach, Parsons stresses that the use of power is only one among several different ways in which one party may secure the compliance of another to a desired course of action. The other ways of obtaining compliance should not be regarded, Parsons stresses, as forms of power; rather it is the case that the use of power (i.e. the activation of 'binding obligations') is one among several ways of ensuring that a party produces a desired response. Parsons distinguishes two main 'channels' through which one party may seek to command the actions of another, and two main 'modes' of such control, yielding a fourfold typology. Ego may try to control the 'situation' in which alter is placed, or try to control alter's 'intentions'; the 'modes' of control depend upon whether sanctions which may be applied are positive (i.e. offer something which alter may desire), or negative (i.e. hold out the threat of punishment):

1. Situational channel, positive sanction: the offering of positive advantages to alter if he follows ego's wishes (*inducement*, e.g. the offering of money).

2. Situational channel, negative sanction: the threat of imposition of disadvantages if alter does not comply. (The use of *power*: in the extreme case, the use of force.)

3. Intention channel, positive sanction: the offering of 'good reasons' why alter should comply (the use of *influence*).

4. Intention channel, negative sanction: the threat that it would be 'morally wrong' for alter not to comply (the appeal to *conscience* or other moral commitments).

There is, Parsons points out, an 'asymmetry' between positive and negative sanctions. When compliance is secured through positive sanctions, because there is some definite reward, the sanctions are obvious. But, in the case of negative sanctions, compliance entails that the sanction is not put into effect; the operation of negative sanctions is generally symbolic rather than actual. In most cases where power is being used, there is no overt sanction employed (instances where force is used, for example, are relatively rare in the exercise of power). It is quite misleading, Parsons emphasizes, to speak of the use of power only when some form of negative sanction has actually been used: and some writers who take the 'zero-sum' notion of power tend to do this, speaking of 'power' only when some form of coercion has been applied. As Parsons says:

(When things are 'running smoothly') to speak of the holder of authority in these circumstances as not having or using power is, in our opinion, highly misleading. The question of his capacity to coerce or compel in case of non-compliance is an independent question that involves the question of handling unexpected or exceptional conditions for which the current power system may or may not be prepared (Parsons, 1964, p. 52).

It is particularly necessary to stress, Parsons argues, that possession and use of power should not be identified directly with the use of force. In Parsons's view, force must be seen as only one means among several, in only one type among several, modes of obtaining compliance. Force tends to be used in stable political systems only as a last resort when other sanctions have proved ineffective. Again using the analogy between money and power, Parsons draws a parallel between centralization of state control over gold, and state monopoly over the instruments of organized force in 'advanced and stable' societies. In the economy, there sometimes occur deflations, in which loss of confidence in the value of money leads to increasing reliance upon gold reserves in order to maintain the stability of the economy. In a similar way, Parsons holds, 'power deflation' can occur when a progressive decrease of confidence in the agencies of political power develops. Such a 'loss of confidence' produces increasing reliance by such agencies upon force to preserve political integration. In both the economic and political case, the undermining of the confidence which is the foundation of money and of power produces a 'regression' towards a 'primitive' standard.

In the subsequent discussion, my principal interest will be to comment on Parsons's analysis of power as such. I shall not attempt to assess in any detail the accuracy of the 'parallels' which Parsons attempts to specify between the polity and economy as 'functional subsystems' of society. If Parsons's conceptual scheme, and the assumptions which underlie it, cannot satisfactorily handle problems of power, then many of these 'parallels' must in any case be declared either invalid or misleading.

Parsons's critique of the 'zero-sum' concept of power does contain a number of valuable contributions and insights. There is no doubt that Parsons is correct in pointing out that the 'zero-sum' concept of power sometimes reinforces a simplistic view which identifies power almost wholly with the use of coercion and force. Such a perspective tends to follow from, although it is not at all logically implied by, the Weberian definition of power, which has probably been the most influential in sociology. In Weber's familiar definition, power is regarded as 'the chance of a man or of a number of men to realize their own will in a communal action even against the resistance of others who are participating in the action'. Such a definition tends to lead to a conception of power relations as inevitably involving incompatible and conflicting interests, since what is stressed is the capacity of a party to realize its *own* (implicitly, sectional) aims, and the main criterion for gauging 'amount' of power is the 'resistance' which can be overcome.

As Parsons correctly emphasizes, this can be extremely misleading, tending to produce an identification of power with the sanctions that are or can potentially be used by the power holder. In fact, very often it is not those groups which have most frequent recourse to overt use of coercion who have most power; frequent use of coercive sanctions indicates an insecure basis of power. This is particularly true, as Parsons indicates, of the sanction of force. The power position of an individual or group which has constant recourse to the use of force to secure compliance to its commands is usually weak and insecure. Far from being an index of the power held by a party, the amount of open force used rather is an indication of a shallow and unstable power base.

However, to regard the use of force in itself as a criterion of power is an error which only the more naïve of social analysts would make. But it is much more common to identify the power held by a party in a social relation with the coercive sanctions it is *capable* of employing against subordinates if called upon to do so – including primarily the capacity to use force. Again Parsons makes an important comment here, pointing out that a party may wield considerable power while at the same time having few coercive sanctions with which to enforce its commands if they are questioned by subordinates. This is possible if the power-holding party enjoys a broad 'mandate' to take authoritative decisions ceded or acquiesced in by those subject to the decisions – i.e. if those over whom the power is exercised 'agree' to subject themselves to that power. In such circumstances, the party in power depends, not on the possession of coercive sanctions with which it can over-ride non-compliance, but sheerly upon the recognition by the subordinate party or parties of its legitimate right to take authoritative decisions. The latter in some sense acquiesce in their subordination. Thus when subordinates 'agree' to allow others to command their actions, and when at the same time those who receive this 'mandate' have few coercive sanctions to employ if their directives are not obeyed, then there exists a situation of power not based upon control of means to coerce. It is because of such a possibility that Parsons emphasizes that the question of 'how much' power a party holds, and the question of what sanctions it is able to bring into play in case of disobedience, are analytically separable. And it must be conceded that lack of capacity to command a defined range of sanctions does not necessarily entail a lack of power; the 'amount' of power held by a party cannot be assessed simply in terms of the effective sanctions it is able to enforce if faced with possible or actual non-compliance. At the same time, it should be pointed out that 'amount' of power wielded in any concrete set of circumstances, and the effective sanctions that can be used to counter non-compliance, are usually closely related. Studies of all types of social structures, from small groups up to total societies, show that power holders always do command or develop sanctions which re-inforce their position: in any group which has a continued existence over time, those in power face problems of dissensus and the possibility of rebellion. The very fact of possession of a 'mandate' from those sub-ordinated to a power relation allows the dominant party to use this 'good will' to mobilize sanctions (even if only the scorn, ridicule, etc., of the conforming majority) against a deviant or potentially deviant minority. If a power-holding party does not possess sanctions to use in cases of disobedience, it tends rapidly to acquire them, and can in fact use its power to do so.

What Parsons is concerned to point out, then, is that the use of power frequently represents a facility for the achievement of objectives which *both* sides in a power relation desire. In this sense, it is clear that the creation of a power system does not *necessarily* entail the coercive subordination of the wishes or interests of one party to those of another. Nor is the use of power necessarily correlated with 'oppression' or 'exploitation'. Quite clearly, in any type of group, the existence of defined 'leadership' positions does 'generate' power which may be used to achieve aims desired by the majority of the members of the group. This possibility is, of course, envisaged in classic Marxist theory, and in most varieties of socialist theory, in the form of 'collective' direction of the instruments of government.

As Parsons recognizes, this kind of power is necessarily legitimate, and so he makes legitimacy part of his very definition of power. Parsons thus rejects the frequently held conception that authority is a 'form' of power, or is 'legitimate power'. This is again a useful emphasis. To regard authority as a 'type' of power leads to a neglect of its principal characteristic: namely that it concerns the *right* of a party to make binding prescriptions. Authority refers to the legitimate position of a party to make binding prescriptions. Authority refers to the legitimate position of an individual or group, and is therefore properly regarded as a *basis* of power (for Parsons, the only basis of power), rather than as a kind of power. It is precisely the confusion of the forms with the bases of power which causes Parsons to specify a very restricted definition of power. Authority is no more a form of power than force is a form of power.

A further valuable aspect of Parsons's analysis is the introduction of the typology of compliant behaviour. It is still quite common for sociologists naïvely to assert or to assume that conformity to any specific course of social action is founded *either* on 'internalization' of appropriate moral values *or* upon some form of coercion. This tendency is strong in the works both of those who follow Parsons and those who are highly critical. The isolation of various modes of securing compliance does allow for other mechanisms of conformity. The importance of the typology is diminished by the lack of any attempt to specify how these different ways of securing compliance are related together in social systems. Nevertheless, within the general context of Parsonian theory, this typology has some significance, marking a more definite recognition of the role of non-normative factors in social action.

But there are other respects in which the Parsons's discussion of power shares some of the basic difficulties and deficiencies of his general theory, and is at least as one-sided as the conception which he wishes to replace. Parsons is above all concerned to emphasize that power does not necessarily entail the coercive imposition of one individual or group over another, and he does indeed point to some valuable correctives for the mainstream of sociological thinking on problems of power. But what slips away from sight almost completely in the Parsonian analysis is the very fact that power, even as Parsons defines it, is always exercised *over* someone! By treating power as necessarily (by definition) legitimate, and thus *starting* from the assumption of consensus of some kind between power holders and those subordinate to them, Parsons virtually ignores, quite consciously and deliberately, the necessarily hierarchical character of power, and the divisions of interest which are frequently consequent upon it. However much it is true that power can rest upon 'agreement' to cede authority which can be used for collective aims, it is also true that interests of power holders and those subject to that power often clash. It is undoubtedly the case that some 'zero-sum' (coercion) theorists tend to argue as if power differentials *inevitably* entail conflicts of interest, and produce overt conflicts – and fail to give sufficient attention to specifying the conditions under which no conflict of either type is present. But it is surely beyond dispute that positions of power offer to their incumbents definite material and psychological rewards, and thereby stimulate conflicts between those who want power and those who have it. This brings into play of course, a multiplicity of possible strategies of coercion, deceit and manipulation which can be used to either acquire, or hold on to, power. If the use of power rests upon 'trust' or 'confidence', as Parsons emphasizes, it also frequently rests upon deceit and hypocrisy. Indeed this is true of all social life; all stable social action, except perhaps for all-out total war, depends upon some kind of at least provisional 'trust' – but this very fact makes possible many sorts of violations and rejections of 'confidence'. *L'enfer c'est les autres*. 'Deceit' and 'mistrust' only have meaning in relation to 'trust' and 'confidence': the former are as ubiquitous a part of social life as the latter are, and will continue to be as long as men have desires or values which are exclusive of each other, and as long as there exist 'scarce resources' of whatever kind. Any sociological theory which treats such phenomena as 'incidental', or as 'secondary and derived', and not as structurally intrinsic to power differentials, is blatantly inadequate. To have power is to have potential access to valued scarce resources, and thus power *itself* becomes a scarce resource. Though the relationships between power and exploitation are not simple and direct, their existence can hardly be denied.

Parsons escapes dealing with such problems largely through a trick of definition, by considering only as 'power' the use of authoritative decisions to further 'collective goals'. Two obvious facts, that authoritative decisions very often do serve sectional interests and that the most radical conflicts in society stem from struggles for power, are defined out of consideration – at least as phenomena connected with 'power'. The conceptualization of power which Parsons offers allows him to shift the entire weight of his analysis away from power as expressing a relation *between* individuals or groups, toward seeing power solely as a 'system property'. That collective 'goals', or even the values which lie behind them, may be the outcome of a 'negotiated order' built on conflicts between parties holding differential power is ignored, since for Parsons 'power' assumes the prior existence of collective goals. The implications of this are clearly demonstrated in Parsons's recent short book, *Societies,* in which he tries to apply some of these ideas to social change in actual historical settings. Social change in its most general aspect, Parsons makes clear, is fundamentally cultural evolution, i.e. change in values, norms and idea systems. And the basic *sources* of change are to be traced to changes in cultural values, and norms *themselves,* not to any sort of 'lower-level' factors, which at the most exert a 'conditioning' effect on social change. In spite of various qualifications and assertions to the contrary, Parsons's theory, as he applies it here, comes down to little more than a kind of idealist orthodoxy. History is moved, societies change, under the guiding direction of cultural values which somehow change, independently of other elements in the structure of social systems and exert a 'cybernetic control' over them. This is hardly consonant with Parsons's conclusion that 'once the problem of casual imputation is formulated analytically, the old chicken and egg problems about the priorities of ideal and material factors simply lose significance'. There is a great deal of difference between the sort of interpretation of social and historical change which Parsons presents in *Societies,* and one which follows a Marxist standpoint. Parsons's account is 'idealist' in the sense that it is based very largely upon an examination of value systems, and changes in them, and displays practically no concern with non-normative factors as causative agents in their formation, maintenance and diffusion. As in Parsons's more general theoretical expositions, such factors are formally recognized as of some importance, but no systematic discussion of the interplay between them and values is presented. As a consequence, Parsons tends to argue as if to show that some kind of logical relationship or 'fit' between a specific value, norm or pattern of behaviour, and some more general value or set of values, consitutes an 'explanation' of the former. This is characteristic also of Parsons's theoretical analysis of power and social change. Thus, for example, at one point in his discussion of political power, he traces 'political democracy' – i.e. universal franchise – to 'the principle of equality before the law', which is a 'subordinate principle of universalistic normative organization', as if this were to explain why or how universal franchise came into being.

In Parsons's conceptualization of power there is one notion which has an explicitly dynamic reference: that of 'power deflation'. This does at least make a conceptual *niche* in the Parsonian system for the possibility of social revolution. It is characteristic, however, that this concept depends upon the prior assumption of consensual 'confidence' in the power system. Power deflation refers to a spiralling diminution of 'confidence' in the agencies of power, so that those subordinate to them come increasingly to question their position. Parsons does not suggest any answers to why power deflations occur, except to indicate that once they get under way they resemble the 'vicious circle' of declining support characteristic of economic crisis. Now the parallel with economic deflation, in the terms in which Parsons discusses it, shows clearly that Parsons conceives the process as basically a psychological one, which is a kind of generalized parallel to the picture of deviance presented in *The Social System*. Power deflation is deviance writ large and in so far as it is focused on legitimate authority. Thus the possibility of explaining power deflation in terms of the mutual interaction of interest groups is excluded. The possibilities of theoretically tying such factors to the mechanics of power deflation, via the typology of means of obtaining compliance, are left aside. The parallels which Parsons is determined to pursue between the polity and the economy serve, in fact, to separate political and economic processes from one another. That economic and other 'material' factors themselves play a key part in power deflation is ignored because Parsons is above all concerned to show how the polity and economy are 'analytically' similar, not how they intertwine. Parsons's many discussions of the relationships between sociology and economics, including his and Smelser's *Economy and Society,* are all stated in terms of highly formal typolitical categories, and rarely suggest any substantive generalizations linking the two. Parsons's method is well illustrated by the entirely abstract character of his typology of modes of securing compliance. A distinction is made between 'inducement' and 'power'. The rationale for the distinction is that these can be considered parallel 'media' in the subsystems of the economy and the polity. Now such a typological distinction might be useful, but the important sociological problem is to apply it. How do inducement and power operate as systematic properties of societies or other social structures? Obviously inducement is often a *basis* of power; and the reverse also may frequently be true – a person or group holding power is often in a position allowing access to various forms of inducement, including the offer of financial reward. The relationship between 'positive' and 'negative' sanctions may be quite complicated as they actually operate in social systems. Thus inducements, offering some definite rewards in exchange for compliance, always offer the possibility of being transformed into negative sanctions; the *withholding* of a reward represents a punishment, and represents a definite form of coercion. But Parsons makes no attempt to draw out such possibilities and apply them to the analysis of power deflation, and in view of this, the process of power deflation is conceived purely as one of psychological 'loss of confidence' in the existing system.

It is significant that Parsons makes very little mention of what factors produce 'power inflation', i.e. the process whereby 'confidence' in a power system is *developed and expanded* in societies. It is just in this area that some of the most crucial problems in the sociology of power lie, and where conflict and coercion may play a major part. In Parsons's treatment of power, coercion and force are pictured as along the end of the line of a progression of corrective sanctions which can be applied to counter any tendency towards power deflation. Force is the sanction which is applied when all else has failed. But it is only when the system shows a lack of 'confidence' that open use of power becomes frequent. Thus, Parsons argues, stable power systems are only based indirectly, or 'symbolically', on the use of force. But in power 'inflation', coercion and force may be the 'foundation' of a consensual order in quite a different way. The history of societies shows again and again that structural arrangements are often at first implemented by force or by some other form of definite coercion, and coercive measures are used to *produce* and reinforce a new legitimacy. It is in this sense that power can grow out of the barrel of a gun. Force allows the manipulative control which can then be used to diminish dependence upon coercion. While this has been in previous ages probably only in part a process of conscious manipulation, in recent times, through the controlled diffusion of propaganda it can become a much more 'deliberate' process. But whether deliberate or not, it is not only the fact that stable power systems rest upon stable legitimation of authority which is the key to the analysis of power but, as the 'zero-sum' theorists have always recognized, just how legitimation is *achieved*. Through defining power as the activation of legitimate obligations, Parsons avoids dealing with the processes whereby legitimacy, and thereby authority and power, are established and maintained. Consensus is assumed, and power conceived to be derivative of it; the determinants of the consensual basis of power are regarded as non-problematic.

This means also that Parsons tends to accept the operations of authority at their face value, as if all 'obligations' of importance were open, public and legitimate. But it is an accepted fact of political life that

those who occupy formal authority positions are sometimes puppets who
have their strings pulled from behind the scenes. It is in the hidden
processes of control that some of the crucial operations of power in
modern societies are located. By defining power as 'the activation of
*legitimate* obligations' Parsons would seem to have to classify those processes as not involving 'power'. But the puppeteers behind the scenes
may be the people who hold real control, and it is not a helpful concept
of power which does not allow us to explore the often complicated relations which pertain between the 'unrecognized' or illegitimate, and the
legitimate, in systems of power.

This may not necessarily stem from Parsons's definition of power *per
se,* since it could be held that those who are *in fact* 'activating legitimate
obligations' are those who are using the individuals in formal authority
positions as a front – that it is the men behind the scenes who really
control those 'legitimate obligations', and thus who really hold 'power'.
But, at any rate, Parsons's own analysis shows an ingenuous tendency to
see nothing beyond the processes which are overt. Parsons's account of
how political support is derived, for example, is given in terms of a
prima facie comparison between government and banking:

Political support should be conceived of as a generalized grant of power
which, if it leads to electional success, puts elected leadership in a position
analogous to a banker. The 'deposits' of power made by constituents are
revocable, if not at will, at the next election....

Thus those in positions of political power have the legitimized right to
'use' the power 'granted' to them by the electorate in the same way as a
banker can invest money deposited with him. Parsons is presumably only
arguing that these two processes are 'analytically' parallel, and would no
doubt recognize the many substantive differences between them. But
nevertheless his anxiety to develop formal similarities between the polity
and economy, and correspondingly between money and power, seems to
have blinded him to the realities of political manipulation and the role
which power itself plays in begetting more *sectional* control. Parsons's
account of power and the electoral process reads like a description of
normative democratic theory in general, and often like an *apologia* for
American democracy in particular.

It is apparent that Parsons's treatment of power, while marking in a few
respects a greater formal recognition of the role of normative 'interests'
in social action, in the main represents a strong retrenchment of his
general theoretical position as set out in *The Social System.* Power now
becomes simply an extension of consensus, the means which a society

uses to attain its 'goals'. But this is surely inadequate. We must assert that power extends as deeply into the roots of social life as do values or norms; if all social relationships involve normative elements, so also do all social relationships contain power differentials. A general theory of social systems must *begin* from the interdependency of norms and power. Parsons's theory of power rests upon the general assertion that integration theory is 'the' theory of social systems, and simply ignores the range of problems which have mainly concerned 'zero-sum' or coercion theorists. The gap between integration and coercion theory appears to yawn as widely as ever.

It is the view of the present writer, however, that some of the differences between integration and coercion theory are more apparent than real. They are what Gurvitch calls 'false problems'. The chief false problem concerns the question of 'value consensus', which has generated so much controversy. In contrasting integration and conflict theory, Dahrendorf makes this the central focus of the distinction between the two perspectives. Integration theory attributes social order to '. . . a general agreement of values, a *consensus omnium* or *volonté générale* which outweighs all possible or actual differences of opinion or interest'; coercion theory 'holds that coherence and order in society are founded on force and constraint, or the domination of some and the subjection of others'. The second recognizes only 'such agreements of value as are required for the very establishment of force'. Parsons seems to accept this categorization (although obviously there are many points at which he would diverge completely from Dahrendorf) since a good deal of the argument in his writings on power is directed against the 'zero-sum' hypothesis that societies are basically 'founded' on coercion and force. But in fact this cloaks the real basis of disagreement between integration and coercion theorists. For most writers whose work could be classified as falling within the category of coercion theory *do* recognize the fundamental significance of 'common value systems' in social integration. Marx's writings can presumably be regarded as the source of the most important stream of coercion theory. Now Marx always recognized the cohering effect of commonly held values and ideas (which, in the Marxist usage, are covered under the generic term 'ideology'), and in fact built much of his theory upon such an assumption. The fact that subordinate groups in society, even if they are subjected to what to an outsider might appear to be extreme exploitation and degradation, *accept their subordination* is evident to any student of society with even a cursory knowledge of history. All societies having some degree of stability of structure develop such ideological systems which serve to 'rationalize' the lines of domination–subordination in society and thereby cohere the social structure. In Marx's theory, the use of force becomes marked only when such legitimate ideologies come under strain – and in this sense Parsons's description of 'power deflation' is not inconsistent with Marx's analysis of revolutionary change. Although, as Dahrendorf remarks, Marx 'assumed the ubiquity of change and conflict as well as dominance and subjection', it is nevertheless true that a crucial part of Marx's theory consists in tracing the integrative functions of ideology.

The main theoretical differences which separate integration and conflict theory do not concern the theoretical significance of 'common-value systems', but centre upon the processes which *give rise* to such systems, and the social mechanisms whereby systems of values and ideas are *linked with other structures of society*. That is, the real problems which have to be tackled, and which lie at the root of much of the debate, concern *how legitimation is mediated in its operation in systems of power*. Whereas coercion theorists argue that value consensus is determined by a combination of coercion and ideological manipulation, integration theory begins from the assumption that consensus derives from natural identity of interest served by some kind of co-operative action. The fundamental questions dividing the two concern *how groups acquire power*, what strategies they use to hold on to power, and how far these are consistent with the ideological basis of their power; the conditions under which those in subordinate groups come to question the legitimacy of those in power, and the channels which they adopt to seek changes in the power system.

It would be foolish to pretend that such questions can be readily resolved, either on a theoretical level or even in relation to concrete empirical problems. But posed in this way it is clear enough that the integration–coercion theory debate does rest upon substantive problems of sociological theory, however much these are related to differential philosophical positions. In other words, these are not two *intrinsically* irreconcilable perspectives. It is not true to say, as Dahrendorf does in *Class and Class Conflict in Industrial Society*, that:

There are sociological problems for the explanation of which the integration theory of society provides adequate assumptions; there are other problems which can be explained only in terms of the coercion theory of society; there are, finally, problems for which both appear adequate (Dahrendorf, 1959, p. 157).

If, say, a specific problem is analysed in terms of, say, Marxian assumptions about the manipulative role played by élite groups in positions of power, then the results are likely to be quite divergent from an analysis which assumes that power is widely diffused in society, and rests upon 'voluntarily' accepted subordination. The first paints a picture of marked divergence between reality and ideology; the second sees the two as correlated. The difference in empirical interpretation this leads to can readily be seen by comparing the divergent portrayals of American society presented by Mills and Parsons.

The degree to which the division between integration and coercion theory can in practice be resolved does not depend upon how far society itself is, as Dahrendorf put it, 'Janus-headed'; it depends upon factors affecting the formulation and validation of sociological theories *generally* – including the inherent difficulties of measurement and control of variables in sociological analysis; and the deep intrusion which 'heteronomous' values make into the process of comparative evaluation of the validity of competing sociological theories.

*Reference*

DAHRENDORF, R. (1959), *Class and Class Conflict in Industrial Society*, Stanford University Press.

PARSONS, T. (1960), 'The distribution of power in American society', in *Structure and Process in Modern Societies*, Free Press.

PARSONS, T. (1963), 'On the concept of political power', *Proc. Amer. Philos. Soc.*, vol. 107.

PARSONS, T. (1964), 'Some reflections on the place of force in social process', in H. Eckstein (ed.), *Internal War*, Free Press.

# 69 Robert K. Merton

Anomie and Social Structure

Excerpt from Robert K. Merton, 'Social structure and anomie', *American Sociological Review*, vol. 3, 1938, pp. 672–80.

There persists a notable tendency in sociological theory to attribute the malfunctioning of social structure primarily to those of man's imperious biological drives which are not adequately restrained by social control. In this view, the social order is solely a device for 'impulse management' and the 'social processing' of tensions. These impulses which break through social control, be it noted, are held to be biologically derived. Nonconformity is assumed to be rooted in original nature. Conformity is by implication the result of an utilitarian calculus or unreasoned conditioning. This point of view, whatever its other deficiencies, clearly begs one question. It provides no basis for determining the nonbiological conditions which induce deviations from prescribed patterns of conduct. In this paper, it will be suggested that certain phases of social structure generate the circumstances in which infringement of social codes constitutes a 'normal' response.

The conceptual scheme to be outlined is designed to provide a coherent, systematic approach to the study of sociocultural sources of deviate behavior. Our primary aim lies in discovering how some social structures *exert a definite pressure* upon certain persons in the society to engage in nonconformist rather than conformist conduct. The many ramifications of the scheme cannot all be discussed; the problems mentioned outnumber those explicitly treated.

Among the elements of social and cultural structure, two are important for our purposes. These are analytically separable although they merge imperceptibly in concrete situations. The first consists of culturally defined goals, purposes and interests. It comprises a frame of aspirational reference. These goals are more or less integrated and involve varying degrees of prestige and sentiment. They constitute a basic, but not the exclusive, component of what Linton aptly has called 'designs for group living'. Some of these cultural aspirations are related to the original drives of man, but they are not determined by them. The second phase of the social structure defines, regulates and controls the acceptable modes of achieving these goals. Every social group invariably couples its scale of desired ends with moral or institutional regulation of permissible and required procedures for attaining these ends. These regulatory norms and moral imperatives do not necessarily coincide with technical or efficiency norms. Many procedures which from the standpoint of *particular individuals* would be most efficient in securing desired values, e.g. illicit oil-stock schemes, theft, fraud, are ruled out of the institutional area of permitted conduct. The choice of expedients is limited by the institutional norms.

To say that these two elements, culture goals and institutional norms, operate jointly is not to say that the ranges of alternative behaviors and aims bear some constant relation to one another. The emphasis upon certain goals may vary independently of the degree of emphasis upon institutional means. There may develop a disproportionate, at times, a virtually exclusive, stress upon the value of specific goals, involving relatively slight concern with the institutionally appropriate modes of attaining these goals. The limiting case in this direction is reached when the range of alternative procedures is limited only by technical rather than institutional considerations. Any and all devices which promise attainment of the all important goal would be permitted in this hypothetical polar case. This constitutes one type of cultural malintegration. A second polar type is found in groups where activities originally conceived as instrumental are transmuted into ends in themselves. The original purposes are forgotten and ritualistic adherence to institutionally prescribed conduct becomes virtually obsessive. Stability is largely ensured while change is flouted. The range of alternative behaviors is severely limited. There develops a tradition-bound, sacred society characterized by neophobia. The occupational psychosis of the bureaucrat may be cited as a case in point. Finally, there are the intermediate types of groups where a balance between culture goals and institutional means is maintained. These are the significantly integrated and relatively stable, though changing, groups.

An effective equilibrium between the two phases of the social structure is maintained as long as satisfactions accrue to individuals who conform to both constraints, viz., satisfactions from the achievement of the goals and satisfactions emerging directly from the institutionally canalized modes of striving to attain these ends. Success, in such equilibrated cases, is twofold. Success is reckoned in terms of the product and in terms of the process, in terms of the outcome and in terms of activities. Continuing satisfactions must derive from sheer *participation* in a competitive order as well as from eclipsing one's competitors if the order itself is to be sustained. The occasional sacrifices involved in institutionalized conduct must be compensated by socialized rewards. The distribution of statuses and roles through competition must be so organized that positive incentives for conformity to roles and adherence to status obligations are provided *for every position* within the distributive order. Aberrant conduct, therefore, may be viewed as a symptom of dissociation between culturally defined aspirations and socially structured means.

Of the types of groups which result from the independent variation of the two phases of the social structure, we shall be primarily concerned with the first, namely, that involving a disproportionate accent on goals. This statement must be recast in a proper perspective. In no group is there an absence of regulatory codes governing conduct, yet groups do vary in the degree to which these folkways, mores and institutional controls are effectively integrated with the more diffuse goals which are part of the culture matrix. Emotional convictions may cluster about the complex of socially acclaimed ends, meanwhile shifting their support from the culturally defined implementation of these ends. As we shall see, certain aspects of the social structure may generate countermores and antisocial behavior precisely because of differential emphases on goals and regulations. In the extreme case, the latter may be so vitiated by the goal-emphasis that the range of behavior is limited only by considerations of technical expediency. The sole significant question then becomes, which available means is most efficient in netting the socially approved value? The technically most feasible procedure, whether legitimate or not, is preferred to the institutionally prescribed conduct. As this process continues, the integration of the society becomes tenuous and anomie ensues.

Thus, in competitive athletics, when the aim of victory is shorn of its institutional trappings and success in contests becomes construed as 'winning the game' rather than 'winning through circumscribed modes of activity', a premium is implicitly set upon the use of illegitimate but technically efficient means. The star of the opposing football team is surreptitiously slugged; the wrestler furtively incapacitates his opponent through ingenious but illicit techniques; university alumni covertly subsidize 'students' whose talents are largely confined to the athletic field. The emphasis on the goal has so attenuated the satisfactions deriving from sheer participation in the competitive activity that these satisfactions are virtually confined to a successful outcome. Through the same process, tension generated by the desire to win in a poker game is relieved by successfully dealing oneself four aces, or, when the cult of success has become completely dominant, by sagaciously shuffling the cards in a game of solitaire. The faint twinge of uneasiness in the last instance and the surreptitious nature of public delicts indicate clearly that the institutional rules of the game *are known* to those who evade them, but that the emotional supports of these rules are largely vitiated by cultural exaggeration of the success goal. They are microcosmic images of the social macrocosm.

Of course, this process is not restricted to the realm of sport. The process whereby exaltation of the end generates a *literal demoralization*, i.e. a deinstitutionalization, of the means is one which characterizes many groups in which the two phases of the social structure are not highly integrated. The extreme emphasis upon the accumulation of wealth as a symbol of success in our own society militates against the completely effective control of institutionally regulated modes of acquiring a fortune. Fraud, corruption, vice, crime, in short, the entire catalogue of proscribed behavior, becomes increasingly common when the emphasis on the *culturally induced* success goal becomes divorced from a coordinated institutional emphasis. This observation is of crucial theoretical importance in examining the doctrine that antisocial behavior most frequently derives from biological drives breaking through the restraints imposed by society. The difference is one between a strictly utilitarian interpretation which conceives man's ends as random and an analysis which finds these ends deriving from the basic values of the culture.

Our analysis can scarcely stop at this juncture. We must turn to other aspects of the social structure if we are to deal with the social genesis of the varying rates and types of deviate behavior characteristic of different societies. Thus far, we have sketched three ideal types of social orders constituted by distinctive patterns of relations between culture ends and means. Turning from these types of *culture patterning*, we find five logically possible, alternative modes of adjustment or adaptation *by individuals* within the culture-bearing society or group. These are schematically presented in the table on page 468, where (+) signifies 'acceptance', (−) signifies 'elimination' and (±) signifies 'rejection and substitution of new goals and standards'.

Our discussion of the relation between these alternative responses and other phases of the social structure must be prefaced by the observation that persons may shift from one alternative to another as they engage in different social activities. These categories refer to role adjustments in specific situations, not to personality *in toto*. To treat the development of this process in various spheres of conduct would introduce a complexity unmanageable within the confines of this paper. For this reason, we shall be concerned primarily with economic activity in the broad sense, 'the production, exchange, distribution and consumption of goods and services' in our competitive society, wherein wealth has taken on a highly

|              | Culture goals | Institutionalized means |
| ------------ | :-----------: | :---------------------: |
| I.   Conformity  | + | + |
| II.  Innovation  | + | − |
| III. Ritualism   | − | + |
| IV.  Retreatism  | − | − |
| V.   Rebellion*  | ± | ± |

* This fifth alternative is on a plane clearly different from that of the others. It represents a *transitional* response which seeks to *institutionalize* new procedures oriented toward revamped cultural goals shared by the members of the society. It thus involves efforts to *change* the existing structure rather than to perform accommodative actions *within* this structure, and introduces additional problems with which we are not at the moment concerned.

symbolic cast. Our task is to search out some of the factors which exert pressure upon individuals to engage in certain of these logically possible alternative responses. This choice, as we shall see, is far from random.

In every society, adaptation I (conformity to both culture goals and means) is the most common and widely diffused. Were this not so, the stability and continuity of the society could not be maintained. The mesh of expectancies which constitutes every social order is sustained by the modal behavior of its members falling within the first category. Conventional role behavior oriented toward the basic values of the group is the rule rather than the exception. It is this fact alone which permits us to speak of a human aggregate as comprising a group or society.

Conversely, adaptation IV (rejection of goals and means) is the least common. Persons who 'adjust' (or maladjust) in this fashion are, strictly speaking, *in* the society but not *of* it. Sociologically, these constitute the true 'aliens'. Not sharing the common frame of orientation, they can be included within the societal population merely in a fictional sense. In this category are *some* of the activities of psychotics, psychoneurotics, chronic autists, pariahs, outcasts, vagrants, vagabonds, tramps, chronic drunkards and drug addicts. These have relinquished, in certain spheres of activity, the culturally defined goals, involving complete aim inhibition in the polar case, and their adjustments are not in accord with institutional norms. This is not to say that in some cases the source of their behavioral adjustments is not in part the very social structure which they have in effect repudiated nor that their very existence within a social area does not constitute a problem for the socialized population.

This mode of 'adjustment' occurs, as far as structural sources are concerned, when both the culture goals and institutionalized procedures have been assimilated thoroughly by the individual and imbued with affect and high positive value but where those institutionalized procedures which promise a measure of successful attainment of the goals are not available to the individual. In such instances, there results a twofold mental conflict in so far as the moral obligation for adopting institutional means conflicts with the pressure to resort to illegitimate means (which may attain the goal) and inasmuch as the individual is shut off from means which are both legitimate *and* effective. The competitive order is maintained, but the frustrated and handicapped individual who cannot cope with this order drops out. Defeatism, quietism and resignation are manifested in escape mechanisms which ultimately lead the individual to 'escape' from the requirements of the society. It is an expedient which arises from continued failure to attain the goal by legitimate measures and from an inability to adopt the illegitimate route because of internalized prohibitions and institutionalized compulsives, *during which process the supreme value of the success goal has as yet not been renounced*. The conflict is resolved by eliminating *both* precipitating elements, the goals and means. The escape is complete, the conflict is eliminated and the individual is asocialized.

Be it noted that where frustration derives from the inaccessibility of effective institutional means for attaining economic or any other type of highly valued 'success', that adaptations II, III and V (innovation, ritualism and rebellion) are also possible. The result will be determined by the particular personality, and thus, the *particular* cultural background, involved. Inadequate socialization will result in the innovation response whereby the conflict and frustration are eliminated by relinquishing the institutional means and retaining the success aspiration; an extreme assimilation of institutional demands will lead to ritualism wherein the goal is dropped as beyond one's reach but conformity to the mores persists; and rebellion occurs when emancipation from the reigning standards, due to frustration or to marginalist perspectives, leads to the attempt to introduce a 'new social order'.

Our major concern is with the illegitimacy adjustment. This involves the use of conventionally proscribed but frequently effective means of attaining at least the simulacrum of culturally defined success – wealth, power and the like. As we have seen, this adjustment occurs when the individual has assimilated the cultural emphasis on success without equally internalizing the morally prescribed norms governing means for its attainment. The question arises: Which phases of our social structure predispose toward this mode of adjustment? We may examine a concrete instance, effectively analysed by Lohman, which provides a clue to the answer. Lohman has shown that specialized areas of vice in the near north side of Chicago constitute a 'normal' response to a situation where the cultural emphasis upon pecuniary success has been absorbed, but where there is little access to conventional and legitimate means for attaining such success. The conventional occupational opportunities of persons in this area are almost completely limited to manual labor. Given our cultural stigmatization of manual labor, and its correlate, the prestige of white-collar work, it is clear that the result is a strain toward innovational practices. The limitation of opportunity to unskilled labor and the resultant low income cannot compete *in terms of conventional standards of achievement* with the high income from organized vice.

For our purposes, this situation involves two important features. First, such antisocial behavior is in a sense 'called forth' by certain conventional values of the culture *and* by the class structure involving differential access to the approved opportunities for legitimate, prestige-bearing pursuit of the culture goals. The lack of high integration between the means-and-end elements of the cultural pattern and the particular class structure combine to favor a heightened frequency of antisocial conduct in such groups. The second consideration is of equal significance. Recourse to the first of the alternative responses, legitimate effort, is limited by the fact that actual advance toward desired success-symbols through conventional channels is, despite our persisting open-class ideology, relatively rare and difficult for those handicapped by little formal education and few economic resources. The dominant pressure of group standards of success is, therefore, on the gradual attenuation of legitimate, but by and large ineffective, strivings and the increasing use of illegitimate, but more or less effective, expedients of vice and crime. The cultural demands made on persons in this situation are incompatible. On the one hand, they are asked to orient their conduct toward the prospect of accumulating wealth and on the other, they are largely denied effective opportunities to do so institutionally. The consequences of such structural inconsistency are psychopathological personality, and/or antisocial conduct, and/or revolutionary activities. The equilibrium between culturally designated means and ends becomes highly unstable with the progressive emphasis on attaining the prestige-laden ends by any means whatsoever. Within this context, Capone represents the triumph of amoral intelligence over morally proscribed 'failure', when the channels of vertical mobility are closed or narrowed *in a society which places a high premium on economic affluence and social ascent for all its members.*

This last qualification is of primary importance. It suggests that other phases of the social structure besides the extreme emphasis on pecuniary success, must be considered if we are to understand the social sources of

antisocial behavior. A high frequency of deviate behavior is not gene-
ated simply by 'lack of opportunity' or by this exaggerated pecuniary
emphasis. A comparatively rigidified class structure, a feudalistic or
caste order, may limit such opportunities far beyond the point which
obtains in our society today. It is only when a system of cultural values
extols, virtually above all else, certain *common* symbols of success *for
the population at large* while its social structure rigorously restricts or
completely eliminates access to approved modes of acquiring these symbols *for a considerable part of the same population*, that antisocial behavior ensues on a considerable scale. In other words, our egalitarian
ideology denies by implication the existence of noncompeting groups
and individuals in the pursuit of pecuniary success. The same body of
success-symbols is held to be desirable for all. These goals are held to
*transcend class lines*, not to be bounded by them, yet the actual social
organization is such that there exist class differentials in the accessibility
of these *common* success-symbols. Frustration and thwarted aspiration
lead to the search for avenues of escape from a culturally induced intolerable situation; or unrelieved ambition may eventuate in illicit attempts
to acquire the dominant values. The American stress on pecuniary success and ambitiousness for all thus invites exaggerated anxieties, hostilities, neuroses and antisocial behavior.

# 70 Ralph H. Turner

## The Nature of Role Interaction

Excerpt from Ralph H. Turner, 'Role-taking: process versus conformity', in Arnold M. Rose (ed.), *Human Behaviour and Social Processes*, Routledge & Kegan Paul, 1962, pp. 32–8.

### Dynamics of self and other

The customary use of the concept of role in sociological and related literature today depicts the dynamic relationship between roles as primarily *conformity*. There are three key terms in this popular model, namely, *conformity*, *expectation* and *approval*. A component of each role is a set of expectations regarding the behaviour of individuals in relevant other-roles. When ego takes the role of alter the aspect of alter's role to which he is crucially sensitive is the set of expectations with respect to his (ego's) role. Ego takes the role of alter in order to conform to alter's expectations. Lack of conformity must be explained by erroneous role taking, or by deficiencies in emphatic ability or opportunities to perceive and judge the role of the other. The confirmation that role taking and role playing have proceeded correctly according to the conformity principle is the registration of approval.

We suggest that the foregoing model is not in itself incorrect; it is merely of insufficient generality. It describes only one of several ways in which the role taking and role playing process may occur, only one of several kinds of dynamic relations which may exist between self- and other-roles. Instead, we propose that the relations between self- and other-roles are interactive in a full sense, the dynamic principles being of several sorts, depending upon the objectives of the role players and upon the character of their relationships with one another. Furthermore the enactment of a given role often involves the simultaneous role taking relationship with several different other-roles, and the dynamic relationship between each self- and other-role may be of a different sort.

In some athletic events such as the game of baseball the roles are highly standardized and the allowance for improvisation is at a minimum, so that the assumption that each role incorporates clear expectations for each other-role is quite valid. But in most situations what the role player expects from the relevant other on the basis of the latter's role is not likely to be a specific action but some behaviour which will be susceptible to interpretation as directed towards the ends associated with the other-role, expressive of the sentiment which dominates the role in question, or as consistent with the values attached to the role. A group torn by internal dissension may turn to someone who it is hoped will enact the role of compromiser. In doing so they have an expectation which identifies the general purpose and sentiment which will guide his actions and some general conception of the kind of behaviour which will contribute to the achievement of compromise and which will not. But they do not have any exact notion of what the specific steps will be.

The articulation of behaviour between roles may be described better by the term 'preparedness' than by the term 'expectation'. The crucial consideration is that ego's role *prepares* him for a loosely definable *range* of responses from alter on the basis of the latter's role. The potential responses of alter, then, divide into those which are readily interpretable upon the basis of the assumed self- and other-roles and those which seem not to make sense from this vantage point. A response which fell outside of the preparedness range would be one of two kinds. It might be a response which was initially perceived as irrelevant, that is, not interpretable as the expression of any role in the context of the present focus of interaction. Or it might be a response which seemed to indicate a different role from that which had been attributed to alter.

The more or less definite expectations for ego's role which are part of alter's role, the preferences, the conceptions of legitimate and illegitimate behaviour and the evaluations, all directed towards ego's role, are a part but not the whole of alter's role. Role taking may or may not concentrate on these aspects, and when it does it has been referred to as reflexive role taking. Role taking is always incomplete, with differential sensitivity to various aspects of the other-role. Only under special circumstances is the sensitization likely to be exclusively to the reflexive aspect. Such sensitization goes along with a conformity relationship, but not necessarily with approval in the simple sense.

The most general purpose associated with sensitization to the reflexive aspects of the other-role is to validate a self-image. The object is to present the self in a fashion which will conform to the relevant other's conception of the role by which the actor seeks to be identified. The role may, however, be one of which the relevant other approves or disapproves or towards which he is neutral. The young 'tough' may be unsure that he has sufficiently exemplified the desired self-image until he provokes a vigorous condemnation from the teacher. The individualist may be dissatisfied until he provokes disagreement from a conventional person.

Elsewhere the kinds of dynamic relationship between roles have been discussed under the headings of role standpoint and reflexive versus non-reflexive role taking. But the most general form of self–other relationship is that in which the relationship is a means to the accomplishment of either some shared goal or separate individual goals. Under such circumstances, the role relationship will be pragmatic, the two roles (or the same role enacted by two interacting individuals) being viewed as an efficient division of labour. In role taking the salient aspects of the other-role will be their instrumental features, and the self-role will be enacted in such a fashion as to combine effectively with the instrumental features of the other-role to accomplish the intended purpose. Conformity to alter's expectations may enter as a partial determinant in this truly inter-active relation but principally because it is an adjunct to the efficient accomplishment of the objective. The conformity principle may also come to be dominant because the effects of the role interaction in the promotion of the group goal are not readily apparent, as in a standby military organization or in an educational organization where no real tests of the effectiveness of the educational process are available. But conformity remains a special instance of the more general interactive principle rather than the general principle itself.

## The normative component of role taking

Roles are often identified as sets of norms applicable to an actor playing a recognizable part. Since norms are at least partially equatable with expectations, such a conception may convey the same simple conformity formula with which we have just dealt. However, there is an essentially normative element in the concept of role which derives from the fact that a minimum of predictability is the precondition of interaction. This interdependency has been well described by Waller and Hill by reference to the 'interlocking habit systems' which develop between marriage partners. To the extent to which one member patterns his behaviour to fit with the past regularities of behaviour in the other, the former's behaviour becomes inappropriate when the latter makes unanticipated alterations in his behaviour. The inappropriateness invokes indignation against the innovator and the charge that he had no right to alter his behaviour. Thus, although no norm originally existed and no explicit commitment had been made, a norm has in fact developed because of the damage which one person's unpredictable behaviour does to the other. The prediction is of two sorts, prediction of the role to be played and prediction that behaviour will continue to exemplify the same role once it is established in interaction. It is the latter which is most fundamental. The basic normative element in role taking and playing is the requirement that the actor be consistent – that his behaviour remain within the confines of a single role. So long as it remains within the role, the other will be generally prepared to cope with the behaviour, whether he approves of it or not.

In institutional contexts, the additional normative element that designates *a priori* what role each individual must play is introduced to insure the required division of labour and to minimize the costs of exploratory role-setting behaviour. But the norm of consistency is the more fundamental since it applies to role taking in both informal and formalized settings, while the norm which assigns roles to persons applies chiefly in the latter.

The norm of consistency is mitigated in operation by an implicit presumption that actors are adhering to the norm. Indications that an actor is from an out-group, special symbols of deviant identity or glaring evidences of 'inconsistency', cause the assumption to be questioned. But in the absence of such cues, the initial presumption that each actor must be adhering to *some* role creates a strong bias in favour of finding a set of interpretations of his behaviour which will allow it to be seen as pertaining to a single role. The bias may go as far as the synthesizing of a partially new role for one of the actors. Once the actor's role has been identified, either on the basis of indications of his position, placing oneself in his situation, or bits of his behaviour, there is a further presumption that his subsequent behaviour represents the same role. The flexibility with which most actions can be interpreted, emphasized and de-emphasized, affords considerable scope for the role taker to find confirmation of his preconceptions.

The normative principle of consistency, then, works both in the direction of enforcing a pattern onto behaviour and in the direction of allowing a range of actions to be subsumed under a given role. The following hypotheses are suggested. The restricting impact of the consistency norm on behaviour tends to be greater under conditions of dominance, whether authoritarian or instrumental, when participants are sensitized to interpret deviations from standard roles as symbolic denials of the dominance–submission relationship. The restricting effect tends to be greater when there is relatively little basis for faith in the role enactor's possession of the appropriate role sentiment. Such faith in turn arises out of prior experience with the other's role performance or out of esteem accorded the other by persons whose judgements are respected.

Many studies of role conflict proceed as if the dynamics of adjustment lie primarily in a choice of which set of expectations to honour in the face of an urgent desire to adhere to two or more incompatible sets. If the view is accepted that conformity is but one type of working adjustment to the other-role, then role conflict should be seen in the light of attempts to establish some kind of working relationship with the roles of relevant others. In its most general sense, role conflict exists when there is no immediately apparent way of simultaneously coping effectively with two different relevant other-roles, whether coping is by conformity to expectation or by some other type of response. The problem of a man whose friend has committed a serious crime need not be primarily or exclusively how to conform to the expectations both of his friend and of the police. The problem is to cope with the roles of each, conformity to expectation being but one of the alternatives before him. The definition of modern woman's problem as primarily how to conform simultaneously to the conflicting expectations of those with traditional and egalitarian views of her role reveals the same limited conception. The problem is more fundamentally how to engage in effective interaction with men, some of whom have modern and some traditional and some mixed conceptions of the masculine role, and with women who may have the same or different conceptions of the feminine role.

## Summary and implications

Role theory, originally depicting a tentative and creative interaction process, has come increasingly to be employed as a refinement of conformity theory. In consequence, the theory has become relatively sterile except with respect to the consequences of role conflict and other forms of deviation from the conventional model of role behaviour. Role taking, however, suggests a process whereby actors attempt to organize their interaction so that the behaviour of each can be viewed as the expression of a consistent orientation which takes its meaning (or consistency) from its character as a way of coping with one or more other actors enacting similarly consistent orientations. Conformity to perceived expectations is but one special way in which an actor's role playing may be related to the role of relevant others. From this viewpoint, role behaviour in formal organizations becomes a working compromise between the formalized role prescriptions and the more flexible operation of the role-taking process. Role conflict is the attempt to devise an orientation from which the actor can cope effectively with multiple other-roles which apparently cannot be dealt with in a 'consistent' fashion.

The conception of role relations as fully interactive rather than merely conforming, harmonizes with current trends in sociology and anthropology to subordinate normative to functional processes in accounting for societal integration. Emphasis on the binding power of the mores and folkways or on the blind adherence to custom corresponds with a society populated by people playing roles principally as sets of expectations with which they must comply. On the other hand, a functional view emphasizes the interdependence of activities in accounting for cultural persistence and social stability. The interactive consequence of role relationships provides the social-psychological mechanism through which the functional principle of social stability operates.

# 71 Edwin M. Lemert

Deviance and Social Control

Excerpts from Edwin M. Lemert, *Human Deviance, Social Problems and Social Control*, Prentice-Hall, 1967, pp. 7–26. First published in Marshall B. Clinard (ed.), *Anomie and Deviant Behavior*, Free Press, 1964.

## Patterned values and social structures

It is theoretically conceivable that there are or have been societies in which values learned in childhood, taught as a pattern and reinforced by structured controls, serve to predict the bulk of the everyday behavior of members and to account for prevailing conformity to norms. However, it is easier to describe the model than it is to discover societies which make a good fit with the model. [. . .] It is safe to say that separatism, federation, tenuous accommodation and perhaps open structuring, are at least as characteristic of known societies of the world as the unified kind of ideal social structure based on value consensus which impressed Durkheim, Parsons and Merton.

## Ethnic pluralism, accommodation and deviation

One form of value pluralism arises when dominant values of a culturally distinct group are extended to become a basis for normative regulation of ethnic or religious populations having divergent values. The resultant social integrations follow from conquest, territorial expansion or migration, and are largely accommodative in nature. By definition or fiat, certain cultural practices of the minority cultural groups become crimes, subject to sanctions and penalties imposed by the dominant group or élite. Sellin called attention to the implication of such facts, years ago, in his discussion of culture conflict and crime. Examples abound in the extension of Soviet law into Siberia, imposition of French law in Algeria, and the establishment of English, French, German and American legal institutions in Pacific Island dependencies. Closer to home can be seen the continuing subjection of American Indians and Mexicans to Anglo-Saxon law, and the consequence of the migration of rural Negroes into northern, urban jurisdictions.

The important conclusion from examination of such pluralistic value situations is that criminal deviation in the ethnic minorities can be explained in the same way as conformity among members of the dominant population segment, i.e. by reference to traditionally patterned values and norms where there is no socially structured restriction of means. Numerous examples of such deviant behavior in our society, without disjunctive ends–means concomitants, can be cited: violations of fish and game laws by Indians; common law marriage, statutory rape, marihuana use and carrying concealed weapons by Mexican migrants; common law marriage, 'totin' ' (petty theft) and assault by rural Negro migrants; gambling and opium use by Chinese; informal sororal polygyny, gambling and statutory rape ('sex sixteen' cases) among Hawaiians; drunkenness among older Japanese in Hawaii; and cockfighting among Filipinos.

This kind of unreflective, subcultural behavior is seen most clearly among newly migrant peoples, whose offenses sometimes seem naïve and childlike in the eyes of law enforcement agents. However, if the law is persistently enforced, its effects will be to create new costs for the traditional means of the minority group, leading to a gradual growth in awareness among the minority peoples of the legal implications of their behavior and introducing valuational phenomena into their behavior. Much, of course, depends upon the way in which the laws are enforced and the subgroups or élites to whom control is delegated.

Conformity of ethnic groups in a pluralistic society, or in situations where intercultural values and norms compete, frequently has to be comprehended as a function of a variety of accommodative relationships which require that subgroup values be satisfied through the instrumental use of associations in the larger, culturally differentiated society. Thus, when native peoples or migrants become involved in a money economy, technological arrangements, and government health and welfare projects, conformities are produced, not through acceptance of dominant values but rather through treating the values and norms of the dominant group as alternative means to their own unchanged ends. Nowhere is this more clearly exemplified than in the sporadic or cyclical patterns of participation of native peoples in the work-money complexes which have been superimposed on their societies by colonizing élites of western nations. Similarly revealing are the uses they make of the money earned by their labors.

### Neo-technic pluralism and social structure

It may be protested that the kinds of deviation and conformity we have just discussed are special problems or are tangential to the main concern of Merton's theory which deals with populations presumed to have been socialized within a common cultural tradition. However, when attention is shifted to a contemporary, urban, secular, technologically based society such as our own, the notion that such a society has a common value hierarchy, either culturally transmitted or structurally induced, strains credulity. [...]

In life-history retrospect, when the individual leaves the arena of primary groups and enters into numerous associations and unstructured situations with individual members representing disparate values, the patterned values acquired in primary groups are overlaid with social interactions which change the meaning of his early experiences. For those who follow patterned values and get the consequences they were taught to expect, the pattern is reinforced in overt behavior and presumably in psychic structure. For those who follow the pristine pattern and meet with other than anticipated consequences there is a modification of either overt behavior or psychic structure, or both.

Because of the disparity in individual members of associations the values which emerge as dominant therein may vary greatly from those of individuals considered distributively. When the association becomes part of an alignment with other associations, the values made dominant in society through the activities of such alignments are even further removed from those of individuals in the various constituent associations. By the same token, the norms set up or legislated to insure the dominance of these remote values may be greatly discrepant or in direct conflict with those held to be appropriate by individuals. It thus becomes doubtful whether study of ideal or presumably indoctrinated values and norms of individuals will generally predict conformity in modern society. Individuals, because they necessarily utilize groups as means to ends, continuously and characteristically conform to norms they have not been taught or to norms whose moral concomitants have been highly attenuated in the course of time. Conformity in groups represents some kind of aggregation of values of individuals, but the form or process of aggregation cannot be presumed from the mere overt facts of conformity. If we are correct that conformity and deviation are complementary aspects of the same phenomena, then much the same generalizations apply to deviation.

### Individual choice in plural society

One objection to Merton's view of choice and action by individuals in our society is that it simplifies something enormously complex. Instead of seeing the individual as a relatively free agent making adaptations pointed toward a consistent value order, it is far more realistic to visualize him as 'captured', to a greater or lesser degree, by the claims of various groups to which he has given his allegiance. It is in the fact that these claims are continually being pre-emptively asserted through group action at the expense of other claims, frequently in direct conflict, that we find the main source of 'pressures' on individuals in modern society, rather than in 'cultural emphasis on goals'. Overt behavior, whether it be conforming or deviant, frequently reflects contingent ordering of values and compromised positioning, and their unresolved dilemmas. The likelihood that these will be similar in any two individuals is small.

The captured position of individuals in modern, pluralistic society sheds light on the choice of means to ends. One general consequence of this position is the increase of calculational behavior and a heightened awareness of alternatives, a necessary willingness to consider a wide variety of values and norms as functional alternatives to ends. In a different type of society, this would not be possible. The pressures for individuals to do this have been paralleled by freedom to do so through the widespread secularization of values, largely a product of science and technology.

Now a very great number of changes in the modern world have altered the traditional means of obtaining man's values. Some of the 'sacred' values of another time have by the development of science become secularized, that is, they are considered as alternatives to other values, and also the means to their achievement can be rationally considered in terms of functionally to achieve them rather than as ends in themselves (Cottrell, 1954, p. 118).

Understanding the way in which illegitimate means are used to satisfy values is complicated by the fact that associations in many areas of choice strive to have, and in many cases succeed in having, their special values advanced, protected or entrenched through enactment of legal norms. Thus, in addition to an older traditional body of criminal laws revolving around sacred values of life, person and property, there is a vast proliferation of criminal statutes having to do with health, welfare, public safety and order, conservation, taxes, banking, fiduciary operations, insurance and transportation, largely representing the specialized values of associations. In many instances the legal norms represent no values of individuals or groups, but rather are the results of compromises reached through group interaction in legislatures.

Our argument here is that criminal laws of the first class can still be regarded as 'sacred', but that those of the latter generally fall into a category of secularized, functional alternatives to ends, irrespective of the fact that they have been given political sanction or public, ethical connotation. It is further contended that it is impossible to speak of a cultural or broadly indoctrinated 'emphasis' on such norms and equally unrealistic to try to classify them in terms of the degree of their compulsiveness, as proposed by Merton. Objective emphasis on such norms is shifting or ephemeral, to a large extent unsteadily resting on associational alignments having access to political power or on illusory ideologies. Subjectively, the emphasis which individuals place upon such norms depends upon the relationship of the individual to the groups whose values the norms have been designed to give dominance. Seen somewhat differently, the emphasis placed on normative means is determined by their cost, that is, by the particular values that must be sacrificed in order to adopt means.

The kind of orientation towards norms emerging in modern society is epitomized in attitudes of the traffic offender toward his punishments. According to one study, he characteristically regards fines either as 'a cost of doing business' or 'an unjust penalty for something he could not have avoided'. Data of my own indicate that fines for violations of weight regulations for trucks in areas of northern California are accepted by companies, as well as by individual truck drivers, as a necessary cost of doing business. Compliance or noncompliance becomes purely a matter of dollars and cents; thus the cost of two trips to move freight from one terminal to another may be higher than the cost of one trip plus fines assessed at so much per pound. Evidence that the illegal alternative is conceived in purely functional terms exists in the formalized arrangements whereby issuance of a certain type of 'trip ticket' insures that the driver's fines will be paid by the company. The reciprocal functionality of attitudes of state officials likewise is revealed by the practice of sending monthly statements to the trucking companies of total fines due.

While it is difficult to determine the extent to which costs become the basis for choosing illegal alternatives to ends in various areas of our society, there seems to be evidence of a growth of 'practical morality', under the influence of the dominant world of business, industry, and the large association. Research is confused by the tendency of persons to continue to pay lip service to older, patterned moral concepts. Some indication of the 'real' situation is gained from one study of chiseling on unemployment compensation, which disclosed that the 'nearness' of persons to the actual conflict situation and the particular issue (sickness) was an important factor in their willingness to regard noncompliance as an acceptable alternative.

### Risk taking and deviant behavior
At this juncture it is possible to bring several of the ideas so far developed into a somewhat different, perhaps novel, concept of deviant

behavior. This concept refers to situations in which persons who are caught in a network of conflicting claims or values choose not deviant alternatives but rather behavioral solutions which carry risks of deviation. Deviation then becomes merely one possible outcome of their actions, but it is not inevitable. It hinges rather on the turn of circumstances or convergence of external factors. Such an explanation has been proposed by Firth to explain suicide – a subject on which Merton is strangely silent.

Taking issue with Durkheim's analysis of suicide, Firth has shown how suicide among people in the island setting of Tikopia cannot be related to rigidities of social structure nor to any consistent psychic states, largely because the persons attempting suicide were responding to a variety of competing values and because the nature of the act of suicide has culturally variable meanings of goodness and badness, depending upon the specific form of an act and the groups viewing it. Furthermore, it is important that the acts differed in their lethal probabilities; only in certain cases could it be ascertained that the person had definitely chosen to end his or her life. In a large range of cases the most that could be said was that death was one possibility, other possibilities being that the act could eventuate as a daring exploit or lead to a reintegration of the individual into the island social life. A not unimportant factor in the outcome was the efficiency and dispatch with which the rescue fleets were organized and put to sea to locate the lone swimmer or canoe voyager – whose behaviors were among the most common forms of suicide-possible acts.

This analysis of suicide suggests the more general possibility that there are many instances in which people do not elect deviant solutions to problems but instead initiate lines of behavior which, according to how circumstances unfold, may or may not become deviant. In other words, risk taking, rather than deviation, is perceived by the conflicting person as a 'way out'. In effect the decision becomes 'let chance decide', which indicates that *several* ends–means possibilities inhere in the behavior. While it would be presumptuous in the absence of supporting research to push this interpretation as a general theory of deviant behavior, nevertheless its pertinence to the facts of suicide in our society seem as great as for suicide among the Polynesians of Tikopia. Evidence that risk taking may be a predominant theme in other forms of deviant behavior comes from the writer's own research on check forgery, in which a substantial number of cases revealed persons who were not motivated to pass bad checks but who simply took chances that under certain circumstances their checks might not be honored. Examples are building contractors who, in anticipation that construction loan payments would be released on schedule, issued checks to laborers and to others for services and materials in such a way that liabilities were created. When the expected payments were not deposited in the bank, their checks became (in California) insufficient funds felony offenses. Although sociology has yet to explore the possibility, it is fair to assume that a considerable amount of risk taking is built into our business culture – particularly in some areas such as contracting, brokerage and commission selling, and salvage and distress merchandising.

## Intervening variables in deviation

If Merton has excessively simplified the complexities of ends and means and their interrelationships in modern society, much the same charge can be made in regard to his treatment of social structure. His theoretical leap from a single, abstracted element of social structure – class-limited access to means – to deviation in its several typologized forms is a broad one, to say the least. However commendable such parsimony may be in the interests of codifying research, it requires at least prima facie evidence that the assumed differential rates of deviation between upper and lower social strata do exist. Furthermore, some logical exercise or empirical argument seems a preliminary necessity to justify the view, certainly tangential to sociology, that deviation is the result of *individual adaptations*.

A general purview of extant research leaves serious doubts that deviant behavior is proportionately more common at lower than at other class levels of our society. The doubts increase as one proceeds away from crime rates, which are the starting point for Merton's formulation. Crime rates are shaky grounds for any theory, largely because of the widely recognized unreliability of crime statistics. Even if it is granted that crime is relatively more frequent for lower-class populations, there are outstanding exceptions when certain types of crimes are noted, such as check forgery, embezzlement, automobile theft and possibly sex offenses. Further difficulties with the assumed priority of class handicaps in the explanation of illegal behavior are met in the equal or greater variations in crime rates when they are computed by age, sex, locality and ethnic identity.

When attention is drawn to such forms of deviation as alcoholism, suicide and drug addiction, there are no consistent data to show that these are more common adaptations of members of lower-class society. Some studies agree with the idea that psychosis rates are inversely related to class or occupational status, but when rates for psychoneuroses are considered, the relationship becomes positive. The contention that radicalism or rebellion are lower-class adaptations is perhaps the most diffi-cult of all to fit the facts. Proclivities of middle-class persons for radical protest and action have long been known to writers on the subject. Cot-trell's case study of the death of a railroad town due to dieselization portrays dramatically how technologically induced crises may evoke a shift towards radicalism or ideological rebellion in the settled, 'moral', propertied class, rather than in the lower class, which in this instance had the low cost alternative of migrating from the town. Geographic location, age and seniority as expressions of technological structure largely determined which persons experienced pressures to deviate.

The degree and rapidity with which technology differentiates social organization in modern society and the difficulty of discovering measures of social status generally applicable to a variety of populations and areas speak of the necessity to use a more discriminating concept or concepts than social class in seeking to explain how social structure in-fluences deviation. It is possible to share with Merton a modest assump-tion that position in social structure is important in determining what means become available to reach ends, but other factors are equally important. Among these are groups, technology, psychic processes and sociobiological handicaps.

## Collective adaptations

Nothing seems more obtrusive in modern society than the dependence of individuals upon groups as means of reaching their ends and the col-lective context in which ends and means assume importance. For this reason we may wonder why Merton made no allusions to groups as dynamic variables in deviant behavior, in his original and revised essays. It was only subsequently, and then in a very limited way, that he recog-nized the need to link theoretically some aspects of deviation to groups. Thus, in order to account for forms of deviation that do not arise from private, 'autistic' adaptations, he advocates the concept of non-conformity as 'a basis for consolidating the theory of deviation and reference group behavior'. Following Cooley, Merton defines this as a kind of conformity in reverse, that is, conformity to values and nor-mative standards of reference groups representing 'an earlier condition of society or that of future society'.

Reference group is a term with several meanings in sociology, but it is employed by Merton to account for the individual's perceptions which are at variance from those expected from an inventory of values of the group or social category of which he is currently a member. The prob-lem in its use is that it easily becomes reductionistic, and in so far as the group becomes an inert repository of values assumed to determine the behavior of the individual for whom it is a referent, the criticism is justifiable. Actually, the 'group' is an illusory variable in Merton's suggested analysis of nonconformist behavior, for it corresponds to no extant or identifiable body of persons. The discrete individual remains for Merton the unit of analysis; the group as an arena of interaction, variably influencing conformity and deviation, nowhere comes to the fore in his treatment.

It seems almost gratuitous to insist that many forms of deviation, professional crime, prostitution, 'vagrancy', skid-row drinking, use of opiates and marihuana smoking, even bureaucratic 'ritualism', are collective acts in which group-derived and group-maintained values, as well as private values, are served. It is equally necessary to see that conformity, as numerous psychological studies and knowledge of monolithic, party-political behavior make plain, is a collective as well as an individual phenomenon.

In struggling with the perplexing problem of the relation of the individual to the group it is wise to note an emphasis in Cooley's figurative prose, other than that singled out by Merton, to wit, that nonconformity 'results from an unusual way of *selecting* and *combining* accessible social influences ...' and that the individual '*tries* to conform to the group standards to which he gives his allegiance'. Seen in this light the issue becomes one of whether the individual conforms or deviates because he shares both values and norms of a deviant subgroup or because he elects to participate in a group whose specialized ends coincide at certain points with his order of values.

A great deal of the confusion and disagreement as to whether juvenile gangs have substantive subcultures classifiable as delinquent comes from a failure to take into account the interaction through which certain values become dominant in a group. It is significant that only a small percentage of such gangs engage in delinquencies, and only a small part of the behavior of so-called delinquent gangs is delinquent. Close analysis discloses that gang members react to many value claims besides those of the gang and that group interaction is highly important in determining the incidence, form and direction of, say, assault or violence.

The need for a theory of associational groups as agencies which fix and alter the order of value satisfaction, as well as shape means to ends, has long been apparent in the study of what has been loosely designated white-collar crime. I once asked E. H. Sutherland whether he meant by this term a type of crime or crime committed by a special class of people. He replied that he was not sure, thus admitting to an ambiguity which, in our estimation, he never resolved. He was not alone, however, for the courts handle antitrust violations in two ways, fining the corporations and also punishing their individual officers. A vast amount of case evidence shows that illegal price fixing, misrepresentation, adulteration, collusive bidding, abetting extortion by labor racketeers, tax evasion, restrictive covenants, as well as a modicum of more traditional crimes, including even behavior chargeable as treason, follow from informal, clandestine, policy decisions of associations. Such decisions, reached through group interaction, reflect an order of values and choice or means not necessarily representative of decision makers considered distributively, and increasingly less representative of persons and groups organizationally removed from the point of policy interaction. The same conclusion is applicable to corruption, crime and radicalism within labor unions, where we have fuller documentation of the control systems and group interaction that create and preserve organizational values inconsistent with member values. In so far as workers narrowly look on the labor union as an effective means to higher wages and better working conditions, they will tolerate, and under certain circumstances will support or even share, criminal practices or communism among their leaders.

The behavior and verbal rationales of corporation executives which so incensed Sutherland – such as their willingness to put profits above patriotism – from our point of view can only be understood in the context of technological and cost imperatives that confront whole associations. Their consequences at the level of individual behavior is illustrated by differences in compliance with axle-load regulations on the part of private and armed forces trucking operations in the northern California area. Generally, private firms seem to disregard the required distribution of weight on axles of trucks, even though this practice shortens the life of trucks and raises maintenance costs. In contrast, truckers working for naval supply in the San Francisco area after the war apparently observed the regulations. The difference in behavior was largely due to the fact that while private firms quickly charged off their depreciated equipment, the Navy pool could not do this, and moreover, it had a relatively low budget for maintenance.

The interplay of technological factors and deviation also appears in problems of determining weight difference in truck loads where moisture content of such materials as sand and gravel cannot be gauged. Trucks loaded in the fields with agricultural produce also make compliance problematical, and it is undoubtedly correct to say that many truck drivers do not know and cannot know whether their equipment is overloaded. Technological factors and costs likewise have a direct influence on disregard for speed limits set for trucks and buses in California. The meeting of schedules for time-conscious customers and passengers can be compromised only at the risk of serious loss of patronage and profits.

The relation of technology to conformity and deviation is unexplored territory so far as sociology is concerned, and our attempts to document its importance can only be faltering. Yet it seems clear from the trend of our analysis that there are numerous aspects of conformity and deviation in which it must be reckoned with as both a limiting and imperative factor.

### Psychic processes and deviation

Although Merton looks upon deviation primarily as the result of individual adaptations, nowhere in his essays does he make allowance for psychic processes as variables that can significantly affect the form of the adaptations. There is but one incidental reference to the possible relevance of such phenomena to deviation, in a comment that 'truly private' nonconformity is a form of 'autism'. However, there is no effort to elaborate this concept or to place it in the larger context of his paradigm.

While culture-personality theory and speculation have yet to prove their worth to sociology, we need not reject the postulate that psychic processes vary with positions occupied by individuals in social structures, particularly when the processes are carefully defined in terms of commitment, involvement and participation. Exclusion from groups and social isolation may be important variables in accounting for the development of certain forms of deviation. Cressey has stressed isolation as one of the variables necessary to explain embezzlement. The present writer has offered what he calls an 'isolation and closure' theory of certain kinds of check forgery, as well as an explanation of paranoia as an interactional product of exclusion. Meier and Bell have suggested, from their research, a more general conclusion that anomie may be a cause rather than an effect of circumscribed life chances. Social isolation from others, arising in a variety of ways, can alter significantly, if only ephemerally, the emphasis placed upon certain values and the perception of means in terms of both their availability and moral acceptability.

The consequence of Merton's omission of any discussion of the psychic process is an unavoidable superficiality in his conception of the deviations that he subsumes as 'retreatist'. We find a certain *tour de force* quality in lumping together activities of such vaguely defined people as 'vagbonds', 'pariahs', 'vagrants' and 'autists' with chronic drunkards and drug addicts and, without specifying what the 'activities' are, attributing to them a common 'escapist' motivation which eventuates in 'asocialized' individuals. Serious difficulties are met in any effort to reduce alcoholism and drug addiction to the simple kind of ends–means relationship which Merton makes a key to understanding deviant behavior. Alcohol and narcotics have manifest physiological and sociopsychological effects which, in ways as yet not well understood, alter the value orders of individuals. With persistent use they frequently become associated with organic and status changes (in our society) which radically modify the perception of the costs of means of reaching ends. Drugs and alcohol at certain stages of use become ends rather than means, a transformation of meaning which must be heeded in explaining how or why drug addicts and alcoholics engage in other forms of deviant behavior, such as petty theft or passing bad checks.

## Sociobiological limits

It would seem that any theory beginning with the idea that limited access to means of adaptation is a source of deviant behavior would turn thought to the limiting effects of biological handicaps and anomalies, if for no other reason than to justify their exclusion. It can, of course, be argued that to bring these into such a theory introduces a synthetic element inconsistent with a disciplinary commitment to study only the 'sociological' factors at work in deviation. More careful analysis and a modicum of familiarity with the data indicate that the central subject matter in question is at least as sociological, or sociopsychological, as it is biological – perhaps more so. Although physical handicaps partially restrict opportunities for achievement, the more critically operating limits come from an overlay of interpersonal and formal social barriers founded on cultural stereotypes about physical defects. As many physically disadvantaged people say, the problem is less the handicap than it is people.

The case is most clear with cosmetic defects, for here there are no biological limitations on behavior or choice in a strict sense. Yet the social exclusion encountered by persons so differentiated and their own withdrawal reactions are no less impressive than those seen in other kinds of physical disabilities. Much the same is true for one of the commonest forms of speech disorder, stuttering, which is almost entirely functional, appearing in otherwise normal children and adults. Equally significant is the fact that there is no necessary relationship between the extent and nature of physical disabilities and the variety of adaptations made to them. Individual responses range from withdrawal, through rebellion, to cynical or 'professional' manipulation of cultural stereotypes and the rehabilitative arrangements organized by society to cope with the 'problems' of the handicapped. Indications are strong that the special status given to the physically handicapped, as well as to many other deviants, differentiates the 'psychic environment' within which they must live. A large part of this consists of imputation of special character qualities to deviant and defective persons, which become an objective framework for the development of subjective limits on meaning and choice.

There is a processual aspect to deviation, whose acknowledgement is forced on us by the fact that with repetitive, persistent deviation or invidious differentiation, something happens 'inside the skin' of the deviating person. Something gets built into the psyche or nervous system as a result of social penalties, or 'degradation ceremonies', or as a consequence of having been made the subject of 'treatment' or 'rehabilitation'. The individual's perception of values, means and estimates of their costs undergoes revision in such ways that symbols which serve to limit the choices of most people produce little or no response in him, or else engender responses contrary to those sought by others.

### Primary and secondary deviation

Considerations of this sort led the present writer, in an earlier paper, to pose a theoretical distinction between primary and secondary deviation. This was devised to bring attention to two different kinds of research problems, the second of which is untouched in Merton's discussions of deviation: (a) *how deviant behavior originates;* (b) *how deviant acts are symbolically attached to persons and the effective consequences of such attachment for subsequent deviation on the part of the person.* Primary deviation is assumed to arise in a wide variety of social, cultural and psychological contexts, and at best has only marginal implications for the psychic structure of the individual; it does not lead to symbolic reorganization at the level of self-regarding attitudes and social roles. Secondary deviation is deviant behavior, or social roles based upon it, which becomes a means of defense, attack or adaptation to the overt and covert problems created by the social reaction to primary deviation. In effect, the original 'causes' of the deviation recede and give way to the central importance of the disapproving, degradational and isolating reactions of society. The distinction between primary and secondary deviation is deemed indispensable to a complete understanding of deviation in modern, pluralistic society. Furthermore, it is held that the second research problem is pragmatically more pertinent for sociology than the first:

In modern society it is difficult or impossible to derive theoretically a set of specific behavioral prescriptions which will in fact be normatively supported, uniformly practised, and socially enforced by more than a segment of the total population. Under such conditions it is not the fact that individuals engage in behaviors which diverge from some theoretically posited 'institutional expectations, or even that such behaviors are defined as deviant by the conventional and conforming members of society. A sociological theory of deviance must focus specifically on the interactions which not only define the behavior as deviant but also organize and activate the application of sanctions by individuals, groups and agencies. For in modern society the socially significant differentiation of deviants from non-deviants is increasingly contingent upon circumstances of situation, place, social and personal biography and bureaucratically organized agencies of social control. (Kitsuse, 1962, p. 256).

## Social control and deviation

We can move now from a kind of revisionist critique of Merton's paradigm to the major theoretical issue between a purely structural conception of deviation and the view of deviation as a consequence of the extent and form of social control. The latter rests upon the assumption that social control must be taken as an independent variable rather than as a constant, or merely reciprocal, societal reaction to deviation. Thus conceived, social control becomes a 'cause' rather than an effect of the magnitude and variable forms of deviation.

Facts are readily marshaled to give body to this conception. Firth, in the previously cited study of suicide in Tikopia, brought out the importance of the organization and dispatch of rescue fleets among other factors determining the lethal probabilities in suicide behavior. In our own society differences in crime rates between communities can be related to variations in available means for policing, as measured, for example, by a ratio of police to population. The differing efficacy of families as supervisory agencies similarly can be shown to have a notable effect on rate differences in juvenile delinquency. Finally, the presence or absence of a 'compliance section' in corporations undoubtedly has something to do with frequency with which antitrust laws are violated.

However, it is necessary to proceed beyond these obvious implications of social control for the incidence of deviation to those more closely connected with its operation in modern pluralistic society. In so doing we would like to note that new ways of thinking can be opened up by assuming that, in the absence of pressures to conform, people will deviate, or more precisely, express a variety of idiosyncratic impulses in overt behavior. When this assumption is joined with our earlier one, that our society increasingly shows fluid and open structuring of situations, categorically different ideas about deviation follow.

An equally flexible conception of norms is required to supplement these assumptions. So considered, norms become little more than a reference point for action or, following Felix Cohen, a set of probabilities that in some situations certain unpleasant things will happen to people either at the hands of associates or from actions of legal or other tribunals. When these probabilities are high we can assume that behavior of an individual and of those reacting to it express patterned values. When they are low we must make other assumptions about the outcome of the individual's actions and of the actions of those who react to him; we must, in so doing, adopt a social-interactional rather than a relationship perspective.

### Constitutive norms

Garfinkel has originated an intriguing set of notions revolving around what he designates as 'constitutive rules of social interaction', which appear to be promising concepts for research on behavior in unstructured situations. These are less specifications of substantive behavior than they are criteria of the possible locale, numbers of participants and order of action an individual assumes must be chosen by himself and others in social interaction. These most nearly resemble ground rules or basic rules of a game. Thus, in a bridge game there are no rules requiring that a given card be played, only rules as to who should play it. Furthermore, players do not respond so much to the act as they do to its meaning in relation to the emerging strategy of the game. It is assumed that constitutive rules are discoverable as interactional guides in the course of daily events as well as in games.

The germane conclusion is that in certain situations it is impossible to determine what is regarded as normal or deviant behavior merely by inspecting its external features. It must be known what rules are the basis of social interaction and at what point the participants are in an interactional sequence. In the course of such interaction, individuals may unilaterally change the rules or the rules may, by group interaction, be shifted to a new ground. In some cases this may take the form of a sliding scale of norms, as at a cocktail party where behavior which would not be allowable at the beginning may become so after 'things get going'. Courtship and sex behavior in general would seem to fall into the category of game-like interaction, in which rules are progressively changed by a variety of subtle cues, dress or sententious silence. Often this applies not only to the courting pair but also to parents and the community.

When constitutive rules are breached, the situation becomes 'confused', which may either lead to withdrawal of persons from interaction or to a redefinition of the unexpected behavior in terms of alternative meanings of what is constitutively 'normal' or acceptable. The interim interaction which culminates in mutual acceptance of new constitutive rules is one of 'normalization'. Normalization takes place between persons who 'trust' one another or who are bonded together by mutual claims, as in family, friendships, reciprocal business and professional relationships, or by informal ties which grow up within formal organizations. It also may occur in what Goffman calls 'encounters', when they are governed by some criteria of politeness or courtesy, or by humanitarian solicitude for physically handicapped persons.

From the point of view of valuational choice, normalization will persist so long as the value satisfactions contingent on the interactional bond are of a higher order than those sacrificed by continued normalization. In such a context anomie becomes the state of confusion during which social interactors are unable to discover alternately acceptable meanings for the departure from the rules. Deviant behavior and the possibility of control action arise from the assignment of unacceptable meanings to behavior in interaction which results in high costs or sacrifices of values to those associated with the bond of trust who have access to means of social control.

Normalization is readily perceived in family interaction where a wide variety of idiosyncratic behavior becomes acceptable by virtue of esoteric rules which evolve out of social interaction. A great deal of behavior which in another context would be defined as 'delinquent' is normalized because the rules of interaction are different. Even more impressive is the normalization of behavior which, when projected against the diagnostic criteria of formal psychiatry, would be looked upon as 'neurotic' or 'psychotic'. Equally revealing is the diversity of meaning of intoxication in courtship, marriage and family settings, or even in occupational situations. One position established by research, as well as theory, in the field of speech disorders is that there is no such thing as abnormal speech among children, and that speech problems are a function of parental perception and evaluation.

There are pressing reasons why primary groups go to what might be thought of as extreme lengths in normalizing the behavior of members. When confronted by a breach of constituted rules, voluntary withdrawal or 'leaving the field' often is impossible for interacting members. Excluding the person who breaches the rules is a drastic step, for it betokens a betrayal of trust, which must be justified to group members as well as to others. The problem is even more critical if the group turns to formal or legal agencies of social control, or when the primary group is forced to interact with such formal agencies due to violation of formal rules by a member.

While there is precious little information to draw from, it is likely that normalization increasingly characterizes internal interaction within large associations. The picture is muddied somewhat by the currency of the concept of the 'organization man' and the assumed high standards of conformity set for him. However, there can be no doubt that accountable losses of time or unfavorable publicity, as well as the complexities of internal situations themselves, lead corporations, for example, often to consider acceptable employee behavior that in other contexts could be defined as deviant. Department stores seem to prefer, or are compelled, to define the unauthorized removal of merchandise by employees as part of losses covered under the accounting concept, 'inventory shrinkage'. While the actions involved in some instances are clear violations of formal rules of the law of theft, in others, where the merchandise is damaged or remaindered, or is taking up space needed for other purposes, it is plausible that the situation is less clearly structured. Distinctions between 'lost' and 'stolen', and between accidental and deliberate breakage on docks and in warehouses, become unimportant to shippers who can adjust their costs or cover losses with insurance. Whether union rules or laws against discrimination in hiring and firing are 'violated' on construction projects often depends on the kind of bargaining interaction which goes on between project supervisors and union representatives. Whether the divergent use of labor and materials authorized for construction projects, particularly public ones, is defined as illegal or contrary to rule often depends upon ephemeral or progressively modified agreements between contractors and supervisors. A revealing topic for examination would be the norms constituted for the use and disposition of military supplies and equipment which became 'salvage' in South Pacific islands after the Second World War.

A recent interpretation by Janowitz of various data on military organization indicates that changing skill structures growing out of technology are revolutionizing military discipline, and that formal rules have less and less of a place in the work of a combat team, which is the prototype of the whole military organization.

The combat soldier, regardless of military arm, when committed to battle, is hardly the model of Max Weber's ideal bureaucrat following rules and regulations. In certain respects he is the antithesis. The combat fighter is not routinized and self-contained. Rather his role is one of contant improvisation, regardless of his service or weapon. Improvisation is the keynote of the individual fighter or combat group. . . . The military organization dedicated to victory is forced to alter its techniques of training and indoctrination. Rather than developing an automatic reaction to combat dangers, it requires training programs to teach men not only to count on instruction from their supervisors but also to exercise their own judgement about the best responses to make when confronted with given types of danger (Janowitz, 1959, pp. 37–8).

It is desirable or even mandatory to ask whether associations in general have not become more or less dedicated to victory or, at least, to vigilant defense in our society. In so far as this is true, and to the degree that goal consciousness pervades organizations, it can be anticipated that their operations will be less and less set by formal rules and that a form of social control appropriate to functionality and loose structuring will emerge.

### Active social control and deviation

Although the concept of social control has never been defined to the full satisfaction of sociologists, usages have pointed either in a kind of positivist, teleological direction, or towards the more conservative thought of W. G. Sumner. In an earlier effort to develop a modern idea of social control, the present author took issue with conceptions of social control fathered by the writings of Sumner, specifically with the notions that folkways, mores and laws are predominant means of social control. Following older ideas of L. M. Bristol, I proposed that such control be termed 'passive', in contrast to 'active' social control. The distinction, a pivotal one for our purposes, makes passive control an aspect of conformity to traditional norms; active social control, on the other hand, is a process for the implementation of goals and values. The former has to do with the maintenance of social order, the latter with emergent social integrations. More precisely stated, active social control is a continuous process by which values are consciously examined, decisions made as to those values which should be dominant, and collective action taken to that end. While it has individual aspects it is more typically a function of group interaction.

The saliency of active social control in modern society must be understood as an outcome of major changes in the nature of innovating processes. Directly contrary to Merton's view of innovation as a deviant or nonconformist response of structurally disadvantaged individuals, are the ubiquitous indications that innovation has become organized or institutionalized in our society. This is reflected in the image and reality of corporations as research-oriented organizations; it can be demonstrated by data showing the changing ratio of patents granted individuals to those granted to corporations. 'Innovate or die' is no idle caveat for the association of today, be it a monster corporation, struggling parochial-school system, or intrenched racial segregationists in Prince Edward County, Virginia.

Organized innovation has given us a dynamic technology which continuously differentiates, undercuts and creates new values, or modifies their order of satisfaction by changing their costs. The dynamics of competition of subgroups within associations, of associations within coalitions and of coalitions of associations within society to advance their values or maintain them in favored positions has no parallel in any society of the past. It demands that a radically different version of social control be brought into our horizons of thought: 'instead of asking how society orders and controls the individual, students of social control might ask how society takes its organization and momentum from its behaving individuals'. We must also ask how society takes its organization and momentum from the interaction of groups. While the shadow of Thomas and Znaniciecki's 'creative man' has grown large, more often than not in society today the shadow cast is that of a creative group.

The implications of active social control of deviation are not easily stated in systematic form, but they can be made apparent by applying an ends–means schema, qualified by cost and other factors, to the agencies and agents of social control. Agencies of social control, not excluding those of law enforcement, when operating in areas of value conflict and in situations complicated by technological change, like other groups in action, select from and implement values in variable ways. The norms that individual agents of social control within organizations are called upon to enforce or follow frequently become functional alternatives to ends. Such individuals seek to gain conformity to norms they do not share, or ignore those they do share, depending upon the availability of means of control, the costs of action and the competition of values within and outside the control agency. Unless such factors are known in particular situations, it is impossible to determine what norms will be invoked to define a given behavior, or a class of behavior, as deviant and to attach the behavior to persons.

Nowhere is the contingent nature of deviation made more apparent in our society than in the action of government regulatory agencies with adjudicative and punitive powers in situations where they are confronted by consequences of technological and organizational change. Large areas of action having to do with business, finance, health, labor, housing, utilities, safety and welfare are subject to control through administrative rules discontinuous in origin from the culturally derived norms which impressed Merton and others seeming to favor a conception of passive social control. The real source of deviation in such areas is not necessarily change in the behavior of the subjects of regulation, but may be the imposition of new rules which define existing behavior, or behavior consistent with older norms, as now deviant. The object of so defining the behavior is to produce change, not to repress it.

Even when the scene changes from administrative agencies to traditional courts, the nonsubstantive nature of legal norms remains clear. The vicissitudes in the interpretation of our anti-trust laws are a record of shifting value dominance, in which court judgements have been taken, or frequently modified, by the perception of intolerable costs which literal enforcement of the laws would impose on socially important or strategic industries. Furthermore, it has had to be recognized that literal application of the laws may have effects opposite to those intended by regulators, so that increasingly, policy or values guide court decisions rather than deviation *per se*.

## Conclusion

The structural conception of deviation as developed by Merton has been criticized on the ground that it rests upon reified ideas of culture and social control. The associated ends–means schema, while it may be valid for the analysis of deviation in situations or societies with patterned values, is insufficient for this purpose in pluralistic value situations. Modern society, by reason of being more pluralistic than hierarchically ordered in regard to values, requires that valuation become a central concept in the explanation of deviation.

It will not escape the reader that Merton and the author concur on the primacy of goals in American social life. However, for Merton, 'goal emphasis' is an initial assumption made by placing American culture at one extreme of a polar typology of cultures. For us, this prevalence on 'ends sought' is derived from postulates concerning the pre-emptive nature of associations in American society, the multiple value claims made on individuals and the underlying dynamics of modern technology. These make it possible to explain the problematical aspects of conformity as well as of deviation and to explain generic deviation, rather than mere differences in rates of deviation, without the necessity to invoke 'inherent' qualities of whole cultures.

In accord with this line of thought we have proposed a risk-taking theory of deviation as an alternative to one emphasizing a single ends–means sequence. This makes deviation (or conformity) an outcome of several ends–means possibilities, with fortuitous factors and active social control being necessary to a complete explanation. This directs attention to the way in which human beings use chance in value conflict situations.

While class structure may be considered an important variable in deviation, equally important are technology, group interaction, sociobiological limits and psychic processes. Discussion of the latter two variables leads to the conclusion that secondary deviations, arising from the societal and subjective reactions to primary, or original, deviation, is one of the more important problems for analysis in modern society.

Meaning assigned to behavior in a context of constitutive norms is, for us, an inseparable part of deviation. Normalization, or conversely, assigning deviant meaning to actions, takes place in informal interaction or through formal agencies of social control. Agencies and agents of social control, actively seeking to advance or defend their values, define deviation and also assign deviant acts to individuals. This frequently, or characteristically in our society, reflects choice, valuation and group interaction.

The most pretentious claim for our point of view is that it opens the way to subsume deviation in a theory of social change. Even more important, it gives a proper place to social control as a dynamic factor or 'cause' of deviation.

*References*

COTTRELL, W. F. (1954), 'Men cry peace', in Q. Wright, W. F. Cottrell and C. H. Boasonn (eds.), *Research for Peace*, Institute for Social Research, Oslo.

JANOWITZ, M. (1959), *Sociology and the Military Establishment*, Russell Sage Foundation.

KITSUSE, J. I. (1962), 'Societal reaction to deviant behavior: problems of theory and method', *Social Problems*, vol. 9

# Acknowledgements

Permission to reprint the papers published in this volume is acknowledged from the following sources:

Reading 1    Oxford University Press, Inc.
Reading 2    Granada Publishing Ltd, Alfred A. Knopf, Inc., and H. Stuart Hughes
Reading 3    Routledge & Kegan Paul Ltd, Harcourt Brace Jovanovich, Inc., and Edward Shils
Reading 4    University of Chicago Press and Thomas S. Kuhn
Reading 5    Aldine Publishing Co. and Anselm L. Strauss
Reading 6    University of California Press and Kenneth Burke
Reading 7    University of Chicago Press and Anselm L. Strauss
Reading 8    Allen Lane The Penguin Press, Doubleday & Co., Inc., Peter L. Berger and Thomas Luckmann
Reading 9    Routledge & Kegan Paul Ltd, London School of Economics and Norbert Elias
Reading 10   Chandler Publishing Co., Intext Publishing and Abraham Kaplan
Reading 11   American Sociological Association
Reading 12   Free Press and Herbert Hyman
Reading 13   University of Chicago Press, Herbert Hyman, Jacob J. Feldman, Mrs Clyde W. Hart and Charles H. Stember
Reading 14   University of Chicago Press and William F. Whyte
Reading 15   Massachusetts Institute of Technology Press, Philip J. Stone, Dexter C. Dunphy, Marshall S. Smith and Daniel Ogilvie
Reading 16   University of Chicago Press
Reading 17   American Anthropological Association and Philippe Garigue
Reading 18   Athlone Press, Raymond W. Firth and Judith Djamour
Reading 19   Plenum Publishing Co. Ltd and Elizabeth Bott
Reading 20   *Manchester School of Economic and Social Studies*, Tom Lupton and C. Shirley Wilson
Reading 21   Harvard University Press and H. Kent Geiger
Reading 22   Her Majesty's Stationery Office
Reading 23   Routledge & Kegan Paul Ltd, Brian Jackson and Dennis Marsden
Reading 24   American Sociological Association and Ralph H. Turner
Reading 25   American Sociological Association
Reading 26   Penguin Books Ltd and Basil Bernstein
Reading 27   Manchester University Press and Colin Lacey
Reading 28   John Wiley & Sons, Inc., and Robert Perrucci
Reading 29   Routledge & Kegan Paul Ltd and Humanities Press, Inc.
Reading 30   *Past and Present* and E. P. Thompson

Reading 31    James Nisbet and Co. Ltd and E. Wight Bakke
Reading 32    Harcourt Brace Jovanovich, Inc.
Reading 33    John Wiley & Sons, Inc., and Reinhard Bendix
Reading 34    Cambridge University Press, J. H. Goldthorpe, David Lockwood,
              Frank Bechhofer and Jennifer Platt
Reading 35    Granada Publishing Ltd and Jeremy Tunstall
Reading 36    Routledge & Kegan Paul Ltd, London School of Economics and
              Robert K. Merton
Reading 37    John Wiley & Sons, Inc., James G. March and Herbert A. Simon
Reading 38    John Wiley & Sons, Inc., and Arthur L. Stinchcombe
Reading 39    Macmillan Co.
Reading 40    Prentice-Hall, Inc., and Amitai Etzioni
Reading 41    Holt, Rinehart & Winston, Inc., and Erving Goffman
Reading 42    Chandler Publishing Co., Intext Publishing, Peter M. Blau and
              W. R. Scott
Reading 43    Institute for Social Research, University of Zambia and B. Kapferer
Reading 44a   Routledge & Kegan Paul Ltd and American Book Co.
Reading 44b   Macmillan Co. and Charles H. Page
Reading 44c   American Sociological Association
Reading 44d   University of Pennsylvania Press and Melvin M. Webber
Reading 44e   University of Chicago Press and Norton E. Long
Reading 45    Harcourt Brace Jovanovich, Inc., and H. M. Lynd
Reading 46    Harvard University Press, Conrad M. Arensberg and Solon T.
              Kimball
Reading 47    University of Toronto Press, Basic Books, Inc., and J. R. Seeley
Reading 48    University of Chicago Press and G. D. Suttles
Reading 49    Clarendon Press and Margaret Stacey
Reading 50    International African Institute and Valdo Pons
Reading 51a   Princeton University Press
Reading 51b   John Wiley & Sons, Inc., A. Vidich and J. Bensman
Reading 52    Routledge & Kegan Paul Ltd and University of Chicago Press
Reading 53    J. & A. Churchill, Anthony de Reuck and Julie Knight
Reading 54    Lewis S. Feuer
Reading 55    Routledge & Kegan Paul Ltd and Free Press
Reading 56    Routledge & Kegan Paul Ltd
Reading 57    University of California Press, Seymour M. Lipset and Reinhard
              Bendix
Reading 58    Doubleday & Co., Inc., and Seymour M. Lipset
Reading 59    George Allen & Unwin Ltd and R. M. Titmuss
Reading 60    Penguin Books Ltd and Henry Pelling
Reading 61a   Macmillan Co.
Reading 61b   Oxford University Press, Inc.
Reading 62    University of Minnesota Press and Theodore Caplow
Reading 63    Basic Books Inc., C. A. Watts & Co. Ltd and T. B. Bottomore
Reading 64    Talcott Parsons
Reading 65    Routledge & Kegan Paul Ltd, Free Press and Edward Shils

Reading 66   Routledge & Kegan Paul Ltd, London School of Economics and
             David Lockwood
Reading 67   Routledge & Kegan Paul Ltd, Humanities Press, Inc., and John
             Rex
Reading 68   Clarendon Press and Anthony Giddens
Reading 69   Robert K. Merton
Reading 70   Routledge & Kegan Paul Ltd, Houghton Mifflin Co. and Ralph
             H. Turner
Reading 71   Free Press and Edwin M. Lemert

# Author Index

# Subject Index

Act, 38–9, 41
Adolescent subculture, 211–14
Agent, agency, 38–9, 41–2
Anti-school culture, 179–82
Authority, 354, 416–22, 455

Behavioural science, programmatic character of, 73
Birth rate
 in French Canada, 134–5
 in U.S.S.R., 168
Bourgeoisie, 359, 361, 362, 363
 'industrial' and 'petty' sections, 363, 364, 374, 368–9
Bureaucracy
 and capitalism, 268, 370
 definition of, 265–6
 and kinship, 163
 and legal authority, 265 ff.
 in non-literate societies, 280–81
 and technical knowledge, 267
Bureaucratization, 264

Caste, 355–8, 366–7
 consciousness, 358
 and status, 397
Central life interests, 237
Charisma, 262, 426
Charismatic retinue, 262–3
Class, 361, 364–5, 366–8, 373–4
 conflict, 25–6, 359–63, 432, 443–4
 and conjugal roles, 147–8, 150
 consciousness, 365
 indicators, 371–5
 intra-class conflict, 362–3, 369
 and the Marxian dialectic, 362
 organizations, 389–91
 and the State, 364
 structure and political power, 362–3, 364, 369–70
 and voting patterns, 380–83

Codes, restricted and elaborated, 195–204
Community
 as a 'constellation of institutions', 300
 as a 'constellation of types of personalities', 300
 definition of, 296–303
 historical definition of, 298
 interest community, 301–3
 local, 297–300, 303–6
 study, 340–49
 territorial basis of, 297, 301–3, 304
Conflict
 between classes, 25–6, 359–63, 432, 443–4
 between kinship and other interests, 163–4
 within classes, 362–3, 369
Conjugal role-relationships, 146–50
 joint and segregated, 147–50
Connectedness
 of social networks, 148–50
Consensus, 405 ff.
Content analysis, 110–14
 inferences from, 111–12, 114
 model of, 111–12
 and study of signs, 113

Decision makers, top, 151–64
Descent, 138–41, 143
Detachment, 59–64
Deviance, 430–33, 464 ff.
Differentiation
 in school, 205–10
Direct tests of relationships, 82–3, 90
 supplementary use of, 90
Discovery, 30–33, 34–7, 69, 71
 context of, 69–70
 logic of, 70–71

Durkheim's suicide, 83–7, 90–91
  as case study of indirect test, 83–6

Education Act, 1944, 179, 184
Educational selection
  at eleven and earlier, 179, 184
  and forms of upward mobility, 183–9
Ego-centrism, 215–16
Élites, 402–4, 416 ff.
  and education, 183–9
Employment, 19–20
  and unemployment, 223 ff.
Ends, 407–14
Ethnic groups, 318–27, 378, 478–9
Experiment, 77–81
  control group, 77–9
  experimental group, 77–9
  feasibility of, 78–81
  randomization, 77–9, 81
Exploitation, 359–62

Fair wage, 229–31
Falsification, 31
Familism,
  values and mobility, 211–14
Family
  domestic, division of labour within,
    127, 146–7, 149–50
  elementary, 136–8, 142–5
  extended, 137, 139, 140, 142
  networks, 148
  Soviet, 165–72
  Soviet ideology and, 166–72
Feudal administration, 263
Feudalism, 353–4
Force, 353, 361
Formal theory, 36, 409–10, 453–4, 461
Function/functional, 429–30, 445–6

Gemeinschaft (community), 295–6, 298
Generalized other, 45–7
Gesellschaft (society), 295–6, 298
Grammar school, 179–82, 184–5, 205–
  210
Grounded theory, 34–7

Idealism
  in medical school, 190–94
Ideology, 25–6, 441, 461–3
  and Soviet family, 166–72
Indirect tests of relationship, 83–9, 91
  supplementary use of, 91
  unique use of, 86–9
Industry
  co-operation in, 332–4
Interests, 443–4
Intersubjectivity, 52–4
Interviewing, 92–101
  error in, 94–102
  organization of, 77
Intuition, 69–70
Involvement, 59–64

Joint conjugal roles, 146–50
Justification, context of, 69

Kin
  frequency of contact with, 123,
    127–130, 132, 310, 338–9
  groups, 132–3, 138–40, 142
  permissive and obligatory relations
    between, 128–30, 132–4, 138, 145
  'priority' kin, 132–4
  services between, 130–31
Kinship
  ambilateral, 141
  bilateral, 140–42
  and bureaucracy, 163
  content of, 130–31, 136, 143
  multilineal, 141
  range of, 137–8
  and residence, 126, 128, 141, 144–5
  and social mobility, 132
  unilineal, 141
  and urbanism, 123, 134–5, 144–5
  variations in knowledge of, 124–6
Knowledge, 22–4, 50–58
  common-sense, 52–3
  pragmatic, 56–7
  social distribution of, 57–8

Values, 60–62, 415 ff.
  grammar school, 181–2, 205–10
  and mobility, 211–14

'White-collar', 369, 372–3, 399–400
Work
  discipline, 222, 224
  and income, 229–31

instrumental orientation to, 235 ff.
  rhythm of, 221–2
  satisfaction at, 226–7, 232–4
  and security, 229–30
  and status, 228–9
Workers, 228 ff.
  affluent, 235 ff.
Working class
  and education, 179–81